BISON
BOOKS

W9-DGW-233

Distant Horizon

DOCUMENTS FROM THE
NINETEENTH-CENTURY AMERICAN WEST

———

COLLECTED AND EDITED BY GARY NOY

UNIVERSITY OF NEBRASKA PRESS
LINCOLN AND LONDON

Acknowledgments for the use of previously
published material appear on pages 445–55

Library of Congress Cataloging-in-Publication Data
Distant horizon: documents from the nineteenth-century
American West / collected and edited by Gary Noy.
p.   cm.
"A Bison original."
Includes bibliographical references (p.   ) and index.
ISBN 0-8032-8371-7 (pbk.: alk. paper)
1. West (U.S.)—History—19th century—Sources.
I. Noy, Gary, 1951–   .
F591.D58   1999
978'.02—dc21   98-30643   CIP

For my
mother and father

VELMA WINKLE NOY
(1927–1985)

HOWARD E. NOY
(1920–1994)

CONTENTS

~

PREFACE

IMAGINE. Driving down a Nevada desert highway in the middle of the night, your headlights provide the only glimmer of illumination, and the sweet smell of sagebrush filters through your open window. It is quiet, lonely, and a little frightening. Suddenly, you crest a rise in the road, and, far in the distance, you spy the inviting lights of a desert town. Their warm glow beckons to you as a refuge, an oasis. Their gleam may be far away but brings a feeling of security, of safety, of recognition. The lights may be on the horizon, but they indicate an attainable goal.

The history of the nineteenth-century American West is much like those lights in the Nevada desert. While the events occurred in relatively recent times—the blink of an eye historically—they are still distant enough that you require significant travel to reach your destination. The history of the American West is on a distant horizon, but it is seemingly within touch nonetheless. The purpose of this book, *Distant Horizon,* is to provide a roadmap for a journey back in time by using the documents, accounts, and reminiscences of those who led the way many years before.

And what a journey it was. The history of the nineteenth-century American West has been dissected, glorified, criticized, denigrated, and romanticized. Its contrasts and contradictions, its successes and faults, have all been grist for the historian's mill. From its earliest inhabitants and immigrants to its present dynamic society, it has been the subject of often microscopic examination.

For the historian, the American West is myth, a hope, a promise, a dream, the rainbow's end—and brutal reality. It is gentility and crudeness, high aspirations and base instincts, a family's faith and a loner's last chance. The American West is the rattle of whiskey glasses, the glimmer of hard-earned mineral riches, a gambler's eyeshades, fortunes gained, fortunes lost. It is fulfilled prophecies, shattered empires, the laughter of success, the quiet tears of failure, and bitter resignation. It is the clatter of wagon wheels, the whine of the railroad whistle, the hiss of a steamboat, and the sharp report of the rifle. The American West is parades in celebration and the foul taste of retreat. It is gunshots in anger, ugly confrontations, discrimination, bigotry, and ways of overcoming these obstacles with grace and dignity. It is fire-cloaked leaves, the scent of wildflowers on the breeze, and the diamond mesh of light on wind-roughened water. It is mud, high water, fire, disease, and death. It is schoolmarms and prostitutes, visionaries and dilettantes, the law and the lawless, the noble and the profane. The American West is boom-town and home, exploitable resource for some, holy ground for others.

Distant Horizon is designed to provide documentary examples of the serendipities and sorrows that combined to form the unique American western mosaic. It describes the motivations of the many and the dreams of a few. It chronicles the dusty world of the cowboy, the hardscrabble existence of the farmer and the settler, and the miner's vision of golden glory. It examines the independent nature of the explorer and mountain man and the sometimes heroic, sometimes cruel existence of the soldier. The book provides insight into the struggle of those who did not move in the mainstream of power—women and westerners of color. It sheds light on the sad fate of victims and the sorry attitudes of victimizers. It investigates the impact of the railroad on the transformation of the region. And it considers the most tragic element of American western history: the concentration, subjugation, and too frequent extermination of the Native American cultures.

This is by no means a comprehensive compilation—a complete record, virtually impossible, would require thousands of pages—but rather a representative sampler. My goal was to provide a foundation of predominantly primary documentation to supplement later historical discussion and analysis. In selecting the content I looked for contemporary accounts, narratives, reminiscences, and so on—texts produced at the time of the events or written by participants in or witnesses to them. Some excerpts from fiction and poetry are included because they highlight an emotional aspect or perception of a historical event. In addition, a handful of selections from secondary sources help to amplify a theme factually or give historical context to other documents.

The materials chosen from the hundreds of items I consulted met two important criteria: (1) applicability to one of my topics, and (2) readability and interest. I make no claim that these are the only or even the most important writings on a particular subject. Nor do I intend to promote any particular historical interpretation or political agenda; on the contrary, I have attempted to offer a reasonably balanced selection, together with introductions and annotations to place the readings in historical context and to provide linkage between them as necessary.

A note of caution to the reader, however: in examining and using these historical documents, one must retain a healthy dose of skepticism, for the primary sources of American western history are frequently a mixture of fact, legend, romance, and personal rationalization and promotion (particularly those dealing with the cowboy culture). I have strived to find items that do not exhibit this combination or at least minimize it acceptably; nevertheless, the contemporary readings must be recognized as snapshots in time, bearing the often prejudiced perspectives of their authors. The story of the American West has thousands of interpretations. It seems that virtually everyone who ever hiked, rode, worked, lived, fought, or bled there wrote an account of some kind—and every one of these memoirs is infused with its writer's individual peculiarities and biases as well as the prejudices of the times. In fact, many of the phrases and personal or racial terms used are distasteful (if not downright odious) to our present-day sensibilities. But it would be historically dishonest to attempt to expunge such references from the documents. To understand the American West, one must also be keenly aware of the racial, social, political, and economic motivations and assumptions of the people involved—no matter how foul. History is much like exploring your grandmother's attic: you will generally find dusty treasures and remarkable artifacts, but if you peer into darkened corners, you may also spy a snarling rat or a black widow spider. It is all part of the experience, and nothing should be avoided or modified to meet our modern views—not even the spelling and grammar that are so often poor and inconsistent in primary documents. Because thorough efforts to parse every syllable or indicate each misspelling would be distracting, the writings are presented with their idiosyncrasies and errors intact and with relatively little corrective interpolation.

Many, if not most, of the primary sources presented here have already been reprinted elsewhere, often more than once, and I owe grateful appreciation to those who have considered and collected these materials in the past. As much as possible, however, I have tried to consult the original document or a faithful reproduction as well. My sources are listed by chapter and reading number at the end of the book, sometimes with a mention of additional informative publications. It is my hope that together, they will help readers understand this important segment of our country's development.

The history of the American West is both a story of grand vistas and epic proportions and the chronicle of simple virtues and everyday people doing the best they could under often difficult conditions. It is a remarkable journey. It is America.

I am grateful to the personnel of the University of Nebraska Press for their tireless, outstanding efforts in the production of *Distant Horizon*. I also want to acknowledge the helpful suggestions and revisions supplied by a remarkable copyeditor, Patricia Sterling.

GARY NOY

DISTANT HORIZON

CHAPTER I

THE SPIRIT AND THE MYTH

IN 1841, the British philosopher Thomas Carlyle observed, "It is the spiritual always which determines the material." So it was with the American West—the spirit animated the physical. It was out of the spiritual motivations of character, heart, poetic sentiment, feverish prospects of instant wealth and economic bounty, good humor, patience, adaptation, independence, determination, and triumph that the history of the West was built. Cutting across all ages, races, and economic conditions, the spirit of the era defined the dream and fleshed out the reality.

Developing from the spirit was the myth of the West. The spirit was a motivator, but it was the emergent myth that encapsulated the westerners' view of themselves. In particular, the cowboy, the Knight of the Plains (as dime novelists called him), came to symbolize western mythology both domestically and internationally. The use and export of this symbol in our popular culture has blurred the border between myth and historical fact. In many cases the myth is less compelling than the fact yet remains the more resonant legacy.

In this chapter the readings examine various aspects of these western historical elements, the "Myth" section focusing exclusively on the impact and the growth of cowboy mythology.

THE SPIRIT

Every great idea or movement must have a catalyst, some spark that motivates someone to think or act. The spark may be the basest instinct or the loftiest aspiration, but the ignition must be there. For the development of the American West, the catalysts were a varied lot: the economic motivations of gold, greed, and geography; the intellectual spur of curiosity and expanding scientific knowledge; the social drive of race, Manifest Destiny, and aggressive nationalism; and the adventurous urge of simply wanting to know what was out there. All combined to form an almost palpable spirit, the idea that the American West represented something special and unique.

THOMAS JEFFERSON'S INSTRUCTIONS TO MERIWETHER LEWIS, 1803

With the unexpected (and largely unconstitutional) purchase of the Louisiana Territory from France in 1803, President Thomas Jefferson was filled with curiosity as to the nature of this new land. Rumors abounded, but knowledge was sketchy. What was out there? What could be done with this land? Was it worth the expenditure? To answer these and the many other questions posed by his fertile mind, Jefferson engaged his personal secretary, Meriwether Lewis, and William Clark, a Kentuckian with military experience, to undertake an expedition to explore this uncharted territory. Jefferson's instructions mirror the wonderment and worry that the West engendered in many Americans of the era.

To Meriwether Lewis, esquire, captain of the first regiment of infantry of the United States of America:

Your situation as secretary of the president of the United States, has made you acquainted with the objects of my confidential message of January 18, 1803, to the legislature; you have seen the act they passed, which, expressed in general terms, was meant to sanction those objects, and you are appointed to carry them into execution.

Instruments of ascertaining, by celestial observations, the geography through which you will pass, have been already provided. Light articles for barter and presents among the Indians, arms for your attendants, say for from ten to twelve men, boats, tents, and other travelling apparatus, with ammunition, medicine, surgical instruments, and provisions, you will have prepared, with such aids as the secretary at war can yield in his department; and from him also you will receive authority to engage among our troops, by voluntary agreement, the number of attendants above-mentioned; over whom you, as their commanding officer, are invested with all the powers the laws give in such a case.

As your movements, while within the limits of the United States, will be better directed by occasional communications, adapted to circumstances as they arise, they will not be noticed here. What follows will respect your proceedings after your departure from the United States.

Your mission has been communicated to the ministers here from France, Spain, and Great Britain, and through them to their governments; and such assurances given them as to its objects, as we trust will satisfy them. The country of Louisiana having been ceded by Spain to France, the passport you have from the minister of France, the representative of the present sovereign of the country, will be a protection with all its subjects; and that from the minister of England will entitle you to the friendly aid of any traders of the allegiance with whom you may happen to meet.

The object of your mission is to explore the Missouri river, and such principal streams of it, as, by its course and communication with the waters of the Pacific ocean, whether the Columbia, Oregan, Colorado, or any other river, may offer the most direct and practicable water-communication across the continent, for the purposes of commerce.

Beginning at the mouth of the Missouri, you will take observations of latitude and longitude, at all remarkable points of the river, and especially at the mouths of rivers, at rapids, at islands, and other places and objects distinguished by such natural marks and characters, of a durable kind, as that they may with certainty be recognised hereafter. The courses of the river between these points of observation may be supplied by the compass, the log-line, and by time, corrected by the observations themselves. . . .

The commerce which may be carried on with the people inhabiting the line you will pursue, renders a knowledge of those people important. You will therefore endeavour to make yourself acquainted, as far as a diligent pursuit of your journey shall admit, with the names of the nations and their numbers;

The extent and limits of their possessions;

Their relations with other tribes and nations;

Their language, traditions, monuments;

Their ordinary occupations in agriculture, fishing, hunting, war, arts, and the implements for these;

Their food, clothing, and domestic accommodations;

The diseases prevalent among them, and the remedies they use;

Moral and physical circumstances which distinguish them from the tribes we know;

Peculiarities in their laws, customs, and dispositions;

And articles of commerce they made need or furnish, and to what extent.

And, considering the interest which every nation has in extending and strengthening the authority of reason and justice among the people around them, it will be useful to acquire what knowledge you can of the state of morality, religion, and information among them; as it may better enable those who may endeavour to civilize and instruct them, to adapt their measures to the existing notions and practices of those on whom they are to operate.

Other objects worthy of notice will be—

The soil and face of the country, its growth and vegetable productions, especially those not of the United States;

The animals of the country generally, and especially those not known in the United States;

The remains and accounts of any which may be deemed rare or extinct;

The mineral productions of every kind, but more particularly metals, lime-stone, pit-coal, and saltpetre; salines and mineral waters, noting the temperature of the last, and such circumstances as may indicate their character;

Volcanic appearances;

Climate, as characterized by the thermometer, by the proportion of rainy, cloudy and clear days; by lightning, hail, snow, ice; by the access and recess of frost; by the winds prevailing at different seasons; the dates at which particular plants put forth, or lose their flower or leaf; times of appearance of particular birds, reptiles, or insects. . . .

In all your intercourse with the natives, treat them in the most friendly and conciliatory manner which their own conduct will admit; allay all jealousies as to the object of your journey; satisfy them of its innocence; make them acquainted with the position, extent, character, peaceable and commercial dispositions of the United States; of our wish to be neighbourly, friendly, and useful to them, and of our dispositions to a commercial intercourse with them; confer with them on the points most convenient as mutual emporiums, and the articles of most desirable interchange for them and us. If a few of their influential chiefs, within practicable distance, wish to visit us, arrange such a visit with them, and furnish them with authority to call on our officers on their entering the United States, to have them conveyed to this place at the public expense. If any of them should wish to have some of their young people brought up with us, and taught such arts as may be useful to them, we will receive, instruct, and take care of them. . . .

As it is impossible for us to foresee in what manner you will be received by those people, whether with hospitality or hostility, so is it impossible to prescribe the exact degree of perseverance with which you are to pursue your journey. We value too much the lives of citizens to offer them to probable destruction. Your numbers will be sufficient to secure you against the unauthorized opposition of individuals, or of small parties; but if a superior force, authorized, or not authorized, by a nation should be arrayed against you further passage, and inflexibly determined to arrest it, you must decline its further pursuit and return. In the loss of yourselves we should also lose the information you have acquired. By returning safely with that, you may enable us to renew the essay with better calculated means. To your own discretion, therefore, must be left the degree of danger you may risk, and the point at which you should decline, only saying, we wish you to err on the side of your safety, and to bring back your party safe, even if it be with less information. . . .

On your arrival on [the Pacific] coast, endeavour to learn if there be any port within your reach frequented by the sea vessels of any nation, and to send two of your trusty people back by sea, in such way as shall appear practicable, with a copy of your notes; and should you be of opinion that the return of your party by the way they went will be imminently dangerous, then ship the whole, and return by sea, by the way either of Cape Horn, or the Cape of Good Hope, as you shall be able. . . .

Should you find it safe to return by the way you go, after sending two of your party round by sea, or with your whole party, if no conveyance by sea can be found, do so; making such observations on your return as may serve to supply, correct, or confirm those made on your outward journey.

On reentering the United States and reaching a place of safety, discharge any of your attendants who may desire and deserve it, procuring for them immediate payment of all arrears of pay and clothing which may have incurred since their departure, and assure them that they shall be recommended to the liberality of the legislature for the grant of a soldier's portion of land each, as proposed in my message to congress, and repair yourself, with your papers, to the seat of government.

To provide, on the accident of your death, against anarchy, dispersion, and the consequent danger to your party, and total failure of the enterprise, you are hereby authorized, by any instrument signed and written in your own hand, to name the person among them who shall succeed to the command on your decease, and by like instruments to change the nomination, from time to time, as further experience of the characters accompanying you shall point out superior fitness; and all the powers and authorities given to yourself are, in the event of your death, transferred to, and vested in the successor so named, with further power to him and his successors, in the manner to name each his successor, who, on the death of his predecessor, shall be invested with all the powers and authorities given to yourself. Given under my hand at the city of Washington, this twentieth day of June, 1803.

Thomas Jefferson,
President of the United States of America.

READING 2
"THE GREAT NATION OF FUTURITY," JOHN O'SULLIVAN, 1839

John Louis O'Sullivan (1813–95) was the editor and publisher of the United States Magazine and Democratic Review. *Established in 1837, the magazine published the literary works of some of the most prominent authors of the day. More important for our purposes, it presented an unfiltered and glorious view of American cultural aspirations. O'Sullivan was one of the first to use the term "Manifest Destiny" in print and to champion its underlying principles. This selection is a typical discussion of what O'Sullivan refers to as the "far-reaching, the boundless future" of American expansionism.*

[O]ur national birth was the beginning of a new history, the formation and progress of an untried political system, which separates us from the past and connects us with the future only; and so far as regards the entire development of the natural rights of man, in moral, political, and national life, we may confidently assume that our country is destined to be *the great nation of futurity.*

It is so destined, because the principle upon which a nation is organized fixes its destiny, and that of equality is perfect, is universal. It presides in all the operations of the physical world, and it is also the conscious law of the soul—the self-evident dictate of morality, which accurately defines the duty of man to man, and consequently man's rights as man. Besides, the truthful annals of any nation furnish abundant evidence that its happiness, its greatness, its duration, were always proportionate to the democratic equality in its system of government. . . .

What friend of human liberty, civilization, and refinement can cast his view over the past history of the monarchies and aristocracies of antiquity, and not deplore that they ever existed? What philanthropist can contemplate the oppressions, the cruelties, and injustice inflicted by them on the masses of mankind and not turn with moral horror from the retrospect?

America is destined for better deeds. It is our unparalleled glory that we have no reminiscences of battlefields, but in defense of humanity, of the oppressed of all nations, of the rights of conscience, the rights of personal enfranchisement. Our annals describe no scenes of horrid carnage, where men were led on by hundreds of thousands to slay one another, dupes and victims of emperors, kings, nobles, demons in the human form called heroes. We have had patriots to defend our homes, our liberties, but no aspirants to crown or thrones; nor have the American people ever suffered themselves to be led on by wicked ambition to depopulate the land, to spread desolation far and wide, that a human being might be placed on a seat of supremacy.

We have no interest in the scenes of antiquity, only as lessons of avoidance of nearly all their examples. The expansive future is our arena and for our history. We are entering on its untrodden space with the truths of God in our minds, beneficent objects in our hearts, and with a clear conscience unsullied by the past. We are the nation of human progress, and who will, what can, set limits to our onward march? Providence is with us, and no earthly power can. We point to the everlasting truth on the first page of our national declaration, and we proclaim to the millions of other lands that the "the gates of hell"—the powers of aristocracy and monarchy—"shall not prevail against it."

The far-reaching, the boundless future, will be the era of American greatness. In its magnificent domain of space and time, the nation of many nations is destined to manifest to mankind the excellence of divine principles; to establish on earth the noblest temple ever dedicated to the worship of the Most High—the Sacred and the True. Its floor shall be a hemisphere—its roof the firmament of the star-studded heavens, and its congregation a Union of many Republics, comprising hundreds of happy millions, calling, owning, no man master, but governed by God's natural and moral law of equality, the law of brotherhood—of "peace and good will amongst men. . . ."

Yes, we are the nation of progress, of individual freedom, of universal enfranchisement. Equality of rights is the cynosure of our nation of states, the grand exemplar of the correlative equality of individuals; and, while truth sheds its effulgence, we cannot retrograde without dissolving the one and subverting the other. We must onward to the fulfillment of the mission—to the entire development of the principle of our organization—freedom of conscience, freedom of person, freedom of trade and business pursuits, universality of freedom and equality. This is our high destiny, and in nature's eternal, inevitable decree of cause and effect we must accomplish it. All this will be our future history, to establish on earth the moral dignity and salvation of man—the immutable truth and beneficence of God. For this blessed mission to the nations of the world, which are shut out from the lifesaving light of truth, has America been chosen; and her high example shall smite unto death the tyranny of kings, hierarchs, and oligarchs and carry the glad tidings of peace and good will where myriads now endure an existence scarcely more enviable than that of beasts of the field. Who, then, can doubt that our our country is destined to be *the great nation* of futurity?

READING 3

SPEECH TO THE UNITED STATES SENATE, THOMAS HART BENTON, 1846

Thomas Hart Benton, United States senator from Missouri, 1821–51, was quite possibly America's greatest proponent of the aggressive nationalist spirit known as Manifest Destiny. An early advocate of western homestead laws, Benton presented the case for the westerner with ringing oratory that clearly reflected the hopes and dreams of millions. In this May 28, 1846, speech, Benton expresses the racial beliefs associated with Manifest Destiny policy.

Since the dispersion of man upon earth, I know of no human event, past or present, which promises a greater, and more beneficent change upon earth than the arrival of the van of the Caucasian race (the Celtic-Anglo-Saxon division) upon the border of the sea which washes the shore of the eastern Asia. The Mongolian, or Yellow race, is there, four hundred millions in number, spreading almost to Europe; a race once foremost of the human family in the arts of civilization; but torpid and stationary for thousands of years. It is a race far above the Ethiopian, or Black—above the Malay, or Brown, . . . and above the American Indian, or Red; it is a race far above all these, but still, far below the White; and like all the rest, must receive an impression from the superior race whenever they come in contact. It would seem that the white race alone received the divine command, to subdue and replenish the earth! for it is the only race that has obeyed it—the only one that hunts out new and distant lands, and even a New World, to subdue and replenish. [They] arrived, after many ages, on the shore of the Atlantic, which they lit up with the lights of science and religion, and adorned with the useful and elegant arts. Three and a half centuries ago, this race, in obedience to the great command, arrived in the New World, and found new lands to subdue and replenish. For a long time, it was confined to the border of the new field . . . and even fourscore years ago the philosophic [Edmund] Burke was considered a rash man because he said the English colonists would top the Alleghenies, and descend into the valley of the Mississippi, and occupy without parchment if the Crown refused to make grants of land. What was considered a rash declaration eighty years ago, is old history, in our young country, at this day. Thirty years ago I said the same thing of the Rocky Mountains and the Columbia; it was ridiculed then; it is becoming history to-day. . . . I cannot murmur at what seems to be the effect of divine law. I cannot repine that this Capitol has replaced the wigwam—this Christian people, replaced the savages—white matrons, the red squaws—and that such men as Washington, Franklin, and Jefferson, have taken the place of Powhattan, Opechonecanough, and other red men, howsoever respectable they may have been as savages. Civilization, or extinction, has been the fate of all people who have found themselves in the track of the advancing Whites, and civilization, always the preference of the Whites, has been pressed as an object, while extinction has followed as the consequence of its resistance.

READING 4
"Texas," Mary Austin Holley, 1831

Among the key "spiritual" elements necessary for successful western development were strength of character and an adventurous heart. In the Texas of the 1820s and 1830s, then a Mexican province, American settlers needed an abundance of both. A December 1831 letter written by visitor Mary Austin Holley, cousin of Texas leader Stephen F. Austin, describes the emerging spirit of a "unique and original" community.

Ones feelings in Texas are unique and original, and very like a dream or youthful vision realized. Here, as in Eden, man feels alone with the God of nature, and seems, in a peculiar manner, to enjoy the rich bounties of heaven, in common with all created things. The animals, which do not fly from him; the profound stillness; the genial sun and soft air,—all are impressive, and are calculated, both to delight the imagination, and to fill the heart, with religious emotions.

With regard to the state of society here, as is natural to expect, there are many incongruities. It will take some time for people gathered from the north, and from the south, from the east, and from the west, to assimilate, and adapt themselves to new situations. The people are universally kind and hospitable, which are redeeming qualities. Everybody's house is open, and table spread, to accommodate the traveller. There are no poor people here, and none rich; that is, none who have much money. The poor and the rich, to use the correlatives, where distinction, there is none, get the same quantity of land on arrival, and if they do not continue equal, it is for want of good management on the one part, or superior industry and sagacity on the other. All are happy, because busy; and none meddle with the affairs of their neighbours, because they have enough to do to take care of their own. They are bound together by a common interest, by sameness of purpose, and hopes. As far as I could learn, they have no envyings, no jealousies, no bickerings, through politics or fanaticism. . . .

The common concerns of life are sufficiently exciting to keep the spirits buoyant, and prevent everything like ennui. Artificial wants are entirely forgotten, in the view of real ones, and self, eternal self, does not alone, fill up the round of life. Delicate ladies find they can be useful, and need not be vain. Even privations become pleasures: people grow ingenious in overcoming difficulties. Many latent faculties are developed. They discover in themselves, powers, they did not suspect themselves of possessing. Equally surprised and delighted at the discovery, they apply to their labours with all that energy and spirit, which new hope and conscious strength, inspire. . . .

[E]ven conceding all the advantages I have claimed for Texas, it does not follow that happiness of all would be promoted, by emigrating to this country. It depends much upon the spirit of the man.

He whose hopes of rising to independence in life, by honourable exertion, have been blasted by disappointment; whose spirit, though depressed, is not discouraged; who longs only for some ample field on which to lay out his strength; who does not hanker after society nor sigh for the vanished illusions of life; who has a fund of resources within himself, and a heart to trust in God and his exertions; who is not particularly sensitive to petty inconveniences, but can bear privations and make sacrifices, of personal comfort—such a person will do well to settle accounts at home, and begin life anew in Texas. He will find, here, abundant exercise for all his faculties, both of body and mind, a new stimulus to his exertions, and a new current for his affections. He may be obliged to labour hard, but riches are a very certain reward of his exertions. He may be generous, without fear of ruin. He will learn to find society in nature, and repose in solitude, health in exertion, and happiness in occupation. If he have a just ambition, he will glow with generous pride, while he is marking out an untrodden path, acting in an unhackneyed sphere, and founding for himself, and his children after him, a permanent and noble independence.

READING 5
WALT WHITMAN AND THE AMERICAN WEST

Everybody realized that westering could be a dangerous experience but also knew that the natural and aesthetic rewards could be enormous as well. Appreciation of the western landscape was more than just an expectation of social and economic opportunity; it was an exclamation of form, sound, color, and awesome beauty. It required a poet's hand to express these elements memorably.

READING 5A
"THE PRAIRIES AND GREAT PLAINS IN POETRY" AND "AMERICA'S CHARACTERISTIC LANDSCAPE," WALT WHITMAN, 1882

Walt Whitman, preeminent poet of his generation, writes of the exhilaration of the western landscape and the American westering spirit in the two vivid descriptions excerpted here.

My Days and nights, as I travel here—what an exhilaration!—not the air alone, and the sense of vastness, but every local sight and feature. Everywhere something characteristic—the cactuses, pinks, buffalo grass, wild sage—the receding perspective, and the far circle-line of the horizon all times of the day, especially forenoon—the clear, pure, cool, rarefied nutriment for the lungs, previously quite unknown—the black patches and streaks left by surface-conflagrations—the deep-plough'd furrow of the "fire-guard"—the slanting snow-racks built all along to shield the railroad from winter drifts—the prairie dogs and the herds of antelope—the curious "dry rivers"—occasionally a "dug-out" or corral—Fort Riley and Fort Wallace—those towns of the northern plains (like ships on the sea), Eagle Tail, Coyote, Cheyenne, Agate, Monotony, Kit Carson—with ever the ant-hill and buffalo-wallow—ever the herds of cattle and the cow-boys ("cow-punchers"), to me a strangely interesting class, bright-eyed as hawks, with their swarthy complexions and their broad-brimm'd hats—apparently always on horseback with loose arms slightly raised and swinging as they ride. . . .

Speaking generally as to the capacity and sure future destiny of the plain and prairie area (larger than any European kingdom) it is the inexhaustible land of wheat, maize, flax, coal, iron, beef and pork, butter and cheese, apples and grapes—land of ten million virgin farms—to the eye at present wild and unproductive—yet experts say that upon it when irrigated may easily be grown enough to feed the world. Then as to the scenery, . . . while I know the standard claim is that Yosemite, Niagara Falls, the upper Yellowstone and the like, afford the greatest natural shows, I am not so sure but the Prairies and the Plains, while less stunning at first sight, last longer, fill the esthetic sense fuller, precede all the rest, and make North America's characteristic landscape.

Indeed through the whole of this journey, with all its shows and varieties, what most impress'd me, and will longest remain with me, are these same prairies. Day after day, and night after night, to my eyes, to all my senses—they silently and broadly unfolded. Even their simplest statistics are sublime.

READING 5B
"PIONEERS! O PIONEERS!" WALT WHITMAN, 1881

In selected stanzas of this poem Whitman embodies the driving impetus of westward expansionist thought.

> All the past we leave behind,
> We debouch upon a newer, mightier world, varied world,
> Fresh and strong the world we seize, world of labor
>   and the march,
>   Pioneers! O Pioneers!

We primeval forests felling
We the rivers stemming, vexing we and piercing deep
        the mines within,
We the surface broad surveying, we the
        virgin soil upheaving,
        Pioneers! O Pioneers!

All the pulses of the world,
Falling in they beat for us, with the
        Western movement beat,
Holding single or together, steady moving to the front,
        all for us,
        Pioneers! O Pioneers!

Till with the sound of trumpet,
Far, far off the day break call—hark! how loud and clear
        I hear it wind,
Swift! to the head of the army!—Swift!
        Spring to your places,
        Pioneers! O Pioneers!

READING 6
"MARVELS OF THE NEW WEST," W. M. THAYER, 1887

For many, the western spirit was based on potential wealth—mineral, timber, and agricultural. The prospect of conquering and utilizing this vast treasure house moved some observers to express emotions approaching rapture. Here W. M. Thayer rhapsodizes about the agricultural potential of the region.

Who has not heard of the cornfields of Kansas and the wheatfields of Dakota? Not that all the mammoth fields of corn and wheat are found in these localities; for the New West, clear to the Pacific coast, challenges the world to survey its empire of golden grain. . . .

The wildest dream has become reality. . . . Nothing is too large for belief. Twenty and even thirty thousand acre farms, and a hundred bushels to the acre, is not an extravagant story now. Corn eighteen feet high, with ears long and heavy enough for a policeman's club, is not questioned now even by the uninitiated. Harvests like an army with banners, waving their golden plumes above the house which the farmer occupies, require no stretch of the imagination to realize.

We have seen Kansas corn several feet higher than the dwelling which the owner occupied. The stocks were marvelously stout as compared with Eastern corn, and seemed to defy ordinary methods of harvesting. An axe appeared as necessary to lay that field of corn flat as in gathering a crop of hoop-poles. . . .

A farm of twenty or thirty thousand acres . . . is divided into sections, with superintendent and army of employees for each section, who go to work with military precision and order. The . . . workers . . . [sweep] forward like a column of cavalry, turning over a hundred acres of soil in an incredibly brief period of time. . . . Under this arrangement the earth is easily conquered by this mighty army of ploughers, who move forward to the music of rattling machines and the tramp of horses. It is an inspiring spectacle,—the almost boundless prairie farm and the cohorts of hopeful tillers marching over it in triumph. Steam also reinforces the battalions of workers on many bonanza farms, largely multiplying the amount of labor performed. . . .

"Necessity is the mother of invention"; and so the wheat-raisers found a way of harvesting their enormous crops. Our forefathers used the sickle, a very slow and unsatisfactory method of gathering grain. Less than a hundred years ago the "cradle" . . . created a revolution in harvesting. . . . But even the "cradle" could not avail much on the vast wheatfields of the New West. . . . One hundred men could cradle but three hundred acres per day at the most; and one hundred days, at this rate, would be required for harvesting. This would "cost more than it comes to." Western farmers could not afford the expense. It was absolutely necessary that some other method of harvesting grain should be discovered, and it was. A machine for cutting, binding, and placing the bundles in an upright position met the needs of the hour. The problem of harvesting the largest fields of grain was solved by this invention. . . . These machines move before the horses,—from twenty to twenty-four horses or mules to each machine,—cut and thresh and sack the grain, and leave the sacks in piles. Four men work them, and cut and thresh from twenty-five to forty acres a day. . . .

The New West . . . is a veritable "Wonderland" as crowded with OP-PORTUNITIES as it is with marvels. Men live rapidly here—a whole month in one day, a whole year in a month. Some have lived a hundred years in the twenty-five or thirty they have spent here. They have seen an empire rise and grow rich and powerful in that time. The changes wrought under their own eyes have been almost as startling as transformations under the wand of a magician,—such strides of progress as usually exist only in dreams. It seems as if God had concentrated His wisdom and power upon this part of our country, to make it His crowning work of modern civilization on this Western Continent. For its history is Providence illustrated,—God in the affairs of men to exhibit the grandeur of human enterprise and the glory of human achievement. . . .

Neither science, art, learning, or religion was competent to handle such marvelous wealth as lay concealed within the domain of the New West.

READING 7
"SILVER FEVER," MARK TWAIN, 1899

It took patience and good humor to prosper in the trans-Mississippi West. Hardships were common, and a dose of hope often provided the only antidote, especially during the various gold and silver rushes of the nineteenth century. Exhilaration led to despair which led to exhilaration again on the rollercoaster of "the fever." Mark Twain humorously describes an aspect of this emotional cycle in a passage from Roughing It.

By and by I was smitten with the silver fever. "Prospecting parties" were leaving for the mountains every day, and discovering and taking possession of rich silver-bearing lodes and ledges of quartz. Plainly this was the road to fortune. The great "Gould and Curry" mine was held at three or four hundred dollars a foot when we arrived; but in two months it had sprung up to eight hundred. The "Ophir" had been worth only a mere trifle, a year gone by, and now it was selling at *four thousand dollars a foot!* Not a mine could be named that had not experienced an astonishing advance in value within a short time. Everybody was talking about these marvels. Go where you would, you heard nothing else, from morning till far into the night. Tom So-and-So had sold out of the "Amanda Smith" for $40,000—hadn't a cent when he "took up" the ledge six months ago. John Jones had sold half his interest in the "Bald Eagle and Mary Ann" for $65,000, gold coin, and gone to the States for his family. The Widow Brewster had "struck it rich" in the "Golden Fleece" and sold ten feet for $18,000—hadn't money enough to buy a crape bonnet when Sing-Sing Tommy killed her husband at Baldy Johnson's wake last spring. The "Last Chance" had found a "clay casing" and knew they were "right on the ledge"—consequence, "feet" that went begging yesterday were worth a brick house apiece today, and seedy owners who could not be trusted for a drink at any bar in the country yesterday were roaring drunk on champagne today and had hosts of warm personal friends in a town where they had forgotten how to bow or shake hands from long-continued want of practice. Johnny Morgan, a common loafer, had gone to sleep in the gutter and waked up worth a hundred thousand dollars, a consequence of the decision in the "Lady Franklin and Rough and Ready" lawsuit. And so on—day in and day out the talk pelted our ears and the excitement waxed better and hotter around us.

I would have been more or less than human if I had not gone mad like the rest. Cart-loads of solid silver bricks, as large as pigs of iron, were arriving from the mills every day, and such sights as that gave substance to the wild talk about me. I succumbed and grew as frenzied as the craziest.

Every few days news would come of the discovery of a brand-new mining region; immediately the papers would teem with accounts of its richness, and away the surplus population would scamper to take possession. By the time I was fairly inoculated with the disease, "Esmeralda" had just had a run and "Humboldt" was beginning to shriek for attention. "Humboldt! Humboldt!" was the new cry, and straightaway Humboldt, the newest of the new, the richest of the rich, the most marvelous of the marvelous discoveries in silver-land, was occupying two columns of the public prints to "Esmeralda's" one. I was just on the point of starting to Esmeralda, but turned with the tide and got ready for Humboldt. That the reader may see what moved me, and what would as surely have moved him had he been there, I insert here one of the newspaper letters of the day. . . .

"But what about our mines? I shall be candid with you. I shall express an honest opinion, based upon a thorough examination. Humboldt county is the richest mineral region upon God's footstool. Each mountain range is gorged with the precious ores. Humboldt is the true Golconda. . . .

"A very common calculation is that many of our mines will yield five hundred dollars to the ton. Such fecundity throws the Gould & Curry, the Ophir and the Mexican, of your neighborhood, in the darkest shadow. I have given you the estimate of the value of a single developed mine. Its richness is indexed by its market valuation. The people of Humboldt county are *feet* crazy. As I write, our towns are near deserted. They look as languid as a consumptive girl. What has become of our sinewy and athletic fellow-citizens? They are coursing through ravines and over mountain tops. Their tracks are visible in every direction. Occasionally a horseman will dash among us. His steed betrays hard usage. He alights before his adobe dwelling, hastily exchanges courtesies with his townsmen, hurries to an assay office and from thence to the District Recorder's. In the morning, having renewed his provisional supplies, he is off again on his wild and unbeaten route. Why, the fellow numbers already his feet by thousands. He is the horse-leech. He has the craving stomach of the shark or anaconda. He would conquer metallic worlds."

This was enough. The instant we had finished reading the above article, four of us decided to go to Humboldt. We commenced to get ready at once. And we also commenced upbraiding ourselves for not deciding sooner—for we were in terror lest all the rich mines would be found and secured before we got there, and we might have to put up with ledges that would not yield more than two or three hundred dollars a ton, maybe. An hour before, I would have felt opulent if I had owned ten feet in a Gold Hill mine whose ore produced twenty-five dollars to the ton; now I was already annoyed at the prospect of having to put up with mines the poorest of which would be a marvel in Gold Hill.

READING 8
FROM *MY ÁNTONIA*, WILLA CATHER, 1918

For the prairie settler, adaptation and independence were key elements the spirit required. Blizzards, freezing temperatures, loneliness, floods, droughts, grasshopper plagues, fire, and dust all contributed to the frontier experience. But the survivors found rewards in their strong sense of accomplishment under difficult conditions. In this excerpt from her novel My Ántonia, *Willa Cather contrasts her own prairie upbringing with the hardships of the immigrant Bohemian family, the Shimerdas. It is a tale of determination, sacrifice, and hope.*

Early the next morning I ran out-of-doors to look about me. I had been told that ours was the only wooden house west of Black Hawk—until you came to the Norwegian settlement, where there were several. Out neighbours lived in sod houses and dugouts—comfortable, but not very roomy. Our white frame house, with a storey and half-storey above the basement, stood at the east end of what I might call the farmyard, with the windmill close by the kitchen door. From the windmill the ground sloped westward, down to the barns and granaries and pig-yards. The slope was trampled hard and bare, and washed out in winding gullies by the rain. Beyond the corncribs, at the bottom of the shallow draw, was a muddy little pond, with rusty willow bushes growing about it. The road from the post-office came directly by our door, crossed the farmyard, and curved round this little pond, beyond which it began to climb the gentle swell of unbroken prairie to the west. There, along the western sky-line it skirted a great cornfield, much larger than any field I had ever seen. This cornfield, and the sorghum patch behind the barn, were the only broken land in sight. Everywhere, as far as the eye could reach, there was nothing but rough, shaggy, red grass, most of it as tall as I.

North of the house, inside the ploughed fire breaks, grew a thick-set strip of box-elder trees, low and bushy, their leaves already turning yellow. This hedge was nearly a quarter of a mile long, but I had to look very hard to see it at all. The little trees were insignificant against the grass. It seemed as if the grass were about to run over them, and over the plum-patch behind the sod chicken-house.

As I looked about me I felt that the grass was the country, as the water is the sea. The red of the grass made all the great prairie the colour of wine-stains, or of certain seaweeds when they are first washed up. And there was so much motion in it; the whole country seemed, somehow, to be running. . . .

I can remember exactly how the country looked to me as I walked beside my grandmother along the faint wagon-tracks on that early September morning. Perhaps the glide of long railway travel was still with me, for more than anything else I felt the motion in the landscape; in the fresh, easy-blowing morning wind, and in the earth itself, as if the shaggy grass were a sort of loose hide, and underneath it herds of wild buffalo were galloping, galloping. . . .

Alone, I should never have found the garden—except, perhaps, for the big yellow pumpkins that lay about unprotected by their withering vines—and I felt very little interest in it when I got there. I wanted to walk straight on through the red grass and over the edge of the world, which could not be very far away. The light air about me told me that the world ended here; only the ground and sun and sky were left and if one went a little farther there would be only sun and sky, and one would float off into them, like the tawny hawks which sailed over our heads making slow shadows on the grass. . . .

I sat down in the middle of the garden, where snakes could scarcely approach unseen, and leaned my back against a warm yellow pumpkin. There were some ground-cherry bushes growing along the furrows, full of fruit. I turned back the papery triangular sheaths that protected the berries and ate a few. All about me giant grasshoppers, twice as big as any I had ever seen, were doing acrobatic feats among the dried vines. The gophers scurried up and down the ploughed ground. There in the sheltered draw-bottom the wind did not blow very hard, but I could hear it singing its humming tune up on the level, and I could see the tall grasses wave. The earth was warm under me, and warm as I crumbled it through my fingers. . . . I kept as still as I could. Nothing happened. I did not expect anything to happen. I was something that lay under the sun and felt it, like the pumpkins, and I did not want to be anything more. I was entirely happy. Perhaps we feel like that when we die and become part of something entire, whether it is sun and air, or goodness and knowledge. At any rate, that is happiness; to be dissolved into something complete and great. When it comes to one, it comes as naturally as sleep. . . .

On Sunday morning Otto Fuchs was to drive us over to make the acquaintance of our new Bohemian neighbours. We were taking them some provisions, as they had come to live on a wild place where there was no garden or chicken-house, and very little broken land. . . .

I could hardly wait to see what lay beyond that cornfield; but there was only red grass like ours, and nothing else, though from the high wagon-seat one could look off a long way. The road ran about like a wild thing, avoiding the deep draws, crossing them where they were wide and shallow. And all along it, wherever it looped or ran, the sunflowers grew. . . .

The Bohemian family, grandmother told me as we drove along, had bought the homestead of a fellow countryman, Peter Krajiek, and paid him more than it was worth. Their agreement with him was made before they left the old country, through a cousin of his, who was also a relative of Mrs. Shimerda. The Shimerdas were the first Bohemian family to come to this part of the country. Krajiek was their only interpreter, and could tell them anything he chose. . . .

"If they're nice people, I hate to think of them spending the winter in that cave of Krajiek's," said grandmother. "It's no better than a badger hole; no proper dugout at all." . . . ·

The land was growing rougher; I was told that we were approaching Squaw Creek, which cut up the west half of the Shimerdas' place and made the land of little value for farming. Soon we could see the broken, grassy clay cliffs which indicated the windings of the stream, and the glittering tops of the cottonwoods and ash trees that grew down in the ravine. Some of the cottonwoods had already turned, and the yellow leaves and the shining white bark made them look like the gold and silver trees in fairy tales.

As we approached the Shimerdas' dwelling, I could still see nothing but rough red hillocks, and draws with shelving banks and long roots hanging out where the earth had crumbled away. Presently, against one of those banks, I saw a sort of shed, thatched with the same wine-coloured grass that grew everywhere. Near it tilted a shattered windmill frame, that had no wheel. We drove up to this skeleton to tie our horses, and then I saw a door and window sunk deep in the drawbank. . . .

The old man was sitting on a stump behind the stove, crouching over as if he were trying to hide from us. Yulka was on the floor at his feet, her kitten in her lap. She peeped out at me and smiled, but, glancing up at her mother, hid again. Ántonia was washing pans and dishes in a dark corner. The crazy boy lay under the only window, stretched on a gunny-sack stuffed with straw. As soon as we entered, he threw a grain-sack over the crack at the bottom of the door. The air in the cave was stifling, and it was very dark, too. A lighted lantern, hung over the stove, threw out a feeble yellow glimmer. . . .

Grandmother went on talking in her polite Virginia way. . . .

"Haven't you got any sort of cave or cellar outside, Ántonia? This is no place to keep vegetables. How did your potatoes get frozen?"

"We get from Mr. Bushy, at the post-office—what he throw out. We got no potatoes," Tony admitted mournfully.

When Jake went out, Marek crawled along the floor and stuffed up the door-crack again. Then, quietly as a shadow, Mr. Shimerda came out from behind the stove. He stood brushing his hand over his smooth grey hair, as if he were trying to clear away a fog about his head. He was clean and neat as usual, with his green neckcloth and his coral pin. He took grandmother's arm and led her behind the stove, to the back of the room. In the rear wall was another little cave; a round hole, not much bigger than an oil barrel, scooped out in the black-earth. When I got up on one of the stools and peered into it, I saw some quilts and a pile of straw. The old man held the lantern. "Yulka," he said in a low, despairing voice, "Yulka; my Ántonia!"

Grandmother drew back. "You mean they sleep in there—your girls?" He bowed his head.

Tony slipped under his arm. "It is very cold on the floor, and this is warm like the badger hole. I like for sleep there," she insisted eagerly. "My *mamenka* have nice bed, with pillows from our own geese in Bohemie. See, Jim?" She pointed to the narrow bunk which Krajiek had built against the wall for himself before the Shimerdas came.

Grandmother sighed, "Sure enough, where *would* you sleep, dear! I don't doubt you're warm there. You'll have a better house after while, Ántonia, and then you will forget these hard times.'"

READING 9
"THE SIGNIFICANCE OF THE FRONTIER,"
FREDERICK JACKSON TURNER, 1893

One function of history is to attempt to interpret, or make sense of, events. In 1893 a young University of Wisconsin history professor presented his view of the frontier experience in a speech before the American Historical Association. Frederick Jackson Turner's interpretation spawned a resurgence of interest in western history and led to the foundation of a school of frontier historians. In recent years his opinions have been challenged as racist and sexist, but few dispute that his was a seminal, catalytic interpretation, a reflection and condensation of the spiritual elements that had defined the American West. Turner's thesis was a curious mixture of a contemporary expansion of the western mythology and a more distant historical consideration of those same themes.

In a recent bulletin of the Superintendent of the Census for 1890 appear the significant words: "Up to and including 1880 the country had a frontier of settlement, but at present the unsettled areas had been so broken into by isolated bodies of settlement that there can hardly be said to be a frontier line. In the discussion of its extent, its westward movement, etc., it can not, therefore, any longer have a place in the census reports." This brief official statement marks the closing of a great historic movement. Up to our own day American history has been in a large degree the history of the colonization of the Great West. The existence of an area of free land, its continuous recession, and the advance of American settlement westward, explain American development.

Behind institutions, behind constitutional forms and modifications, lie the vital forces that call these organs into life and shape them to meet changing conditions. The peculiarity of American institutions is the fact that they have been compelled to adapt themselves to the changes of an expanding people—to the changes involved in crossing a continent, in winning a wilderness, and in developing at each area of this progress out of the primitive economic and political conditions of the frontier into the complexity of city life. . . . All peoples show development; the germ theory of politics has been sufficiently emphasized. In the case of most nations, however, the development has occurred in a limited area; and if the nation has expanded, it has met other growing people whom it has conquered. But in the case of the United States we have a different phenomenon. Limiting our attention to the Atlantic Coast, we have the familiar phenomenon of the evolution of institutions in a limited area, such as the rise of representative government; the differentiation of simple colonial governments into complex organs; the progress from primitive industrial society, without division of labor, up to the manufacturing civilization. But we have in addition to this a recurrence of the process of evolution in each western area reached in the process of expansion. Thus American development has exhibited not merely advance along a single line, but a return to primitive conditions on a continually advancing frontier line, and a new development for that area. American social development has been continually beginning over again on the frontier. This perennial rebirth, this fluidity of American life, this expansion westward with its new opportunities, its continuous touch with the simplicity of primitive society, furnish the forces dominating American character. The true point of view in the history of this nation is not the Atlantic Coast, it is the Great West. . . .

The frontier is the line of the most rapid and effective Americanization. The wilderness masters the colonist. It finds him European in dress, industries, tools, modes of travel, and thought. It takes him from the railroad car and puts him in the birch canoe. It strips off the garments of civilization and arrays him in the hunting shirt and the moccasin. It puts him in the log cabin of the Cherokee and Iroquois and runs an Indian palisade around him. Before long he has gone to planting Indian corn and plowing with a sharp stick; he shouts the war cry and takes the scalp in orthodox Indian fashion.

In short, at the frontier the environment is at first too strong for the man. He must accept the conditions which it furnishes, or perish, and so he fits himself into the Indian clearings and follows the Indian trails. Little by little he transforms the wilderness, but the outcome is not the old Europe. . . . The fact is, that here is a new product that is American. At first, the frontier was the Atlantic Coast. It was the frontier of Europe in a very real sense. Moving westward, the frontier became more and more American. As successive terminal moraines result from successive glaciations, so each frontier leaves its traces behind it, and when it becomes a settled area the region still partakes of the frontier characteristics. Thus the advance of the frontier has meant a steady movement away from the influence of Europe, a steady growth of independence on American lines. And to study this advance, the men who grew up under these conditions, and the political, economic, and social results of it, is to study the really American part of our history. . . .

The United States lies like a huge page in the history of society. Line by line as we read this continental page from West to East we find the record of social evolution. It begins with the Indian and the hunter; it goes on to tell of the disintegration of savagery by the entrance of the trader, the pathfinder of civilization; we read the annals of the pastoral stage in ranch life; the exploitation of the soil by the raising of unrotated crops of corn and wheat in sparsely settled farming communities; the intensive culture of the denser farm settlement; and finally the manufacturing organization with city and factory system. . . .

The Atlantic frontier was compounded of fisherman, fur-trader, miner, cattle-raiser, and farmer. Excepting the fisherman, each type of industry was on the march toward the West, impelled by an irresistible attraction. Each passed in successive waves across the continent. Stand at Cumberland Gap and watch the procession of civilization, marching single file—the buffalo following the trail to the salt springs, the Indian, the fur-trader and the hunter, the cattle-raiser, the pioneer farmer—and the frontier has passed by. Stand at South Pass in the Rockies a century later and see the same procession with wider intervals between. The unequal rate of advance compels us to distinguish the frontier into the trader's frontier, the rancher's frontier, or the miner's frontier, and the farmer's frontier. When the mines and the cow pens were still near the fall line the trader's pack trains were tinkling across the Alleghenies, and the French on the Great Lakes were fortifying their posts, alarmed by the British trader's birch canoe. When the trappers scaled the Rockies, the farmer was still near the mouth of the Missouri. . . .

It was this nationalizing tendency of the West that transformed the democracy of Jefferson into the national republicanism of Monroe and the democracy of Andrew Jackson. The West of the War of 1812, the West of Clay, and Benton and Harrison, and Andrew Jackson, shut off by the Middle States and the mountains from the coast sections, had a solidarity of its own national tendencies. On the tide of the Father of Waters, North and South met and mingled into a nation. Interstate migration went steadily on—a process of cross-fertilization of ideas and institutions. The fierce struggle of the sections over slavery on the western frontier does not diminish the truth of this statement; it proves the truth of it. Slavery was a sectional trait that would not down, but in the West it could not remain sectional. It was the greatest of frontiersmen who declared: "I believe this government can not endure permanently half slave and half free. It will become all of one thing or all of the other." Nothing works for nationalism like intercourse within the nation. Mobility of population is death to localism, and the western frontier worked irresistibly in unsettling population. . . .

But the most important effect of the frontier has been in the promotion of democracy here and in Europe. As has been indicated, the frontier is productive of individualism. Complex society is precipitated by the wilderness into a kind of primitive organization based on the family. The tendency is anti-social. It produces antipathy to control, and particularly to any direct control. The tax-gatherer is viewed as a representative of oppression. Prof. Osgood, in an able article, has pointed out that the frontier conditions prevalent in the colonies are important factors in the explanation of the American Revolution, where individual liberty was sometimes confused with absence of all effective government. The same conditions aid in explaining the difficulty of instituting a strong government in the period of the confederacy. The frontier individualism has from the beginning promoted democracy. . . .

From the conditions of frontier life came intellectual traits of profound importance. The works of travelers along each frontier from colonial days onward describe certain common traits, and these traits have, while softening down, still persisted as survivals in their place of origin, even when a higher social organization succeeded. The result is that to the frontier the American intellect owes its striking characteristics. That coarseness and strength combined with acuteness and inquisitiveness; that practical, inventive turn of mind, quick to find expedients; that masterful grasp of material things, lacking in the artistic but powerful to effect great ends; that restless, nervous energy; that dominant individualism, working for good and for evil, and withal that buoyancy and exuberance which comes with freedom—these are the traits of the frontier, or traits called out elsewhere because of the existence of the frontier. Since the days when the fleet of Columbus sailed into the waters of the New World, America has been another name for opportunity, and the people of the United States have taken their tone from the incessant expansion which has not only been open but has been forced upon them. He would be a rash prophet who should assert that the expansive character of American life has now entirely ceased. Movement has been its dominant fact, and, unless this training has no effect upon a people, the American energy will continually demand a wider field for its exercise. But never again will such gifts of free land offer themselves. For a moment, at the frontier, the bonds of custom are broken and unrestraint is triumphant. There is not *tabula rasa*. The stubborn American environment is there with its imperious summons to accept its conditions; the inherited ways of doing things are also there; and yet, in spite of the environment, and in spite of custom, each frontier did indeed furnish a new field of opportunity, a gate of escape from the bondage of the past; and freshness, and confidence, and scorn of older society, impatience with its restraints and its ideas, and indifference to its lessons, have accompanied the frontier. What the Mediterranean Sea was to the Greeks, breaking the bond of custom, offering new experiences, calling out new institutions and activities, that, and more, the ever retreating frontier has been to the United States directly, and to the nations of Europe more remotely. And now, four centuries after the discovery of America, at the end of a hundred years of life under the Constitution, the frontier has gone, and with its going has closed the first period of American history.

THE MYTH

The American West is populated with a vast rainbow of ethnic groups from all economic strata and of many political philosophies, but they all seem to give way to the symbol of the West—the cowboy. No specific person is associated with this mythology; rather, an

attitude provides the substance. The cowboy (and, by extension, the westerner) is indepen-
dent, laconic, forthright, and loyal. There is a timeless quality to this image from the past,
a sense of immutable values and endless geographic and personal vistas. The cowboy
represents the vision of westerners as they would prefer to see themselves, with the warts
hidden and the nobility shining. This section looks at the development of the cowboy legend
and the translation of this ultimate Western myth into popular culture.

READING 10

FROM *THE VIRGINIAN*, OWEN WISTER, 1902

Owen Wister drew upon the traditions of the West to expand the image of the
cowboy as the heroic prairie cavalier, staring down danger with a quip and a faint
smile. In this well-known passage from his 1902 novel, Wister evokes the tension
and the honor of the cowboy card game—a contest of both face cards and self-
preservation.

This time the two card dealers that I stood near began to give a part of their
attention to the group that sat in the corner. There was in me a desire to
leave this room. So far my hours at Medicine Bow had seemed to glide
beneath a sunshine of merriment, of easy-going jocularity. This was suddenly gone, like the wind changing to north in the middle of a warm day. But
I stayed, ashamed to go.

Five or six players sat over in the corner at a round table where counters
were piled. Their eyes were close upon their cards, and one seemed to be
dealing a card at a time to each, with pauses and betting between. Steve was
there and the Virginian; the others were new faces.

"No place for amatures," repeated the voice; and now I saw it was the
dealer's. There was in his countenance the same ugliness that his words
conveyed.

"Who's that talkin'?" said one of the men near me, in a low voice.

"Trampas."

"What's he?"

"Cow-puncher, bronco-buster, tin-horn, most anything."

"Who's he talkin' at?"

"Think it's the black-headed guy he's talkin' at."

"This ain't supposed to be safe, is it?"

"Guess we're all goin' to find out in a few minutes."

"Been trouble between 'em?"

"They've not met before. Trampas don't enjoy losing to a stranger."

"Fello's from Arizona, yu' say?"

"No. Virginia. He's recently back from havin' a look at Arizona. Went down there last year for a change. Works for the Sunk Creek outfit." And then the dealer lowered his voice still further and said something in the other man's ear, causing him to grin. After which they both looked at me.

There had been silence over in the corner; but now the man Trampas spoke again.

"*And* ten," said he, sliding out some chips from before him. Very strange it was to hear him, how he contrived to make these words a personal taunt. The Virginian was looking at his cards. He might have been deaf.

"*And* twenty," said the next player, easily.

The next threw down his cards.

It was now the Virginian's turn to bet, or leave the game, and he did not speak at once.

Therefore Trampas spoke. "Your bet, you son-of-a- ——."

The Virginian's pistol came out, and his hand lay on the table, holding it unaimed. And with a voice as gentle as ever, the voice that sounded almost like a caress, but drawling a very little more than usual, so that there was almost a space between each word, he issued his orders to the man Trampas:—

"When you call me that, *smile!*" And he looked at Trampas across the table.

Yes, the voice was gentle. But in my ears it seemed as if somewhere the bell of death was ringing; and silence, like a stroke, fell on the large room. All men present, as if by some magnetic current, had become aware of this crisis. In my ignorance, and the total stoppage of my thoughts, I stood stock-still, and noticed various people crouching, or shifting their positions.

"Sit quiet," said the dealer, scornfully to the man near me. "Can't you see he don't want to push trouble? He has handed Trampas the choice to back down or draw his steel."

Then, with equal suddenness and ease, the room came out of its strangeness. Voices and cards, the click of chips, the puff of tobacco, glasses lifted to drink,—this level of smooth relaxation hinted no more plainly of what lay beneath than does the surface tell the depth of the sea.

For Trampas had made his choice. And that choice was not to "draw his steel." If it was knowledge that he sought, he had found it, and no mistake! We heard no further references to what he had been pleased to style "amatures." In no company would the black-headed man who had visited Arizona be rated a novice at the cool art of self-preservation.

One doubt remained: what kind of man was Trampas? A public backdown is an unfinished thing,—for some natures at least. I looked at his face, and thought it sullen, but tricky rather than courageous.

Something had been added to my knowledge also. Once again I had heard applied to the Virginian that epithet which Steve so freely used. The same words, identical to the letter. But this time they had produced a pistol. "When you call me that, *smile!*" So I perceived a new example of the old truth, that the letter means nothing until the spirit gives it life.

READING 11

FROM *THE OLD-TIME COWHAND*, RAMON F. ADAMS, 1961

> *As time marches on, the true nature of the Old West cowboy becomes more remote and even more difficult to portray with historical accuracy. Even when the cowboy culture was at its height, however, many who knew these cowhands ascribed to them a certain nobility of character and other wholly admirable personality traits. The myth of the independent, individualistic cowboy (and westerner) came early to the popular culture and has never faded. In this excerpt Ramon F. Adams comments on the development of the cowboy persona.*

No class of men were ever so unfaithfully represented, and in consequence so misunderstood and unfairly judged by people generally, as the old-time cowboy has been. He suffered severely from the bad publicity of ill-informed writers who had no real conception of his life and work. They pictured the rough, crude, brutal aspects of the cattle country; the reckless, happy-go-lucky visits to town, the careless use of the six-shooter, the drinkin', the fightin', practical jokes that were rough, the gamblin', and the profanity. All them things were subjects for the writer who painted, in the most lurid colors, slanderous accounts for eager Eastern readers. . . . but still, in spite of all that's been wrote 'bout 'im, them who knowed 'im best and lived with 'im found 'im to be good-natured and a rollickin' whole-souled feller, quick to do a kindness, and as quick to resent an insult.

"THE COW-BOY," TEXAS JACK, 1877

In 1877 a former scout for Buffalo Bill Cody named John Burwell Omohundro Jr.
wrote a series of newspaper articles about the American western culture. Under
the name Texas Jack he wrote lovingly about the cattle drives and the dangers of
bucking broncos, river crossings, stampedes, and the necessity of singing to the
cattle at night. Not all their contemporaries found cowboys admirable, but in this
passage Texas Jack discusses the (to his mind) justifiable attachment of "the
noblest qualities" to the cowboy myth.

The Cow-Boy! How often spoken of, how falsely imagined, how greatly despised (where he is not known), how little understood! I've been there considerable. How sneeringly referred to, and how little appreciated, although his title has been gained by the possession of many of the noblest qualities that form the romantic hero of the poet, novelist, and historian; the plainsman and the scout.

"COWBOY HALLOWEEN IN THE DAKOTA BADLANDS," 1885

The cowboy myth includes a characterization of the cowhand as hard-living, hard-
drinking, carousing, hell-bent for leather, with just a touch of piety thrown in to
leaven the mix. Westerners of all stripes like to feel that they are the spiritual
descendants of this psychological hodgepodge. That portrait has considerable basis
in fact, however. Cowboys did exhibit all these traits at one time or another, and
they were duly reported, as this perhaps slightly exaggerated 1885 newspaper
account of a Halloween celebration in the Dakota Badlands attests.

The cowboys of the Badlands favored the stars and gaudy buttes of that land of earthen goblins with a celebration, which for brilliancy and spontaneity surpasses any thing of the kind on record. True, there were no maidens to add the feminine charm to the occasion, but the pistol decorated gentlemen of the ranges were equal to every emergency. . . . A number of the bovine guardians agreed to don the female attire, and while away the evening hours. . . . They could skim the jagged pasture land on their half breed plugs and rip the ambient air up the back with shouts and whoops and leaden balls. A general fusilade was indulged in, the meeting adjourning when the lamps were shot to pieces.

READING 14
"The Cowboy Dance House," Joseph G. McCoy, 1874

Among observers who did not subscribe to the romantic concept of the cowboy myth, Joseph G. McCoy in his Sketches of the Cattle Trade *presented a decidedly different view. His book, generally considered the earliest narrative of the cowboy culture, depicted a wild and unglamorous figure. And yet McCoy's evocations of the cowboy lifestyle added to the myth of the cowhand as a rollicking frontier rogue. This passage provides one of the best descriptions of the dance halls frequented by cowboys and the zealous nature of their entertainment.*

That institution known in the west as the dance house, is there found also. When the darkness of the night is come to shroud their orgies from public gaze, these miserable beings gather into the halls of the dance house, and "trip the fantastic toe" to wretched music, ground out of dilapidated instruments, by beings fully as degraded as the most vile. . . . Few more wild, reckless scenes of abandoned debauchery can be seen on the civilized earth, than a dance house in full blast in one of the many frontier towns. To say they dance wildly or in an abandoned manner is putting it mild.

READING 15
"On a Western Ranche," John Baumann, 1887

In the American West, myth could rapidly become reality. Long before the frontier was officially declared closed in 1890 the Knight of the Sagebrush, the Cavalier of the Plains, the Lonesome Cowpoke was already part of the American experience. It is not difficult to find contemporary descriptions of this western icon like the one in this passage by John Baumann, a British visitor.

The cowboy has at the present time become a personage; nay, more, he is rapidly becoming a mythical one. Distance is doing for him what lapse of time did for the heroes of antiquity. His admirers are investing him with all manner of romantic qualities; they descant upon his manifold virtues and his pardonable weaknesses as if he were a demi-god, and I have no doubt that before long there will be ample material for any philosophic inquirer who may wish to enlighten the world as to the cause and meaning of the cowboy myth. Meanwhile, the true character of the cowboy has been obscured, his genuine qualities are lost in fantastic tales of impossible daring and skill, of daring equitations and unexampled endurance. Every member of his class is pictured as a kind of Buffalo Bill, as a long-haired ruffian who, decked out in gaudy colors, and tawdry ornaments, booted like a cavalier, chivalrous as a Paladin, his belt stuck full of knives and pistols, makes the world to resound with bluster and braggadocio.

READING 16

"No life can be pleasanter," Theodore Roosevelt, 1893

One of the greatest proponents of the American western lifestyle was Theodore Roosevelt, who during the 1880s owned and operated cattle ranches in the Dakota Badlands. His lyrical and detailed accounts enthralled readers of such magazines as Century *and* Harper's. *Here Roosevelt describes his view of an idyllic cowboy world.*

No life can be pleasanter than life during the months of fall on a ranch in the northern cattle country. The weather is cool; in the evenings and on the rare rainy days we are glad to sit by the great fireplace, with its roaring cotton-wood logs. But on most days not a cloud dims the serene splendor of the sky; and the fresh pure air is clear with the wonderful clearness of the high plains. We are in the saddle from morning to night.

The long, low, roomy ranch-house, of clean hewed logs, is as comfortable as it is bare and plain. We fare simply but well; for the wife of my foreman makes excellent bread and cake, and there are plenty of potatoes grown in the forlorn little garden-patch on the bottom. We also have jellies and jams, made from wild plums and buffalo berries; and all the milk we can drink. For meat, we depend on our rifles; and, with an occasional interlude of ducks or prairie-chickens, the mainstay of each meals is venison—roasted, broiled, or fried.

RECIPE FOR THE WESTERN MOVIE,
CHARLES W. HARRIS AND BUCK RAINEY, 1976

*By the turn of the twentieth century the cowboy myth was firmly ingrained in the
American consciousness. The cowboy as romantic adventurer of the prairie came
to represent what westerners, in particular, wanted to feel about themselves and
their accomplishments. Songs, books, stage plays, and Wild West shows reinforced
the mythology, and early in the new century a new medium—the motion picture—
not only adopted it hook, line, and sinker but expanded it. Today, most of our
beliefs about the cowboy culture (and our views of contemporary American western
behavior) come from the impact of the movies and their stepchild, television. It is
the myth in grand scale, legend served with popcorn. In this passage the editors of*
The Cowboy: Six-Shooters, Songs, and Sex *discuss the commonly accepted
ingredients of the western movie—many of which we, the audience, matter-of-factly
regard as representing at least aspects of accurate western history.*

Clean, unlingering, unsuffering deaths. Did you ever stop to wonder why everyone died so conveniently quick, sparing our hero the frustration and responsibility associated with caring for a villain he has shot out on the range
somewhere?

Cowless cowboys. Where did all the cows go? And why did we call them
cowboys when, in fact, most of the time they were marshals or Texas
Rangers or just drifters? Only in a minority of Westerns was the cowboy star
ever depicted as a working cowboy.

Well-lodged hats. Yes, neither gravity, force, or "all hell turned loose"
seemed to be able to separate a cowboy's Stetson from his head. It was an
interesting phenomenon when you stop to think about it.

Unerring accuracy. In spite of the poor weapons of the late nineteenth
century, our nonchalant heroes seemed always able to shoot the gun out of a
man's hand at fifty yards, without aiming and without hitting the antago-
nist's hand.

Perpetual summers. I wonder why there was never winter in the West? Like
the bears, the cowboy seemed to hibernate in the winter, and our only
glimpse of him or of the West was invariably in a summer setting.

Corpses galore! As Duncan Renaldo (of Cisco Kid fame) once said, "There
have been more people killed in Westerns than ever populated the West!"
Killing seemed to be taken nonchalantly in many Westerns, as if it were an

everyday occurrence. And hardly ever was there an inquest or legal red tape for our hero, who might have finished off six or seven men in as many minutes—nor did such killings ever seem to rest heavily on his mind.

Biological freaks. Most of the heroines in Westerns had but a single parent, nearly always a father. Less than one percent of them ever had a living mother in the film.

Perpetual-firing six-shooters. The "six-shooters" that fired fifteen times without reloading would certainly be a collector's dream today if we could get our hands on them. I wonder where the Durango Kid got that pistol anyway?

Sarsaparilla drinking, girl-shy heroes. It was always strange that the cowboys thought asexual thoughts only—must have been all that sarsaparilla!

"Fists only" heroes. A guy, cowboy hero or not, had to be a little stupid not to pick up a chair, break a whiskey bottle, run, or pull a gun in the face of a dozen hoodlums out to kill him.

Full musical orchestrations. I never could figure out where all the music was coming from out there on the desert when Gene Autry or Roy Rogers was riding along singing to his horse. I could have sworn that either the whole Lawrence Welk Orchestra or Bob Wills and his Texas Playboys were hidden behind a boulder somewhere.

Superior social graces. Where did the cowboy heroes obtain the culture they displayed—speech, etiquette, education? Certainly not out in the barn, or behind it in the haystack with the neighbor girl, or closely trailing the south end of a herd of cattle headed north along The Chisholm Trail.

Ambiguous movie titles. A title such as "Outlaws of Cherokee Pass" for some reason seemed odd at times when there was neither a town nor a "pass" by that name in the movie. And downright misleading were such titles as "Conquest of Cheyenne" when the heroine, it turns out, is named "Cheyenne" and is the subject of the conquest rather than a booming, lawless frontier town.

Instantaneous recovery. After a bruising battle with several badmen weighing no less than two hundred pounds each, the hero would come up with all his teeth intact, bloodless, his clothes immaculately clean, and with a smile on his face. . . .

Ridiculous wearing apparel. Can you believe a cowboy in the 1870s wearing a costume like that of Gene Autry, Tom Mix, Roy Rogers, or William Boyd? Well, really! Not if he wanted to live long.

Bullet-proof horses. I wonder why, with all the bullets flying around, the horses never got hit, but only the humans? Those horses sure knew how to duck!

Happy endings only. You could always count on the fact that the hero would be vindicated, win the girl, and bring about the downfall of the lawless element. The hero's luck in this respect never wavered.

Physical Adonises. Why was the hero nearly always six feet tall, muscular, clean shaven, handsome? Anyway, was it necessary for him, at the conclusion of a knock-down-and-drag-out encounter with two dozen villains in a Western drinking hell, to appear in his close-ups as though he had just left the beauty shop?

Unencumbered heroes. Very seldom was the hero of a B-Western laden with the responsibilities that beset the ordinary man. He seldom was married, seldom presented as a widower with children, and almost never had a mother or father or maiden aunt to see after.

Simple plot structures. A dusty one-street town; one young, beautiful woman; one outlaw gang headed by the town's leading citizen; one saloon serving as a social gathering place; and one hero. Very seldom was there a deviation from this basic structure—yet Western towns came in all sizes; some of them had several beautiful women worth fighting for or rescuing; some had more than one outlaw gang; and, upon occasion, a town might even have several heroes capable of thwarting the nefarious plans of the villain and of vying for the affections of the girl(s).

READING 18

"ARIZONA NATURE MYTH," JAMES MICHIE, 1959

The skill of poets can encapsulate the grandest concept in minimal words and images. In this poem James Michie consolidates many western myths into a few sparse but evocative lines. The landscape of the American West can be bare but spectacular, and the image of the cowboy or sheriff often taciturn and steely. Michie succeeds in presenting the combination.

Up in the heavenly saloon
Sheriff sun and rustler moon
Gamble, stuck in the sheriff's mouth
The fag end of an afternoon.

There in the bad town of the sky
Sheriff, nervy, wonders why
He's let himself wander so far West
On his own; he looks with a smoky eye

At the rustler opposite turning white,
Lays down a king for Law, sits tight
Bluffing. On it that crooked moon
Plays an ace and shoots for the light.

Spurs, badge and uniform red,
(It looks like blood, but he's shamming dead),
Down drops the marshal, and under cover
Crawls out dogwise, ducking his head.

But Law that don't get its man ain't Law.
Next day, faster on the draw,
Sheriff creeping up from the other side
Blazes his way in through the back door.

But moon's not there. He'd ridden out on
A galloping phenomenon,
A wonder horse, quick as light,
Moon's left town. Moon's clean gone.

CHAPTER 2

EXPLORERS AND MOUNTAIN MEN

IT CAN BE like a drug. It can trigger a surge of adrenalin. It can enrapture. It can lead to doom. "It" is the urge to discover what is out there, somewhere. In the American West this urge was personified in the explorers and mountain men. These adventurers—a mixture of semiprimitives, scholarly advocates, visionary dreamers, and crafty entrepreneurs—plunged into the uncharted territory of the West with high hopes. Their motives were mixed, but all took with them the basic attitude expressed by the writer and editor O. S. Marden in this way: "There is no medicine like hope, no incentive so great, and no tonic so powerful as expectation of something tomorrow."

This chapter examines the aspirations and recollections of the men who embarked on journeys to lands that seemed to the dominant culture as remote as the moon. Women, too, often played a crucial role in these explorations as guides and cultural intermediaries.

READING 1

AT THE GREAT FALLS OF THE MISSOURI, MERIWETHER LEWIS, 1805

The 1804–6 Lewis and Clark Expedition, which explored the Louisiana Purchase lands and went on to the Pacific coast, provided a wealth of information about the trans-Mississippi West. The expedition was fraught with danger and endless toil but was also a romantic adventure comparable to those depicted in the most florid novels of the time. The impending rush of future development that would soon change this vast land forever seems far away as Meriwether Lewis describes his party's arrival at the Great Falls of the Missouri in his journal entry of June 13, 1805.

This morning we set out about sunrise after taking breakfast off our venison and fish. we again ascended the hills of the river and gained the level country.

the country through which we passed for the first six miles tho' more rolling than that we had passed yesterday might still with propryety be deemed a level country; our course as yesterday was generally S W. the river from the place we left it appeared to make a considerable bend to the South. from the extremity of this rolling country I overlooked a most beatifull and level plain of great extent or at least 50 or sixty miles; in this there were infinitely more buffaloe than I had ever before witnessed at a view. nearly in the direction I had been travling or S. W. two curious mountains presented themselves of square figures, the sides rising perpendicularly to the hight of 250 feet and appeared to be formed of yellow clay; their tops appeared to be level plains; these inaccessible hights appeared like the ramparts of immence fortifications; I have no doubt but with very little assistance from art they might be rendered impregnable. fearing that the river boar to the South and that I might pass the falls if they existed between this and the snowey mountains I altered my course nealy to the South leaving those insulated hills to my wright and proceeded through the plain; I sent Feels on my right and Drewyer and Gibson on my left with orders to kill some meat and join me at the river where I should halt for dinner. I had proceded on this course about two miles with Goodrich at some distance behind me whin my ears were saluted with the agreeable sound of a fall of water and advancing a little further I saw the spray arrise above the plain like a collumn of smoke which would frequently dispear again in an instant caused I presume by the wind which blew pretty hard from the S. W. I did not however loose my direction to this point which soon began to make a roaring too tremendious to be mistaken for any cause short of the great falls of the Missouri. here I arrived about 12 OClock having traveled by estimate about 15 Miles. I hurryed down the hill which was about 200 feet high and difficult of access, to gaze on this sublimely grand spectacle. I took my position on the top of some rocks about 20 feet high opposite the center of the falls. this chain of rocks appear once to have formed a part of those over which the waters tumbled, but in the course of time has been separated from it to the distance of 150 yards lying prarrallel to it and forming a butment against which the water after falling over the precipice beats with great fury; this barrier extends on the right to the perpendicular clift which forms that board [bound? border?] of the river but to the distance of 120 yards next to the clift it is but a few feet above the level of the water, and here the water in very high tides appears to pass in a channel of 40 yds. next to the higher part of the ledg of rocks; on the left it extends within 80 or ninty yards of the lard [larboard]. Clift which is also perpendicular; between this abrupt extremity of the ledge of rocks and the perpendicular bluff the whole body of water passes with incredible swiftness. immediately at the cascade the river is about 300 yds. wide; about ninty or a hundred yards of this next the Lard. bluff is a smoth even sheet of water falling over a precipice of at least eighty feet, the remaining part of about 200 yards on my right formes the grandest sight I ever beheld, the hight of the fall is the same of the other but the irregular and somewhat projecting rocks below receives the water in it's passage down and brakes it into a perfect white foam which assumes a thousand forms in a moment sometimes flying up in jets of sparkling foam to the hight of fifteen or twenty feet and are scarcely formed before large roling bodies of the same beaten and foaming water is thrown over and conceals them. in short the rocks seem to be most happily fixed to present a sheet of the whitest beaten froath for 200 yards in length and about 80 feet perpendicular. the water after decending strikes against the butment before mentioned or that on which I stand and seems to reverberate and being met by the more impetuous courant they role and swell into half formed billows of great hight which rise and again disappear in an instant. this butment of rock defends a handsom little bottom of about three acres which is deversified and agreeably shaded with some cottonwood trees; in the lower extremity of the bottom there is a very thick grove of the same kind of trees which are small, in this wood there are several Indian lodges formed of sticks. a few small cedar grow near the ledge of rocks where I rest. below the point of these rocks at a small distance the river is divided by a large rock which rises several feet above the water, and extends downwards with the stream for about 20 yards. about a mile before the water arrives at the pitch it decends very rappidly, and is confined on the Lard. side by a perpendicular clift of about 100 feet, on Stard. [starboard] side it is also perpendicular for about three hundred yards above the pitch where it is then broken by the discharge of a small ravine, down which the buffaloe have a large beaten road to the water, for it is but in very few places that these anamals can obtain water near this place owing to the steep and inaccessible banks. I see several skelletons of the buffaloe lying in the edge of the water near the Stard. bluff which I presume have been swept down by the current and precipitated over this tremendious fall. about 300 yards below me there is another butment of solid rock with a perpendicular face and abot 60 feet high which projects from the Stard. side at right angles to the distance of 134 yds. and terminates the lower part nearly of the bottom before mentioned; there being a passage arround the end of this butment between it and the river of about 20 yardes; here the river again assumes it's usual width soon spreading to near 300 yards but still continues it's rappidity. from the reflection of the sun on the spray or mist which arrises from these falls there is a beatifull rainbow produced which adds not a little to the beauty of this majestically grand senery. after wrighting this imperfect description I again viewed the falls and was so much disgusted with the imperfect idea which it conveyed of the scene that I determined to draw my pen across it and begin agin, but then reflected that I could not perhaps succeed better than pening the first impressions of the mind; I wished for the pencil of Salvator Rosa or the pen of Thompson, that I might be enabled to give to the enlightened world some just idea of this truly magnifficent and sublimely grand object, which has from the commencement of time been concealed from the view of civilized man; but this was fruitless and vain. I most sincerely regreted that I had not brought a crimee [camera] obscura with me by the assistance of which even I could have hoped to have done better but alas this was also out of my reach; I therefore with the assistance of my pen only indeavoured to trace some of the stronger features of this seen by the assistance of which and my recollection aided by some able pencil I hope still to give to the world some faint idea of an object which at this moment fills me with such pleasure and astonishment, and which of it's kind I will venture to ascert is second to but one in the known world. I retired to the shade of a tree where I determined to fix my camp for the present and dispatch a man in the morning to inform Capt. C. and the party of my success in finding the falls and settle in their minds all further doubts as to the Missouri. the hunters now arrived loaded with excellent buffaloe meat and informed me that they had killed three very fat cows about ¼ of a mile hence. I directed them after they had refreshed themselves to go back and butcher them and bring another load of meat each to our camp determining to employ those who remained with me in drying meat for the party against their arrival. in about 2 hours or at 4 OClock P. M. they set out on this duty, and I walked down the river about three miles to discover if possible some place to which the canoes might arrive or at which they might be drawn on shore in order to be taken by land above the falls; but returned without effecting either of these objects; the river was one continued sene of rappids and cascades which I readily perceived could not be encountered with our canoes, and the Clifts still retained their perpendicular structure and were from 150 to 200 feet high; in short the river appears here to have woarn a channel in the process of time through a solid rock. on my return I found the party at camp; they had butchered the buffaloe and brought in some more meat as I had directed. Goodrich had caught half a douzen very fine trout and a number of both species of the white fish. these trout are from sixteen to twenty three inches in length, precisely resemble our mountain or speckled trout in form and the position of their fins, but the specks on these are of a deep black instead of the red or goald colour of those common to the U.' States. these are furnished long sharp teeth on the pallet and tongue and have generally a small dash of red on each side behind the front ventral fins; the flesh is of a pale yellowish red, or when in good order, of a rose red.—

I am induced to believe that the Brown, the white and the Grizly bear of this country are the same species only differing in colour from age or more probably from the same natural cause that many other anamals of the same family differ in colour. one of those which we killed yesterday was of a creemcoloured white while the other in company with it was of the common bey or rdish brown, which seems to be the most usual colour of them. the white one appeared from it's tallons and teath to be the youngest; it was smaller than the other, and although a monstrous beast we supposed that it had not yet attained it's growth and that it was a little upwards of two years old. the young cubs which we have killed have always been of a brownish white, but none of them as white as that we killed yesterday. one other that we killed sometime since which I mentioned sunk under some driftwood and was lost, had a white stripe or list of about eleven inches wide entirely arround his body just behind the shoalders, and was much darker than these bear usually are. the grizly bear we have never yet seen, I have seen their tallons in possession of the Indians and from their form I am perswaded if there is any difference between this species and the brown or white bear it is very inconsiderable. There is no such animal as a black bear in this open country or of that species generally denominated the black bear

my fare is really sumptuous this evening; buffaloe's humps, tongues and marrowbones, fine trout parched meal pepper and salt, and a good appetite; the last is not considered the least of the luxuries.

Manuel Lisa and the Fur Trade

Although Lewis and Clark's was the first organized and government-sponsored Anglo-American expedition into the American West, they were by no means its first white explorers. For years there had been commerce on the Missouri River involving British, French, and Spanish traders. In some respects these European activities paved the way for Lewis and Clark, even though they did not have the same romantic sweep and lasting resonance.

Among the best-known of the early merchant-capitalists was Manuel Lisa (1772–1820), the first to explore along the Missouri River in search of furs and trade. His efforts provided important contributions in the development of that trade and in giving impetus to events that followed.

By 1798 Lisa, born in New Orleans and of Spanish descent, had established permanent residence in St. Louis. By 1802 he was requesting permission of the Spanish governor of the province of Louisiana to establish a fur-trading enterprise. Following the transfer of Louisiana to American control in 1803, Lisa led the first trading and fur-trapping expedition northward in 1807. In 1808—in partnership with William Clark, among others—he formed the unsuccessful St. Louis Missouri Fur Company, reorganized in 1812 as the Missouri Fur Company; financial difficulties and the looming War of 1812 led to its failure in 1814. In that year William Clark, then head of Indian Affairs in the Louisiana Territory, named Manuel Lisa subagent for tribes along the Missouri River, enabling Lisa to maintain amicable relationships with Indian nations in the region. In 1819 he formed a second Missouri Fur Company. It failed as well, but Lisa did not live to see the failure; he died in 1820.

Manuel Lisa is credited with being the first in the American era to envision and develop the Missouri River for purposes of commerce and the first to station trappers in the mountains as employees of a fur-trading company, thus creating the fur-trapping "mountain men."

"The commerce in question," Manuel Lisa
to Governor General Salcedo, 1802

On June 4, 1802, Manuel Lisa petitioned the Spanish governor of the province of Louisiana, General Salcedo, for permission to develop and exploit the fur-trading

resources of the Missouri River region. Lisa is asking the governor to end the
absolute fur-trading rights previously granted to a competitor and soliciting for
himself exclusive rights to that trade in a region of the Missouri River basin, with
permission to equip hunters.

New Orleans
June 4, 1802
Senor Governor General

That impelled by the laudable intentions of obviating the repeated public wrongs occasioned to these representatives and their fellow citizens by the exclusive privilege of fur trade granted to Don Augusto Chouteau, because of this individual alone reaping the benefit from a branch of trade in the promotion of which all the inhabitants are interested, or, rather, in which they are interested for their subsistence. . . . [We request that] you might be pleased to restore to them the former general liberty of the said trade with absolute extinction of the exclusive grants. . . . [We ask that the Governor use his office] . . . to conciliate their own interests and those of almost all the inhabitants of those districts with the right which the privileged ones might have acquired to the commerce in question. It is, that Your Excellency concede to the exponents [of this letter] the exclusive trade corresponding to the post of the Big and Little Osages situated at a half day's journey from the Missouri river about forty or fifty leagues from its mouth, with power to equip the hunters who might wish to enter that river. . . .

The commendable proposals of dividing the benefit of the exclusive trade which is solicited . . . also offers to the state an advantage of consideration in the greater facility of restraining and subjecting the incursions of the Indians, it being verified that they will do so because of their own interest, as they promise it with greater security and force than if the privilege were to be conceded to one individual alone. For this purpose they [the authors of the letter] will sacrifice their lives and estates for the sake of an object so plausible and interesting to His Majesty no less than the common and individual welfare of those inhabitants

It can be affirmed without temerity that the foregoing propositions assure to the exponents the public esteem for honor and patriotism which has led them to this representation, and which could confer upon them grave injury by considering them ambitious and clothing themselves in the name of common happiness.

And in view of all this they beg Your Excellency that through your kindness you may be pleased to concede them the aforesaid exclusive trade in the stated terms for the period of five years and in consequence to issue strict orders to the commandant of St. Louis, in order that for no reason may he forbid the representatives to have the use of the said privileges soon as they return to that post, which will be about August or September in view of the fact that it is within the appointed time for making commerce and the suspension of this trade is necessary at the beginning of November on account of the considerable cold and ice which is frequent in that climate. Therefore they are hoping for it from Your Excellency's bountiful beneficence.

May God guard Your Excellency's important life many years for the happiness of the colony.

Manuel Lisa [and three others]

Lisa's petition was granted, but his competitor, Chouteau, did not yield his Osage trade without a fight and continued to control it despite Lisa's fondest hopes. Ironically, Lisa and Chouteau later became partners in the St. Louis Missouri Fur Company.

READING 2B
A STANDARD FUR HUNTER'S CONTRACT, 1809

This typical document, translated from French, details the nature of the relationship in 1809 between Alexis Doza, a fur trapper and essentially an independent contractor, and Pierre Menard, agent for the Missouri Fur Company.

Articles of Contract, & Agreement made today Between pierre Menard of Kaskaskias Agent of the Missouri Fur Company of the one part; & Alexis Doza also of Kaskaskias territory of the Illinois of the other part, Witness; That the said Alexis Doza voluntarily engages himself in the capacity of Hunter, & fisherman of Beaver, to embark and follow a voyage from St. Louis, to the headwaters of the Missouri, or other places on the waters of the said River, to do, & to assist the said Company or Society; in the transportation of baggage loading and unloading of the boats & all connected things, relative to the safeguarding of men baggage, merchandise which will be transported from the city of St. Louis to the headwaters of the said Missouri River; & that at his arrival at his destination, he is obliged to Hunt, and trap the Beaver of the Missouri the best that he can, to gather together the meat of the furred animals, & peltries, & to remain with the said Company or Society, & to hunt in all the environs that he will find the most suitable on the waters of the missouri for the interest and advantage of the said Society, as also for the said Company, change of place or encampment, he is obliged as above to assist to transport the Baggage, Merchandise &c. . . . in the reloading & unloading; finally he is obliged to do, to obey, to execute with promptness, & diligence all reasonable orders which can be given by those in command of the expedition.

And the said Pierre Menard, to the same name, & for the said Company agrees & is obliged to the said Alexis Doza to furnish him with five traps which will be in good condition & repaired at the expense of the said Society besides which he will furnish for (one) year a Horse, ten pounds of powder, twenty pounds of lead, four knives hatchets, —— awls, kettle, —— and if for his risk the said Doza shall find it shall be for the interest of the said Society to take with him the engages of the said Society, he will be given at his choice, in payment by the said Doza one half of their wages for the time he will keep them, & according to the price he will have given those engages he will take with him; as also if the said Doza wants to go downriver after having stayed two years he will be the master of it, besides the said Alexis Doza is obliged to remit & return to the fort of the said Society before or (on) the fifteenth of June of each year with all the pelts, furs, that he will be able to have made in this time, upon which peltries, & furs he will have the half for his services those which will go downriver in the boats of the Society without having paid any part, nor expense, but they will go down at the risk and peril of the said Alexis Doza —— & the other half of the said peltries & furs will belong to the said Society. This present engagement will remain in full force and virtue for three years unless it should be revoked before by the Society or the said Doza at the expiration of two years, to follow the specific conditions in the said agreement under penalty of five hundred Piastres of damages by those who will break the said conditions, cause their good faith to be doubted, presence of witnesses at Kaskaskias the 8 May 1809

"Articles of Association and Copartnership of the St. Louis Missouri Fur Company," 1809

The fur trade was conducted not as a romantic adventure but as coldhearted commerce. As these provisions from the Articles of Association and Copartnership of the St. Louis Missouri Fur Company demonstrate, the enterprise was designed for profit, not out of a sense of history; the adventurous spirit is not clearly evident here, but the commercial impulse certainly is. Established in 1808 by ten partners, the two best known being Manuel Lisa and William Clark, the company was dogged by resistance from Blackfoot Indians, financial instability, transportation difficulties, and an inadequate supply network. The more conservative partners eventually bailed out, and Lisa reorganized the firm into the limited-partnership and short-lived Missouri Fur Company in 1812.

The Articles of Association, as shown by these selected clauses, were designed to spell out in legalistic detail the responsibilities and obligations of the partners and to describe the company's area of operation. The provisions were approved and signed on March 7, 1809, and witnessed by the governor of the Louisiana Territory, Meriwether Lewis.

Articles of Association and Copartnership made and entered into by and between Benjamin Wilkinson, Pierre Chouteau, senior, Manuel Lisa, Auguste Chouteau, junior, Reuben Lewis, William Clark and Sylvester Labbadie all of the Town of St. Louis and Territory of Louisiana and Pierre Menard and William Morrison of the town of Kaskaskia in the Territory of Indiana and also Andrew Henry of Louisiana for the purpose of trading and hunting up the river Missouri and to the headwaters thereof or at such other place or places as a majority of the subscribing co-partners may elect, viz:

Article 1st. This Association shall be called and known by the style & firm of the St. Louis Missouri Fur Company; each member of which shall sign and subscribe these articles of association, and shall be bound to furnish for the joint benefit of the company to compose the outfits requisite for such expedition, and generally to pay equal proportions of all and every expense whatsoever, which may be deemed expedient by the aforesaid majority of the company in order to carry out the above mentioned objects of trading and hunting.

Article 2nd. Each member of the association shall be obliged to accompany the expedition in person or to send some person or persons, to be approved of by a majority of the company; and each member of the company failing to do so, shall pay the sum of five hundred dollars per annum for the benefit of and to be divided amongst such of the co-partners as may accompany the expedition.

Article 3rd. Each partner binds and obliges himself to do every thing which may be in his power for the joint benefit of the company during the period of time fixed upon for the existence of these articles of association; to refrain from trading directly or indirectly with all and every party or nations of Indians or the men employed by the company contrary to the true spirit and meaning of these articles of co-partnership or contrary to the joint interest and benefit of the company. And it is expressly agreed and understood that if any member of the company shall during the existence of these articles, be discovered or be known to traffic or trade for his own separate or individual interest or contrary to the true spirit and meaning of these articles of association he shall not only forfeit & pay for the joint benefit of the Company all his portion of the stock and profits but also to be forever thereafter excluded from the Company. Provided however that a majority of all members agree to such forfeiture and expulsion. . . .

Article 5th. And whereas the above named Manuel Lisa, Pierre Menard and William Morrison were lately associated in a trading expedition up the said River Missouri and have now a fort established on the waters of the Yellow Stone River, a branch of the Missuory, at which said fort they have as is alleged by them a quantity of Merchandise and also a number of horses.

Now therefore it is agreed that this Company is to accept from them the said Manuel Lisa, Pierre Menard and William Morrison all the merchandise they may have on hand at the time of the first expedition to be sent up by this Company shall arrive at said fort. Provided however that the same is not then damaged, and if the same or any part thereof shall be damaged then the Company shall only be bound to receive such parts and parcels thereof as may be fit for trading or such parts as may be received by a majority of the other members of this company then present this company is to allow and pay them the said Manuel Lisa, Pierre Menard & William Morrison one hundred per centum of the first cost.

Article 6th. The present company is also bound from the said Manuel Lisa, Pierre Menard & William Morrison the number of thirty eight horses which it is alleged had been left by them at the said fort when Manuel Lisa took his departure from there or so many of the said Horses as a majority of the other members of this Company then present may approve of, and allow and pay them the sum of thirty dollars for each Horse so approved and accepted. This Company is also bound to receive from them the said Manuel Lisa, Pierre Menard & William Morrison such other Horses the number and quantity of which is to be approved of in like manner as may have been purchased by their agent for them at the said fort, at the time the aforesaid expedition shall arrive there and which may then be delivered for which this Company is to allow and pay the first cost of the merchandise paid for such Horses and also one hundred per centum of the first cost thereof. . . .

Article 9th. When [an] expedition shall arrive at or above the Mandan nation of Indians, each partner accompanying the expedition shall be bound to proceed & reside at such post or place as may be designated for him by a majority of the Company then present and also when there to do and perform as far as may be possible all those duties required of him by such a majority of the Company. Each member failing to comply with this article shall be bound to forfeit and pay to the Company one thousand Dollars per annum to be computed from the time of the first breach of this article in each year untill he shall comply with the aforesaid duties required of him by such a majority.

Article 10th. The members of this association having contracted with his Excellency governor Lewis to convey the Chief of the Mandan Indians now at St. Louis to his nation: It is hereby agreed that Pierre Chouteau senior shall have the command and complete control of the present expedition: to have the full direction of the march; to have command of such officers as may be appointed under him; to point out their duties and give each officer his command agreeably to rank—so far as the Company is bound by the aforesaid contract with the Executive to observe Military Discipline. . . .

Article 14th. William Clark is hereby appointed agent of this company to reside at the Town of St. Louis. He is to receive all Peltries, furs, monies or other property sent or delivered to him by the Company or any member thereof; and the same to keep & preserve in the best manner he can for the interest of the Company and said agent shall be paid and allowed all necessary expenditures made by him.

Article 15th. Whenever any Peltries, furs or other property belonging to the company shall be sent down and delivered to said agent, the same shall be (as speedily thereafter as may be) divided equally between all the partners, and their respective proportions paid to them or their agents on demand....

Article 20th. The foregoing articles of association and Copartnership are to have effect and continue in force for and to the full end and expiration of the term of three years and after the date hereof subject to alterations as a majority of the Company may deem necessary.

In testimony of which we & each of us have hereunto subscribed our names at the Town of St. Louis this seventh day of March eighteen hundred and nine. ...

	Pierre Chouteau
	Manuel Lisa
	Ben Wilkinson
	Stre Labbadie
Signed in presence of	A. P. Chouteau
Meriwether Lewis	Ben Wilkinson for Reuben Lewis
Requirer	Wm Clark
	Manuel Lisa pr Pierre Menard
	Manuel Lisa pr William Morrison
	Andrew Henry

READING 3

THE MOUNTAIN-MEN, GEORGE RUXTON, 1849

It was the beaver that made the mountain men. In the early to middle nineteenth century, desire for beaver pelts and beaver hats propelled trappers into the American West. Probably less than a thousand individuals, the mountain men explored the mountain passes and brought the first taste of the dominant culture to the land of Manifest Destiny. Some names are legendary—Kit Carson, Jim Bridger, James Beckwourth, Jedediah Smith—and their exploits came to be equally legendary. But perhaps the reality of their existence was even more fascinating. In 1847 George Ruxton, an Englishman, spent some time with the mountain men and recounted his experiences in Adventures in Mexico and the Rocky Mountains, *from which this selection is taken.*

The trappers of the Rocky Mountains belong to a "genus" more approximating the primitive savage than perhaps any other class of civilized man.

Their lives being spent in the remote wilderness of the mountains, with no other companion than Nature herself, their habits and character assume a cast of simplicity mingled with ferocity, appearing to take their colouring from the scenes and objects which surround them. Knowing no wants save those of nature, their sole care is to procure sufficient food to support life, and the necessary clothing to protect them from the rigorous climate. This, with the assistance of their trusty rifles, they are generally able to effect, but sometimes at the expense of great peril and hardship. When engaged in their avocation, the natural instinct of primitive man is ever alive, for the purpose of guarding against danger and the provision of necessary food.

Keen observers of nature, they rival the beasts of prey in discovering the haunts and habits of game, and in their skill and cunning in capturing it. Constantly exposed to perils of all kinds, they become callous to any feeling of danger, and destroy human as well as animal life with as little scruple and as freely as they expose their own. Of laws, human or divine, they neither know nor care to know. Their wish is their law, and to attain it they do not scruple as to ways and means. Firm friends and bitter enemies, with them it is "a word and a blow," and the blow often first. They may have good qualities, but they are those of the animal; and people fond of giving hard names call them revengeful, bloodthirsty, drunkards, . . . gamblers, . . . in fact, "White Indians." However, there are exceptions, and I *have* met honest mountain-men. Their animal qualities, however, are undeniable. Strong, active, hardy as bears, daring, expert in the use of their weapons, they are just what uncivilised white man might be supposed to be in a brute state, depending upon his instinct for the support of life. Not a hole or corner in the vast wilderness of the "Far West" but has been ransacked by these hardy men. From the Mississippi to the mouth of the Colorado of the West, from the frozen regions of the North to the Gila in Mexico, the beaver-hunter has set his traps in every creek and stream. All this vast country, but for the daring enterprise of these men, would be even now a *terra incognita* to geographers, as indeed a great portion still is; but there is not an acre that has not been passed and repassed by the trappers in their perilous excursions. The mountains and streams still retain the names assigned to them by the rude hunters; and these alone are the hardy pioneers who paved the way for the settlement of the western country.

Trappers are of two kinds, the "hired hand" and the "free trapper": the former hired for the hunt by the fur companies; the latter, supplied with animals and traps by the company, is paid a certain price for his furs and peltries.

There is also the trapper "on his own hook"; but this class is very small. He has his own animals and traps, hunts where he chooses, and sells his peltries to whom he pleases.

On starting a hunt, the trapper fits himself out with the necessary equipment, either from the Indian trading-forts, or from some of the petty traders—coureurs des bois—who frequent the western country. This equipment consists usually of two or three horses or mules—one for saddle, the others for packs—and six traps, which are carried in a bag of leather called a *trap-sack*. Ammunition, a few pounds of tobacco, dressed deer-skins for mocassins, &c., are carried in a wallet of dressed buffalo-skin, called a possible-sack. His "possibles" and "trap-sack" are generally carried on the saddle-mule when hunting, the others being packed with the furs. The costume of the trapper is a hunting-shirt of dressed buckskin, ornamented with long fringes; pantaloons of the same material, and decorated with porcupine-quills and long fringes down the outside of the leg. A flexible felt hat and mocassins clothe his extremities. Over his left shoulder and under his right arm hang his powder-horn and bullet-pouch, in which he carries his balls, flint and steel, and odds and ends of all kinds. Round the waist is a belt, in which is stuck a large butcher-knife in a sheath of buffalo-hide, made fast to the belt by a chain or guard of steel; which also supports a little buckskin case containing a whetstone. A tomahawk is also often added; and, of course, a long heavy rifle is part and parcel of his equipment. I had nearly forgotten the pipe-holder, which hangs around the neck, . . . and a triumph of squaw workmanship, in the shape of a heart, garnished with beads and porcupine-quills.

Thus provided, and having determined the locality of his trapping-ground, he starts to the mountains, sometimes alone, sometimes with three or four in company, as soon as the breaking up of the ice allows him to commence operations. Arrived on his hunting-grounds, he follows the creeks and streams, keeping a sharp look-out for "sign." If he sees a prostrate cotton-wood tree, he examines it to discover if it be the work of beaver—whether "thrown" for the purpose of food, or to dam the stream. The track of the beaver on the mud or sand under the bank is also examined; and if the "sign" be fresh, he sets his trap in the run of the animal, hiding it under water, and attaching it by a stout chain to a picket driven in the bank, or to a bush or tree. A "float-stick" is made fast to the trap by a cord a few feet long, which, if the animal carry away the trap, floats on the water and points out its position. The trap is baited with the "medicine," an oily substance obtained from a gland in the scrotum of the beaver, but distinct from the testes. A stick is dipped into this and planted over the trap; and the beaver, attracted by the smell, and wishing a close inspection, very foolishly puts his leg into the trap, and is a "gone beaver."

When a lodge is discovered, the trap is set at the edge of the dam, at the point where the animal passes from deep to shoal water, and always under water. Early in the morning the hunter mounts his mule and examines the traps. The captured animals are skinned, and the tails, which are a great dainty, carefully packed into camp. The skin is then stretched over a hoop or framework of osier-twigs, and is allowed to dry, the flesh and fatty substance being carefully scraped (grained). When dry, it is folded into a square sheet, the fur turned inwards, and the bundle, containing about ten to twenty skins, tightly pressed and corded, and is ready for transportation.

During the hunt, regardless of Indian vicinity, the fearless trapper wanders far and near in search of "sign." His nerves must ever be in a state of tension, and his mind ever present at his call. His eagle eye sweeps round the country, and in an instant detects any foreign appearance. A turned leaf, a blade of grass pressed down, the uneasiness of the wild animals, the flight of birds, are all paragraphs to him written in nature's legible hand and plainest language. All the wits of the subtle savage are called into play to gain an advantage over the wily woodsman; but with the natural instinct of primitive man, the white hunter has the advantages of a civilised mind, and, thus provided, seldom fails to outwit, under equal advantages, the cunning savage.

Sometimes, following on his trail, the Indian watches him set his traps on a shrub-belted stream, and, passing up the bed, . . . so that he may leave no track, he lies in wait in the bushes until the hunter comes to examine his carefully-set traps. Then, waiting until he approaches his ambushment within a few feet, whiz flies the home-drawn arrow never failing at such close quarters to bring the victim to the ground. For one white scalp, however, that dangles in the smoke of an Indian's lodge, a dozen black ones, at the end of the hunt, ornament the camp-fires of the rendezvous.

At a certain time, when the hunt is over, or they have loaded their pack-animals, the trappers proceed to the "rendezvous," the locality of which has been previously agreed upon; and here the traders and agents of the fur companies await them, with such assortment of goods as their hardy customers may require, including generally a fair amount of alcohol. The trappers drop in singly and in small bands, bringing their packs of beaver to this mountain market, not unfrequently to the value of a thousand dollars each, the produce of one hunt. The dissipation of the "rendezvous," however, soon turns the trapper's pocket inside out. The goods brought by the traders, although of the most inferior quality, are sold at enormous prices. . . .

The "beaver" is purchased at from two to eight dollars per pound; the Hudson's Bay Company alone buying it by the pluie, or "plew," that is, the whole skin, giving a certain price for skins, whether of old beaver or "kittens."

The rendezvous is one continued scene of drunkenness, gambling, and brawling and fighting, as long as the money and credit of the trappers last. Seated, Indian fashion, round the fires, with a blanket spread before them, groups are seen with their "decks" of cards, playing at "euker," "poker," and "seven-up," the regular mountain-games. The stakes are "beaver," which here is the current coin; and when the fur is gone, their horses, mules, rifles, and shirts, hunting-packs, and *breeches,* are staked. Daring gamblers make the rounds of the camp, challenging each other to play for the trapper's highest stake,—his horse, his squaw (if he have one), and, as once happened, his scalp. . . . A trapper often squanders the produce of his hunt, amounting to hundreds of dollars, in a couple of hours; and, supplied on credit with another equipment, leaves the rendezvous for another expedition, which has the same result time after time; although one tolerably successful hunt would enable him to return to the settlements and civilised life, with an ample sum to purchase and stock a farm, and enjoy himself in ease and comfort the remainder of his days.

An old trapper, a French Canadian, assured me that he had received fifteen thousand dollars for beaver during a sojourn of twenty years in the mountains. Every year he resolved in his mind to return to Canada, and, with this object, always converted his fur into cash; but a fortnight at the "rendezvous" always cleaned him out, and, at the end of twenty years, he had not even credit sufficient to buy a pound of powder.

These annual gatherings are often the scene of bloody duels, for over their cups and cards no men are more quarrelsome than your mountaineers. Rifles, at twenty paces, settle all differences, and, as may be imagined, the fall of one or other of the combatants is certain, or, as sometimes happens, both fall to the word "fire."

READING 4
THE FUR HUNTERS, ALEXANDER ROSS, 1855

In the Pacific Northwest the fur trade brought the greatest profits and the greatest source of friction. Europeans competed among themselves for this lucrative commerce, and this in turn caused conflict within the Native American population. Alexander Ross, originally a trapper with John Jacob Astor's Pacific Fur Company and later with the North West Fur Company, describes how a large fur-trapping party worked in Indian territory.

A safe and secure spot, near wood and water, is first selected for the camp. Here the chief of the party resides with the property. It is often exposed to danger or sudden attack, in the absence of the trappers, and requires a vigilant eye to guard against the lurking savages. The camp is called head-quarters. From hence all the trappers, some on foot, some on horseback, according to the distance they have to go, start every morning in small parties in all directions ranging the distance of some twenty miles around. Six traps is the allowance for each hunter, but to guard against wear and tear, the complement is more frequently ten. These he sets every night and visits again in the morning, sometimes oftener, according to the distance of the circumstances. The beaver taken in the traps are always conveyed to the camp, skinned, stretched, dried, folded up with the hair in the inside, laid by, and the flesh used for food. No sooner, therefore, has a hunter visited his traps, set them again, and looked out for some other place, than he returns to the camp to feast and enjoy the pleasures of an idle day.

There is, however, much anxiety and danger in going through the ordinary routine of a trapper's duty. For as the enemy is generally lurking about among the rocks and hiding-places, watching an opportunity, the hunter has to keep a constant lookout, and the gun is often in one hand while the trap is in the other. But when several are together, which is often the case in suspicious places, one-half set the traps and the other half keep guard over them. Yet notwithstanding all their precautions some of them fall victims to Indian treachery.

The camp remains stationary while two-thirds of the trappers find beaver in the vicinity, but whenever the beaver becomes scarce the camp is removed to some more favorable spot. In this manner the party keeps moving from place to place during the whole season of hunting. Whenever serious danger is apprehended, all the trappers make for the camp. Were we, however, to calculate according to the numbers, the prospects from such an expedition would be truly dazzling: say seventy-five men with each six traps, to be successfully employed during the five months; that is, two in the spring, and three in the fall, equal to 131 working days, the result would be 58,950 beaver! Practically, however, the case is very different. The apprehension of danger at all times is so great that three-fourths of their time is lost in the necessary steps taken for their own safety. There is also another serious drawback unavoidably accompanying every large party. The beaver is a timid animal. The least noise, therefore, made about its haunt will keep it from coming out for nights together, and noise is unavoidable when the party is large. But when the party is small the hunter has a chance of being more or less successful. Indeed, were the nature of the ground such as to admit of the trappers moving about in safety at all times, and alone, six men with six traps each would in the same space of time and at the same rate kill as many beaver—say 4,716—as the whole seventy-five could be expected to do! And yet the evil is without a remedy, for no small party can exist in these parts. Hence the reason why the beaver are so numerous.

READING 5

A BUFFALO HUNT, JOHN C. FREMONT, 1843

John C. Fremont, soldier, political leader, and explorer, perhaps best exemplifies the impact of American western adventures on the national culture and society. From 1841 to 1844 Fremont and his band (including his guide Kit Carson) roamed the West on congressionally sponsored expeditions. His enthusiastic reports created remarkable interest in and impetus for settlement of these regions. All told, Fremont led three expeditions westward, exploring the Rocky Mountains and the Oregon Territory; he also led the mapping of the Oregon Trail. In recounting an 1843 event, Fremont describes a buffalo hunt in the plains.

A few miles brought us into the midst of the buffalo, swarming in immense numbers over the plains, where they had left scarcely a blade of grass standing. Mr. Preuss, who was sketching at a distance in the rear, had at first noted them as large groves of timber. In the sight of such a mass of life, the traveler feels a strange emotion of grandeur. We had heard from a distance a dull and confused murmuring, and, when we came in view of their dark masses, there was not one among us who did not feel his heart beat quicker. It was the early part of the day, when the herds were feeding; and everywhere they were in motion. Here and there a huge old bull was rolling in the grass, and clouds of dust rose in the air from various parts of the bands, each the scene of some obstinate fight. . . . The wind was favorable; the coolness of the morning invited to exercise; the ground was apparently good, and the distance across the prairie (two or three miles) gave us a fine opportunity to charge them before they could get among the river hills. It was too fine a prospect for a chase to be lost; and, halting for a few moments, the hunters were brought up and saddled, and Kit Carson, Maxwell and I started together. They were now somewhat less than a half a mile distant, and we rode easily along within about three hundred yards, when a sudden agitation, a wavering in the band, and a galloping to and fro of some which were scattered along the skirts, gave us the intimation that we were discovered. We started together at a hand gallop, riding steadily abreast of each other, and here the interest of the chase became so engrossingly intense that we were sensible of nothing else. We were now closing upon them rapidly, and the front of the mass was already in rapid motion for the hills, and in a few seconds the movement had communicated itself to the whole herd.

A crowd of bulls, as usual, brought to the rear, and every now and then some of them faced about, and then dashed on after the band a short distance, and turned and looked again, as if more than half inclined to stand and fight. In a few moments, however, during which we had been quickening our pace, the rout was universal, and we were going over the ground like a hurricane. When at about thirty yards, we gave the usual shout (the hunter's battle cry) and broke into the herd. We entered on the side, the mass giving away in every direction in their heedless course. Many of the bulls, less active and less fleet than the cows, paying no attention to the ground, and occupied solely with the hunter, were precipitated to the ground with great force, rolling over and over with the violence of the shock, and hardly distinguishable in the dust. We separated on entering, each singling out his game.

My horse was a trained hunter, famous in the West under the name of Proveau, and, with his eyes flashing and the foam flying from his mouth, sprang on after the cow like a tiger. In a few moments he brought me alongside of her, and, rising in the stirrups, I fired at the distance of a yard, the ball entering at the termination of the long hair, and passing near the heart. She fell headlong at the report of the gun, and checking my horse, I looked around for my companions. At a little distance, Kit was on the ground, engaged in tying his horse to the horns of a cow which he was preparing to cut up. Among the scattered bands, at some distance below, I caught a glimpse of Maxwell; and while I was looking, a light wreath of white smoke curled away from his gun, from which I was too far to hear the report.

Nearer, and between me and the hills, toward which they were directing their course, was the body of the herd, and giving my horse the rein, we dashed after them. A thick cloud of dust hung upon their rear, which filled my mouth and eyes, and nearly smothered me. In the midst of this I could see nothing, and the buffalo were not distinguishable until within thirty feet. They crowded together more densely still as I come upon them, and rushed along in such a compact body, that I could not obtain an entrance—the horse almost leaping after them. In a few minutes the mass divided to the right and left, the horns clattering with a noise heard above everything else, and my horse darted into the opening. Five or six bulls charged on us and we dashed along the line, but were left far behind; singling out a cow, I gave her my fire, but struck too high. She gave me a tremendous leap, and scoured on swifter than before. I reined up my horse, and the band swept on like a torrent, and left the place quiet and clear.

Our chase had led us into dangerous ground. A prairie-dog village, so thickly settled there were three or four holes in every twenty yards square, occupied the whole bottom for nearly two miles length. Looking around, I saw one of the hunters, nearly out of sight, and the dark line of our caravan crawling along, at three or four miles distance.

READING 6

THE DISCOVERY OF BECKWOURTH PASS, JAMES BECKWOURTH, 1892

Adventurers frequently lent their names to geographic features and landmarks. James Beckwourth—an African-American mountain man who liked to call himself "Mountaineer, Scout, Pioneer, and Chief of the Crow Nation of Indians"—"discovered" a pass through the Sierra Nevada that still bears his name. His experiences are a classic microcosm of the mountain man / explorer world, for the activities of the mountain men varied from the sublime to the suspect. Beckwourth's explorations and assistance to western settlement were dangerous and perhaps noble endeavors, but he also conspired with other mountain men, trappers, and some Indians to steal property and livestock from ranches for trade and resale. In this excerpt from his autobiography Beckwourth relates the story of Beckwourth Pass.

We proceeded in an easterly direction, and all busied themselves in searching for gold; but my errand was of a different character; I had come to discover what I suspected to be a pass.

It was the latter end of April when we entered upon an extensive valley at the northwest extremity of the Sierra range. . . . Swarms of wild geese and ducks were swimming on the surface of the cool crystal stream, which was the central fork of the Rio de las Plumas [Feather River], or sailed the air in clouds over our heads. Deer and antelope filled the plains, and their boldness was conclusive that the hunter's rifle was to them unknown. Nowhere visible were any traces of the white man's approach, and it is probable that our steps were the first that ever marked the spot. We struck across this beautiful valley to the waters of the Yuba, from thence to the waters of the Truchy. . . . This, I at once saw, would afford the best waggon-road into the American Valley approaching from the eastward, and I imparted my views to three of my companions in whose judgment I placed the most confidence. They thought highly of the discovery, and even proposed to associate with me in opening the road. We also found gold, but not in sufficient quantity to warrant our working it. . . .

On my return to the American Valley, I made known my discovery to a Mr. Turner, proprietor of the American Ranch, who entered enthusiastically into my views; it was a thing, he said, he had never dreamed of before. If I could but carry out my plan, and divert travel into that road, he thought I should be a made man for life. Thereupon he drew up a subscription-list, setting forth the merits of the project, and showing how the road could be made practicable to Bidwell's Bar, and thence to Marysville. . . . He headed the subscription with two hundred dollars.

When I reached Bidwell's Bar and unfolded my project, the town was seized with a perfect mania for the opening of the route. The subscriptions toward the fund required for its accomplishment amounted to five hundred dollars. . . . While thus busily engaged I was seized with erysipelas [a bacterial disease characterized by skin inflammation], and abandoned all hopes of recovery; I was over one hundred miles away from medical assistance, and my only shelter was a brush tent. I made my will, and resigned myself to death. Life still lingered in me, however, and a train of waggons came up, and encamped near where I lay. I was reduced to a very low condition, but I saw the drivers, and acquainted them with the object which had brought me out there. They offered to attempt the new road if I thought myself sufficiently strong to guide them through it. The women, God bless them! came to my assistance, and through their kind attentions and excellent nursing I rapidly recovered from my lingering sickness, until I was soon able to mount my horse, and lead the first train, consisting of seventeen waggons, through "Beckwourth's Pass." . . .

In the spring of 1852 I established myself in Beckwourth Valley, and finally found myself transformed into a hotel-keeper and chief of a trading-post. My house is considered the emigrant's landing-place, as it is the first ranch he arrives at in the golden state, and is the only house between this point and Salt Lake.

READING 7

THE MORMONS

Exploration can take many forms. It can be scientific, commercial, spiritual, military, legal, or any of a dozen other manifestations. For the Church of Jesus Christ of Latter-Day Saints—the Mormons—exploration and settlement in the American West constituted a search for a safe haven and freedom from persecution.

Founded in Fayette, New York, in 1830 by the Mormon prophet Joseph Smith, the Mormons became (along with the Catholics) a much discussed and feared religious sect in nineteenth-century America. Following the tenets of the Book of Mormon, *the church proselytized throughout New England, Canada, the Old Northwest, and Great Britain; by the mid-1830s the Mormons claimed more than eight thousand converts. Their presence brought controversy and violence. Mormon leaders and settlers were successively forced out of New York, Ohio, and Missouri. The church established a large community in Nauvoo, Illinois. However, in 1844 a mob, which included members of the Illinois State Militia, stormed the Carthage, Illinois, jail where Joseph Smith and his brother were being held on the charge of inciting a riot and murdered them. Within weeks a new leader, Brigham Young, organized an expedition to find a new, more hospitable settlement to the west. In 1847–48 about two thousand church members arrived in the isolated Great Salt Lake basin, and by 1860 there were some forty thousand Mormons in the region.*

Controversy followed them to their Utah homeland. Throughout America their practice of inhibiting non-Mormon commerce, their insular religious community and behavior, their system of "voluntary consecrations" (tithing), their attempt to monopolize the political structure at the expense of non-Mormons, and especially the practice of "plural marriage," or polygamy, were sources of endless curiosity and concern in the non-Mormon world. To state that the dominant public opinion of the "Gentiles" toward the Mormons was hostile is an understatement. By 1857 the United States government viewed the church leaders as failing to cooperate with federal authority. President James Buchanan declared that the Mormons were in "a state of substantial rebellion" and sent the U.S. Army to occupy the Territory of Utah; they remained until the outbreak of the Civil War in 1861.

In 1887 the federal government passed the Edmunds-Tucker Act to limit Mormon political and business control in Utah. The law disincorporated the church, regulated elections and business practices, stripped the vote from Mormon women (which had been granted in 1870), and required seizure of much Mormon property. In 1890 Mormon leaders agreed to refrain from performing plural marriages, to disband the church's political apparatus, and to not operate church-supported business. In recognition of these actions, Utah was granted statehood in 1896.

The following readings detail the religious visions of Joseph Smith, the power and influence of Brigham Young, the story of the "Handcart Pioneers," and criticism of Mormon practices, most notably that of "plural marriage."

READING 7A
"HIS NAME WAS MORONI," JOSEPH SMITH, 1838

In 1838 Joseph Smith recorded his testimony, in which he relates the circumstances of the 1823 "divine visitation" that had prompted him to found the Church of Jesus Christ of Latter-Day Saints.

On the evening of the . . . twenty-first of September [1823] . . . I betook myself to prayer and supplication to Almighty God. . . .

While I was thus in the act of calling upon God, I discovered a light appearing in my room, which continued to increase until the room was lighter than at noonday, when immediately a personage appeared at my bedside, standing in the air, for his feet did not touch the floor.

He had on a loose robe of the most exquisite whiteness. It was a whiteness beyond anything earthly I had ever seen; nor do I believe that any earthly thing could be made to appear so exceedingly white and brilliant. His hands were naked, and his arms also, a little above the wrists; so, also, were his feet naked, as were his legs, a little above the ankles. His head and neck were also bare. I could discover that he had no other clothing on but this robe, as it was open, so that I could see his bosom.

Not only was his robe exceedingly white, but his whole person was glorious beyond description, and his countenance truly like lightning. The room was exceedingly light, but not very bright as immediately around his person. When I first looked upon him, I was afraid; but the fear soon left me.

He called me by name, and said unto me that he was a messenger sent from the presence of God to me, and that his name was Moroni; that God had a work for me to do; and that my name should be had for good and evil among all nations, kindreds, and tongues, or that it should be both good and evil spoken of among all people.

He said there was a book deposited, written upon gold plates, giving an account of the former inhabitants of this continent, and the source from whence they sprang. He also said that the fulness of the everlasting Gospel was contained in it, as delivered by the Savior to the ancient inhabitants.

Also, that there were two stones in silver bows—and these stones, fastened to a breastplate, constituted what is called the Urim and Thummim—deposited with the plates, and the possession of these stones were what constituted *Seers* in ancient or former times; and that God had prepared them for the purpose of translating the book. . . .

Again, he told me, that when I got those plates of which he had spoken—for the time that they should be obtained was not yet fulfilled—I should not show them to any person; neither the breastplate with the Urim and Thummim; only to those to whom I should be commanded to show them; if I did I should be destroyed. While he was conversing with me about the plates, the vision was opened to my mind that I could see the place where the plates were deposited, and that so clearly and distinctly that I knew the place again when I visited it.

After this communication, I saw the light in the room begin to gather immediately around the person of him who had been speaking to me, and it continued to do so, until the room was again left dark, except just around him, when instantly I saw . . . a conduit open right up into heaven, and he ascended until he entirely disappeared, and the room was left as it had been before this heavenly light had made its appearance.

I lay musing on the singularity of the scene, and marveling greatly at what had been told to me by this extraordinary messenger; when, in the midst of my meditation, I suddenly discovered that my room was again beginning to get lighted, and in an instant . . . the same heavenly messenger was again at my bedside.

He commenced, and again related the very same things which he had done at his first visit, without the least variation, which having done, he informed me of great judgments which were coming upon the earth, with great desolations by famine, sword, and pestilence; and that these grievous judgments would come on the earth in this generation. Having related these things, he again ascended as he had done before.

By this time, so deep were the impressions made on my mind, that sleep had fled from my eyes, and I lay overwhelmed in astonishment at what I had both seen and heard. . . .

[On his fourth visitation, Moroni instructed Smith to tell his father about the visions.] I obeyed; I returned to my father in the field, and rehearsed the whole matter to him. He replied to me that it was of God, and told me to go and do as commanded by the messenger. I left the field, and went to the place where the messenger had told me the plates were deposited; and owing to the distinctness of the vision which I had had concerning it, I knew the place the instant that I arrived there.

Convenient to the village of Manchester, Ontario county, New York, stands a hill of considerable size, and the most elevated of any in the neighborhood. On the west side of this hill, not far from the top, under a stone of considerable size, lay the plates, deposited in a stone box. This stone was thick and rounding in the middle on the upper side, and thinner towards the edges, so that the middle part of it was visible above the ground, but the edge all around was covered with earth.

Having removed the earth, I obtained a lever, which I got fixed under the edge of the stone, and with a little exertion raised it up. I looked in, and there indeed did I behold the plates, the Urim and Thummim, and the breastplate, as stated by the messenger. The box in which they lay was formed by laying stones together in some kind of cement. In the bottom of the box were laid two stones crossways of the box, and on these stones lay the plates and the other things with them.

I made an attempt to take them out, but was forbidden by the messenger, and was again informed that the time for bringing them forth had not yet arrived, neither would it, until four years from that time; but he told me that I should come to that place precisely in one year from that time, and that he would there meet with me, and that I should continue to do so until the time should come for obtaining the plates.

Accordingly as I had been commanded, I went at the end of each year, and at each time I found the same messenger there, and received instruction and intelligence from him at each of our interviews, respecting what the Lord was going to do, and how and in what manner His kingdom was to be conducted in the last days. . . .

At length the time arrived for obtaining the plates, the Urim and Thummim, and the breastplate. On the twenty-second day of September [1827] . . . having gone as usual at the end of another year to the place where they were deposited, the same heavenly messenger delivered them up to me with this charge: That I should be responsible for them; that if I should let them go carelessly, or through any neglect of mine, I should be cut off; but that if I would use all my endeavors to preserve them, until he, the messenger, should call for them, they should be protected.

I soon found out the reason why I had received such strict charges to keep them safe, and why it was that the messenger had said that when I had done what was required at my hand, he would call for them. For no sooner was it known that I had them, than the most strenuous exertions were used to get them from me. Every stratagem that could be invented was resorted to for that purpose. The persecution became more bitter and severe than before, and multitudes were on the alert continually to get them from me if possible. But by the wisdom of God, they remained safe in my hands, until I had accomplished by them what was required at my hand. When, according to arrangements, the messenger called for them, I delivered them up to him; and he has them in his charge until this day, being the second of May [1838].

Soon after he supposedly received the plates, Joseph Smith showed them to seven other people. All eight men signed a document that claimed they had personally seen and handled the gold plates, concluding with the words, "And we lie not, God bearing witness to it."

Horace Greeley Interviews Brigham Young, 1859

With the death of Joseph Smith in 1844, Brigham Young assumed the mantle of leadership. He organized and led the journey to the Great Salt Lake basin, where he gained nearly dictatorial control of the Utah Mormon empire in its early years. Young fascinated observers of the time with his power and influence. In 1861 French writer Jules Remy called him "the Mormon Pope." Mark Twain in Roughing It *referred to Utah as "an absolute monarchy" where "Brigham Young is King." In 1859 the famous newspaper editor Horace Greeley—whose admonition "Go west, young man, and grow with the country" was one of many sparks igniting the westward movement—traveled to Utah as part of his own western journey. In Salt Lake City he met with the Mormon leader for about two hours. Greeley described Brigham Young as "very plainly dressed in thin summer clothing, and with no air of sanctimony or fanaticism. In appearance, he is a portly, frank, good-natured, rather thickset man of fifty-five, seeming to enjoy life and to be in no particular hurry to get to heaven." This is Greeley's account of their interview.*

Horace Greeley—Am I to regard Mormonism (so-called) as a new religion, or as simply a new development of Christianity?

Brigham Young—We hold that there can be no true Christian Church without a priesthood directly commissioned by, and in immediate communication with the Son of God and Savior of mankind. Such a church is that of the Latter-day Saints, called by their enemies Mormons; we know no other that even pretends to have present and direct revelations of God's will.

H.G.—Then I am to understand that you regard all other churches professing to be Christian as the Church of Rome regards all churches not in communion with itself—as schismatic, heretical, and out of the way of salvation?

B.Y.—Yes, substantially.

H.G.—Apart from this, in what respect do your doctrines differ essentially from those of our orthodox Protestant churches—the Baptist or Methodist, for example?

B.Y.—We hold the doctrines of Christianity, as revealed in the Old and New Testaments—also in the Book of Mormon, which teaches the same cardinal truths, and those only.

H.G.—Do you believe in the doctrine of the Trinity?

B.Y.—We do, but not exactly as it is held by other churches. We believe in the Father, the Son, and the Holy Ghost as equal, but not identical—not as one person. We believe in all the Bible teaches on this subject.

H.G.—Do you believe in a personal devil—a distinct, conscious, spiritual being whose nature and acts are essentially malignant and evil?

B.Y.—We do. . . .

H.G.—Do you make removal to these valleys obligatory on your converts?

B.Y.—They would consider themselves greatly aggrieved if they were not invited hither. We hold to such a gathering together of God's people as the Bible foretells, and that this is the place and now is the time appointed for its consummation. . . .

H.G.—What is the position of your church with respect to slavery?

B.Y.—We consider it of divine institution and not to be abolished until the curse pronounced on Ham shall have been removed from his descendants.

H.G.—Are any slaves now held in this territory?

B.Y.—There are.

H.G.—Do your territorial laws uphold slavery?

B.Y.—These laws are printed; you can read for yourself. If slaves are brought here by those who owned them in the states, we do not favor their escape from the service of those owners.

H.G.—Am I to infer that Utah, if admitted as a member of the federal Union, will be a slave state?

B.Y.—No; she will be a free state. Slavery here would prove useless and unprofitable. I regard it generally as a curse to the masters. I myself hire many laborers and pay them fair wages; I could not afford to own them. I can do better than subject myself to an obligation to feed and clothe their families, to provide and care for them in sickness and health. Utah is not adapted to slave labor.

H.G.—Let me now be enlightened with regard more especially to your church policy. I understand that you require each member to pay over one-tenth of all he produces or earns to the church.

B.Y.—That is a requirement of our faith. There is no compulsion as to the payment. Each member acts in the premises according to his pleasure, under the dictates of his own conscience.

H.G.—What is done with the proceeds of this tithing?

B.Y.—Part of it is devoted to building temples and other places of worship;

part to helping the poor and needy converts on their way to this country; and the largest portion to the support of the poor among the saints. . . .

H.G.—Can you give me any rational explanation of the aversion and hatred with which your people are generally regarded by those among whom they have lived and with whom they have been brought directly in contact?

B.Y.—No other explanation than is afforded by the crucifixion of Christ and the kindred treatment of God's ministers, prophets, and saints of all ages.

H.G.—I know that a new sect is always decried and traduced; that it is hardly ever deemed respectable to belong to one; that the Baptists, Quakers, Methodists, Universalists, etc., have each in their turn been regarded in the infancy of their sect as the offscouring of the earth; yet I cannot remember that either of them were ever generally represented and regarded by the older sects of their early days as thieves, robbers, murderers.

B.Y.—If you will consult the contemporary Jewish account of the life and acts of Jesus Christ, you will find that He and His disciples were accused of every abominable deed and purpose, robbery and murder included. Such a work is still extant and may be found by those who seek it.

H.G.—What do you say of the so-called Danites, or Destroying Angels, belonging to your church?

B.Y.—What do *you* say? I know of no such band, no such persons or organization. I hear of them only in the slanders of our enemies.

The Danites, or "Destroying Angels," were allegedly a secret group of Mormon operatives under the control of the church hierarchy who were to violently avenge wrongs against the church and to intimidate or permanently silence opposition. The church leadership always denied their existence, but significant evidence exists that such a band did operate in Utah.

H.G.—With regard, then, to the grave question on which your doctrines and practices are avowedly at war with those of the Christian world—that of a plurality of wives—is the system of your church acceptable to the majority of its women?

B.Y.—They could not be more adverse to it than I was when it was first revealed to us as the divine will. I think they generally accept it, as I do, as the will of God.

H.G.—How general is polygamy among you?

B.Y.—I could not say. Some of those present (heads of the church) have each but one wife; others have more; each determines what is his individual duty.

H.G.—What is the largest number of wives belonging to any one man?

B.Y.—I have fifteen; I know no one who has more; but some of those sealed to me are old ladies whom I regard rather as mothers than wives, but whom I have taken home to cherish and support.

H.G.—Does not the apostle Paul say that a bishop should be "the husband of one wife"?

B.Y.—So we hold. We do not regard any but a married man as fitted for the office of bishop. But the apostle does not forbid a bishop having more wives than one.

READING 7C

The Handcart Pioneers, *Report of the Second Handcart Company*, 1856

The Mormons who came to the Great Salt Lake basin were searching for a new start and new opportunities as much as any other explorers and settlers who trekked to the American West. The earliest Mormons arrived on roads and trails carved out by the emigrants themselves in territory that was largely unexplored or avoided; later on, newcomers arrived with some ease over what became the well-worn Mormon Trail. But others, meanwhile, desperate to take their place among the "Saints," were willing to endure greater hardships. The "Handcart Pioneers," as they were called, came to Salt Lake City from 1856 to 1860. In 1855 thousands of converted Europeans, mostly Scandinavian, arrived on the East Coast and transferred to rail lines to begin their trip to Utah. At the end of the lines in Missouri most were poverty-stricken and without any means of further transportation. Brigham Young wrote, upon hearing of their predicament: "They will be provided with handcarts on which to haul their provisions and clothing. We will send experienced men . . . to aid them. . . . [T]hey are expected to walk and draw their carts across the plains. Sufficient teams will be furnished to haul the aged, infirm, and those unable to walk. A few good cows will be sent along to furnish milk and some beef cattle." Each emigrant was allowed seventeen pounds of belongings. Most endeavored to travel during the late spring and summer if possible, but some encountered snow and starvation.

The Handcart Pioneers continued for several years until they were replaced by church-sponsored wagon trains. They were significant not only for their unique mode of travel but also in the development of the Mormon emigration history, the heroic legends that would form the core of the community's shared values and experiences.

This selection from the Report of the Second Handcart Company, May– September 1856, was written by one of its leaders, Daniel D. McArthur. The Second Company had 222 members. On this journey seven would die, and one would disappear.

Our carts, when we started, were in an awful fix. They moaned and groaned, screeched and squealed, so that a person could hear them for miles. You may think this is stretching things a little too much, but it is a fact, and we had them to eternally patch, mornings, noons, and nights. . . . Our train consisted of 12 yoke of oxen, 4 wagons, and 48 carts; we also had 5 beef and 12 cows; flour, 55 lbs. per head, 100 lbs. rice, 550 lbs. sugar, 400 lbs. dried apples, 125 lbs. tea, and 200 lbs. salt for the company. . . .

After three months on the trail, the Second Handcart Company split into two divisions. We had six tents in each division and a president over each tent, who were strict in seeing that singing and prayer was attended to every morning and night, and that peace prevailed. I must say that a better set of saints to labor with I never saw. They all did the best they could to forward our journey. When we came to a stream, no matter how large it might be, the men would roll up their trousers and into it they would go, and the sisters would follow, if the men were smart [quick] enough to get ahead of them, which the men failed many times to do. If the water was high enough to wet things on the carts, the men would get one before the cart and one behind it and lift it up slick and clean, and carry it across the stream. . . .

. . . On the 16th [of August 1856], while crossing over some sand hills, Sister Mary Bathgate was badly bitten by a large rattlesnake, just above the ankle, on the back part of her leg. She was about a half a mile ahead of the camp at the time it happened, as she was the ring leader of the footmen or those who did not pull the handcarts. She was generally accompanied by Sister Isabella Park. They were both old women, over 60 years of age, and neither of them had ridden one inch, since they left Iowa camp ground. Sister Bathgate sent a little girl back to me as quickly as possible to have me and Brothers Leonard and Crandall come with all haste, and bring the oil with us, for she was bitten badly. As soon as we heard the news, we left all things, and, with the oil, we went post haste. When we got to her she was quite sick, but said that there was power in the Priesthood, and she knew it. So we took a pocket knife and cut the wound larger, squeezed out all the bad blood we could, and there was considerable, for she had forethought enough to tie her garter around her leg above the wound to stop the circulation of the blood. We then took and anointed her leg and head, and laid our hands on her in the name of Jesus and felt to rebuke the influence of the poison, and she was full of faith. We then told her that she must get into the wagon, so she called witnesses to prove that she did not get into the wagon until she was compelled to by the cursed snake. . . . Sister Bathgate continued to be quite sick, but was full of faith, and after stopping one and a half hours we hitched up our teams. As the word was given for the teams to start, old Sister Isabella Park ran in before the wagon to see how her companion was. The driver, not seeing her, hallooed at his team and they being quick to mind, Sister Park could not get out of the way, and the fore wheel struck her and threw her down and passed over both her hips. Brother Leonard grabbed hold of her to pull her out of the way and the hind wheels passed over her ankles. We all thought that she would be all mashed to pieces, but to the joy of us all, there was not a bone broken, although the wagon had something like two tons burden on it, a load for 4 yoke of oxen. We went right to work and applied the same medicine to her that we did to the sister who was bitten by the rattlesnake, and although quite sore for a few days, Sister Park got better, so that she was on the tramp before we got into this Valley [Great Salt Lake basin], and Sister Bathgate was right at her side, to cheer her up. Both were as smart as could be long before they got here, and this is what I call good luck, for I know that nothing but the power of God saved the two sisters and they traveled together, they rode together, and suffered together. . . . While we were leading our handcart companies through the States and on the plains, we were called tyrants and slave drivers, and everything else that could be thought of, both by Gentiles and apostates.

READING 7D

RICHARD BURTON EXAMINES THE DOCTRINE OF POLYGAMY, 1862

Mormon beliefs and activities were sufficiently foreign to mainstream America that detractors ignored the successes of the cooperative effort in Utah and focused on perceived abnormalities—whether real or imagined. Critics commented, often harshly, on every aspect of the Mormon community from obstruction of non-Mormon commerce and politics, to Destroying Angels, to the origin of the Book of Mormon, *to the church's refusal to accede to federal authority. In 1857, when troops were sent to occupy the Mormon community in response to its resistance to federal jurisdiction, the prominent Illinois senator Stephen Douglas denounced the church as "a pestiferous disgusting cancer" and its members as "alien enemies and outlaws engaging in treasonable, disgusting and bestial practices."*

What elicited by far the largest amount of criticism was the practice of plural marriage. In this selection from his book The City of Saints and Across the Rocky Mountains, *the well-known British author Richard Burton turns an inquisitive eye on Mormon marital habits.*

It will, I suppose, be necessary to supply a popular view of the "peculiar institution," at once the bane and blessing of Mormonism—plurality. I approach the subject with a feeling of despair, so conflicting are opinions concerning it, and so difficult is it to naturalise in Europe the customs of Asia, Africa, and America, or to reconcile the habits of the 19th century A.D. with those of 1900 B.C. A return to the patriarchal ages . . . has its disadvantages.

There is a prevailing idea . . . that the Mormons are Communists or Socialists; . . . that wives are in public, and that a woman can have as many husbands as the husbands can have wives—in fact, to speak colloquially, that they "all pig together." The contrary is notably the case. The man who . . . murders, in cold blood, his wife's lover, is invariably acquitted, the jury declaring that civil damages mark the rottenness of other governments, and that "the principle, the only one that beats and throbs through the heart of the *entire inhabitants* (!) of this Territory is simply this: *The man who seduces his neighbour's wife must die, and her nearest relation must kill him.*" Men . . . slain for the mortal sin, perish for their salvation; the Prophet, were they to lay their lives at his feet, would because unable to hang or behead them, counsel them to seek certain death in a righteous cause as an expiatory sacrifice; which may save their souls alive. Their two mortal sins are: 1. Adultery; 2. Shedding innocent blood.

This severity of punishing an offence, which modern society looks upon rather in the light of a sin than of a crime, is clearly based upon the Mosaic code. It is also . . . the "common mountain law," a "religious and social custom," and a point of personal honour. Another idea underlies it: The Mormons hold, like the Hebrews of old, "children of shame" in extreme dishonour. . . . They would expel all impurity from the Camp of Zion, and they adopt every method of preventing what they consider a tremendous evil, viz. the violation of God's temple in their own bodies. . . .

The first wife, as among polygamists generally, is *the* wife, and assumes the husband's name and title. Her "plurality"-partners are called sisters—such as sister Anne or sister Blanche—and are aunts of her children. The first wife is married for [all] time, the others are sealed for eternity. Hence, according to the Mormons, arose the Gentile calumny concerning spiritual wifedom, which they distinctly deny. Girls rarely remain single past sixteen—in England the average marrying age is thirty—and they would be the pity of the community, if they were doomed to a waste of youth so unnatural. . . .

The "chaste and plural marriage" being once legalised, finds a multitude of supporters. The anti-Mormons declare that it is at once fornication and adultery—a sin which absorbs all others. The Mormons point triumphantly to the austere morals of their community, their superior freedom from maladive influences, and the absence of that uncleanness and licentiousness which distinguish the cities of the civilized world. They boast that if it be an evil they have at least chosen the lesser evil, that they practise openly as a virtue what others do secretly as a sin . . . [and] that their plurality has abolished the necessity of concubinage, cryptogamy, contubernium, celibacy, . . . with their terrible consequences, infanticide, and so forth. . . . Like its sister institution Slavery, the birth and growth of a similar age, Polygamy acquires *vim* by abuse and detraction; the more turpitude is heaped upon it, the brighter and more glorious it appears to its votaries.

There are rules and regulations of Mormonism . . . which disprove the popular statement that such marriages are made to gratify licentiousness, and which render polygamy a positive necessity. All sensuality in the married state is strictly forbidden beyond the requisite for ensuring progeny. . . .

The other motive for polygamy in Utah is economy. Servants are rare and costly; it is cheaper and more comfortable to marry them. Many converts are attracted by the prospect of becoming wives. . . . The old maid is . . . an unknown entity. Life in the wilds of Western America is a course of severe toil; a single woman cannot perform the manifold duties of housekeeping, cooking, scrubbing, washing, darning, child-bearing, and nursing a family. A division of labour is necessary, and she finds it by acquiring a sisterhood. . . .

For the attachment of the women of the Saints to the doctrine of plurality there are many reasons. The Mormon prophets have expended all their arts upon this end, well knowing that without the hearty co-operation of mothers and wives, sisters and daughters, no institution can live long. They have bribed them with promises of Paradise—they have subjugated them with threats of annihilation. With them once a Mormon always a Mormon. I have said that a modified reaction respecting the community of Saints has set in throughout the States; people no longer wonder that their missionaries do not show horns and cloven feet, and the Federal officer, the itinerant politician, the platform orator, and the place-seeking demagogue, can no longer make political capital by bullying, oppressing, and abusing them. The tide has turned, and will turn yet more. But the individual still suffers: the apostate Mormon is looked upon by other people as a scamp or a knave, and the woman worse than a prostitute. . . . The Mormon household has been described by its enemies as a hell of envy, hatred, and malice—a den of murder and suicide. The same has been said of the Moslem harem. Both, I believe, suffer from the assertions of prejudice or ignorance. The temper of the new is so far superior to that of the old country, that, incredible as the statement may appear, rival wives do dwell together in amity; and do quote the proverb "the more the merrier." . . .

I am conscious that my narrative savours of incredibility; the fault is in the subject, not in the narrator.

READING 8

OREGON FEVER, JESSE APPLEGATE, 1877

> *The famous explorers of the American West often get the recognition, but perhaps the most courageous of all these adventurers were the common folk who were seeking a new life in a new place. The urge to "wester" had been a longstanding phenomenon in the dominant culture; for many, the possibilities in that region seemed endless, or at least better. When the Oregon Territory became a popular destination in the 1840s, thousands formed caravans for the journey across the trackless plains, motivated by an incurable bug known as Oregon Fever. With precision and organization, these adventurers prepared and formed structured companies under captains, lieutenants, and "pilots." In 1843 one of the largest expeditions set out for Oregon with nearly a thousand travelers and more than five thousand cattle. Soon after departure the assemblage split in two, one group moving faster and the other taking a more leisurely pace. The captain of the second group, known as the "Cow Column," was Jesse Applegate. In this selection Applegate describes events on the trail.*

It is four o'clock A.M.; the sentinels on duty have discharged their rifles—the signal that the hours of sleep are over; and every wagon and tent is pouring forth its night tenants, and slow-kindling smokes begin largely to rise and float away on the morning air. Sixty men start from the corral, spreading as they make through the vast herd of cattle and horses that form a semi-circle around the encampment, the most distant perhaps two miles away.

The herders pass to the extreme verge and carefully examine the trails beyond, to see that none of the animals have strayed or been stolen during the night. This morning no trails lead beyond the outside animals in sight, and by five o'clock the herders begin to contract the great moving circle and the well-trained animals move slowly toward camp, clipping here and there a thistle or tempting bunch of grass on the way. In about an hour five thousand animals are close up to the encampment, and the teamsters are busy selecting their teams and driving them inside the "corral" to be yoked. The corral is a circle one hundred yards deep, formed with wagons connected strongly with each other, the wagon in the rear being connected with the wagon in front by its tongue and ox chains. It is a strong barrier that the most vicious ox cannot break, and in case of an attack of the Sioux would be no contemptible entrenchment.

From six to seven o'clock is a busy time; breakfast is to be eaten, the tents struck, the wagons loaded, and the teams yoked and brought up in readiness to be attached to their respective wagons. All know when, at seven o'clock, the signal to march sounds, that those not ready to take their proper places in the line of march must fall into the dusty rear for the day.

There are sixty wagons. They have been divided into fifteen divisions or platoons of four wagons each, and each platoon is entitled to lead in its turn. The leading platoon of today will be the rear one tomorrow, and will bring up the rear unless some teamster, through indolence or negligence, has lost his place in the line, and is condemned to that uncomfortable post. It is within ten minutes of seven; the corral but now a strong barricade is everywhere broken, the teams being attached to the wagons. The women and children have taken their places in them. The pilot (a borderer who has passed his life on the verge of civilization, and has been chosen to the post of leader from his knowledge of the savage and his experience in travel through the roadless wastes) stands ready in the midst of the pioneers, and aids, to mount and lead the way. Ten or fifteen young men, not today on duty, form another cluster. They are ready to start a buffalo hunt, are well mounted, and well armed as they need be, for the unfriendly Sioux have driven the buffalo out of the Platte [River basin], and the hunters must ride fifteen or twenty miles to reach them. The cow drivers are hastening, as they get ready, to the rear of the charge, to collect and prepare them for the day's march.

It is on the stroke of seven; the rushing to and fro, the cracking of the whips, the loud command to oxen, and what seems to be the inextricable confusion of the last ten minutes has ceased. Fortunately every one has been found and every teamster is at his post. The clear notes of the trumpet sound in the front; the pilot and his guards mount their horses, the leading division of wagons move out of the encampment, and takes up the line of march, the rest fall into their places with the precision of clock work, until the spot so lately full of life sinks back into that solitude that seems to reign over the broad plain and rushing river as the caravan draws its lazy length toward the distant El Dorado. . . .

The caravan has been about two hours in motion and is now extended as widely as a prudent regard for safety will permit. First, near the bank of the shining river, is a company of horsemen; they seem to have found an obstruction, for the main body has halted while three or four ride rapidly along the bank of the creek or slough. They are hunting a favorable crossing for the wagons; while we look they have succeeded; it has apparently required no work to make it passable, for all but one of the party has passed on and he has raised a flag, no doubt a signal to the wagons to steer their course to where he stands. The leading teamster sees him though he is yet two miles off, and steers his course directly towards him, all the wagons following in his track. They (the wagons) form a line three quarters of a mile in length; some of the teamsters ride upon the front of their wagons, some walk beside their teams; scattered along the line companies of women and children are taking exercise on foot; they gather bouquets of rare and beautiful flowers that line the way; near them stalks a stately greyhound or an Irish wolf dog, apparently proud of keeping watch and ward over his master's wife and children.

Next comes a band of horses; two or three men or boys follow them, the docile and sagacious animals scare needing their attention, for they have learned to follow in the rear of the wagons, and know that at noon they will be allowed to graze and rest. Their knowledge of the time seems as accurate as of the place they are to occupy in the line, and even a full-blown thistle will scarcely tempt them to straggle or halt until the dinner hour has arrived. Not so with the large herd of horned beasts that bring up the rear; lazy, selfish and unsocial, it has been a task to get them in motion, the strong always ready to domineer over the weak, halt in the front and forbid the weaker to pass them. They seem to move only in fear of the driver's whip; though in the morning full to repletion, they have not driven an hour before their hunger and thirst seem to indicate a fast of day's duration. Through all the long days their greed is never sated nor their thirst quenched, nor is there a moment of relaxation of the tedious and vexatious labors of their drivers, although to all others the march furnishes some season of relaxation or enjoyment. For the cow-drivers there is none. . . .

The pilot, by measuring the ground and timing the speed of the wagons and the walk of his horses, has determined the rate of each, so as to enable him to select the nooning place, as nearly as the requisite grass and water can be had at the end of five hours' travel of the wagons. Today, the ground being favorable, little time has been lost in preparing the road, so that he and his pioneers are at the nooning place an hour in advance of the wagons, which time is spent in preparing convenient watering places for the animals and digging little wells near the bank of the Platte. As the teams are not unyoked, but simply turned loose from the wagons, a corral is not formed at noon, but the wagons are drawn up in columns, four abreast, the leading wagon of each platoon on the left—the platoons being formed with that view. This brings friends together at noon as well as night.

Today an extra session of the Council is being held, to settle a dispute that does not admit of delay, between a proprietor and a young man who has undertaken to do a man's service on the journey for bed and board. Many such engagements exist and much interest is taken in the manner this high court, from which there is no appeal, will define the rights of each party in such engagements. The Council was a high court in the most exalted sense. It was a Senate composed of the ablest and most respected fathers of the emigration. It exercised both legislative and judicial powers, and its laws and decisions proved it equal and worthy of the high trust reposed in it. Its sessions were usually held on days when the caravan was not moving. It first took the state of the little commonwealth into consideration; revised or repealed rules defective or obsolete, and exacted such others as the exigencies seemed to require. The commonwealth being cared for, it next resolved itself into a court, to hear and settle private disputes and grievances. The offender and aggrieved appeared before it, witnesses were examined, and the parties were heard by themselves and sometimes by counsel. The judges thus being made fully acquainted with the case, and being in no way influenced or cramped by technicalities, decided all cases according to their merits. There was but little use for lawyers before this court, for no plea was entertained which was calculated to defeat the ends of justice. Many of these judges have since won honors in higher spheres. They have aided to establish on the broad basis of right and universal liberty two of the pillars of our great Republic in the Occident. Some of the young men who appeared before them as advocates have themselves sat upon the highest judicial tribunals, commanded armies, been Governors of States, and taken high positions in the Senate of the nation.

It is now one o'clock; the bugle has sounded, and the caravan has resumed its westward journey. It is in the same order, but the evening is far less animated than the morning march; a drowsiness has fallen apparently on man and beast; teamsters drop asleep on their perches and even walking by their teams, and the words of command are now addressed to the slowly creeping oxen in the softened tenor of women or the piping treble of children, while the snores of teamsters make a droning accompaniment. . . .

The sun is now getting low in the west, and at length the painstaking pilot is standing ready to conduct the train in the circle which he has previously measured and marked out, which is to form the invariable fortification for the night. The leading wagons follow him so nearly round the circle, that but a wagon length separates them. Each wagon follows in its tracks, the rear closing on the front until its tongue and ox chains will perfectly reach from one to the other, and so accurate the measurement and perfect the practice, that the hindmost wagon of the train always precisely closes the gateway. As each wagon is brought into position it is dropped from its team (the teams being [pastured] inside the circle), the team unyoked, and the yokes and chains are used to connect the wagon strongly with that in its front. Within ten minutes from the time the leading wagon halted, the barricade is formed, the teams unyoked and driven out to pasture.

Everyone is busy preparing fires of buffalo chips to cook the evening meal, pitching tents and otherwise preparing for the night.

READING 9
GEORGE BUSH ON THE ROAD TO OREGON, JOHN MINTON, 1901

Although the experiences recounted by Jesse Applegate (reading 8) appear to constitute an organized, almost seamless adventure, underlying problems on the

Oregon Trail reflected societal concerns. In particular, racial tensions became apparent. One traveler to the Oregon Territory in September 1844 was a free black named George Bush, who had been a soldier in Andrew Jackson's army at the Battle of New Orleans. One of Bush's party on the Oregon journey, a white named Michael Simmons, later secured 640 acres for Bush in Oregon. A traveler in another party, John Minton, met Bush at the journey's starting point in Missouri and again on the way west. Minton recounts his impressions of George Bush's concerns.

I struck the road again in advance of my friends near Soda Springs. There was in sight, however, G. W. Bush, at whose camp table Rees and I had received the hospitalities of the Missouri rendezvous. Joining him, we went to the Springs. Bush was a mulatto, but had means, and also a white woman for a wife, and a family of five children. Not many men of color left a slave state so well to do, and so generally respected; but it was not in the nature of things that he should be permitted to forget his color. As we went along together, he riding a mule and I on foot, he led the conversation to this subject. He told me he should watch, when we got to Oregon, what usuage was awarded to people of color, and if he could not have a free man's rights he would seek the protection of the Mexican Government in California or New Mexico. He said there were few in that train he would say as much to as he had just said to me. I told him I understood. This conversation enabled me afterwards to understand the chief reason for Col. M. T. Simmons and his kindred, and Bush and [Gabriel] Jones determining to settle north of the Columbia [River]. It was understood that Bush was assisting at least two of these to get to Oregon, and while they were all Americans, they would take no part in ill treating G. W. Bush on account of his color.

[Minton indicates that when the party heard rumors that any African American attempting to enter the Oregon Territory might be whipped, they agreed to fight to protect Bush.] No act of Colonel Simmons as a legislator was more creditable to him than getting Mr. Bush exempt from the Oregon law, intended to deter mulattoes or Negroes from settling in Oregon—a law, however, happily never enforced.

SACAJAWEA, MERIWETHER LEWIS AND WILLIAM CLARK, 1805–1806

Often overlooked is the role of women in explorations and their importance to the success of the early explorers. Mountain men frequently took Native American or Hispanic women as wives, and they served as interpreters, negotiators, and cultural intermediaries. Since a miscalculation caused by a misunderstood word or custom could lead to economic failure or even physical danger, these women provided knowledge and a soothing demeanor in often tense discussions. Journals of the time pointedly remark that the presence of a woman signaled that the explorers or mountain men had peaceful intentions.

Women who accompanied explorations into country they were familiar with often provided leadership in recognizing landmarks or suggesting routes. The most famous was undoubtedly Sacajawea, the Shoshone woman who traveled with Lewis and Clark. Sacajawea was a captive who was purchased by and became the "wife" of Touissant Charbonneau, a French guide on the Lewis and Clark Expedition. The importance of her role has long been debated by historians. Some claim that she recognized few landmarks and was more an interesting oddity in the otherwise all-male party than a significant contributor. Other historians argue that she was crucial to the expedition's success, particularly in cementing positive relations with Indian tribes along the route.

The journals of Meriwether Lewis and William Clark present Sacajawea in a very positive light. Products of a culture that had little regard for the capabilities of women and even less admiration for Native Americans, the two expedition leaders show respect for Sacajawea's courage, tenacity, and spunk. These excerpts comment on her significant contributions, particularly in recognizing familiar territory and in easing tensions as the explorers encountered various Indian cultures.

[Lewis, February 11, 1805]

about five Oclock this evening one of the wives of Charbono was delivered of a fine boy [this was Sacajawea; Charbonneau had two other wives from the Mandan tribe]. it is worthy of remark that this was the first child which this woman had boarn, and as common in such cases her labour was tedious and the pain violent; Mr. Jessome [Rene Jessaume, a trader who lived among the Mandans] informed me that he had frequently administered a small portion of the rattle of the rattle-snake, which he assured me had never failed to produce the desired effect, that of hastening the birth of the child; having the rattle of a snake by me I gave it to him and he administered two rings of it to the woman broken into small pieces with the fingers and added to a small quantity of water. Whether this medicine was truly the cause or not I shall not undertake to determine, but I was informed that she had not taken it more than ten minutes before she brought forth.

[Lewis, May 14–16, 1805]

Lewis describes the aftermath of an accident where a pirogue, a river-running canoe with sails, capsized and threatened to destroy many important articles and notes. The boat was being steered by Charbonneau, whom Lewis exclaimed "cannot swim and is perhaps the most timid waterman in the world."

we now took every article out of her and lay them to drane as well we could for the evening, baled out the canoe and secured her, there were two other men beside Charbono on board who could not swim, and who of course must also have perished had the perogue gone to the bottom. . . . After having all the matters arranged for the evening as well as the nature of the circumstances would permit, we thought it a proper occasion to console ourselves and cheer the spirits of our men and accordingly took a drink of grog and gave each man a gill of sperits. . . .

The morning was fair and the day proved favorable to our operations; by 4 Oclock in the evening our Instruments, Medicine, merchandize provision & c, were perfectly dryed, repacked and put on board the perogue. the loss we sustained was not so great as we had at first apprehended; our medicine sustained the greatest injury, several articles of which were intirely spoiled; and many others considerably injured, the ballance of our losses consisted of some gardin seeds, a small quantity of gunpowder, and a few culinary articles which fell overboard and sunk. the Indian woman [Sacajawea] to whom I ascribe equal fortitude and resolution, with any person onboard at the time of the accedent, caught and preserved most of the light articles which were washed overboard.

[Lewis, May 20, 1805]

The hunters returned this evening and informed us that the country continued much the same in appearance as that we saw where we were or broken, and that about five miles abe [above] the mouth of shell river a handsome river of about fifty yards in width discharged itself into the shell river on the Stard. or upper side; this stream we called Sah-ca-ger we-ah [Sacajawea] or bird woman's River, after our interpreter the Snake [Shoshone] woman.

[Lewis, June 16–19, 1805]

Lewis describes the serious illness and treatment of Sacajawea as the expedition neared the Great Falls of the Missouri. Both he and Clark went to unusual lengths to restore Sacajawea to health. Clark first noted Sacajawea's illness on June 14, 1805: "Her case is somewhat dangerous," he recorded in his diary. Lewis continues on June 16, 1805:

I found that two dozes of barks and opium which I had given her . . . had produced an alteration in her pulse for the better; they were now fuller and more regular. I caused her to drink the mineral water [of a nearby spring] altogether. wen I first came down [from the Great Falls] I found that her pulse were scarcely perceptible, very quick frequently irregular and attended with strong nervous symptoms, that of the twitching of the fingers and leaders of the arm; now the pulse had become regular much fuller and a gentle perspiration had taken place; the nervous symptoms have also in a great measure abated, and she feels herself much freer from pain. she complains principally of the lower region of the abdomen, I therefore continued the cataplasms of barks and laudnumn which had been previously used by my friend Capt. Clark. I beleive her disorder originated principally from an obstruction of the mensis in consequence of taking could. . . .

[The next day] the Indian woman much better; . . . I have still continued the same course of medecine; she is free from pain clear of fever, her pulse regular, and eats as heartily as I am willing to permit her of broiled buffaloe well seasoned with pepper and salt and rich soope of the same meat; I think therefore that there is every rational hope of her recovery. . . .

[Two days later] The Indian woman is recovering fast. she sat up the greater part of the day and walked out for the fi[r]st time since she arrived here; she eats hartily and is free from fever or pain. I continue same course of medecine and regimen except that I added one doze of 15 drops of the oil of vitriol today about noon. . . .

the Indian woman was much better [the next morning] . . . she walked out and gathered a considerable quantity of the white apples of which she eat so heartily in their raw state, together with a considerable quantity of dryed fish without my knowledge that she complained very much and her fever again returned. I rebuked Sharbono severely for suffering her to indulge herself with such food he being privy to it and having been previously told what she must only eat. I now gave her broken dozes of diluted nitre untill it produced perspiration and at 10 P.M. 30 drops of laudnum which gave her a tolerable nights rest. [She recovered quickly after this last attack.]

[Lewis, July 22, 1805]
The Indian Woman recognizes the country and assures us that this is the river on which her relations live, and that the three forks are at no great distance, this peice of information has cheered the sperits of the party who now begin to console themselves with the anticipation of shortly seeing the head of the missouri yet unknown to the civilized world.

[Lewis, July 28, 1805]
Our present camp is precisely on the spot that the Snake [Shoshone] Indians were encamped at the time the Minnetares of the Knife R. first came in sight of them five years since. from hence they retreated about three miles up Jeffersons river and concealed themselves in the woods, the Minnetares pursued, attacked them, killed 4 men 4 women a number of boys, and mad[e] prisoners of all the females and four boys. Sah-cah-gar-we-ah o[u]r Indian woman was one of the female prisoners taken at that time; tho' I cannot discover that she shews any immotion of sorrow in recollecting this event, or of joy in being again restored to her native country; if she has enough to eat and a few trinkets to wear I beleive she would be perfectly content anywhere.

[Lewis, August 8, 1805]
the Indian woman recognized the point of a high plain to our right which she informed us was not very distant from the summer retreat of her nation on a river beyond the mountains which runs to the west. this hill she says her nation calls the beaver's head [Beaverhead Rock in present-day Montana] from a conceived re[se]mblance of it's figure to the head of that animal. she assures us that we shall either find her people on this river or on the river immediately west of it's source; from which it's present size cannot be very distant.

[Lewis, August 16–17, 1805]

In one of the great coincidences of American history, the band of Shoshones the expedition encountered was Sacajawea's band, and the chief was her brother, Kameawait. These Indians provided important assistance to the expedition.

I had mentioned to the chief several times that we had with us a woman of his nation who had been taken prisoner by the Minnetares, and that by means of her I hoped to explain myself more fully than I could do signs. . . .

an Indian who had straggled some little distance down the river returned and reported that the whitemen were coming, that he had seen them just below. they all appeared transported with joy, & the ch[i]ef repeated his fraturnal hug. I felt quite as much gratifyed at this information as the Indians appeared to be. Shortly after Capt. Clark arrived with the Interpreter Charbono, and the Indian woman, who proved to be a sister of the Chief Cameahwait. the meeting of these people was really affecting, particularly between Sah-cah-gar-we-ah and an Indian woman, who had been taken prisoner at the same time with her and who, had afterwards escaped from the Minnetares and rejoined her nation.

[Clark, August 17, 1805]

Clark records the meeting with Kameawait in his very terse style. Clark reflected more of his military experience in his reports which are short and to the point. Lewis was more fully descriptive in his accounts.

The Great Chief of this nation proved to be the brother of the *woman* with us and is a man of Influence, Sence & easey & reserved manners.

[Clark, October 19, 1805]

[On the Columbia River the Walla walla] Indians came out & Set by me and smoked They said we came from the clouds &c &c and were not men &c &c. this time Capt. Lewis came down with the canoes in which the Indian[s were riding], as Soon as they Saw the Squar [squaw] wife of the interpreter [Sacajawea] they pointed to her and informed those who continued yet in the Same position I first found them, they imediately all came out and appeared to assume new life, the sight of This Indian woman, wife to one of our interprs. confirmed those people of our friendly intentions, as no woman ever accompanies a war party of Indians in this quarter.

On November 24, 1805, the expedition made plans for its winter quarters, to be called Fort Clatsop, near the mouth of the Columbia. Its location was determined by the vote of everyone in the party, including York, Clark's black slave, and Sacajawea (whom Clark now referred affectionately to as "Janey"). This election, probably unthinkable on the Atlantic seaboard, reflects the increasing admiration of Lewis and Clark for the sacrifices of the expedition's members.

[Clark, November 30, 1805]
Clark describes a gift from Sacajawea, of whom he had become increasingly fond.

The squar gave me a piece of bread made of flour which She had reserved for her child and carefully Kept untill this time, which had unfortunately got wet, and a little Sour. this bread I eate with great satisfaction, it being the only mouthfull I had tasted for Several months past.

[Lewis, January 6, 1806]
Lewis reports the expedition's trip to the Pacific Ocean, where they shared the blubber of a whale with a local Indian band. Sacajawea accompanied them.

Capt. Clark set out after an early breakfast with the party in two canoes as had been concerted the last evening; Charbono and his Indian woman were also of the party; the Indian woman was very impo[r]tunate to be permitted to go, and was therefore indulged; she observed that she had traveled a long way with us to see the great waters, and that now that monstrous fish [a whale] was also to be seen, she thought it very hard she could not be permitted to see either (she had never yet been to the Ocean.)

[Clark, August 17, 1806]
By August 1806 the expedition had nearly completed its grand adventure. The leaders were paying off its members and taking steps to dismantle the project. Lewis and Clark's respect for Sacajawea's efforts and her fortitude is evident in Clark's final encounter with Sacajawea and the remarkable bargain they struck.

we also took leave of T. Charbono, his Snake Indian wife and their child [a son] who had accompanied us on our rout to the pacific ocean in the capacity of interpreter and interpret[r]e[s]s. T. Charbono wished much to accompany us in the said Capacity if we could have provailed [upon] the

Minnetare chiefs to dec[e]nd the river with us to the U. States, but [as] none of those Chiefs of whoes language he was Conversant would accompany us, his services were no longer of use to the U. States and he was therefore discharged and paid up. we offered to convey him down to the Illinois if he chose to go, he declined proceeding on at present, observing that he had no acquaintance or prospects of makeing a liveing below, and must continue to live in the way that he had done. I offered to take his little son [named Pompy] a butifull promising child who is 19 months old to which they both himself & wife were willing provided the child had been weened. they observed that in one year the boy would be sufficiently old to leave his mother & he would then take him to me if I would be so freindly as to raise the child for him in such a manner as I thought proper, to which I agreed.

Clark remembered his promise. Sacajawea, he said "desirved a greater reward for her attention and services on that rout than we had in our power to give her at the Mandans." In 1810 the young boy, now named Jean-Baptiste, was brought to Clark, who "adopted" him and put him in school. In 1824 Jean-Baptiste traveled to Europe with a visiting German Prince, Paul of Württemberg. He eventually became an interpreter and guide among the Indians; on one expedition he would guide Clark's son Jefferson.

Sacajawea's final years are partially clouded in mystery. Some claim she lived to be one hundred years old and died in the mountains of central Wyoming, but it is more likely that she died years earlier. In a journal entry from 1828, Clark, who had kept close contact with the family, recorded "Se car ja we au Dead."

CHAPTER 3

FARMERS AND TOWNSFOLK

IF THERE was one single element that connected all facets of the American western experience, it was the land. From the unspoiled buffalo prairies of yesteryear to today's metropolitan centers, respect for, possession of, or use of the land has been a primary motivator of western history. During the nineteenth century the farming frontier and the development of towns helped to define the American West. Stories of rich soil, unfettered personal freedom, a new start, hope, and possibilities touched a resonant chord in the American mind—the belief that out there, to the west, was the landscape of opportunity.

Dreams soon gave way to reality, however, and the experience was often more tribulation than triumph, more long hours than leisure, more dust than destiny. But the perseverance of both farmers and townsfolk added a significant chapter to the history of the American West.

In this chapter the readings chronicle the development of farms and communities from the basic construction of the soddy through the development of a sophisticated and influential political protest movement that expressed farmers' demands and frustrations—Populism.

READING 1

"THIS IS A SOD HOUSE," KANSAS HOMESTEADER, 1877

Shelter is always one of the first requirements in the establishment of any community, and many settlers on the plains constructed their first houses of the most available building material—sod. Lumber was a scarce commodity on the rolling plains, but sod was everywhere. In this letter a Kansas homesteader describes the process of building a "soddy"—a process repeated by thousands of settlers making what they hoped would be a temporary residence until they could save enough money to buy or build a more substantial home.

At Snyder's, Kill Creek, Kansas

March 27, 1877

This is a sod house, plastered inside. The sod wall is about 2 feet thick at the ground, and slopes off on the outside to about 14 inches at the top. The roof is composed of a ridge pole and rafters of rough split logs, on which is laid corn stalks, and on top of those are two layers of sod. The roof has a very slight pitch, for if it had more, the sod would wash off when there is a heavy rain.

Perhaps you would be interested in the way a sod house is built. Sod is the most available material, in fact, the only material the homesteader has at hand, unless he happens to be one of the fortunates who secured a creek claim with timber suitable for house logs.

Occasionally a new comer has a "bee," and the neighbors for miles around gather at his claim and put up his house in a day. Of course there is no charge for labor in such cases. The women come too, and while the men lay up the sod walls, they prepare dinner for the crowd, and have a very sociable hour at noon. A house put up in this way is very likely to settle and get out of shape, but it is very seldom deserted for that reason.

The builder usually "cords up" the sods, though sometimes he crosses the layers, making the walls about two feet thick, but a little experience shows that the extra thick walls are of no real advantage. When the prairie is thoroughly soaked by rain or snow is the best time for breaking sod for building. The regulation thickness is 2½ inches, buffalo [grass] sod preferred on account of its superior toughness. The furrow slices are laid flat and as straight as a steady-walking team can be driven. These furrow slices, 12 inches wide, are cut with a sharp spade into 18-inch lengths, and carefully handled as they are laid in the wall, one length reaching across the wall, which rises rapidly even when the builders are green hands. Care must be taken to break joints and bind the corners of the house. "Seven feet to the square" is the rule, as the wall is likely to settle a good deal, especially if the sod is very wet when laid. The [wooden] door and window frames are set in place first and the wall built around them. Building such a house is hard work.

When the square is reached, the crotches (forks of a tree) are set at the ends and in the middle of the house and the ridge pole—usually a single tree trunk the length of the building, but sometimes spliced—is raised to its place by sheer strength of arm, it being impossible to use any other power. Then rails are laid from the ridge log to the walls and covered with any available material—straight sorghum stalks, willow switches, and straw, or anything that will prevent the sod on the roof from falling between the rafters. From the comb of the roof to the earthen floor is usually about nine feet.

The gables are finished before the roof is put on, as in roofing the layer of sod is started at the outer edge of the wall. If the builder is able, he has sawed cottonwood rafters and a pine or cottonwood board roof covered with sod. Occasionally a sod house with a shingle roof is seen, but of course this costs more money.

At first these sod houses are unplastered, and this is thought perfectly all right, but such a house is somewhat cold in the winter, as the crevices between the sods admit some cold air; so some of the houses are plastered with a kind of "native lime," made of sand and a very sticky native clay. This plaster is very good unless it happens to get wet. In a few of the houses this plaster is whitewashed, and this helps the looks very much. Some sod houses are mighty comfortable places to go into in cold weather, and it don't take much fire to keep them warm. I will have to be contented with a very modest affair for a while, but perhaps I can improve it later. . . .

April 10, 1877

I made out an estimate of the cost of our house. This does not include what was paid for in work: Ridgepole and hauling (including two loads of firewood) $1.50; rafters and straw, 50 [cents]; 2 lb. nails, 15 [cents]; hinges 20 [cents]; window 75 [cents]; total cash paid, $4.05. Then there was $4 worth of lumber, which was paid for in work, and $1.50 for hauling it over, which, together with hauling the firewood, 50 [cents], makes $10.05 for a place to live in and enough firewood to last all summer.

READING 2
"THE LITTLE OLD SOD SHANTY," 1870S

The sod house was such a familiar sight on the plains that it became a symbol of western settlement. Since Americans tend to make the familiar an integral part of their popular culture, by the end of the nineteenth century the soddy had entered the literature of the West, as these song lyrics attest.

I am looking rather seedy now while holding down my claim
And my victuals are not always served the best;

And the mice play shyly round me as I nestle down to rest
In the little old sod shanty on my claim.

Oh, the hinges are of leather and the windows have no glass,
And the board roof lets the howling blizzard in,
And I hear the hungry "kiyote" as he slinks up thru the grass
Round my little old sod shanty on my claim.

When I left my eastern home, a bachelor so gay,
To try to win my way to wealth and fame,
I never thought I'd come to burning twisted hay
In the little old sod shanty on my claim.

But I rather like the novelty of living in this way
Though my bill-of-fare is always rather tame,
And I'm happy as a clam on the land of Uncle Sam,
In the little old sod shanty on my claim.

My clothes are plastered o'er with mud, I'm looking like a fright,
And every thing is scattered round the room,
Still I wouldn't give the freedom that I have out in the West
For the comfort of the eastern man's old home.

Still I wish some kind-hearted girl would pity on me take,
And relieve me from the mess that I am in;
The angel, how I'd bless her if this her home she'd make
In the little old sod shanty on my claim.

We would make our fortunes on the prairies of the West
Just as happy as two lovers we'd remain;
We'd forget the trials and troubles we endured at the first
On the little old sod shanty on our claim.

Oh, the hinges are of leather, and the windows have no glass,
And the board roof lets the howling blizzard in;
And I hear the hungry "kiyote" as he slinks up thru the grass
Round my little old sod shanty on my claim.

And if fate would bless us with now and then an heir,
To cheer our hearts with honest pride and fame;
Oh, then we'd be contented for the toil that we had spent
In the little old sod shanty we call home.

"THE CHEROKEE STRIP," SETH K. HUMPHREY, 1893

Land was the lure that drew many to the American West. The last part of the region to be opened for settlement by the dominant Anglo-American culture was the Cherokee Strip in Oklahoma Territory (formed from part of Indian Territory in 1889). This six-million-acre area was owned by the Cherokee Indians until 1891, when the United States government purchased it. Seth K. Humphrey, who participated in the remarkable land rush that occurred at the Cherokee Strip, here describes this extraordinary event of September 16, 1893. Those rushers who waited for the cannon shot signaling the beginning of the land grab were called "Boomers"; those who sneaked in early to stake a claim were called "Sooners."

The Cherokee Strip—more correctly, the Cherokee Outlet—was a stretch of prairie country about sixty miles wide extending for two hundred miles along the north line of the Indian Territory. North of it was Kansas; on the south, the four-year-old Territory of Oklahoma. Its great extent and its location next to settled country drew the biggest crowd of adventurers ever gathered for the single purpose of collecting a farm from the government. There were also a few farmers present. . . .

The rush was to be made from a line-up on both the Kansas and Oklahoma boundaries. I chose the Kansas state line, since two of my brothers, land men like myself, were living within twenty miles of the Cherokee border. At this point a railroad crossed the strip, running southward to Oklahoma and Texas. My older brother and I, being landowners and therefore ineligible as homesteaders, were making the run solely for the fun of it; and to get an extra kick out of the experience we were going in on bicycles. . . .

Days before the run matters began to look ominous. Already there were twice as many waiting boomers as waiting farms, and heaven knew what the proportion would be on the day of the rush. The idea was penetrating the deluded crowd that this was to be a race, not a prairie schooner parade to a happy new home. . . .

At last the eventful morning broke, a day exactly like all the rest, hot and dry, a south wind rising with the sun—dead ahead, and a hard proposition for bicyclists. We had stayed overnight in the little hotel of the town within a mile of the border, several of us in one room; but at least we two of the bicycle corps did not have to mix up with the jam of horses about the place. And we had another decided advantage in not having horses to look after in a hot prairie wilderness where there was not a well, scarcely a stream not gone to a dry bed, and only an occasional water tank on the one railroad running south to Texas. This water would be of service only to the comparative few who could locate near by.

Naturally there was a wild eagerness to make the run next to the railroad, not only because of its water tanks in a dry country, but because farm land near it was desirable, as well as the town lots in the several sites that had been laid out near the tank stations. A boomer could take a farm or a town lot, but not both.

So at this point in the waiting line an immense number of "town siters" were added to the crowd of land-seekers. For this special accommodation a train of ten cattle cars was to be run, which was to stop for a moment at each town site. Its engine toed the starting line, along with all the rest of us, waiting, with steam up and loaded to the cow catcher with a human swarm, for the crack of the gun at twelve o'clock noon. The train was to run no faster than eight miles an hour, so as to have no advantage over the horsemen; but a flock of dollar bills fluttering around the engine warped the trainmen's judgement and they ran it at fifteen. Another fight-provoker, this, in the already hectic scrap for land. My brother and I, out for excitement, found ourselves in the right spot to get it.

A quarter to twelve. The line stiffened and became more quiet with the tension of waiting. Out in front a hundred yards and twice as far apart were soldiers, resting easily on their rifles, contemplating the line. I casually wondered how they could manage to dodge the onrush; perhaps they were wondering that too. The engine, a few hundred feet away, coughed gently at the starting line; its tender and the tops of its ten cattle cars trailing back into the state of Kansas, were alive with men. Inside the cars the boomers were packed standing, their arms sticking out where horns ought to be. . . .

Five minutes. Three minutes. The soldiers now stood with rifles pointing upward, waiting for the first sound of firing to come along their line from the east. A cannon at its eastern end was to give the first signal; this the rifles were to take up and carry on as fast as sound could travel the length of the Cherokee Strip.

All set!

At one minute before twelve o'clock my brother and I, noticing that the soldier out in front was squinting upward along his rifle barrel and intent on the coming signal, slipped out fifty feet in front of the line, along the railroad embankment. It was the best possible place from which to view the start. It has been estimated that there were somewhere around one hundred thousand men in line on the Kansas border. Within the two-mile range of vision that we had from our point of vantage there were at least five thousand and probably nearly eight.

Viewed from out in front the waiting line was a breath-taking sight. We had seen it only from within the crowd or from the rear. The back of the line was ragged, incoherent; the front was even, smooth, solid. It *looked* like the line-up that it was. I thought I had sensed the immensity of the spectacle, but that one moment out in front gave me the unmatched thrill of an impending race with six thousand starters in sight.

First in line was a solid bank of horses; some had riders, some were hitched to gigs, buckboards, carts, and wagons, but to the eye there were only the two miles of tossing heads, shiny chests, and restless front legs of horses. The medley of grotesque speed outfits, the stupendous gamble, the uniqueness of the farce and the tragedy of it—these were submerged in the acute expectancy of a horse race beyond words, incomparable.

While we stood, numb with looking, the rifles snapped and the line broke with a huge, crackling roar. That one thundering moment of horseflesh by the mile quivering in its first leap forward was a gift of the gods, and its like will never come again. The next instant we were in a crash of vehicles whizzing past us like a calamity. . . .

The funniest of the starters was the engine with its ten carloads of men. From our stand fifty feet directly in front of it I was contemplating it as the chief absurdity of the race when the rush began. The engine tooted incessantly and labored hard, but of course she could not get under way with anything like the quickness of the horses. They left her as good as tied to her cattle train. The incongruity of starting a contrivance like that with a lot of horses and calling it a race made us laugh—not only because she waddled behind so ridiculously at the start but because we knew the crowd aboard intended to be far ahead of the horsemen long before the finish of the race, if moral suasion or cash inducement could make the old girl cough a little faster than the rule allowed.

Of course everybody on the train was mad with excitement, particularly since they were packed in without a chance to vent their emotions in any but some noise-making way. With the first toots of the engine came revolver shots from the crowd all along the tops of the cars, and at least a few from those penned up inside. The fusillade, which kept up all the while the train was pulling out past us, had a most exhilarating effect; my old gun, I suddenly noticed, was barking with the rest of them. . . .

At six o'clock we were only twenty miles in; but that twenty miles loomed up like a day's work. Inflating and mending tires had taken a good deal of time, for we had been riding on the sharp stubble left by the fires [probably set deliberately to provide open ground]; this hard ride over burned ground we could not have foreseen. The deflation of our own energy by the rough prairie and a head wind, too, had slowed us down to little better than a walk. Six miles ahead was Pond Creek, the first town site of any importance. We could make that in the morning, after taking in the hectic first-night events on the prairie. . . .

Very soon after sunset came darkness and with it a multitude of stars such as the heavens display only in a dry atmosphere. There was a blaze of light above, but it was pitch dark below; the brilliant starlight of an exceedingly clear air seems to have little power to illuminate the earth. But these sights did not even interest us. Dog-tired, we rolled up in our blankets, rested our heads on our bicycle wheels, and dropped off to sleep.

A little before midnight, we woke to a distant clatter of hoofs, shouting, and shooting. "Number—section—township—range—. Keep off and get off!" Then crack! crack! went the rifles, after each call, from the pretty country we had been admiring at sundown. . . .

After a hearty breakfast we pumped up our sorry tires and packed up to start for the town sites. Ever since daybreak boomers had been straggling northward, bound for Kansas and all points east. One young fellow who stopped for a moment while we were eating breakfast was a fair sample of the crowd. He asked for water, and we gave him a biscuit, for we hadn't a drop of water left. He had staked a claim in our nice little valley, along with a half dozen others on the same tract; and of course, as in such cases all over the Strip, nobody under heaven could know who had arrived first. But for him the delicate question had been settled by the . . . horsemen in the pitch darkness of the night before. By the time they were through with him he felt assured that he must have arrived about a week late.

"I wouldn't live here next to such neighbors, anyway," he told us with considerable heat. At this safe distance and in the daylight his feelings had turned to indignation, but he was still trembling a little.

We did our best to soothe him by pointing out that he had escaped several years of doubtful litigation by accepting the hint of the clean-up crowd to vacate; but there was no need to tell him, since he had lost his claim, that even if he had stayed he never would have had those men for neighbors. Farming in the Cherokee Strip was the last thing any of those gun-toters, to say nothing of the speed sports and most of the others, intended to do. True, somebody would have to live on these claims as homesteaders, but not they; their plan was to get possession, file on it, then sell their relinquishments to farmers.

In the Cherokee Strip was to be repeated the history of every move in the prairie frontier; a first crop of settlers, mostly fly-by-nights, followed by a second contingent, composed largely of true farmers.

READING 4
THE HOMESTEAD ACT, 1862

The United States government promoted the settlement of the western lands with the passage of "An Act to secure Homesteads to actual settlers on the Public Domain," more commonly known as the Homestead Act of 1862. Under this legislation, adult "citizens of the United States" (meaning whites only) and those who declared their intention to become citizens could be allotted 160 acres of government-controlled land in the public domain of the West. Only those who had fought for the Confederacy were excluded from the program. The land was free, except for small title fees, as long as the possessors made certain improvements within five years. Although many homesteaders "went bust" on their new lands, the act did spur settlement of the West and served as a powerful symbolic statement of the government's intent to fulfill Manifest Destiny through legislative fiat, if necessary. Here is the text of the legislation.

Be it enacted by the Senate and House of Representatives of the United States of America in Congress assembled, That any person who is the head of a family, or who has arrived at the age of twenty-one years, and is a citizen of the United States, or who shall have filed his declaration of intention to become such, as required by the naturalization laws of the United States, and who has never borne arms against the United States Government or given aid and comfort to its enemies, shall, from and after the first of January, eighteen hundred and sixty-three, be entitled to enter one quarter section or a less quantity of unappropriated public lands, upon which said person may have filed a preemption claim, or which may, at the time the application is made, be subject to preemption at one dollar and twenty-five cents, or less, per acre; or eighty acres or less of unappropriated lands, at two dollars and fifty cents per acre, to be located in a body, in conformity to the legal subdivisions of the public lands, and after the same shall have been surveyed: *Provided,* That any person owning and residing on land may, under the provisions of this act, enter other land lying contiguous to his or her said land, which shall not, with the land already owned and occupied, exceed in the aggregate one hundred and sixty acres.

Sec. 2. And be it further enacted, That the person applying for the benefit of this act shall, upon application to the register of the land office in which he or she is about to make such entry, make affidavit before such register or receiver that he or she is the head of the family, or is twenty-one years or more of age, or shall have performed service in the army or navy of the United States, and that he has never borne arms against the Government of the United States or given aid and comfort to its enemies, and that such application is made for his or her exclusive use and benefit, and that said entry is made for the purpose of actual settlement and cultivation, and not either directly or indirectly for the use or benefit of any other person or persons whomsoever; and upon filing the said affidavit with the register or receiver, and on payment of ten dollars, he or she shall thereupon be per-mitted to enter the quantity of land specified; *Provided, however,* That no certificate shall be given or patent issued therefor until the expiration of five years from the date of such entry; and if, at the expiration of such time, or at any time within two years thereafter, the person making such entry; or, if he be dead, his widow; or in the case of her death, his heirs or devisee, or in case of a widow making such entry, her heirs or devisee, in case of her death; shall prove by two credible witnesses that he, she, or they have resided upon or cultivated the same for the terms of five years immediately succeeding the time of filing the affidavit aforesaid, and shall make affidavit that no part of said land has been alienated, and that he has borne true allegiance to the

Government of the United States; then, in such case, he, she, or they, if at the time a citizen of the United States, shall be entitled to a patent, as in other cases provided for by law; *And provided, further,* That in case of the death of both father and mother, leaving an infant child, or children, under twenty-one years of age, the right and fee shall enure to the benefit of said infant child or children; and the executor, administrator, or guardian may, at any time within two years after the death of the surviving parent, and in accordance with the laws of the State in which such children for the time being have their said domicil, sell said land for the benefit of said infants, but for no other purpose; and the purchaser shall acquire the absolute title by the purchase, and be entitled to a patent from the United States, on payment of the office fees and sum of money herein specified.

Sec. 3. And be it further enacted, That the register of the land office shall note all such applications on the tract books and plats of his office, and keep a register of all such entries, and make return thereof to the General Land Office, together with the proof upon which they have been founded.

Sec. 4. And be it further enacted, That no lands acquired under the provisions of this act shall in any event become liable to the satisfaction of any debt or debts contracted prior to the issuing of the patent therefor.

Sec. 5. And be it further enacted, That if, at any time after the filing of the affidavit, as required by the second section of this act, and before the expiration of the five years aforesaid, it shall be proven, after due notice to the settler, to the satisfaction of the register of the land office, that the person having filed such affidavit shall have actually changed his or her residence or abandoned the said land for more than six months at any time, then and in that event the land so entered shall revert to the government.

Sec. 6. And be it further enacted, That no individual shall be permitted to acquire title to more than one quarter section under the provision of this act; and that the Commissioner of the General Land Office is hereby required to prepare and issue such rules and regulations, consistent with this act, as shall be necessary and proper to carry its provisions into effect; and that the registers and receivers of the several land offices shall be entitled to receive the same compensation for any lands entered under the provisions of this act that they are now entitled to receive when the same quantity of land is entered with money, one half to be paid by the person making the application at the time of so doing, and the other half on the issue of the certificate by the person to whom it may be issued; but this shall not be construed to enlarge the maximum of compensation now prescribed by law for any register or receiver; *Provided,* That nothing contained in this act shall be so construed as to impair or interfere in any manner whatever with existing preemption rights: *And provided, further,* That all persons who may have filed their applications for a preemption right prior to the passage of this act, shall be entitled to all privileges of this act: *Provided, further,* That no person who has served, or may hereafter serve, for a period of not less than fourteen days in the army or navy of the United States, either regular or volunteer, under the laws thereof, during the existence of an actual war, domestic or foreign, shall be deprived of the benefits of this act on account of not having attained the age of twenty-one years.

Sec. 7. And be it further enacted, That the fifth section of the act entitled "An act in addition to an act more effectually to provide for the punishment of certain crimes against the United States, and for other purposes," approved the third of March, in the year eighteen hundred and fifty-seven, shall extend to all oaths, affirmations, and affidavits, required or authorized by this act.

Sec. 8. And be it further enacted, That nothing in this act shall be so construed as to prevent any person who has availed him or herself of the benefits of the first section of this act, from paying the minimum price, or the price to which the same may have graduated, for the quantity of land so entered at any time before the expiration of the five years, and obtaining a patent therefor from the government, as in other cases provided by law, on making proof of settlement and cultivation as provided by existing laws granting preemption rights.

Approved, May 20, 1862.

READING 5
"POOR MEANS NEARLY ALL HOMESTEADERS,"
MARY CHAFFEE ABELL, 1871–1875

The Homestead Act provided the legal basis for settling the American West, but it was the perseverance and grit of the early settlers that provided the drama. In this series of letters to her family Mary Chaffee Abell describes the conditions she encountered on the Kansas frontier.

[To Mary's sister, June 29, 1871]
Robert has got a piece of land that suits him, and so near market that we can get every thing just as cheap as we could in Lawrence. It seems so fortu-

nate. . . . There is a house to be built, fences to make—a well to be dug and a cow to be got beside a living—for the first year on a homestead brings in nothing—for the sod has to rot a year before a crop can be put in. I really cannot see how we are to get along—but in some way I hope. . . .

[To her sister, January 18, 1873]
Here we have been shut up all winter. Have not been anywhere since I was out to Miriam's last fall, do you wonder that I get nervous shut up so week after week with the children in a room 10 x 11 for that is every inch of room we have. Em talks about being crowded, but let her try keeping house in the further bedroom with four small children—a bedstead—bed on the floor—stove—table—big trunk, three chairs (stowed on the bed part of the time) and things you can't get along without, and no sort of a storeroom and half a window to light it all and then what about being crowded, and yet we are just in that predicament. I have to cook and do everything right here. Get milk—make butter, eat, sleep, etc., etc. . . .

[To her mother, October 11, 1873]
I helped Rob in with the last of his hay Friday. Yesterday I cleaned all the lower part of the house excepting washing the doors and windows and mopping the other room floor. I was tired enough when night came. Nevertheless sat up till half past ten o'clock mending clean clothes for the little ones. They have all had the bowel complaint this fall, but are well and hearty again now. Baby has cut four double teeth at once. I felt motion soon after I wrote you last. Am over five months along, shall be sick the first part of Feb I expect—seems as if I have all I can tend to now. . . . Have been at work all day even though it has been the Sabbath—washed the children all over, heads and all and put clean clothes on them—cut Rob's hair and whiskers etc. . . . I have been his sole help in getting up and stacking at least 25 tons of hay and oats—some of the time I was deathly sick and faint while loading, but finally got through it. . . .

[To her family, October 16, 1873]
I feel very little like writing, but you will be wanting to know the whys of course. One of those dreadful prairie fires, accompanied by a hurricane of wind swept through here . . . and took everything but our house and stock (horses and cattle). All our hay and oats that Rob and I had worked so hard

to get up and stack, harness, saddle, bridle, stable, 26 hens and chickens that I had had such work to raise—all the wooden part to the mower, hay rack post planks all burned etc. At least a hundred dollars worth swept away in a few moments. The flames came rolling in, in huge billows . . . but no one could stand before this blinding smoke, heat and cinders. I burned the right side of my face raw. One of my eyes is half shut, it is so badly swollen. . . .

Rob is blue enough—and who wouldn't be?

[To her parents, November 28, 1873]
Imagine yourselves for instance with nothing but land, house, and stock—for that's where we are. Not a tree, particle of water, grass, stable, fence or any thing else. Comfortable though right on the verge of winter—and the wherewith to get it with, about as vague. Eastern people may think us homesteaders are doing a fine thing to get 160 acres for nothing—all but the nothing. Oh, the suffering that the poor endure here, and the privations you have not the remotest idea of, and poor means nearly all homesteaders.

[To her father, November 21, 1874]
We've been obliged to tell the children that Santa Claus will not come here this year, everybody is so poor, and need food and clothes so much it wont pay him to bring any playthings. I shall try and sell butter to get them some candy etc. . . . I have aches and pain somewhere all the time, and with all am cross and nervous. If I was only where I could run home once or twice a year and get a rest—but I am here and here I must stay, how long?

[To her mother, February 16, 1875]
Your two kind letters have been received. I am sorry you worry about me so, but can't blame you. I am not as bad as I was in that coldest weather because I can sit up more, but I have no strength to do anything and the least little thing tires me all out. Baby has been quite sick for three days, and he is so heavy that the lifting and care of him has quite used me up. . . . The weather here is colder than with you, for the cold is a fierce north wind which will freeze man or beast that happen to be out. The children had to wear their hoods nights. My eyelids froze together so I picked off the ice, the tops of the sheets and quilts and all our beds were frozen stiff with the breath. The cold was so intense we could not breath the air without pain.

School Life in 1870s Eastern Iowa, Hamlin Garland, 1925

With settlement came institutions, and often the first to be established was a school. They may have been rude affairs but the journey to literacy was as important as westward expansion in the nineteenth century. In this excerpt from his autobiography the novelist Hamlin Garland reaches back to his Iowa childhood of the 1870s to describe school life on the prairie, especially during the winter months.

The school-house which was to be the center of our social life stood on the bare prairie . . . and like thousands of other similar buildings in the west, had not a leaf to shade it in summer nor a branch to break the winds of savage winter. . . . It was merely a square pine box painted a glaring white on the outside and a desolate drab within; at least drab was the original color, but the benches were mainly so greasy and hacked that original intentions were obscured. It had two doors on the eastern end and three windows on each side.

A long square stove (standing on slender legs in a puddle of bricks), a wooden chair, and a rude table in one corner, for the use of the teacher, completed the moveable furniture. The walls were roughly plastered and the windows had no curtains.

It was a barren temple of the arts even to the residents of Dry Run, and Harriet and I, stealing across the prairie one Sunday morning to look in, came away vaguely depressed. We were fond of the school and never missed a day if we could help it, but this neighborhood center seemed small and bleak and poor. . . .

The school-house which stood at the corner of our new farm was less than half a mile away, and yet on many of the winter days . . . we found it quite far enough. Hattie was now thirteen, Frank nine and I a little past eleven but nothing, except a blizzard . . . could keep us away from school. Facing the cutting wind, wallowing through the drifts, battling like small intrepid animals, we often arrived at the door moaning with pain yet unsubdued, our ears frosted, out toes numb in our boots, to meet others in similar case around the roaring hot stove.

Often after we reached the school-house another form of suffering overtook us in the "thawing out" process. Our fingers and toes, swollen with blood, ached and itched, and our ears burned. Nearly all of us carried sloughing ears and scaling noses. Some of the pupils came two miles against these winds.

The natural result of all this exposure was of course, chilblains! Every foot in the school was more or less touched with this disease to which our elders alluded as if it were an amusing trifle, but to us it was no joke.

After getting thoroughly warmed up, along about the middle of the forenoon, there came into our feet a most intense itching and burning and aching, a sensation so acute that keeping still was impossible, and all over the room an uneasy shuffling and drumming arose as we pounded our throbbing heels against the floor or scraped our itching toes against the edge of our benches. The teacher understood and was kind enough to overlook this disorder. . . .

It was always too hot or too cold in our schoolroom and on certain days when a savage wind beat and clamored at the loose windows, the girls, humped and shivering, sat upon their feet to keep them warm, and the younger children with shawls over their shoulders sought permission to gather close about the stove.

Our dinner pails (stored in the entry way) were often frozen solid and it was necessary to thaw our mince pie as well as our bread and butter by putting it on the stove. I recall, vividly, gnawing, dog-like, at the mollified outside of a doughnut while still its frosty heart made my teeth ache.

Happily all days were not like this. There were afternoons when the sun streamed warmly into the room, when long icicles formed on the eaves, adding a touch of grace to the desolate building, moments when the jingling bells of passing wood-sleighs expressed the natural cheer and buoyancy of our youthful hearts.

READING 7
"THE ESSENTIAL TRAGIC FUTILITY OF THEIR
EXISTENCE," HAMLIN GARLAND, 1925

In 1925 Hamlin Garland, revisiting the home of his youth, mused about life in the Dakota of the 1880s and its effect on the people. He recalled the difficulties of his mother on these endless plains and came to the sad conclusion of "the futility of woman's life on a farm." He addresses these issues in a poignant and melancholy recollection of the place and time.

All that day I had studied the land, musing upon its distinctive qualities, and while I acknowledged the natural beauty of it, I revolted from the graceless-ness of its human habitations. The lonely box-like farmhouses on the ridges suddenly appeared to me like the dens of wild animals. The lack of color, of charm in the lives of the people anguished me. I wondered why I had never before perceived the futility of woman's life on the farm. . . .

Looking at the sky above me, feeling how much I had dared and how little, how pitifully little I had won. Over me the ragged rainclouds swept, obscuring the stars and in their movement and in the feeling of the dawn lay something illimitable and prophetic. Such moments do not come to men often—but to me for an hour, life was painfully purposeless. "What does it all mean?" I asked myself. . . .

As I walked the street I met several neighbors from Dry Run as well as acquaintances from the Grove. Nearly all, even the young men, looked worn and weather-beaten and some appeared silent and sad. Laughter was curi-ously infrequent and I wondered whether in my days on the farm they had all been as rude of dress, as misshapen of form and as wistful of voice as they now seemed to me to be. "Have times changed? Has a spirit of unrest and complaining developed in the American farmer?"

I perceived the town from the triple viewpoint of a former resident, a man from the city, and a reformer, and every minutest detail of dress, tone, and gesture revealed new meaning for me. . . . At the moment nothing [could shield] the essential tragic futility of their existence. . . .

In those few days, I perceived life without its glamor. I no longer looked upon these toiling women with the thoughtless eyes of youth. I saw no humor in the bent forms and graying hair of the men. I began to understand that my own mother had trod a similar slavish round with never a full day of leisure, with scarcely an hour of escape from the tugging hands of children, and the need of mending and washing clothes. I recalled her as she passed from the churn to the stove, from the stove to the bedchamber, and from the bedchamber back to the kitchen, day after day, year after year, rising at daylight or before, and going to he bed only after the evening dishes were washed and the stockings and clothing mended for the night.

AN IOWA FARM OF THE 1870S, HERBERT QUICK, 1925

Farm life was difficult. The unexpectedly fertile plains soil could yield a rich bounty, but often the harvest could be hardship and heartbreak as well. The agricultural world of the nineteenth century involved many perils—harsh weather, droughts, dust, insect plagues—but perhaps the greatest threats were shifts in the economy and political philosophy, which could spell danger ahead for the struggling farmer. Herbert Quick recalls his childhood on an Iowa farm of the 1870s and the challenges faced by the farm community.

We grew wonderful wheat at first; the only problem was to get it to market and to live on the proceeds when it was sold. My father hauled wheat from the Iowa River to Waterloo, and even to Iowa City, when it was the railhead for our part of the country; hauled it slowly over mere trails across the prairie. It took him three days to market a load of wheat in Waterloo. . . .

But the worst, however, was yet to come. A harvest came when we found something was wrong with the wheat. No longer did the stalks stand clean and green as of old until they went golden in the sun. The broad green blades were spotted red and black with rust. Still it grew tall and rank; but as it matured it showed signs of disease. The heads did not fill well. Some blight was at work on it. However, we thought next year all would be well again. And when it grew worse year by year, it became a blight not only on the life of the grain but on human life as well. Wheat was almost our sole cash crop. If it failed, what should we do? And it was failing!

We were incurring, of course, the penalty for a one-crop system. We ought to have known it was inevitable. . . .

This . . . gave me my first contact with the phenomenon which puzzles so many city people. If the farmers are losing money on a certain crop, why in the world don't they change to something else? It is not so easy to change as the city man may think. The wheat growers of the Central States at the time of this writing have been losing money on their wheat for years; but if they endeavor to change, they are confronted by a great problem. Such a change means the adoption of an entirely new rotation of crops. They have for years used a three- or four-year rotation—wheat, then corn, then clover. The sowing of the wheat gives them the chance to put in their fertilizer. They are used to this system. Any change from it involves the risking of a new crop on which losses are also probable. . . .

The fields of wheat had always been a delight to me. . . . But now all the poetry went out of it. There was no joy for the soul of the boy who was steeped in such poetry as he could stumble upon, in these grain-fields threatened by grasshoppers, eaten by chinchbugs, blacked with molds and rusts, their blades specked as with the shed blood of the husbandman, their gold dulled by disease, their straw crinkling down in dead brittleness instead of rising and falling and swaying with the beautiful resiliency of health and abundance. . . .

All this time, while we were playing the role of tortured victims in the tragedy of the wheat, we were feeling our way toward some way out. We knew that our fields would grow great crops of maize—it was good corn country. But if there was more than one person who grew and fed cattle for the market there, I did not know of it. The average small farmer grew into the combination of hogs and corn. Gradually we changed over from wheat farming to big cornfields and populous hog lots. And then the price of both corn and pork went down, down, down, until corn sold for less than ten cents a bushel in our depreciated money and hogs for even less than three cents a pound. We had not found out about the balanced ration and the hog's need of pasture; and after a few generations of a diet of corn, the swine lost vitality and the crop of young pigs failed save where there was milk for them. The villain of misfortune still pursued us. . . .

Gradually we worked out a better *modus vivendi*—worked it out in a welter of debt and a depression which has characterized the rural mind to this day. Corn and hogs came to pay us as little as had wheat; yet for a while they were our only recourse, for the soil refused to grow wheat. For a long time there was plenty of open prairie on which the cattle could be grazed freely. . . . Then the expanding acres of wheat land cut us off from any extended range of free grass. We had no fencing until barbed wire came in. So our cows were picketed on the prairie, led to water and cared for much as the Danes handle their cows now.

In spite of these difficulties, however, it gradually dawned on us that by the sale of butter we were getting a little money from time to time. And though eggs were sometimes as low as eight cents a dozen, they brought us in some funds. The skim milk restored our hogs to health. Without con-scious planning, we were entering the business of mixed farming. My moth-er's butter was famed in all the nearby villages. In view of all the pains she took with it, it should have been; for she met the hot weather of our Iowa summers by hanging both cream and butter down the well where it was cool. Finally a creamery was started in Holland, a small town near us; and by this time we had a nice little herd of cows. A tank was made where water could be pumped through it and in this we set our cans of milk; and the cream hauler of the creamery came, skimmed off the cream, gave us tickets for it and hauled it away, thus giving us the cash when we went to town and saving the women the work of making the butter. It was the first contact of the factory system with the Iowa farm.

All this made life easier as to labor and money. But it was not our only amelioration. We began to have a better food supply . . . [as] our strawberries, raspberries, grapes, gooseberries, currants and cherries yielded abundantly. I had a patch of raspberries which I pruned and tended on a system of my own which gave us all we could consume and furnished dividends for our friends. In place of the old regimen of dried fruits and just dry groceries, we were surfeited on jams, jellies, preserves and other delicious viands; and with our supply of milk and cream, found the pioneer epoch definitely past so far as the larder was concerned. The prairie had been tamed. Iowa had been civilized. Our eighty-acre farm was furnishing us a real living for the first time. . . .

The farmer is often accused by the city dweller of being a confirmed calamity howler. He is. He is such because almost every calamity which comes on the land hits him sooner or later. Whenever any other industry shifts from under an economic change it shifts in part upon the farmer; and the farmer is unable to shift it in his turn; while most other shiftees can, by adding to prices or wages, get from under the load. The farmer is so placed that there is nothing beyond him but the wall. He is crushed against it. There is nothing under him but the earth. He is pressed into it. He is the end of the line in the economic game of crack the whip, and he is cracked off.

READING 9

"FARMING IS AN HONORABLE OCCUPATION," JOHN READ, 1881

In 1881 John Read, a midwestern farmer and author, published a handbook titled Farming for Profit *in which he provided example after example of the methods needed for success in the often harsh environment of the plains. Toward the end of the book, in philosophizing on the way to inculcate farm values and virtues in children, Read presents the essential ideology and attitude toward their calling of the farmers of the late nineteenth century.*

How to keep boys on the farm and induce them cheerfully to choose farming as their occupation for life is a question of deep interest to many parents. The stampede of young men from the country to the cities and large towns is not an evil which finds its limit in domestic circles which they leave, but is one which extends through society and makes its depressing influence felt everywhere. How to check this evil is a question of great importance and is well worthy of consideration.

In order to induce the boys to stay on the farm they must be informed of the true relation which exists between the city and the country. They must be shown that the expenses of living are so high that the city clerk, whom they envy because of his large salary, can hardly keep out of debt. And the fact that the man in the city is tied to his business a great deal more closely than the farmer is to his work should be set before them. . . .

Boys should be taught that farming is an *honorable occupation*. It is very true that the calling does not make the man, and that a man should not be respected because he follows one honest occupation or despised because he follows another. Character is what a man is, and cannot always be determined by reference to the kind of work which he performs. The farmer may be a gentleman or he can be a boor, he may build up a noble character or he may be a villain. He makes his own choice in these respects. Merely being a farmer will make him neither a good man nor a bad one. Still, farming is a business which does not open to its followers so many evil influences, and expose them to as many temptations, as some lines of business. It is the kind of labor which GOD directly marked out for man, and upon the cultivation of the soil the civilization and happiness of mankind must, in great measure, depend. As far as occupation is concerned, the farmer has no occasion to "look up to" the merchant, manufacturer, or professional man. Clergymen and teachers are doing a work the value of which is beyond all price, and many boys will be called from the farm to fill the ranks of these professions. . . . But before a boy leaves the farm to become a merchant, or to go to a city as a laborer, or to engage in business of any kind, he should very carefully consider the question whether there is any good prospect that he can do better than the thousands of those who have preceded him, and who soon have been led to repent that they ever left the farm. . . .

The girls must be taught to respect farming as an occupation, and be required to help their mothers in the work of the house and the dairy. When farmers educate their girls in a manner which will fit them to become farmers' wives, and teach them that farming is one of the most honorable of all occupations, and that the girl who marries a farmer does fully as well as one who marries a merchant or a lawyer, they will thereby do a great deal towards keeping their boys on the farm. . . .

We are well aware that many farmers' wives have been terribly overworked, and we can sympathize with the mother who desires an easier lot for her child. But we know that this excessive labor is not an absolute necessity, and that with the aid of the labor-saving implements of the present day a farmer's wife can live as easily as the wives of men engaged in many other pursuits. . . . The wife of the farmer ought to be willing to work in order to help him, and if the man is what he should be he will see to it that she does not go beyond her strength.

READING 10

"CONSIDERATIONS THAT MAKE IRRIGATION ATTRACTIVE
TO THE AGRICULTURIST," JOHN WESLEY POWELL, 1878

Development of the West's natural resources was of intense interest to both western settlers and the federal government, but attempts to formulate a rational plan often bumped up against powerful special interests and the sometimes rabidly independent American western mind-set. In 1878 Congress authorized John Wesley Powell—a one-armed Civil War veteran and leader of the first successful expedition to float the entire length of the Colorado River canyons—to examine the issues involved. His subsequent Report on the Lands of the Arid Region of the United States *amounted to a regional planning map. As an energetic advocate of government planning for the American West, he argued for a "wise prevision" in development and called for government-sponsored districts for mining, logging, grazing, agriculture, dams, and—most important for the farmer—irrigation. Powell recognized that political power and the social future of the American West lay in the control and utilization of water resources, and much of his argument focused on that issue. He even included examples of proposed legislation for irrigation districts. Controversies engendered by his recommendations—Would big farmers prosper at the expense of the smallholder? Would local government or federal authority be paramount? Was Powell advocating government control at the expense of private development?—would scuttle most of Powell's grand plan. As an expression of government concern over the often haphazard direction of western development, however, his report remains a watershed. In part because of his influence and arguments, federal government interest in regulating and controlling the development of the region became public policy—and remains a national concern today; vast acreages and water courses in the American West continue to be under federal control.*

This excerpt from Powell's report deals with the advisability of irrigation districts in arid regions. Note that Powell advocates cooperative—not independent laissez-faire—development for these districts and presents the Mormons' Utah experience as a successful example.

Advantages of Irrigation

There are two considerations that make irrigation attractive to the agriculturist. Crops thus cultivated are not subject to the vicissitudes of rainfall; the farmer fears no droughts; his labors are seldom interrupted and his crops rarely injured by storms. This immunity from drought and storm renders agricultural operations much more certain than in regions of greater humidity. Again, the water comes down from the mountains and plateaus freighted with fertilizing materials derived from the decaying vegetation and soils of the upper regions, which are spread by flowing water over the cultivated lands. It is probable that the benefits derived from this source alone will be full compensation for the cost of the process. Hitherto these benefits have not been fully realized, from the fact that the methods employed have been more or less crude. When the flow of water over the land is too great or too rapid the fertilizing elements borne in the waters are carried past the fields, and a washing is produced which deprives the lands irrigated of their most valuable elements, and little streams cut the fields with channels injurious in diverse ways. Experience corrects these errors and the irrigator soon learns to flood his lands gently, evenly, and economically. It may be anticipated that all the lands redeemed by irrigation in the Arid Region will be highly cultivated and abundantly productive, and agriculture will be but slightly subject to the vicissitudes of scant and excessive rainfall.

A stranger entering this Arid region is apt to conclude that the soils are sterile, because of their chemical composition, but experience demonstrates the fact that all the soils are suitable for agricultural purposes when properly supplied with water. It is true that some of the soils are overcharged with alkaline materials, but these can in time be "washed out." Altogether the fact suggests that far too much attention has heretofore been paid to the chemical constitution and too little to those physical conditions by which moisture and air are supplied to the roots of growing plants.

Cooperative Labor or Capital Necessary for the Development of Irrigation
Small streams can be taken out and distributed by individual enterprise, but cooperative labor or aggregated capital must be employed in taking out the larger streams.

The diversion of a large stream from its channel into a system of canals demands a large outlay of labor and materials. To repay this all waters so taken out must be used, and large tracts of land thus become dependent upon a single canal. It is manifest that a farmer depending upon his own labor cannot undertake this task. To a great extent the small streams are already employed, and but a comparatively small portion of the irrigable lands can be thus redeemed; hence the chief future development of irrigation must come from the use of the larger streams. Usually the confluence of brooks and creeks which form a large river takes place within the mountain district which furnishes its source before the stream enters the lowlands where the waters are to be used. The volume of water carried by the small streams that reach the lowlands before uniting with the great rivers, or before they are lost in the sands, is very small when compared with the volume of the streams which emerge from the mountains as rivers. This fact is important. If the streams could be used along their upper ramifications while the several branches are yet small, poor men could occupy the lands, and by their individual enterprise the agriculture of the country would be gradually extended to the limit of the capacity of the region; but when farming is dependent upon larger streams such men are barred from these enterprises until cooperative labor can be organized or capital induced to assist. Before many years all the available smaller streams throughout the entire region will be occupied in serving the lands, and then all future development will depend on the conditions above described.

In Utah Territory cooperative labor, under ecclesiastical organization, has been very successful. Outside of Utah there are but few instances where it has been tried; but at Greeley, in the State of Colorado, this system has been eminently successful.

"The test of trying to live happily
ever after," Jessie Rowland, c. 1870

Building a home or community was one thing, but trying to build a life together
was another on the often harsh frontier. Jessie Rowland, as the daughter of a
Kansas justice of the peace, was frequently present at the simple, stark marriage
ceremonies of plains pioneers who often had dreams but little else. The wedding
she describes demonstrates the hardscrabble existence that many encountered. It
also reflects the wise observation of the English poet Alexander Pope that "hope
springs eternal."

My father, being one of the early pioneers and a justice of the peace, was
called upon many times to report "Wilt thou, Mary?" and "Wilt thou,
John?" Then came the test of trying to live happily ever after.

On one of those occasions my father was asked to preside at a wedding
ten miles away from our home and my mother received an invitation to
accompany him. Upon arriving at their destination they were ushered down
six steps into a dugout, where the mother of the bride was preparing a
wedding feast. There was but one room and the furniture consisted of two
chairs, one with only two rounds to the back and bottoms. A bed made of
scantlings, a board table, a short bench, a stove, and a motto hung over the
door, "God Bless Our Home."

There was no floor, and a sheet had been stretched across one corner of
the room. The bride and groom were stationed behind this, evidently under
the impression it would not be proper to appear until time for the ceremony,
but they were in such close quarters and the sheet was so short it put one in
mind of an ostrich when it tries to hide by sticking its head in the sand.

Mrs. Brown, we will call her, was grinding something in a coffee mill but
arose to receive her guests with all the dignity of the first lady of the land.
She placed one chair for my mother and one for my father; seating herself
upon the bench, she continued turning the coffee grinder. Soon after some
of the neighbors came in and at the appointed time the bride and groom
emerged arm in arm from behind the temporary curtain and, stepping
forward to where my father was sitting, all became quiet and he pronounced
the words that made them one.

Soon after all sat down to the wedding supper. The sheet that hung across
the corner of the room was taken down and spread over the table for a cloth.

Mrs. Brown's efforts at the coffee mill had turned out some delicious coffee, made of dried carrots. There were seven different kinds of sauce, all made out of wild plums put up in seven different ways. The rest of the menu was quite simple and consisted of plain bread and butter, and fried pork. The table was shoved close to the bed and three sat on that side while three sat on the bench. The chairs were occupied and two or three kegs finished out the number of seats.

After supper the bridegroom took my father to one side and asked him to accept some potatoes in payment for performing the ceremony. He readily accepted and returned home.

READING 12

TEXAS CATTLE KINGDOM HOUSES OF
THE 1840S, WILLIAM BANTA, 1893

The primary function of towns and housing in the western settlements was to provide safety and security; the form these took was often the product of the dominant economic activity of a given region. Where mining was dominant, for instance, mine boomtowns would grow. In Texas, cattle raising was predominant, and the dwellings constructed showed characteristics of that culture. William Banta, who arrived in Texas in 1839, remembered years later the look and purpose of the Cattle Kingdom houses.

The houses were from fourteen to sixteen feet square; the first six logs were fourteen feet in length, the next four rounds sixteen feet long; thus the house had the appearance of a big house set on a smaller one, forming what was then called a block house. . . . The doors were made of split and hewed puncheons pinned together with an auger, and hung to the log wall with wooden hinges. On the inside of the house they were fastened by heavy wooden bars in such a manner that it was impossible for any one to get into the house from the outside. The cracks of the house were stopped with pieces of timber split for the purpose and driven in with an axe, then pinned fast with wooden pins, leaving two or three holes in each side and end between the chinking, called port holes, used for the purpose of shooting outside in case of attack. . . . The object of the projecting wall above was to be able to shoot straight down from the upper floor; and in fact this position commanded any approach from the outside.

BUSTED IN KANSAS, *EMPORIA GAZETTE*, JUNE 15, 1895

For many the West proved to be a dream dashed. The Homestead Act provided the land, but success was often elusive in semiarid land that was difficult to cultivate and even more difficult to profit from. Hundreds of hopeful settlers gave up their claims and returned to the East, chastened and disheartened. William Allen White, in 1895 just starting his distinguished journalistic career, describes one such surrender.

There came through Emporia yesterday two old-fashioned "mover wagons," headed east. The stock in the caravan would invoice four horses, very poor and tired; one mule, more disheartened than the horses; and one sad-eyed dog, that had been compelled to rustle his own precarious living for many a long and weary day.

A few farm implements of the simpler sort were in the wagon, but nothing that had wheels was moving except the two wagons. All the rest of the impedimenta had been left upon the battlefield, and these poor stragglers, defeated but not conquered, were fleeing to another field, to try the fight again.

These movers were from western Kansas—from Gray County, a country which holds the charter from the state to officiate as the very worst, most desolate, God-forsaken, man-deserted spot on this sad old earth. They had come from the wilderness only after a ten years' hard, vicious fight, a fight which had left its scars on their faces, had beat their bodies, had taken the elasticity from their steps, and left them crippled to enter the battle anew.

For ten years they had been fighting the elements. They had seen it stop raining for months at a time. They had heard the fury of the winter wind as it came whining across the short burned grass, and their children huddling in the corner. They have strained their eyes watching through the long summer days for the rain that never came. They have seen that big cloud roll up from the southwest about one o'clock in the afternoon, hover over the land, and stumble away with a few thumps of thunder as the sun went down. They have tossed through hot nights wild with worry, and have arisen only to find their worst nightmares grazing in reality on the brown stubble in front of their sun-warped doors.

They had such high hopes when they went out there; they are so desolate now—no, not now, for now they are in the land of corn and honey. They have come out of the wilderness, back to the land of promise. They are now in God's country down on the Neosho, with their wife's folks, and the taste of apple butter and good cornbread and fresh meat and pie—pie—plant pie like mother used to make—gladdened their shrunken palates last night. And real cream, curdling on their coffee saucers last night for supper, was a sight so rich and strange that it lingered in their dreams, wherein they walked beside the still water, and lay down in green pastures.

READING 14

"Wrong Side Up," J. K. Howard, 1943

The soil of much of the prairie was anchored with thick prairie or buffalo grass. Slicing through it provided access to the rich topsoil underneath but also made the soil vulnerable to wind and erosion. It was a damned if you do, damned if you don't situation. Eventually so much topsoil was turned over and so much wind blew that portions of the American West turned into the Dust Bowl of the 1930s. The devastated economies of these regions prompted new migrations westward to new landscapes of opportunity. Here journalist J. K. Howard describes an 1883 incident that later became a minor western legend.

One day in the spring of 1883 as a Scandinavian farmer, John Christiansen, plowed his fields in Montana's neighbor state of North Dakota, he looked up to find he was being watched . . . by an old and solemn Sioux Indian.

Silently the old Indian watched as the dark soil curled up and the prairie grass was turned under. Christiansen stopped, leaned against the plow handle, pushed his black Stetson back on his head, rolled a cigarette. He watched amusedly as the old Indian knelt, thrust his fingers into the plow furrow, measured its depth, fingered the sod and the buried grass.

The old Indian straightened up, looked at the farmer.

"Wrong side up," he said, and went away.

For a number of years that was regarded as a very amusing story indeed, betraying the ignorance of the poor Indian. Now [1943] there's a marker on Highway No. 10 in North Dakota on the spot where the words were spoken—a little reminder to the white man that his red brother was not so dumb.

"THE EXODUSTERS," HENRY KING, 1880

Following the Civil War, thousands of former slaves journeyed westward in an
"exodus" led by Benjamin Singleton and other African-American visionaries.
They established small farming communities in Kansas, Oklahoma, and
Colorado. Like other settlers, they faced hard times struggling with the soil,
weather, and economic conditions; many of these "Exodusters" were burdened in
addition by the yoke of racial discrimination. As a result, most had little success
as farmers and often gravitated toward the cities of the North and West. Henry
King's eyewitness account of the Exodus of 1879 into Kansas is a story of
admiration for the migrants. (For the perspective of many black migrants
themselves, see chapter 9, reading 8.)

One morning in April, 1879, a Missouri steamboat arrived at Wyandotte,
Kansas, and discharged a load of colored men, women, and children, with
divers barrels, boxes, and bundles of household effects. It was a novel,
picturesque, pathetic sight. They were of all ages and sizes; . . . their garments were incredibly patched and tattered, stretched, and uncertain; . . .
and there was not probably a dollar in money in the pockets of the entire
party. The wind was eager, and they stood upon the wharf shivering. . . .
They looked like persons coming out of a dream. And, indeed, such they
were . . . for this was the advance guard of the Exodus.

Soon other and similar parties came by the same route, and still others,
until, within a fortnight, a thousand or more of them were gathered there at
the gateway of Kansas—all poor, some sick, and none with a plan of future
action. . . .

The case was one to appeal with force to popular sympathy. . . . So
temporary shelter was speedily provided for them; food and facilities for
cooking it were furnished them in ample measure. . . . Then came more of
them. The tide swelled daily. . . .

The closing autumn found at least 15,000 of these colored immigrants in
Kansas. Such of them as had arrived early in the spring had been enabled to
do something toward getting a start, and the thriftier and more capable ones
had made homestead-entries and contrived, with timely aid, to build cabins;
in some cases, small crops of corn and garden vegetables were raised. . . .

. . . Numerous cabins of stone and sod were constructed while the cold season lasted; . . . in many cases, the women went to the towns and took in washing, or worked as house-servants . . . while the men were doing the building. Those who could find employment on the farms about their "claims," worked willingly and for small wages, and in this way supported their families, and procured now and then a calf, a pig, or a little poultry; others obtained places on the railroads, in the coal-mines, and on the public works of Topeka. Such as got work at any price, did not ask assistance; those who were compelled to apply for aid did it slowly, as a rule, and rarely came a second time. Not a single colored tramp was seen in Kansas all winter; and only one colored person was convicted of any crime. . . .

. . . [T]heir savings were not remarkable, to be sure, but they are creditable, and not to be lightly passed over. The wonder is that they have anything whatever to show for . . . twelve months of hand-to-mouth hardship and embarrassment.

READING 16

"Ranch and Mission Days in Alta
California," Guadalupe Vallejo, 1890

*Despite the very real hardships that farming communities faced, it was inevitable
that early life in the West would be looked back upon with nostalgia by some.
This seemed particularly true in California; Spanish and Mexican Americans
fondly remembered the simplicity and graciousness of the old days prior to the
"American conquest" of the 1840s and 1850s. Invariably, however, such
reminiscences were written by the children of the upper class; one must view them
critically not as romantic tales from the laborer or lower class but as the roseate
remembrances of the well-to-do. Other European Americans also wrote loving
narratives of their farming past, but the descriptions of the Hispanic agricultural
frontier are among the most poetic and colorful. This December 1890 selection
from the* Century Magazine *was written by Guadalupe Vallejo, nephew of the
wealthy Mariano Vallejo, a major figure in Mexican Californian history and one
of the largest landowners of this time period.*

It seems to me that there never was a more peaceful or happy people on the face of the earth than the Spanish, Mexican, and Indian population of Alta California before the American conquest. We were the pioneers of the Pacific coast, building towns and Missions while George Washington was carrying on the war of the Revolution, and we often talk together of the days when a few hundred large Spanish ranches and Mission tracts occupied the whole country from the Pacific to the San Joaquin. No class of American citizens is more loyal than the Spanish Californians, but we shall always be especially proud of the traditions and memories of the long pastoral age before 1840. Indeed, our social life still tends to keep alive a spirit of love for the simple, homely, outdoor life of our Spanish ancestors on this coast, and we try, as best we may, to honor the founders of our ancient families, and the saints and heroes of our history since the days when Father Junípero [Serra] planted the cross at Monterey [1770].

The leading features of Old Spanish life at the Missions, and on the large ranches of the last century, have been described in many books of travel, and with many contradictions. I shall confine myself to those details and illustrations of the past that no modern writer can possibly obtain except vaguely, from hearsay, since they exist in no manuscript, but only in the memories of a generation that is fast passing away. My mother has told me much, and I am still more indebted to my illustrious uncle, General Vallejo, of Sonoma, many of whose recollections are incorporated in this article. . . .

No one need suppose that the Spanish pioneers of California suffered many hardships or privations, although it was a new country. They came slowly, and were well prepared to become settlers. All that was necessary for the maintenance and enjoyment of life according to the simple and healthful standards of those days was brought with them. They had seeds, trees, vines, cattle, household goods, and servants, and in a few years their orchards yielded abundantly and their gardens were full of vegetables. Poultry was raised by the Indians, and sold very cheaply; a fat capon cost only twelve and a half cents. Beef and mutton were to be had for the killing, and wild game was very abundant. At many of the Missions there were large flocks of tame pigeons. At the Mission San Jose the father's doves consumed a cental of wheat daily, besides what they gathered in the village. The doves were of many colors, and they made a beautiful appearance on the red tiles of the church and the tops of the dark garden walls.

The houses of the Spanish people were built of adobe, and were roofed with red tiles. They were very comfortable, cool in summer and warm in winter. The clay used to make the bricks was dark brown, not white or yellow, as the adobes in the Rio Grande region and in parts of Mexico. Cut straw was mixed with the clay, and trodden together by the Indians. . . .

In the old days every one seemed to live out-doors. There was much gaiety and social life even though people were widely scattered. We traveled as much as possible on horseback. Only old people or invalids cared to use the slow cart, or *carreta*. Young men would ride from one ranch to another for parties, and whoever found his horse tired would let him go and catch another. In 1806 there were so many horses in the valleys around San Jose that seven or eight thousand were killed. Nearly as many were driven into the sea at Santa Barbara in 1807, and the same thing was done at Monterey in 1810. Horses were given to the runaway sailors, and to trappers and hunters who came over the mountains. . . .

Nothing was more attractive than the wedding cavalcade on its way from the bride's house to the Mission church. The horses were more richly caparisoned than for any other ceremony, and the bride's nearest relative or family representative carried her before him, she sitting on the saddle with her white satin shoe in a loop of golden or silver braid, while he sat on the bear-skin covered *anquera* behind. The groom and his friends mingled with the bride's party, all on the best horses that could be obtained, and they rode gaily from the ranch house to the Mission, sometimes fifteen or twenty miles away. In April or May, when the land was covered with wildflowers, the light-hearted troop rode along the edges of the uplands, between hill and valley, crossing the streams, and some of the young horsemen, anxious to show their skill, would perform all the feats for which the Spanish-Californians were famous. . . .

In these days of trade, bustle, and confusion, when many thousands of people live in the Californian valleys, which formerly were occupied by only a few Spanish families, the quiet and happy domestic life of the past seems like a dream. We, who loved it, often speak of those days, and especially the duties of the large Spanish households, where so many dependents were to be cared for, and everything was done in a simple and primitive way.

There was a group of warm springs a few miles distant from the old adobe house in which we lived. It made us children happy to be waked before sunrise to prepare for the "wash-day expedition" to the *Agua Caliente*. The night before the Indians had soaped the clumsy carreta's great wheels. Lunch was placed in baskets, and the gentle oxen were yoked to the pole. We climbed in, under the green cloth of an old Mexican flag which was used as an awning, and the white-haired Indian *ganan,* who had driven the carreta since his boyhood, plodded beside with his long *garrocha,* or ox-goad. The great piles of soiled linen were fastened on the backs of the horses, led by other servants, while the girls and women who were to do the washing trooped along by the side of the carreta. All in all, it made an imposing cavalcade, though our progress was slow, and it was generally sunrise before we had fairly reached the spring. . . .

We watched the women unload the linen and carry it to the upper spring of the group, where the water was best. Then they loosened the horses, and let them pasture on the wild oats, while the women put home-made soap on the clothes, dipped them in the spring, and rubbed them on the smooth rocks until they were white as snow. Then they were spread out to dry on the tops of the low bushes growing on the warm, windless, southern slopes of the mountain. There was sometimes a great deal of linen to be washed, for it was the pride of every Spanish family to own much linen, and the mother and daughters almost always wore white. I have heard strangers speak of the wonderful way in which Spanish ladies of the upper classes in California always appeared in snow-white dresses, and certainly to do so was one of the chief anxieties of every household. When there were no warm springs the servants of the family repaired to the nearest *arroyo*, or creek, and stood knee-deep in it, dipping and rubbing the linen, and enjoying the sport. . . . To me, at least, one of the dearest of my childish memories is the family expedition from the great thick-walled adobe, under the olive and fig trees of the Mission, to the *Agua Caliente* in early dawn, and the late return at twilight, when the younger children were all asleep in the slow carreta, and the Indians were singing hymns as they drove the linen-laden horses down the dusky ravines.

READING 17

THE BUILDING OF MAIN STREET, BARBARA RUTH BAILEY, 1982

Most American western towns went through roughly the same stages of development. The building materials might display regional variations, but the physical dimensions and outward appearance of western towns show remarkable similarities. In her 1982 study of the development of small towns in northeastern Oregon during the 1890–1920 era, historian Barbara Ruth Bailey analyzes their typical stages of development. The Oregonian model could easily be transplanted to virtually any nineteenth-century western locale.

Buildings enter into this study principally as indicators of the main street development process. For this purpose, only the basic facts about them—their relative dimensions, basic style and construction materials—are necessary; a careful analysis of the style and architecture has not been included. . . . Buildings were similar in character, repeating basic architectural patterns seen widely throughout the West. What makes these buildings interesting is the sequence of their appearance in a town, information useful in interpreting main street evolution. . . .

In their physical evolution, main streets passed through several stages. These corresponded to the town's growth, involving the progression from a relatively open building pattern to a denser one. Four stages of development can be identified in the small towns examined in northeastern Oregon. . . . These stages are not differentiated by any single feature; rather, each stage represents a different composite of characteristics that developed over the years. As the streets were built and rebuilt, some characteristics from earlier stages lingered while others, more typical of later stages, emerged. . . . Nevertheless, a definite sequence of development changed main streets from a pioneer row of widely spaced, gable-end and false-front frame structures to a solid row of two-story brick business buildings.

Through a main street's history, one element remained fairly constant: the portion of the street included in the business district. It was usually two blocks. This two-block length appeared even along the earliest streets. As a business district developed, its length remained the same but the gaps between the buildings were filled with increasing numbers of wider, deeper, taller buildings. Only in the largest towns did the main street business district ever expand to three or more blocks. The history of main street involves increasingly intense land use; therefore the four stages of development relate to building density and height. . . .

STAGE I

[T]he main street of a new town was often the first developed area. Towns were founded as trading centers and merchants usually built the first buildings. In a new town the standard business district stretched about two blocks along main street; merchants bought property within that area, selecting non-adjacent lots and creating a main street with many gaps along its length. Their buildings were usually a frame construction with a gable end to the street. Some had false fronts. . . .

The pioneer town was a small settlement consisting of a main street with a few wooden frame buildings spread along it, accompanied by a few houses off to the side. The towns that survived soon passed this stage as they grew and their main streets filled in with more buildings.

STAGE 2

A number of northeastern Oregon's towns still possess stage 2 main streets, lined with one- and two-story wood-frame buildings among which a few stone or brick buildings are interspersed. Although buildings stand on nearly all of the lots, there is still . . . open space between them, even where lots have been divided and contain two structures. The main streets were busy despite the towns' small populations, which peaked at from 200 to 450 people. . . .

Towns with stage 2 main streets are remarkably similar. . . . They had comparable economic bases. Their main streets looked much alike. Since these towns' early years their fates have differed, but the fundamental character of their main streets remains much the same.

STAGE 3

Stage 3 main streets occurred in towns with economies based on some form of industry as well as on the provision of goods and services to the immediately surrounding area. These towns were linked with the regional economy and, to some degree, the national economy.

Main streets of this stage were lined by buildings that filled the street frontage but did not extend to a lot's full depth. Little open space remained between these buildings, which were becoming increasingly substantial. New buildings generally stood two stories high and they were likely to be brick, although a few frame structures continued to be built. By stage 3, main streets began to look like those typical of large towns. And in fact, these towns were larger than those of stage 2 streets. Their peak population ranged from 450 to 1,000 people, many of whom were employed by local industries such as a lumber company or the railroad. [Maps of these Oregon towns included] a number of features indicative of stage 3 main streets and the kind of regional economy that supported a stage 3 town. The park was installed at the insistence of the ladies of [the town] and a pagoda . . . was used for band concerts. The depot was combined with a hotel, and the platform beyond was used for loading [agricultural products]. . . .

With densely built-up main streets, whose wooden structures were being replaced by more expensive and durable brick, stone and concrete buildings, these towns' physical appearance reflected their relative prosperity and greater regional roles.

STAGE 4

Stage 4 towns had main streets lined with numerous two-story brick buildings, many of which completely filled their lots. Several blocks may have been solidly packed with brick buildings. As a whole, however, the main street showed variety in the height, materials and lot depth of the buildings lining it. Despite this variety, records of stage 4 main streets reveal a consistently higher skyline and denser patter of ground use than those in towns of the preceding stage.

. . . All rapid-growth towns, they emerged as among the largest in the region within 15 years of their founding, at their peak housing between 1,000 and 2,000 people. Each served an area larger than its immediate environs. [Many served as county seats.] . . .

As the towns grew, their main street progressed quickly through the first three stages of main street development. It was actually possible to see characteristics of all stages at the same time along these streets as they shifted from one to the next. . . .

SUMMARY

Although [towns were] founded for a variety of reasons—either to make money for their founders, or to serve passing traffic, or to supply the surrounding districts—the underlying motive was always economic. Since most of a town's economic activity revolved around its main street business district, founders realized that their town's growth and prosperity depended on that street's development, and planned accordingly.

Thus, main street was the first part of a new town to develop. The earliest towns consisted of a row of commercial and domestic buildings along the main street (often, for financial reasons, both functions were under one roof). A few houses were scattered through the rest of the platted town; perhaps a church completed the new town. As the town grew, its main street filled in with more buildings. The nature of the buildings changed as the street evolved, showing a progression in style and materials. Town size, economic base and main street character were linked, and each stage of main street development reflected distinct steps in the town's growth.

"The Triple Nationalities," Frederick Law Olmsted, 1857

Cities and towns may be constructed of brick and mortar, but it is the human aspect that energizes a community. The interplay between hopes and realities and, in some cases, diverse cultural elements is what gives a town life and identity. In 1857 Frederick Law Olmsted, famous landscape architect and observant social critic, traveled through Texas. His description of San Antonio is testament to the impact of humanity on a town's character.

The principal part of the town lies within the sweep of the river upon the other side. We descend to the bridge, which is close down upon the water, as the river, owing to its particular source, never varies in height or temperature. We irresistibly stop to examine it, we are so struck with its beauty. It is of a rich blue and pure as crystal, flowing rapidly but noiselessly over pebbles and between reedy banks. One could lean for hours over the bridge-rail.

From the bridge we enter Commerce Street, the narrow principal thoroughfare, and here are American houses, and the triple nationalities break out in the most amusing display, till we reach the main plaza. The sauntering Mexicans prevail on the pavements, but the bearded Germans and the sallow Yankees furnish their proportion. The signs are German by all odds, and perhaps the houses, trim-built, with pink window-blinds. The American dwellings stand back, with galleries and jalousies and a garden picket-fence against the walk, or rise, next door, in a three-story brick to respectable city fronts. The Mexican buildings are stronger than those we saw before but still of all sorts, and now put to all sort of new uses. They are all low, of adobe or stone, washed blue and yellow, with flat roofs close down upon their single story. Windows have been knocked in their blank walls, letting the sun into their dismal vaults, and most of them are stored with dry goods and groceries, which overflow around the door. Around the plaza are American hotels, and new glass-fronted stores, alternating with sturdy battlemented Spanish walls, and confronted by the dirty, grim old stuccoed stone cathedral, whose cracked bell is now clunking for vespers in a tone that bids us no welcome, as more of the intruding race who have caused all this progress on which its traditions, like its imperturbable dome, frown down.

We have no city except perhaps New Orleans that can vie, in point of the picturesque interest that attaches to odd and antiquated foreignness, with

San Antonio. Its jumble of races, costumes, languages, and buildings; its religious ruins, holding to an antiquity for us indistinct enough to breed an unaccustomed solemnity; its remote, isolated, outposted situation, and the vague conviction that it is the first of a new class of conquered cities into whose decaying streets our rattling life is to be infused, combine with the heroic touches in its history to enliven and satisfy our traveler's curiosity.

. . . [W]e strolled, by moonlight, about the streets. They are laid out with tolerable regularity, parallel with the sides of the main plaza, and are pretty distinctly shared among the nations that use them. On the plaza and the busiest streets, a surprising number of old Mexican buildings are converted, by trowel, paintbrush, and gaudy carpentry, into drinking-places, always labeled "Exchange," and conducted on the New Orleans model. About these are loitered a set of customers, sometimes rough, sometimes affecting an "exquisite" dress, by no means attracting to a nearer acquaintance with themselves or their haunts. Here and there was a restaurant of a quieter look, where the traditions of Paris are preserved under difficulties by the exiled Gaul.

The doors of the cabins of the real natives stood open wide, if indeed they exist at all, and many were the family pictures of jollity or sleepy comfort they displayed to us as we sauntered curious about. The favorite dress appeared to be dishabille, and a free-and-easy, loloppy sort of life generally seemed to have been adopted as possessing, on the whole, the greatest advantages for a reasonable being. The larger part of each family appeared to be made up of black-eyed, olive girls, full of animation of tongue and glance, but sunk in a soft embonpoint, which added a somewhat extreme good-nature to their charms. Their dresses seemed lazily reluctant to cover their plump persons, and their attitudes were always expressive of the influences of a Southern sun upon national manners. The matrons, dark and wrinkled, formed a strong contrast to their daughters, though, here and there, a fine cast of feature and a figure erect with dignity, attracted the eye. The men lounged in roundabouts and cigaritos . . . and in fact the whole picture lacked nothing that is Mexican.

A Typical County Seat, Luther A. Lawhon, c. 1865

The largest town in a western county (which was sometimes the only town in the county, particularly in the cattle regions of the Southwest) would be designated the county seat; social and economic activity would generally gravitate to this center of legal and governmental responsibility. In 1865 Luther A. Lawhon, a Texas cattle rancher, remembered the design of the typical Texas county seat in the years leading to the Civil War. It was a pattern of development repeated numerous times throughout the American West with very little modification.

[The typical Texas county seat had] its rock or lumber court house, which was rarely two stories, and near by, as an adjunct, a one-cell rock or lumber jail. Around the public square were built the few unpretentious store houses, that flaunted the proverbial signs, "Dry Goods and Groceries" or "Dry Goods, Boots and Shoes," as the case might be. That the weaknesses as well as the social predelictions of the sturdy citizenship might be readily and conveniently catered to, a saloon or perhaps several, could always be found on or near the public square. Clustered about the commercial center, and growing further apart as the distance increased, were private residences which went to make up the hamlet. After the court house and jail, the hotel—generally a two-story building—was considered the most important, as it was frequently the most imposing structure in the village. In addition to the official and business edifices, there was always a well-constructed school house (there were no free schools in those days) and a commodious, comfortable church house.

READING 20

The Populist Platform, 1892

In the early 1890s difficult physical conditions, low prices, outrageous railroad freight rates, and political indifference toward their plight led farmers to form organizations to express and redress their grievances. Since the mid-nineteenth century, farmers had developed political and social organizations—the Patrons of Husbandry, or the Granger Movement, and the Farmers' Alliances—but these had little clout and disbanded or faded from view. In the 1890s, however, remnants of them banded with the labor movement and other reformers to form the Populist movement, which argued the reform agenda of the age and sought to reinvigorate farmers' wrath. In 1892 farm and labor delegates met in Omaha, Nebraska, to put their ideals into action by founding a political arm—the People's Party—and nominating General James Weaver of Iowa for the presidency. In the election that fall Weaver polled over one million popular votes and won twenty-two electoral votes.

Despite their significant efforts, the Populists failed to unite farmers in a viable political force. As an expression of their frustration, however, the Populist platform of 1892, adopted at Omaha on July 4, is an eloquent and heartfelt document.

Assembled upon the 116th anniversary of the Declaration of Independence, the People's Party of America, in their first national convention, invoking upon their action the blessing of Almighty God, put forth in the name and on behalf of the people of this country, the following preamble and declaration of principles:

PREAMBLE

The conditions which surround us best justify our co-operation; we meet in the midst of a nation brought to the verge of moral, political, and material ruin. Corruption dominates the ballot-box, the Legislatures, the Congress, and touches even the ermine of the bench. The people are demoralized; most of the States have been compelled to isolate the voters at the polling places to prevent universal intimidation and bribery. The newspapers are largely subsidized or muzzled, public opinion silenced, business prostrated, homes covered with mortgages, labor impoverished, and the land concentrating in the hands of capitalists. The urban workmen are denied the right to organize for self-protection, imported pauperized labor beats down their wages, a hireling standing army, unrecognized by our laws, is established to shoot them down, and they are rapidly degenerating into European conditions. The fruits of the toil of millions are boldly stolen to build up colossal fortunes for a few, unprecedented in the history of mankind; and the possessors of those, in turn, despise the Republic and endanger liberty. From the same prolific womb of governmental injustice we breed the two great classes—tramps and millionaires.

The national power to create money is appropriated to enrich bondholders; a vast public debt payable in legal tender currency has been funded into gold-bearing bonds, thereby adding millions to the burdens of the people.

Silver, which has been accepted as coin since the dawn of history, has been demonetized to add to the purchasing power of gold by decreasing the value of all forms of property as well as human labor, and the supply of currency is purposely abridged to fatten usurers, bankrupt enterprise, and enslave industry. A vast conspiracy against mankind has been organized on two continents, and it is rapidly taking possession of the world. If not met and overthrown at once it forebodes terrible social convulsions, the destruction of civilization, or the establishment of an absolute despotism.

We have witnessed for more than a quarter of a century the struggles of the two great political parties for power and plunder, while grievous wrongs have been inflicted upon the suffering people. We charge that the controlling influences dominating both these parties have permitted the existing dreadful conditions to develop without serious effort to prevent or restrain them. Neither do they now promise us any substantial reform. They have agreed together to ignore, in the coming campaign, every issue but one. They propose to drown the outcries of a plundered people with the uproar of a sham battle over the tariff, so that capitalists, corporations, national banks, rings, trusts, watered stock, the demonetization of silver and the oppressions of the usurers may all be lost sight of. They propose to sacrifice our homes, lives, and children on the altar of mammon; to destroy the multitude in order to secure corruption funds from the millionaires.

Assembled on the anniversary of the birthday of the nation, and filled with the spirit of the grand general and chief who established our independence, we seek to restore the government of the Republic to the hands of "the plain people," with which class it originated. We assert our purposes to be identical with the purposes of the National Constitution; to form a more perfect union and establish justice, insure domestic tranquility, provide for the common defence, promote the general welfare, and secure the blessings of liberty for ourselves and our posterity.

We declare that this Republic can only endure as a free government while built upon the love of the whole people for each other and for the nation; that it cannot be pinned together by bayonets; that the civil war is over, and that every passion and resentment which grew out of it must die with it, and that we must be in fact, as we are in name, one united brotherhood of free men.

Our country finds itself confronted by conditions for which there is no precedent in the history of the world; our annual agricultural productions amount to billions of dollars in value, which must, within a few weeks or months, be exchanged for billions of dollars' worth of commodities consumed in their production; the existing currency supply is wholly inadequate to make this exchange; the results are falling prices, the formation of combines and rings, the impoverishment of the producing class. We pledge ourselves that if given power we will labor to correct these evils by wise and reasonable legislation, in accordance with the terms of our platform.

We believe that the power of government—in other words, of the people—should be expanded (as in the case of the postal service) as rapidly and as far as the good sense of an intelligent people and the teachings of experience shall justify, to the end that oppression, injustice, and poverty shall eventually cease in the land.

While our sympathies as a party of reform are naturally upon the side of every proposition which will tend to make men intelligent, virtuous, and temperate, we nevertheless regard these questions, important as they are, as secondary to the great issues now pressing for solution, and upon which not only our individual prosperity but the very existence of free institutions depend; and we ask all men to first help us determine whether we are to have a republic to administer before we differ as to the conditions upon which it is to be administered, believing that the forces of reform this day organized will never cease to move forward until every wrong is remedied and equal rights and equal privileges securely established for all the men and women of this country.

PLATFORM

We declare, therefore—

First.—That the union of labor forces of the United States this day consummated shall be permanent and perpetual; may its spirit enter into all hearts for the salvation of the Republic and the uplifting of mankind.

Second.—Wealth belongs to him who creates it, and every dollar taken from industry without an equivalent is robbery. "If any will not work, neither shall he eat." The interests of rural and civic labor are the same; their enemies are identical.

Third.—We believe that the time has come when the railroad corporations will either own the people or the people must own the railroads, and should the government enter upon the work of owning and managing all railroads, we should favor an amendment to the Constitution by which all persons engaged in the government service shall be placed under a civil-service regulation of the most rigid character, so as to prevent the increase of the power of the national administration by the use of such additional government employees.

Finance.—We demand a national currency, safe, sound, and flexible, issued by the general government only, a full legal tender for all debts, public and private, and that without the use of banking corporations, a just, equitable, and efficient means of distribution direct to the people, at a tax not to exceed 2 per cent per annum, to be provided as set forth in the sub-treasury plan of the Farmers' Alliance, or a better system; also by payments in discharge of its obligations for public improvements.

1. We demand free and unlimited coinage of silver and gold at the present legal ratio of 16 to 1.

2. We demand that the amount of circulating medium be speedily increased to not less than $50 per capita.

3. We demand a graduated income tax.

4. We believe that the money of the country should be kept as much as possible in the hands of the people, and hence we demand that all State and national revenues shall be limited to the necessary expenses of the government, economically and honestly administered.

5. We demand that postal savings banks be established by the government for the safe deposit of the earnings of the people and to facilitate exchange.

Transportation.—Transportation being a means of exchange and a public necessity, the government should own and operate the railroads in the interest of the people. The telegraph, telephone, like the post-office system, being a necessity for the transmission of news, should be owned and operated by the government in the interest of the people.

Land.—The land, including all the natural sources of wealth, is the heritage of the people and should not be monopolized for speculative purposes, and alien ownership of land should be prohibited. All land now held by railroads and other corporations in excess of their actual needs, and all lands now owned by aliens should be reclaimed by the government and held for actual settlers only.

Your Committee on Platform and Resolutions beg leave unanimously to report the following:

WHEREAS, Other questions have been presented for our consideration, we hereby submit the following, not as part of the Platform of the People's Party, but as resolutions expressive of the sentiment of this Convention:

1. *Resolved,* That we demand a free ballot and a fair count in all elections, and pledge ourselves to secure it to every legal voter without Federal intervention, through the adoption by the States of the unperverted Australian or secret ballot system.

2. *Resolved,* That the revenue derived from a graduated income tax should be applied to the reduction of the burden of taxation now levied upon the domestic industries of this country.

3. *Resolved,* That we pledge our support to fair and liberal pensions to ex-Union soldiers and sailors.

4. *Resolved,* That we condemn the fallacy of protecting American labor under the present system, which opens our ports to the pauper and criminal classes of the world and crowds out our wage-earners; and we denounce the present ineffective laws against contract labor, and demand the further restriction of undesirable emigration.

5. *Resolved,* That we cordially sympathize with the efforts of organized workingmen to shorten the hours of labor, and demand a rigid enforcement of the existing eight-hour law on Government work, and ask that a penalty clause be added to the said law.

6. *Resolved,* That we regard the maintenance of a large standing army of mercenaries, known as the Pinkerton system, as a menace to our liberties, and we demand its abolition; and we condemn the recent invasion of the Territory of Wyoming by the hired assassins of plutocracy, assisted by Federal officers.

7. *Resolved,* That we commend to the favorable consideration of the people and the reform press the legislative system known as the initiative and referendum.

8. *Resolved,* That we favor a constitutional provision limiting the office of the President and Vice-President to one term, and providing for the election of Senators of the United States by a direct vote of the people.

9. *Resolved,* That we oppose any subsidy or national aid to any private corporation for any purpose.

10. *Resolved,* That this convention sympathizes with the Knights of Labor and their righteous contest with the tyrannical combine of clothing manufacturers of Rochester, and declare it to be the duty of all who hate tyranny and oppression to refuse to purchase the goods made by the said manufacturers, or to patronize any merchants who sell such goods.

CHAPTER 4

BURY ME IN A TREE

The Mining Frontier

MANY YEARS ago a Cornish hard-rock miner confided to his colleagues his last wish. "When I die," he said, "bury me in a tree—I've spent too much time underground already." The history of the American western mining frontier has spent too much time underground as well. Almost without exception, miners and mining companies have been viewed historically as environmental despoilers or racist and capitalistic exploiters. As with history generally, the true story is much more complex and comprehensive. Negative elements did exist, of course, but most miners (and a majority of mining companies) were simply doing a day's work with its cosmic ramifications far from conscious thought. What linked the participants on the mining frontier was the visceral lust for the yellow flake, the gleam of gold in the pan, the golden vein in the quartz, the silver lining in the country rock, and the copper bonanza just a shovelful away. Dreams.

Among the thousands of documents that chronicle the dozens of mineral "rushes" in the American West, this chapter focuses on the emotional impact of discovery, the anticipation of great wealth, the boomtown culture, the hardscrabble working conditions, the violence between miner and owner, the development of corporate mining, and racial and ethnic tensions. The California gold rush of 1848–50 provides the jumping-off point.

READING 1

THE CALIFORNIA GOLD DISCOVERY, JAMES MARSHALL, 1848

On January 24, 1848, the California gold rush began. James Marshall, an employee of John Sutter at Sutter's Mill on the American River in Coloma, discovered gold in the tailrace of the sawmill—which, he said later, made him "think right hard." Little did he know that a tidal wave of humanity would engulf California over the next few years, or that his chance find would bring him fame but little else. He failed as a miner, mostly because other miners followed him everywhere, hoping to have a little of Marshall's Midas touch rub off. He attempted several other professions with little success and was eventually reduced to selling his autograph for a livelihood. Today a monument to James Marshall stands in Coloma, where it all began. A statue of him, proudly atop a column, points to the spot where he discovered gold. Here he describes his discovery.

One morning in January, it was a clear cold morning; I shall never forget that morning, as I was taking my usual walk along the race, after shutting off the water, my eye was caught by a glimpse of something shining in the bottom of the ditch. There was about a foot of water running there. I reached my hand down and picked it up; it made my heart thump for I felt certain it was gold. The piece was about half the size and of the shape of a pea. Then I saw another piece in the water. After taking it out, I sat down and began to think right hard. I thought it was gold, and yet it did not seem to be of the right color; all the gold coin I had seen was of a reddish tinge; this looked more like brass. I recalled to mind all the metals I had ever seen or heard of, but I could find none that resembled this. Suddenly the idea flashed across my mind that it might be iron pyrites ["fool's gold"]. I trembled to think of it! This question could soon be determined. Putting one of the pieces on hard river stone, I took another and commenced hammering it. It was soft and didn't break; it therefore must be gold, but largely mixed with some other metal, very likely silver; for pure gold, I thought, would certainly have a brighter color.

When I returned to our cabin for breakfast I showed the two pieces to my men. They were all a good deal excited, and had they not thought that the gold existed in small quantities they would have abandoned everything and left me to finish the job alone. However, to satisfy them, I told them that as soon as we had the mill finished we would devote a week or two to gold hunting and see what we could make out of it.

While we were looking in the race after this discovery, we always kept a sharp lookout, and in the course of three or four days we had picked up about three ounces—our work still progressing as lively as ever, for none of us imagined at that time that the whole country was sowed with gold.

About a week's time after the discovery I had to take another trip to the fort; and to gain what information I could respecting the real value of the metal, took all we had collected with me and showed it to Mr. Sutter, who at once declared it was gold, but thought with me, it was greatly mixed with some other metal. It puzzled us a great deal to hit upon the means of telling the exact quantity contained in the alloy; however, we at last stumbled on an old American cyclopedia where we saw the specific gravity of all the metals, and rules given to find the quantity of each in a given bulk. After hunting the whole fort and borrowing from some of the men, we got three dollars and a half in silver, and with a small pair of scales we soon cyphered it out that there was no silver nor copper in the gold, but that it was entirely pure.

This fact being ascertained, we thought it our best policy to keep it as quiet as possible till we should have finished the mill, but there was a great number of disbanded Mormon soldiers in and about the fort, and when they came to hear of it, why, it just spread like wildfire, and soon the whole country was in a bustle. I had scarcely arrived at the mill again till several persons with pans, shovels and hoes, and those that had not iron picks but wooden ones, all anxious to fall to work and dig up our mill; but this we would not permit. As fast as one party disappeared another would arrive, and sometimes I had the greatest kind of trouble to get rid of them. I sent them all off in different directions, telling them about such and such places, where I was certain there was plenty of gold if they would only take the trouble of looking for it. At that time I never imagined the gold was so abundant. I told them to go to such and such places, because it appeared that they would dig nowhere but in such places as I pointed out, and I believe such was their confidence in me that they would have dug on the very top of yon mountain if I had told them to do so.

So there, stranger, is the entire history of the gold discovery in California—a discovery that hasn't yet been of much benefit to me.

READING 2
"CAPTAIN SUTTER'S ACCOUNT OF THE
FIRST DISCOVERY OF GOLD," 1854

James Marshall's employer was the imperious land baron John Augustus Sutter, a transplanted Swiss citizen who had received a 40,000-acre land grant from the Mexican authorities. It was on his property, located in the Sacramento Valley and up into the foothills of what came to be called the Mother Lode region, that Marshall discovered gold, triggering the California gold rush. Sutter's land was soon overrun by "argonauts," his cattle butchered, and his rights ignored. He spent the rest of his life seeking redress from the American government, to little avail. This is Sutter's account of his fateful meeting with Marshall soon after the gold discovery.

I was sitting one afternoon just after my siesta, engaged, by-the-bye, in writing a letter to a relation of mine at Lucern, when I was interrupted by Mr. Marshall, a gentleman with whom I had frequent business trans-actions—bursting into the room. From the unusual agitation in his manner I imagined that something serious had occurred, and, as we involuntarily do in this part of the world, I at once glanced to see if my rifle was in its proper place. You should know that the mere appearance of Mr. Marshall at that moment in the [Sutter's] Fort, was quite enough to surprise me, as he had but two days before left the place to make some alterations in a mill for sawing pine planks, which he had just run up for me some miles higher up the Americanos [River]. When he had recovered himself a little, he told me that, however great my surprise might be at his unexpected reappearance, it would be much greater when I heard the intelligence he had come to bring me. "Intelligence," he added, "which if properly profited by, would put both of us in possession of unheard-of wealth—millions and millions of dollars, in fact." I frankly own, when I heard this that I thought something had touched Marshall's brain, when suddenly all my misgivings were put to an end by his flinging on the table a handful of scales of pure virgin gold. I was fairly thunderstruck and asked him to explain what all this meant, when he went on to say, that according to my instructions, he had thrown the mill-wheel out of gear, to let the whole body of the water in the dam find a passage through the tail race, which was previously too narrow to allow the water to run off in sufficient quantity, whereby the wheel was prevented from efficiently performing its work. By this alteration the narrow channel was considerably enlarged, and a mass of sand & gravel carried off by the force of the torrent. Early in the morning after this took place, Mr. Marshall was walking along the left bank of the stream when he perceived something which he at first took for a piece of opal—a clear transparent stone, very common here—glittering on one of the spots laid bare by the sudden crum-bling away of the bank. He paid no attention to this, but while he was giving directions to his workmen, having observed several similar glittering frag-ments, his curiosity was so far excited, that he stooped down & picked one of them up. "Do you know," said Mr. Marshall to me, "I positively debated within myself two or three times whether I should take the trouble to bend my back to pick up one of the pieces and had decided on not doing so when further on, another glittering morsel caught my eye—the largest of the pieces now before you. I condescended to pick it up, and to my astonishment found that it was a thin scale of what appears to be pure gold." He then gathered some twenty or thirty pieces which on examination convinced him that his suppositions were right. His first impression was, that this gold had been lost or buried there, by some early Indian tribe—perhaps some of those mysterious inhabitants of the West, of whom we have no account, but who dwelt on this continent centuries ago, and built those cities and temples, the ruins of which are scattered about these solitary wilds. On proceeding, however, to examine the neighbouring soil, he discovered that it was more or less auriferous. This at once decided him. He mounted his horse, and rode down to me as fast as it could carry him with the news.

At the conclusion of Mr. Marshall's account, and when I had convinced myself, from the specimens he had brought with him, that it was not exaggerated, I felt as much excited as himself. I eagerly inquired if he had shown the gold to the work people at the mill and was glad to hear that he had not spoken to a single person about it. We agreed not to mention the circumstance to any one and arranged to set off early the next day for the mill. On our arrival, just before sundown, we poked the sand around in various places, and before long succeeded in collecting between us more than an ounce of gold, mixed up with a good deal of sand. I stayed at Mr. Marshall's that night, and the next day we proceeded some little distance up the South Fork, and found that gold existed along the whole course, not only in the bed of the main stream, where the [water] had subsided but in every little dried-up creek and ravine. Indeed I think it is more plentiful in these latter places, for I myself, with nothing more than a small knife, picked out from a dry gorge, a little way up the mountain, a solid lump of gold which weighed nearly an ounce and a half.

Notwithstanding our precautions not to be observed, as soon as we came back to the mill, we noticed by the excitement of the working people that we had been dogged about, and to complete our disappointment, one of the Indians who had worked at the gold mine in the neighbourhood of La Paz cried out in showing us some specimens picked up by himself,—"Oro!—Oro—Oro!!!"

"THE WORLD'S RAFFLE," HENRY DAVID THOREAU, 1852

Generally, the announcement of a gold strike or any discovery of precious metal would send observers into paroxysms of anticipation and delight. The possibilities of sudden wealth and endless leisure usually occasioned a writer's most purple prose. Not everyone agreed; Henry David Thoreau, for one, thought the California gold rush symptomatic of (as he put it) "the greatest disgrace of mankind"—namely, wealth gained without a concomitant contribution to societal welfare. His views, however, were shared by very few.

The recent rush to California and the attitude of the world, even of its philosophers and prophets, in relation to it appears to me to reflect the greatest disgrace on mankind. That so many are ready to get their living by the lottery of gold-digging without contributing any value to society, and that the great majority who stay at home justify them in this both by precept and example! It matches the infatuation of the Hindoos who have cast themselves under the car of the Juggernaut. I know of no more startling development of the morality of trade and all the modes of getting a living than the rush to California affords. Of what significance the philosophy, or poetry, or religion of a world that will rush to the lottery of California gold-digging on the receipt of the first news, to live by luck, . . . without contributing any value to society? And that is called enterprise, and the devil is only a little more enterprising! The philosophy and poetry and religion of such a mankind are not worth the dust of a puffball. The hog that *roots* his own living, and so makes manure, would be ashamed of such company. If I could command the wealth of all the worlds by lifting my finger, I would not pay such a price for it. It makes God to be a moneyed gentleman who scatters a handful of pennies in order to make mankind scramble for them. Going to California. It is only three thousand miles nearer to hell. I will resign my life sooner than live by luck. The world's raffle. A subsistence in the domains of nature a thing to be raffled for! No wonder they gamble there. I never heard that they did anything else there. What a comment, what a satire, on our institutions! The conclusion will be that mankind will hang itself upon a tree. And who would interfere to cut it down? And have all the precepts in all the bibles taught men only this? and is the last and most admirable invention of the Yankee race only an improved muck-rake?—patented too! If one came hither to sell lottery tickets, bringing satisfactory credentials, and the prizes were seats in heaven, this world would buy them with a rush.

Did God direct us so to get our living, digging where we never planted,—and He would perchance reward us with lumps of gold? . . . The gold of California is a touchstone which has betrayed the rottenness, the baseness, of mankind. Satan, from one of his elevations, showed mankind the kingdom of California, and they entered into a compact with him at once.

READING 4

LIFE IN THE GOLDFIELDS, DANIEL B. WOODS, 1849

The mining experience could often be a frustrating and unprofitable one. Success was more frequently based on serendipity than on skill, and the life was hard at best, as attested to by Daniel B. Woods's account of two days in the Mother Lode goldfields.

July 9th

Today we made $20 each. One of the conclusions at which we are rapidly arriving is that the chances of making a fortune in the gold mines are about the same as those in favor of our drawing a prize in a lottery. No kind of work is so uncertain. A miner may happen upon a good location in his very first attempt and in a very few days make hundreds or thousands, while the experienced miners about him may do nothing. An instance of this kind happened recently when two men who had been some time in the mines started a dispute as to a small space between their claims. As they could not amicably settle the dispute they agreed to leave it to a newcomer who happened by who had not yet done an hour's work in the mines. He measured off ten feet—the amount allowed by custom—to each of the claimants, taking for his trouble the narrow strip of land between them. In a few hours the larger claims belonging to the older miners were abandoned as useless while the newcomer discovered a deposit which yielded him $7,435.

July 10th

We made $3.00 each today. This life of hardships and exposure has affected my health. Our diet consists of hard tack, flour we eat half cooked, and salt pork, with occasionally a salmon which we purchase from the Indians. Vegetables are not to be procured. Our feet are wet all day, while a hot sun shines down upon our heads and the very air parches the skin like the hot air of an oven. Our drinking water comes down to us thoroughly impregnated with the mineral substances washed through the thousand cradles above us. After our days of labor, exhausted and faint, we retire—if this word may be applied to the simple act of lying down in our clothes—robbing our feet of their boots to make a pillow of them, and wrapping our blankets about us, on a bed of pine boughs, or on the ground beneath the clear, bright stars of the night. Near morning there is always a change in the temperature and several blankets become necessary. The feet and the hands of a novice in this business become blistered and lame, and the limbs are stiff. Besides all these causes of sickness, the anxieties and cares which wear away the lives of so many men who leave their families to come to this land of gold, contribute, in no small degree, to the same result.

READING 5

"NATURE'S GREAT LOTTERY SCHEME," DAME SHIRLEY, 1852

> *There was no great mystery as to how to strike it rich in the goldfields—it took luck, hard work, and more luck. The process mixed drudgery with high expectation. Letters written by the wife of a physician at a mining camp, Louise Amelia Knapp Smith Clappe—better known by her pseudonym of Dame Shirley—describe the miners' work habits and techniques.*

From Our Log Cabin,
Indian Bar, April 10, 1852
Having got our gold mines discovered, and claimed, I will try to give you a faint idea of how they work them. Here, in the mountains, the labor of excavation is extremely difficult, on account of the immense rocks which form a large portion of the soil. Of course no man can work out a claim alone. For that reason, and also for the same that makes partnerships desirable, they congregate in companies of four or six, generally designating themselves by the name of the place from whence they emigrated; as, for example, the Illinois, Bunker Hill, Bay State, etc., companies. In many places the surface soil, or in mining phrase, the top dirt, pays when worked in a Long-Tom. This machine (I have never been able to discover the derivation of the name) is a trough, generally about twenty feet in length and eight inches in depth, formed of wood, with the exception of six feet at one end, called the "riddle" (query, why "riddle?"), which is made of sheet-iron perforated with

holes about the size of a large marble. Underneath this colander-like portion of the long-tom, is placed another trough, about ten feet long, the sides six inches, perhaps, in height, which, divided through the middle by a slender slat, is called the riffle-box. It takes several persons to manage properly a long-tom. Three or four men station themselves with spades at the head of the machine, while at the foot of it stands an individual armed "wid de shovel an' de hoe." The spadesmen throw in large quantities of the precious dirt, which is washed down to the riddle by a stream of water leading into the long-tom through wooden gutters or sluices. When the soil reaches the riddle, it is kept constantly in motion by the man with the hoe. Of course, by this means, all the dirt and gold escapes through the perforations into the riffle-box below, one compartment of which is placed just beyond the riddle. Most of the dirt washes over the sides of the riddle-box, but the gold, being so astonishingly heavy, remains safely at the bottom of it. When the machine gets too full of stones to be worked easily, the man whose business it is to attend to them throws them out with his shovel, looking carefully among them as he does so for any pieces of gold which may have been too large to pass through the holes of the riddle. I am sorry to say that he generally loses his labor. At night they pan out the gold, which has been collected in the riffle-box during the day, many of the miners decline washing the top dirt at all, but try to reach as quickly as possible the bed-rock, where are found the richest deposits of gold. The river is supposed to have formerly flowed over this bed-rock, in the crevices of which it left, as it passed away, the largest portions of the so eagerly sought for ore. The group of mountains amidst which we are living is a spur of the Sierra Nevada, and the bed-rock, which in this vicinity is of slate, is said to run through the entire range, lying, in the distance varying from a few feet to eighty or ninety feet, beneath the surface of the soil. On Indian Bar the bed-rock falls in almost perpendicular benches, while at Rich Bar the friction of the river has formed it into large, deep basins, in which the gold, instead of being found, as you would naturally suppose, in the bottom of it, lies, for the most part, just below the rim. A good-natured individual bored *me,* and tired *himself,* in a hopeless attempt to make me comprehend that this was only a necessary consequence of the under-current of the water, but with my usual stupidity upon such matters I got but a vague idea from his scientific explanation, and certainly shall not mystify *you* with my confused notions thereupon.

When a company wish to reach the bed-rock as quickly as possible, they sink a shaft (which is nothing more nor less than digging a well) until they "strike it." They then commence drifting coyote holes, as they call them, in search of crevices, which, as I told you before, often pay immensely. These coyote holes sometimes extend hundreds of feet into the side of the hill. Of course, they are obliged to use lights in working them. They generally proceed until the air is so impure as to extinguish the lights, when they return to the entrance of the excavation and commence another, perhaps close to it. When they think that a coyote hole has been faithfully worked, they clean it up, which is done by scraping the surface of the bed-rock with a knife, lest by chance they have overlooked a crevice, and they are often richly rewarded for this precaution.

Now I must tell you how those having claims on the hills procure the water for washing them. The expense of raising it in any way from the river is too enormous to be thought of for a moment. In most cases it is brought from ravines in the mountains. A company, to which a friend of ours belongs, has dug a ditch about a foot in width and depth, and more than three miles in length, which is fed in this way. I wish you could see this ditch. I never beheld a *natural* streamlet more exquisitely beautiful. It undulates over the mossy roots and the gray old rocks like a capricious snake, singing all the time a low song with the "liquidest murmur," and one might almost fancy it the airy and coquettish Undine herself. When it reaches the top of the hill, the sparkling thing is divided into five or six branches, each one of which supplies one, two, or three long-toms. There is an extra one, called the waste-ditch, leading to the river, into which the water is shut off at night and on Sundays. This race (another and peculiar name for it) has already cost the company more than five thousand dollars. They sell the water to others at the following rates: Those that have the first use of it pay ten per cent upon all the gold that they take out. As the water runs off from their machine, (it now goes by the elegant name of "tailings"), it is taken by a company lower down, and as it is not worth so much as when it was clear, the latter pay but seven per cent. If any others wish the tailings, now still less valuable than at first, they pay four per cent on all the gold they take out, be it much or little. The water companies are constantly in trouble, and the arbitrations on the subject are very frequent. . . .

Gold mining is Nature's great lottery scheme. A man may work in a claim for many months, and be poorer at the end of the time than when he commenced, or he may take out thousands in a few hours. It is a matter of chance.

"No complaints of rheumatism or cold,"
William Tecumseh Sherman, 1875

What often impressed observers of the mineral rushes was the incredible amount of labor necessary to find even the smallest speck of "color." In his memoirs General William Tecumseh Sherman, who had been instrumental in the establishment of Sacramento in the 1850s and gained fame during the Civil War, recalled his experiences in the California gold rush. From 1848 until 1853 Sherman served as an army administrative officer and commissary captain in California. Here he describes the working conditions of the miners he encountered and expresses admiration for their uncomplaining efforts. Dreams of wealth can quiet even the most rabid complainer.

I recall the scene as perfectly today as though it were yesterday. In the midst of a broken country, all parched and dried by the hot sun of July [1848], sparsely wooded with live oaks and straggling pines, lay the valley of the American River, with its bold mountain stream coming out of the Snowy Mountains to the east. In this valley is a flat, or gravel bed, which in high water is an island, or is overflown, but at the time of our visit was simply a level gravel bed of the river. On its edges men were digging, and filling buckets with the finer earth and gravel, which was carried to a machine made like a baby's cradle, open at the foot, and at the head a plat of sheet iron or zinc, punctured full of holes. On this metallic plate was emptied the earth, and water was then poured on it from buckets, while one man shook the cradle with violent rocking by a handle. On the bottom were nailed cleats of wood.

With this rude machine four men could earn from forty to one hundred dollars a day, averaging sixteen dollars, or a gold ounce, per man per day. While the sun blazed down on the heads of the miners with tropical heat, the water was bitter cold, and all hands were either standing in the water or had their clothes wet all the time; yet there were no complaints of rheumatism or cold.

We made our camp on a small knoll, a little below the island, and from it we could overlook the busy scene. A few bush huts nearby served as stores, boarding houses, and for sleeping; but all hands slept on the ground, with pine leaves and blankets for bedding. As soon as word spread that the

Government was there, persons came to see us, and volunteered all kinds of information, illustrating it by samples of the gold, which was of a uniform kind, "scale gold" [thin plates or flakes], bright and beautiful. A large variety, of every conceivable shape and form, was found in the smaller gulches round about, but the gold in the river bed was uniformly scale gold. . . . That evening we all mingled freely with the miners, and witnessed the process of cleaning up and "panning" out, which is the last process for separating the pure gold from the fine dirt and black sand.

The next day we continued our journey up the valley of the American Fork, stopping at various camps, where mining was in progress; and about noon we reached Coloma, the place where gold had first been discovered. The hills were higher, and the timber of better quality. The river was narrower and bolder, and but few miners were at work there, by reason of [sawmill foreman James] Marshall's and [sawmill owner John] Sutter's claims to the site. There stood the sawmill unfinished, the dam and the tail-race just as they were left when the Mormons [Marshall's workforce] ceased work. Marshall and his family of wife and half a dozen tow-head children were there, guarding their supposed treasure; living in a house made of clapboards. . . .

The next day we crossed the American River to its north side, and visited many small camps of men in what were called the "dry diggings." Little pools of water stood in the beds of the streams, and these were used to wash the dirt; and there the gold was in every conceivable shape and size, some of the specimens weighing several ounces. . . . Sometimes a lucky fellow would hit upon a "pocket," and collect several thousand dollars in a few days, and then again he would be shifting about from place to place, prospecting, and spending all he had made. Little stores were being opened at every point, where flour, bacon, etc., were sold; everything a dollar a pound, and a meal usually costing three dollars. Nobody paid for a bed, for he slept on the ground, without fear of cold or rain.

READING 7
"A man I could respect," Mary McNair Mathews, 1880

At least in the early mining camps, almost as rare as the mineral finds were women. In California, 95 percent or more of the rushers were men. Women came primarily as laundresses, seamstresses, and restaurant proprietors; contrary to

conventional wisdom, only a handful were prostitutes. Scholars consider that
women generally provide the "civilizing" influence in boomtowns and the impetus
for reform (see chapter 8). In boomtown Virginia City, Nevada, in the 1870s
Mary McNair Mathews—a college-educated widow of forty-five who had a young
son—owned a boardinghouse, took in sewing and laundry, and also organized a
soup kitchen. In this Comstock Lode community, as she recounts, Mathews had
plenty of suitors—most of whom had practicality in mind, not romance. Although
her experiences were not uncommon for women of the period and place, her
independent, blunt dismissal of these advances was out of the ordinary.

I never lived in a place where the people dressed more richly or more extrav-
agantly than in Virginia City. It is not only a few millionaires who indulge in
it, but every woman on the Comstock who has a husband earning $4 to $6 a
day. . . . And many families live up to every cent of their wages or salary.

Some of my friends were very extravagant, and I used often to tell them
so, and in return they would call me a miser, because I would not follow all
of the silly fashions.

Mrs. Calvin often laughed at me, and said: "If you would go down in that
old stocking, and get out some of the gold you have hoarded up, and put it
on your back in fine clothes, you would stand some show to get a rich
husband, for they would know then that you did have something; and now
they don't know you are worth anything."

I would tell her I was not in the market, for I had determined never to
bring a stepfather over my child, no matter how good he might be. I told her
that if I ever married, it would be after my boy had grown to be a man, and
then it would not be a fortune-hunter, but a *man* I could respect.

I do believe that if I could have married every man that she and Mrs. Beck
picked out and tried to make a match with for me, I would have had as many
husbands as old Brigham Young ever had wives.

They finally gave up all hopes of ever dancing at my wedding, although
both offered to be bridesmaids, and furnish the wedding supper. But I told
them I had too much business on hand to get married.

[Though I never appeared] shabbily dressed . . . I never bought needless
finery, as I had other uses for my money; besides, I never believed in dressing to catch a husband. I think this is one reason of so many divorces in
California and Nevada. . . .

[It was not that] I never had an offer, for I have had several. . . .

Mathews tells of several suitors. One merchant wanted a wife simply to take care of his "four or five children"; to press his suit, he offered her discounts at his store. When she dismissed him with "I dislike other children," she no longer received the discounts. Another applicant from England asked Mathews to marry him primarily so he could save the $40 a month he was paying for housekeeping. She suggested that he hire a Chinese housekeeper for $15 per month.

Another man came and took a room at my house for a month. After he had been there a week, he came one day and rapped at the sitting-room door, I opened it, thinking perhaps he had called for something I had left out of his room, and stood waiting to see what it was; and to my astonishment, he came in and sat down, and asked me if I owned the place. I said I did. . . .

I expected the next question would be, Do you want to sell? But no such question came. His next words were: "Well, you want to get some nice man to take care of it for you. I heard you were a widow, and came and took a room on purpose to get acquainted with you."

Well, sir, said I, I am afraid you will have your labor for your pains. I made this property, and I think I can take care of it without the assistance of any man. Good-day sir! said I, holding the door open for him.

The next day he called and paid my week's rent.

He had his trunk by the handle dragging it along.

Are you moving? said I.

"Yes; I am off."

I thought you wanted the room for a month.

"Well, I did; but you know I have been terribly disappointed."

Indeed, said I. Perhaps you will have better success the next time you go fortune-hunting.

This is about the way one-third of the people of the coast propose and are accepted. This is the reason why their honeymoons end in divorce. It is no trouble for a woman in any class of society to get married.

READING 8
"Tommyknockers—Elves of the
Hardrock Mines," Gary Noy, 1989

Miners brought not only their experience to the West but also their diverse cultures. Cornish miners, in particular, added unique cultural elements to the society. Their belief that certain supernatural powers protected their efforts was heartfelt and real. An article from Sierra Heritage *magazine describes this fascinating phenomenon.*

Belief is a powerful force. It makes you see things that aren't there, hear things in the silence, and feel things that do not exist. For the hard-rock, or underground, miners of the Gold Rush, the dangers of their work led them to believe wholeheartedly in the existence of underground elves known as tommyknockers.

Tommyknockers were imported to Gold Country by the Cornish, the most experienced, skillful, and sought after of hard-rock miners. Centuries of labor in the tin mines of Cornwall, England, had given these hardy workers a vast knowledge of tunneling and other mining techniques—know-how that proved perfectly suited to the mines of northern California. Along with mining skills, the Cornish brought their colorful language, festive personalities, ironic view of life, and mining superstitions.

Life in the mines was dirty, dangerous, and often unproductive. The Cornish miner approached the task with irony and good cheer. As one Cornishman once replied when asked how to find a rich pocket of gold: "Well, where gold is, it is, and where it hain't, there be I." The difficult and often mysterious nature of mining led the Cornish to develop their belief in the tommyknockers—a superstition that helped explain the unexplainable.

Originating in legend, tommyknockers were said to be direct descendants of ancient elves known as Vugs and Piskies. After emigrating to the Gold Country, the elves became Americanized and grew to be as important to the miner as his tin lunchbox, hard hat, carbide lamp, and double jack. Many Cornish miners refused to enter a mine until assured that tommyknockers were on duty, providing warnings, and helpful directions.

According to stories handed down from one generation of miners to the next, two kinds of tommyknockers inhabited the mines—the friendly, helpful elf and the mischievous nuisance elf. Both are described as "little men about two feet high" dressed in miniature mining attire complete with tiny picks, hard hats, and lunch buckets. The elves who befriended the miners were said to watch over the miners' children; and, more important, to work alongside the miners deep in the mines, leading them to rich ore veins, testing shaft conditions, prying down loose rocks, and issuing life-saving warnings of cave-ins, water leaks, and runaway carts by tapping on air pipes or timber supports.

Many miners could recount times when tommyknockers saved their lives.

Frank Crampton, in his classic reminiscence of life as a miner, *Deep Enough,* specifically credits the tommyknockers with saving his life in a mining accident. Crampton had just squeezed into a tiny underground crawl space to load 20 sticks of dynamite for blasting. After carefully placing the dynamite, Crampton lit the fuse and then, in his words, "The tommyknockers began to raise hell [with warning noises], and instead of crawling out cautiously, I put on a head of steam to get out as fast as I could, caution or no caution. Just as I made the opening . . . the whole thing let go and came down. The [dynamite] powder had been struck by a boulder or ore, and a cap shot the powder prematurely. The blast tore out [the tunnel] . . . and the drift was loaded with splinted timber and muck. . . . I was lucky to get off with a few cuts and bruises from flying rock. . . . I owed my life to the tommyknockers, those unseen, wee, small folk, . . . as they had warned me when I had [lit] the fuse."

In another incident, at Grass Valley's Empire Mine, a massive cave-in collapsed hundreds of feet of tunnel and caused extensive flooding—all during a shift change. The miners firmly believed that tommyknockers had held up the rock until the crew got out, and then released it, and as was their common practice, the miners expressed this belief to the mine management.

In a 1957 interview for the *Sacramento Bee,* retired miner Fred Nettell, a member of a pioneer Grass Valley Cornish family, describes the miners' attitude toward tommyknockers: "When a Cornish miner of the old school tells you how his life was saved by a tommyknocker's warning, he is not being facetious. His respect and feeling toward these underground elves is almost religious."

As a token of gratitude to the helpful tommyknockers, the miners often left behind in the mines pieces of their traditional lunch of Cornish meat pasties.

But the activities of the nuisance tommyknockers, it was said, were meant to bedevil. Stories abound of blown out candles, upset lunch buckets, hidden tools, or even of miners reaching around rock ledges for tools and encountering instead the handshake of tiny hands. Mischievous tommyknockers, miners believed, sometimes held all-night jamborees in the mine's mule barns. Thus, on days of low productivity, miners could report to critical shift bosses that their tired mules had been kept up all night by reveling tommyknockers.

Some unromantic engineers and geologists explained the manifestations of tommyknockers as natural phenomena. Sounds in the tunnel depths, they said, can be greatly magnified, and what could be interpreted as the distant tapping of an elf was simply a creaking timber or the metallic drip of water onto ore. These literal-minded souls found, however, that trying to persuade Cornish miners to their view was like trying to shovel smoke.

In the late 1950s when the Empire Mine was closed, concerned miners and other bearers of the legend lobbied for the transfer of the tommy-knockers to active mines elsewhere in the Mother Lode. Eventually, the general manager of a Sierra County mining company agreed to accept the Empire's tommyknockers as welcome and permanent residents.

The fate of the tommyknockers is closely tied to the fortunes of hard-rock mining in the Gold Country. With the decline and virtual extinction of underground mining in California, the tommyknockers' activities ceased. But the little men live on as legend, and if the mines ever reopen, who knows where they will turn up, tapping on timbers or snitching tools.

READING 9
"The Extractive Industries," Michael
Malone and Richard Etulain, 1989

In the beginning, mining exploited the surface minerals. For example, "placer" gold found in streambeds and rock crevices allowed the independent prospector to flourish. As mining became more expensive and labor-intensive, however, the lone miner gave way to mining companies and then to corporate control. This was especially true for the newly dominant copper industry, which grew dramatically with the advent of the telephone and increasing electrical usage. Corporate mining brought greater profitability to the industry but also increased environmental damage and gave rise to social and labor turmoil. This selection from the book The American West *chronicles the development of corporate mining.*

The West's basic extractive industries resembled its agriculture in that, with the revolutionary application of new technologies, they surged in productivity during the first two decades of the twentieth century, and then faced serious problems of overproduction and low prices by the 1920s. In that oldest of the region's extractive industries, metal mining, the earlier focus on highly valuable precious metals—gold and silver—increasingly gave way to an emphasis on the industrially important base metal, copper.

In the wake of the Panic of 1893, precious metals faced a dreary future: the best high-grade veins had, for the most part, been mined out, and silver had lost its primary market when the federal government stopped coining silver dollars. At select locations, precious metal mines still worked on a large scale, as at the Homestake gold district in the Black Hills, the Coeur d'Alene silver district in north Idaho, the Cripple Creek, Colorado, and Mercur, Utah, gold operations, or the new, post-1900 Nevada boomtowns of Tonopah and Goldfield. The cyanide process of gold extraction now made lower-grade ores profitable to work; and in California and elsewhere, mining outfits continued to extract surface gold by such environmentally disastrous methods as blasting away stream banks with large hydraulic hoses and digging up stream beds with floating dredges.

In 1899, Henry Rogers of Standard Oil and other millionaire speculators formed the American Smelting and Refining Company in an effort to merge the West's silver-lead smelters into one great "super-trust." They soon lost control of ASARCO to the powerful family of Meyer Guggenheim and his seven sons, who had started out in Colorado and Mexico. The Guggenheims prospered, extracting metals fortunes from Alaska to Latin American; but ASARCO never succeeded in monopolizing this increasingly marginal industry.

Western copper came to command U.S. and world markets during the 1890s in the wake of the Butte, Montana, district's ascendancy over the formerly dominant Michigan mines. As the "red metal" expanded in usage with the rising electrical and telephone industries, first Montana, dominated by the Anaconda Copper Mining Company, and then Arizona, led by Phelps Dodge, boomed as copper provinces. In 1899, the diabolical Rogers of Standard Oil and others who were collaborating in the founding of ASARCO formed the Butte-based Amalgamated Copper Company in a similar effort to corner the production of this metal. However, the Rogers group got into a nasty political fight with independent Butte operators W. A. Clark and F. Augustus Heinze, and though Amalgamated Copper (later reverting to Anaconda again) did gain control of the Butte District, it failed to corner the American copper market.

The main explanation for Amalgamated's failure to become the U.S. Steel of copper lay in new technologies, which so inflated production that no firm could control it. The use of electricity made mining machinery, both above and below ground, much more efficient. And whereas the concentration of copper ores by the new "flotation" method of releasing them in oil vats made it much easier and cheaper to reduce lower-grade ores, so did the application of electrolysis to refining simplify the process of removing the final impurities from smelted copper.

By far the most important innovations took place at the old Bingham Canyon mining district, near Salt Lake City. Here, a dynamic group of engineers and investors led by Daniel Jackling formed the Utah Copper Company and in 1903–4 proved a dramatic new way of mining very low grade (as low as 1 percent, or even less) ores. Employing giant steam-shovels to dig and rails to haul the ore, and erecting giant concentrators and smelters to reduce it, Jackling demonstrated that huge amounts of previously worthless low-grade ores could be mined profitably in open pits. Bingham Canyon prospered and grew into what John D. Rockefeller once called "the greatest industrial sight on Earth." . . .

Open-pit mining clearly represented the wave of the future, and though labor-intensive tunnel mines continued to deepen where rich veins prevailed, pit mining spread rapidly across the West. . . . By 1907, the deep mines of Butte had lost their preeminence as Arizona, with its many centers, became the nation's copper leader. Soon Utah too surpassed Montana to occupy the number two position.

The extent to which copper now dominated the glamorous old precious metals can be seen in two interesting facts. For many years, Bingham Canyon ranked as America's second-greatest gold mine, behind the Homestake; and Anaconda similarly ranked number two in silver, behind the Coeur d'Alenes. Copper, in other words, reigned supreme, and the precious metals faded in importance to become in large part by-products of copper operations. Mining of all kinds boomed during World War I. With a government-guaranteed price of twenty-three cents a pound, the copper industry paid huge dividends during the war, even despite angry confrontations with labor. After the war, though, the copper miners, like the farmers, faced glutted markets and low prices, due especially to portentous, cheap imports from new mines in South America and Africa. As the price of their product fell toward a disastrous five cents per pound, they too fretted about the future of their uncontrolled industry.

READING 10

THE ENVIRONMENTAL IMPACT, *WOODRUFF V.*
NORTH BLOOMFIELD GRAVEL MINING CO., 1884

In the largely unregulated economy of the nineteenth century, mining companies adopted techniques that could and did wreak havoc on the landscape. The most dramatically destructive of these, used primarily in northern California gold

mines, was hydraulic mining, whereby whole hillsides were washed away with
water from powerful, high-pressure nozzles called monitors. The tons of rock and
debris flushed away to obtain small amounts of gold ore were channeled into
nearby rivers, clogging their drainage fields, spilling out into farmland
downstream, and fouling the water for human or animal use. When the damage
could no longer be overlooked, some largely halfhearted attempts were made to
discover a way to end the destruction, but in 1884 farmers took the mining
companies to court to find a legal solution. The case detailed the destructive path of
hydraulic mining debris in California's Feather River basin and established the
legal precedent for shutting down a grossly polluting industry, as shown in
excerpts from the sixty-page decision.

Circuit Court, D. California. January 7, 1884.

I. PUBLIC AND PRIVATE NUISANCE FROM MINING DEBRIS.
[Three California rivers are in question here: the Yuba River, which dumps
into the Feather River, which ultimately empties into the Sacramento River.
The North Bloomfield Mining Company] have for several years been and
they are still engaged in hydraulic mining, to a very great extent, in the Sierra
Nevada mountains, and have discharged and they are discharging their
mining *debris,*—rocks, pebbles, gravel, and sand,—to a very large amount
into the head-waters of the Yuba, whence it is carried down, by the ordinary
current and by floods, into the lower portions of that stream, and into the
Feather and the Sacramento. The *debris* thus discharged has produced the
following effects: It has filled up the natural channel of the Yuba above
the level of its banks and of the surrounding country, and also the Feather
below the mouth of the Yuba, to the depth of 15 feet or more. It has buried
with sand and gravel and destroyed all the farms of the riparian owners on
either side of the Yuba, over a space two miles wide and twelve miles long.
[Further destruction is partially prevented downstream] . . . by means of a
system of levees, erected at great public expense, . . . which levees continually and yearly require to be enlarged and strengthened to keep pace
with the increase in the mass of *debris* thus sent down, at a great annual
cost. . . . It has polluted the naturally clear water of these streams so as to
render them wholly unfit to be used for any domestic or agricultural purpose. . . . All these effects have been constantly increasing during the past
few years, and their still further increase is threatened by the continuance of

the defendant's said mining operations. *Held,* that these acts . . . constitute a public and private nuisance, destructive, continuous, increasing, and threatening to continue, increase, and be still more destructive.

2. SPECIAL INJURIES TO THE COMPLAINANT

During all this time the complainant [Woodruff] was and he is now owner . . . of a block of buildings in Marysville [California], . . . about 500 feet from the levee on the Yuba. Originally the steam-boat landing for the city was on the Yuba, nearly opposite to his [buildings], but by reason of the filling up of that river its navigation has been prevented, and the landing is now in the Feather, three-fourths of a mile from [his buildings.] By a break in the levee of the Yuba during one of its annual floods, the water stood several feet deep, . . . *debris* was deposited in it, its underpinning was washed out so that the roof fell in. . . . The complainant also owns two farms,—one of 952 acres, . . . the other of 720 acres. . . . Seventy-five acres of one of these tracts and 50 acres of the other have been completely buried and destroyed by the *debris,* and the remaining portions are only protected from destruction by the levees, which on several occasions have broken, and the lands have been damaged by water charged with *debris,* and they are in danger of being overflowed and injured in a similar manner from a breach of the levees at any flood. The value of [Woodruff's] land has been depreciated from these causes; his access to the river from his farms for the purpose of shipping or receiving freights has been cut off; he has been obliged to pay an extraordinary, onerous, annual tax for the erection and maintenance of the levees to protect his property from the constantly increasing danger of loss or destruction. *Held,* that these facts constitute special injuries to the complainant, which entitle him to maintain a suit in equity to restrain the further commission of the public nuisance by the defendants. . . .

[From the opinion of Justice Sawyer]
Hydraulic mining as used in this opinion, is the process by which a bank of gold-bearing earth and rock is excavated by a jet of water, discharged through the converting nozzle of a pipe, under great pressure, the earth and *debris* being carried away by the same water, through sluices, and discharged on lower levels into the natural streams and water-courses below. Where the gravel or other material of the bank is cemented, or where the bank is composed of masses of pipe-clay, it is shattered by blasting with powder,

sometimes from 15 to 20 tons of powder being used at one blast to break up a bank. In the early periods of hydraulic mining, as in 1855, the water was discharged through a rubber or canvas hose, with nozzles of not more than an inch in diameter; but later, upon the invention of the "Little Giant" and the "Monitor" machines, the size of the nozzle and the pressure was greatly increased, till now the nozzle is from four to nine inches in diameter, discharging from 500 to 1,000 inches of water under a pressure of from three to four to five hundred feet. For example, an eight-inch nozzle, at the North Bloomfield mine discharges 185,000 cubic feet of water in an hour, with a velocity of 150 feet per second. The excavating power of such a body of water, discharged with such velocity, is enormous; and, unless the gravel is very heavy or firmly cemented, it is much in excess of its transporting power. At some of these mines, as at North Bloomfield, several of these Monitors are worked, much of the time, night and day, the several levels upon which they are at work being brilliantly illuminated by electric lights, the electricity being generated by water power. A night scene of the kind, at the North Bloomfield mine, is in the highest degree weird and startling, and it cannot fail to strike strangers with wonder and admiration. The amount of *debris* discharged into the rivers by these operations can only be duly appreciated by actual observation. . . .

Dr. Teegarden's lands afford a very striking example of individual injuries inflicted by this mining *debris*. Dr. Teegarden . . . owned 1,275 acres on the Yuba bottoms, some three or four miles above Marysville, on the north side. All except 75 acres now lying outside the levee have been buried from three to five feet deep with sand, and utterly destroyed for farming purposes; for which injuries he received no remuneration. . . . Dr. Teegarden testifies that the main filling up was in 1879 and 1880; but that there has been a constant addition to it ever since, and that, during the last year, it has filled up faster than at any other time; that he built three miles of levee to protect it, but it proved insufficient; and that the land is five to six feet higher with sand and sediment on the river, or inside the levee, than on the outside, where he lives. . . .

It is proposed to erect a barrier in the narrows of the Yuba, upon a bed of *debris* now 60 feet deep, just out of the foot-hills, 150 feet high,—as high as Niagara,—over which its waters, concentrated in a narrow gorge, charged at times to their full carrying capacity with heavy material, on occasions of great floods will pour in volumes equal, perhaps, or nearly so, to those pouring over an equal space at Niagara. It is said this dam will be a *debris-dam*, and less dangerous than a water-dam. . . . The danger shown by the testimony will be, not so much from the pressure above as from the force and effects of the water charged with *debris,* sometimes with stones of greater or lesser dimensions, falling over and down a dam so great a distance. . . . According to the testimony of some intelligent witnesses, only about 70 per cent of the *debris* would be retained by any dam, as all that the water is capable of carrying in suspension would pass over under any circumstances. This percentage of the enormous quantity yet to be mined would add a great deal to the amount now in the streams. A large amount, at all events, would necessarily pass over. Dams, such as are proposed, properly constructed, and not carried too high, may well be safe, and extremely valuable in keeping back the *debris* now in the stream, . . . even though utterly inadequate to protect the valleys below, in case hydraulic mining is continued, and enormous quantities of *debris* be added to that already accumulated. But there are no dams now of any appreciable service in protecting the rights of the complainant from further injury, either from the *debris* already in the streams, or such further accumulations as may arise from a continuance of hydraulic mining as now pursued. There is, therefore, no alternative to granting an injunction. . . .

After an examination of the great questions involved, as careful and thorough as we are capable of giving them, with a painfully anxious appreciation of the responsibilities resting upon us, and of the disastrous consequences to the [mining company], we can come to no other conclusion than that [Woodruff] is entitled to a perpetual injunction. But as it is possible that some mode may be devised in the future for obviating the injuries, either one of those suggested or some other, and successfully carried out, so as to be both safe and effective, a clause will be inserted in the decree giving leave on any future occasion, when some such plan has been successfully executed, to apply to the court for a modification or suspension of the injunction.

Let a decree be entered accordingly.

Mining and Milling Terms,
Homestake Mining Company, 1876–1976

Since every industry or economic activity has its own unique vocabulary, one gold-mining company offers definitions of commonly used mining and milling terms.

ADIT—A horizontal tunnel driven into the side of a mountain through which a mineral deposit can be explored and developed.

ADSORPTION—Adhesion of molecules of a liquid or dissolved substance to a surface of solid bodies, [e.g.,] gold to activated carbon.

ASSAY—The testing of a sample of minerals or ore to determine the content of valuable minerals in the sample.

BACK—The ceiling of any underground excavation.

BACKFILL—Sand portion of the milled ore used to support the walls of a stope and provide a working platform after the removal of the ore.

BALL MILL—A milling machine used to grind ore into small particles which uses steel balls as the grinding medium.

BEDROCK—The solid rock of the earth's crust, generally covered by overburden of soil or water.

BULLION—Gold or other precious metal in bars or similar form.

CAGE—An elevator-type conveyance which moves people and materials up and down a mine shaft.

CHUTE—An opening into a stope through which ore is dropped after it is first mined to waiting mine ore cars for transportation to a shaft.

COLLAR—The term applied to the timbering or concrete around the mouth of a shaft; also used to describe the top of a drill hole.

CROSSCUT—A lateral or horizontal tunnel made underground that cuts across the ore body.

CUT-AND-FILL—A stoping method in which the ore is removed in slices or "lifts," after which the excavation is filled with sand backfill before the next slice is mined. The backfill supports the walls of the stope.

DEPLETION—The [steady decline of the] amount of ore in a deposit or property resulting from production. Minerals are said to be a "depleting resource" because, once mined, they cannot be replaced.

DEVELOPMENT—Bringing a mining property to the production stage.

DRIFT—A horizontal underground tunnel in such a direction that it follows or "drifts" with the ore or an ore vein.

ELECTROLYTIC PROCESS—Pertaining to a refining process in which not quite pure gold is suspended in a cell containing a liquid known as electrolyte. The metal to be refined forms a positive post or "anode" and is deposited on the negative post, called the "cathode," by the electric current fed into the anode.

FOOTWALL—The wall or rock on the undercut of a stope.

GANGUE—The worthless minerals associated with valuable minerals in the ore deposit.

HANGING WALL—The wall or rock on the upper or top side of an ore deposit.

HOIST—A machine which raises and lowers the cage and skips in a shaft.

LEVELS—Horizontal passageways or tunnels in the mine leading from shafts. They are established at regular intervals.

MARGINAL ORE—Lower grade ore which is close to being uneconomic to mine.

METALLURGY—The various methods of preparing gold or other metals for use by separating them from their ores.

MINERAL—A substance which may, or may not, be of economic value, that occurs naturally in the earth. It is homogeneous, has [a] certain chemical makeup and usually appears in crystal or grain form.

ORE—A mixture of minerals and gangue from which at least one of the minerals can be extracted at a profit.

ORE RESERVES—The tonnage of ore of a certain grade which is estimated for the mine or certain sections of it.

OUNCES, TROY—Unit of weight used in the precious metals industry. 14.583 troy ounces equal 1 pound avoirdupois.

PROSPECT—A mining property, the value of which has not been proved by exploration.

PULP—A liquid and ore mixture.

RAISE—A vertical underground tunnel that has been excavated from the bottom upward.

REFINING—The final purification process of a metal or mineral.

ROCKBOLTING—The act of consolidating walls and back by means of anchoring and tensioning steel bolts in holes drilled for the purpose.

ROD MILL—A rotating cylindrical mill which employs steel rods as a medium for grinding ore into small pieces.

SHAFT—An opening cut downward from the surface for transporting personnel, equipment, supplies, ore, and waste. It is also used for ventilation and as an auxiliary exit. It is equipped with a surface hoist system which lowers and raises a cage in the shaft, as well as "skips" or containers for bringing up ore and waste. A shaft generally has more than one compartment.

SHRINKAGE STOPE—A method of stoping which utilizes part of the broken ore as a working platform and as support for the walls.

SKIP—A self-dumping type of bucket used in a shaft for hoisting ore or rock.

SLIME—Fine fraction of the ground ore.

SLURRY—A liquid and ore mixture.

SLUSHER—A mechanical drag shovel used to move ore or waste in a stope.

SQUARE SET—A set of timbers used for support in underground mining.

STOPE—An opening underground in which ore or waste is blasted and broken.

TAILINGS—Waste material from the milling process.

VEIN—An opening, fissure or crack in rock, containing mineralized material.

WASTE—Material that is too low in grade to be of economic value.

WINZE—A vertical or inclined opening from a point inside a mine. Similar to a shaft, but the latter starts at a surface.

READING 12

THE GOLD RECOVERY PROCESS, HOMESTAKE MINING COMPANY, 1976

The large corporate mines both expanded previous mining techniques and developed newer, more efficient methods—among them the cyanidation process for recovering gold and silver. Using cyanide solutions increased the yield of these precious metals significantly but led to overproduction problems as well, followed by downturns in the mining industry in the 1920s. The process itself and the refining that followed, however, were excellent examples of the application of advancing technology to an age-old profession. This selection from the one hundredth anniversary publication of the Homestake Mining Company of the Black Hills (America's largest and most successful gold mine) describes the developing process of gold recovery.

The gold is recovered from the ore by two methods; gravity concentration and cyanidation. Gravity concentration depends upon the fact that the gold particles are much heavier than rock particles and settle out of the pulp much faster. Steel trough-like boxes called launders, with traps built in the bottom, are situated so that the finely ground pulp flows out of the ball mills and through the launders on its way to mechanical separation of the ore particles. Some of the gold particles settle into these traps and are periodically removed from the traps and taken to the Refinery for further treatment to produce high purity gold bars.

The Cyanidation Process—

Cyanidation is a process which depends upon the fact that gold and silver are soluble in cyanide solutions, such as either potassium, calcium or sodium compounds in cyanide. Here at Homestake, a very weak solution of sodium cyanide ranging from one-fiftieth of one percent to one-twentieth of one percent [is] used to dissolve the gold. [Homestake Mine] has been using the cyanidation process since 1901, and recover over 70 percent of gold from each ton of the ore by this method.

Before cyanidation, the particles of finely ground ore are separated by classifying them into "sands" and "fines" (slimes), each for treatment in different plants.

The coarser more granular sands amount to about 59 per cent of the ore and are treated in buildings known as "sand plants." The finer slime-like portions, which are so fine they are almost clay-like, amount to about 41 per cent of the ore and are treated in a new section called the "carbon-in-pulp plant."

In order to dissolve gold with sodium cyanide solution, certain conditions both chemical and physical must be observed. Chemically, it is necessary that oxygen be present in order to dissolve the gold. Lime is added to the sand as it is delivered to the leaching vats. Its function is to neutralize the acidity of the ore as acid destroys cyanide. Physically, it is important to separate the coarser granular sand particles from the extremely fine slime particles, because an excessive amount of the very fine slime in the sand charge would retard the downward percolation of the cyanide solution as it is introduced on top of the sand.

In the sand plants large vats are filled with the granular sand particles. The vats have canvas filter bottoms. There are 35 vats; some contain 750 tons of sand, others 780 tons. After a vat is filled with sand, most of the included water is drained off through the bottom. This draining is then followed by forcing compressed air upward through the sand. Four periods of drain, air and solution followed by a clear-water wash complete the cyanide treatment. The gold bearing solutions pass through the canvas filters in the bottom of the vats and flow to further processing equipment.

Recovery of the gold from this cyanide solution is then made by adding a small amount of very fine zinc powder which precipitates the gold as a dark brown powder, and this product is filtered from the solution in a filter-press. The powder, known as "precipitate" is then treated in the Refinery to produce pure gold. The weakened sodium-cyanide solution (with the gold removed) is saved, regenerated, and re-used.

The sand, with the gold removed, is then washed out of the vats, collected in reservoirs and returned to the mine as needed to backfill mined-out areas.

. . . In August 1973, a new process to treat the "slime" was instituted in and adjoining the sand treatment plants. In this process the gold is dissolved by cyanide by conventional methods in large agitation tanks, and then the gold is adsorbed from the solution by particles of granular activated carbon in suspension in the slurry or pulp. The term adsorption applies to a surface phenomenon in which gold ions are attracted to the surface of the carbon particles and held there by electrostatic forces. Carbon particles are then screened from the pulp and washed, and the gold stripped from the carbon with hot caustic cyanide cathodes, and then deposited by electrolysis on steel-wool cathodes. A gold sponge is formed with the steel-wool which is then later converted to gold bullion in the Refinery.

Refining—

Refining is the last of the many steps necessary to produce pure gold and some silver each year from the over three billion pounds of tough hard ore that was mined, hoisted, crushed, ground and chemically treated. The Refinery is a small smelting plant containing various types of furnaces, electrolytic and other special equipment.

Here, free gold from the mill launders, precipitates from the sand treatment plants and the steel-wool gold-sponge are processed until pure gold and almost pure silver are the end results. When the three products begin their refining process they are mixed with suitable fluxes and smelted to remove impurities such as iron, zinc, and copper. The resulting gold is referred to as crude bullion. It contains silver and traces of iron, zinc, copper, etc. Further refining takes place when chlorine gas is blown into the molten crude bullion to separate the silver from the gold and flux is added to remove the last traces of impurities. The chlorine reacts with the silver to form silver chloride which is lighter than gold and floats to the surface. It is then removed by skimming. When all the silver chloride has been removed the gold is poured into small bars weighing 17.14 pounds or 250 troy ounces. Each bar represents the final product of the total operation including mining, hoisting, crushing, grinding, and cyanidation of over 2,170,000 pounds of ore.

Some of the almost-pure bars are then refined to purity by a complex electrolytic process.

READING 13

"This was his property," Antonio Franco Coronel, 1849

Violence, both personal and industrial, followed the mineral rushes. Hope and frustration produced an explosive mixture; additionally, prejudice and hatred were frequently part of a miner's kit. If a fuse was lit on this emotional powder keg, the innocent and the guilty would both be caught in the aftermath. During the early days of the California gold rush, social justice was a more difficult ore to mine than gold. In particular, the Californios, or Mexican Americans, often found their lands overrun by argonauts and their lives subjected to racial and ethnic tensions that could lead to violence. Of the few existing narratives by Californios about these problems, the best known was written by Antonio Franco Coronel in 1849. Coronel was a prominent figure in those days; he eventually served as mayor of Los Angeles and member of the city council, and then as California's state treasurer. In 1848 he and his companions began mining at Placer Seco (Dry Diggins) and achieved, as he put it, "brilliant results." Returning after the winter of 1849, he found his claim filled with newcomers. Here Coronel describes the resulting tensions and the changes they produced for the Californios.

I arrived at the Placer Seco and began to work at a regular digging.

In this place there was already a numerous population of Chileans, Peruvians, Californians, Mexicans, and many Americans, Germans, etc. The camps were almost separated according to nationalities. All, some more, some less, were profiting from the fruit of their work. Presently news was circulated that it had been resolved to evict all of those who were not

American citizens from the placers because it was believed that the foreigners did not have the right to exploit the placers.

One Sunday, [documents] appeared in writing in Los Pinos and in several places, that anyone who was not an American citizen must abandon the place within twenty-four hours and that he who did not comply would be obliged to by force. This was supported by a gathering of armed men, ready to make that warning effective.

There was a considerable number of people of various nationalities who understood the order to leave—they decided to gather on a hill in order to be defensive in case of any attack. On the day in which the departure of the foreigners should take place, and for three or four more days, both forces remained prepared, but the thing did not go beyond cries, shots, and drunken men. Finally all fell calm and we returned to continue our work. Daily, though, the weakest were dislodged from their diggings by the strongest.

After this agitation had calmed down, a Frenchman named Don Augusto and a Spaniard named Luis were seized—persons with whom I had dealt and who appeared to me to be honorable and of fairly good upbringing. All who had known them had formed the same opinion as I, and this seizure caused great surprise. Some of the most prominent people met together and commissioned me to investigate the reason for these arrests. I went to an American I had known in Los Angeles, one Richard, who had been a cavalry sergeant—I asked him to look into it for me. He answered immediately that they had been accused by an Irish fellow . . . of having stolen from him four pounds of gold from the place where he had buried it. I gave an account of my constituents and then, without loss of time, five pounds of gold was gathered from among all of us to see if payment would set the prisoners free. I approached the leader, whose appearance was disagreeable and ferocious. Wanting to vindicate the two men, I presented my plan to him through an interpreter. I told him we knew them as good men who had sufficient resources of their own and no need to appropriate those of another. Nevertheless, I had here five pounds of gold, one more than the old Irishman said they had stolen from him. He took the five pounds of gold and told me that he would go to report to his group—that I should return in the afternoon, some two or three hours later. Before the hour he had indicated to me, we saw the movement of armed men, the major part under the influence of liquor. Afterward we saw a cart leave with our two unfortunates, their arms tied behind their backs. Two men guarded them from on top of the cart, which was followed by a large crowd, some on foot, and others on horseback. On the cart there was an inscription, poorly written in charcoal or something similar, which said that whoever might intercede for them would suffer the same punishment. They reached an oak tree where the execution was to take place. When the ropes had been hung around their necks, they asked me to write something to their families and to arrange their affairs. For having made this request, one of the men received a slap in the face. Then, suddenly, they moved the cart and the unlucky men were hanged.

This act horrified me and it had the same effect upon many others—in two days I raised camp and headed toward the northern placers.

The reason for most of the antipathy against the Spanish race was that the greater portion was composed of Sonorans [a common term for any Spanish-speaking miners] who were men accustomed to prospecting and who consequently achieved quicker, richer results—such as the Californios had already attained by having arrived first and acquiring understanding of this same art. Those who came later, were possessed by the terrible fever to obtain gold, but they did not get it because their diggings yielded little or nothing, or because their work did not correspond to what they took out. Well, these men aspired to become rich in a minute and they could not resign themselves to view with patience the better fortune of others. Add to this fever that which the excessive use of liquor gives them. Add that generally among so many people of all nationalities there are a great number of lost people, capable of all conceivable crimes. The circumstance that there were no laws nor authorities who could protect the rights and lives of men gave to these men advantages over peaceful and honorable men. Properly speaking, there was no more law in those times than that of force, and finally, the good person, in his own defense, had to establish the law of retaliation. . . .

I arrived at Sacramento with my mules, loaded them, and headed north to the place where I had left my tent in charge of my brother.

Some fourteen miles distant from Sutter's mill, toward the north, I met my brother and the servants, and several others of the Spanish race, coming, fleeing on foot. They told me a party of armed foreigners had run them out quickly, without permitting them to take either their animals or other things. I returned to the mill where there was a small population—there I had some acquaintances. My aim was to see if I could sell the cargo that I carried, in order to leave the placers. I sold the goods in different places, almost all the mules, etc., at prices so low that I lost two-thirds of the gold they had cost me. These people took advantage of the situation in which I found myself.

At this time, Juan Manso arrived there with some Sonorans, still of the party of Andres Pico—Ramon Carillo, with some other companions from Sonoma, came also. Concerning the alternatives of continuing, or of retreating as I had been going to do, one Fisher, a merchant of Sutter's Mill and an old acquaintance of mine from Los Angeles, together with other merchants from the place, began to persuade us that this measure did not represent the feeling of the greater part of the people who lived in these parts and that these acts must have come from some party of highwaymen; because it was published thus, it was understood that the Californians were considered the same as the rest of the Americans that they would give us a credential signed by the outstanding people from here in which we would be commended as such citizens and worthy of respect. I did not agree, but at this insistence of the others, I acceded to return and set about anew to take out gold from the placers. . . .

Coronel recounts his band's success in finding gold and explains that under his direction the Californios adopted a code of secrecy in order to prevent further incidents of violence. The miners were unmolested for a week—until, on a Saturday night, a member of Carillo's group, a trusted Irishman, got drunk and disappeared.

[The Irishman] went to Sutter's Mill, he got drunk, and revealed all of our affair, plans, rules, etc. On the following Monday, we staked out new diggings and proceeded to work them immediately. The work was harder because the gold was much deeper and there was more rock, but on the other hand the gold turned out to be denser and in greater quantity. Almost everyone had to occupy the week working his diggings in order to reach the gold. But, during this time, a large number of armed men gathered daily, taking account as before. They had such complete knowledge of our business that on Saturday of this week armed men began to slip in, making their camp immediately next to ours. Then I thought about the goal of those people and I charged everyone in our camp to be very prudent and moderate so that they not give the others a pretext to bother us.

Now all of us were piling up our dirt, which was rather rich and promised us better results than the first week. About ten in the morning all of these merciless people, numbering more than 100, invaded our diggings at a moment when all of us were inside of them. The invaders were so courteous that they asked who the leader of our party was. When I was pointed out to them, their leader and some eight more surrounded my digging. . . . All of these men raised their pistols, their Bowie knives; some had rifles, other[s] pickaxes and shovels.

Their leader spoke to me, introducing himself and two others with pickaxes and shovels in my digging. He led me to understand that this was theirs because before we took the place, one or two months before, he with his men took possession of this same and that a boundary had been marked out from one side of the river to the other. He told me several things in English so that I did not understand him immediately, but all amounted to saying that this was his property. Excited, I answered him harshly, but fortunately he did not understand me. I was able to reflect for a moment that the gold was not worth risking my life in this way.

The rest of the invaders took possession of the other diggings in the same way. My companions ran to our camp before me and armed themselves. I knew their hostile intentions. Already they had ordered that a number of horses be saddled. I arrived where they were and persuaded them to calm down. Indeed, whatever attempt they might make would be fruitless. For me the placers were finished.

We mounted our horses and left the place. The entire party dispersed and I left for Los Angeles without stopping in any place longer than was necessary.

READING 14
VIOLENCE IN COEUR D'ALENE, *SPOKANE (WA) WEEKLY REVIEW*, 1892

As the independent placer miner gave way to mining companies, violence was often the result. Particularly in mountain communities of the West, conflict between the working-class miner and mine management spawned industrial violence. In 1891 the mine workers in Coeur d'Alene, Idaho, a lead and silver mining town in the Rockies, organized a union to demand uniform wages. The companies responded by forming a Mine Owners Protective Association, a possible strikebreaking force. In early 1892 the owners offered a new contract with a 25 percent cut in wages. The regular workers rejected it and were locked out. The owners then hired

hundreds of strikebreakers, or "scabs," and private guards to protect them. In
consequence, strikers intimidated scabs, hired Pinkerton agents killed strikers,
rebellious miners killed guards, potentially violent protest marches surrounded
mine operations. Finally, the governor of Idaho declared a state of insurrection
and sent the National Guard to patrol the region. This force, supported by federal
troops, protected the strikebreakers, rounding up six hundred of the most openly
hostile strikers and herding them into detention centers known as "bullpens."
Local political figures sympathetic to the strikers were removed from office, and all
active union operatives were fired from their mine jobs. Court orders freed most of
the detained strikers, mine owners found they could not run their operations
without skilled workers, and eventually most recognized the union. But anarchy
was the rule for a considerable part of 1892, as reflected in this account of events in
Coeur d'Alene on July 14. It was a pattern repeated throughout the West for
years to come.

Wallace, Idaho, July 11. [Special.]

This has been the most exciting day in the history of the Coeur d'Alene. The hitherto peaceful canyons of these mountains have echoed with the sharp and deadly report of the rifle, and the cliffs of Canyon Creek have reverberated with the detonations of bomb and dynamite used in the destruction of valuable property.

The long-dreaded conflict between the forces of the strikers and the non-union men who have taken their places has come at last. As a result five men are known to be dead and 16 are already in the hospital; the Frisco mill on Canyon Creek is in ruins; the Gem Mine has surrendered to the strikers, the arms of its employees have been captured, and the employees themselves have been ordered out of the country. Flushed with the success of these victories the turbulent element among the strikers are preparing to move upon other strongholds of the non-union men and will probably show their hand at Wardner tomorrow.

About 6 o'clock this morning a non-union miner from the Gem mine, at the town of Gem, was fired upon at a point near the Frisco mine. He ran back to the Gem mine and afterward died of his wound.

This shot seemed to be the signal for the non-union forces, who quickly gathered in considerable numbers and marched upon the mine, a lively firing being kept up by both sides. The attacking forces, however, were too strong for the besieged forces, and to avoid further bloodshed the mine was surrendered, the arms given up and the non-union men were marched down the canyon and sent out of the district.

In the meantime a similar attack was made upon the property of the Helena and San Francisco company at the same place, and with a like result. The men in the mine and mill surrendered, and the besiegers then went up the hill and sent down a lot of dynamite on the tramway, expecting it to explode and wreck the mill. They did this in revenge for the severe manner in which Mr. Esler has spoken of their cause and themselves, but the first attempt failed. They then shot a bomb down the iron water flume, and when it struck the bottom there was a tremendous explosion that wrecked the mill and destroyed $125,000 worth of property.

After this a sort of truce was held and hostilities were suspended. The arms of the non-union men were stacked and placed in charge of one man, from each side, but they were afterward taken by the strikers, the mine owners claiming in violation of the agreement.

The dead, wounded, and prisoners were then placed aboard a special train and taken down to Wallace, and Canyon Creek is now in complete control of the strikers, and no one is permitted to invade the district.

The blackest feature of the direful conflict in the Coeur d'Alene was the tragedy enacted at the Old Mission on the Coeur d'Alene River and in Fourth of July Canyon. After driving many of the fugitive non-union men into the canyon and the river the desperate and impassioned strikers followed them up and shot them down like deer. Among those shot down was Foreman Monaghan of the Gem mine, who was coming out with his family. The family was spared, but Monaghan was run into the bush and shot through the back. He was picked up yesterday morning and taken back to the mines. It is thought he will die. It is reported that 12 bodies have already been recovered in Fourth of July Canyon. The non-union men had been entirely disarmed and were at the mercy of their pursuers. The boat that came down the lake yesterday picked up 30 more of the fugitives who had taken to the river and bush. They tell tales of frightful cruelty. Some of them were beaten with revolvers and many were robbed of all their valuables.

A middle-aged man who escaped the hands of the executioner at Mission had a doleful story to relate of his sufferings and privations after getting away from the strikers. He asked that his name be withheld, as he fears further acts of revenge.

"After the shooting began," said he, "we started and ran like so many sheep. We were taken completely by surprise and dumbfounded. I made for the railroad track and got into a car. The car was crowded with men and women, too. I saw Mrs. Monaghan crouching down between two seats. Pretty soon a big burly fellow made his appearance at the door of the car with a Winchester rifle, 'Git out of the car, you d——d s—— —— ——,' said he, and we all began scrambling for the door. I heard Mrs. Monaghan crying, 'For God's sake, don't take my life; I have two daughters here some-where, and I've lost them.' The fellow told her she could stay. That's the last I heard in the car. The next moment I was crowded out of the door and made off as fast as I could run. There was a party of us together. Pretty soon shots began to whistle around our heads, but we kept on running, through fields and brush, the shots following us like a hail storm.

"Our party began to separate and then there were only two of us together. We came to a fence, and as we were both crowding through an opening a shot swished past my companion's ear, and he shouted: 'Oh, God, I'm shot!'

"After a bit I saw one of our men drop in the distance. I ran past where he was lying. He looked up at me and said; 'Tell Abbott I'm killed.' He was the son of Nighwatchman Abbott. I could do nothing for him.

"When night came we found ourselves in a swamp, with water up to our knees. We lost our bearing entirely and were afraid to move for fear of being discovered. As the night wore out we began to move, and when dawn appeared we saw a man with a dog. At first we were afraid to let him see us, but gradually our courage returned, and besides, we were starving to death. We went up to the man and told him our story. At first he refused to give us anything to eat, but after we promised him $3 he took us to his house, where we got a bowl of bread and milk, and he rowed us over the river on a raft. We wandered along a mile or two, and were finally picked up by the boat."

READING 15
PREAMBLE AND MANIFESTO, INDUSTRIAL
WORKERS OF THE WORLD, 1905

By the end of the nineteenth century, mine workers had experienced a diverse set of working conditions: some had remained independent prospectors, but many others toiled for the corporate interests that had come to control the industry. Violent incidents between miners and clashes between miners and owners had become all too frequent. The differences with corporate ownership often revolved around

traditional labor-management issues—safer working conditions, better hours,
higher wages—but sometimes a deeper and more philosophical issue was at the
root of the troubles: respect for the miner's effort. As a result of these conflicts,
miners' organizations and labor unions—some local, some regional, such as the
Western Federation of Miners—sprang up throughout the West. They varied
dramatically in philosophy and tactics—some preferred political action; others
preferred strikes and sabotage—but all shared the same goal: a better life, a
respected life for the miner.

The most radical of these labor organizations was the Industrial Workers of
the World, known as "the Wobblies." The Wobblies believed in direct, aggressive
action to settle their differences with management, advocating labor violence as a
way to topple capitalism and improve the miners' conditions. Their leadership was
composed of socialists, militant unionists, Western Federation of Miners members,
and others who felt that one big union could address all the issues most effectively.
The Wobblies would sponsor strikes and actions in Colorado mines, lumber
camps in the Pacific Northwest, textile mills in Massachusetts and New Jersey,
and steel mills in Pennsylvania. Their strikes were often successful, but their
tactics scared even their own members; the IWW rolls never exceeded 150,000 at
any one moment. The Wobblies were subject to opposition vigilante attacks and
prosecution under federal and state laws for espionage, sedition, and criminal
syndicalism. Hence their influence dwindled, and by 1919 Communism had
become the preferred venue for the committed radical laborer. The more
conservative Western Federation of Miners broke with the Wobblies over what it
considered their socialist, anti-American stance.

It was all but over by 1920 for the Wobblies. Yet however brief their period of
influence, it illustrates the frustration many in the mining community felt toward
corporate ownership and working conditions in general. There is no clearer
expression of the anger of the worker of that age than the Preamble and
Manifesto produced by the IWW's January 1905 convention.

THE PREAMBLE

The working class and the employing class have nothing in common. There
can be no peace so long as hunger and want are found among millions of
working people, and the few, who make up the employing class, have all the
good things of life.

Between these two classes a struggle must go on until all the toilers come
together on the political as well as on the industrial field, and take and hold

that which they produce by their labor, through an economic organization of the working class, without any affiliation with any political party.

The rapid gathering of wealth and the centering of the management of industries into fewer and fewer hands make the trade-unions unable to cope with the ever-growing power of the employing class, because the trade-unions foster a state of things which allows one set of workers to be pitted against another set of workers in the same industry, thereby helping defeat one another in wage wars. The trade-unions aid the employing class to mislead the workers into the belief that the working class have interests in common with their employers.

These sad conditions can be changed and the interests of the working class upheld only by an organization formed in such a way that all its members in any one industry, or in all industries, if necessary, cease work whenever a strike or lockout is on in any department thereof, thus making an injury to one an injury to all.

MANIFESTO

Social relations and groupings only reflect mechanical and industrial conditions. The *great* facts of present industry are the displacement of human skill by machines and the increase of capitalist power through concentration in the possession of the tools with which wealth is produced and distributed.

Because of these facts trade division among laborers and competition among capitalists are alike disappearing. Class divisions grow ever more fixed and class antagonisms more sharp. Trade lines have been swallowed up in a common servitude of all workers to the machines which they tend. New machines, ever replacing less productive ones, wipe out whole trades and plunge new bodies of workers into the ever-growing army of tradeless, hopeless unemployed. As human beings and human skill are displaced by mechanical progress, the capitalists need use the workers only during that brief period when muscles and nerves respond most intensely. The moment the laborer no longer yields the maximum of profits, he is thrown upon the scrap pile, to starve alongside the discarded machine. A *dead* line has been drawn, and an age-limit established, to cross which, in this world of monopolized opportunities, means condemnation to industrial death.

The workers, wholly separated from the land and the tools, with his skill of craftsmanship rendered useless, is sunk in the uniform mass of wage slaves. He sees his power of resistance broken by craft divisions, perpetuated from outgrown industrial stages. His wages constantly grow less as his hours grow longer and monopolized prices grow higher. Shifted hither and thither by the demands of profit-takers, the laborer's home no longer exists. In this hopeless condition he is forced to accept whatever humiliating conditions his master may impose. He is subjected to a physical and intellectual examination more searching than was the chattel slave when sold from the auction block. Laborers are no longer classified by differences in trade skill, but the employer assigns them according to the machines to which they are attached. These divisions, far from representing differences in skill or interests among the laborers, are imposed by the employers that workers may be pitted against one another and spurred to greater exertion in the shop, and that all resistance to capitalist tyranny may be weakened by artificial distinctions.

While encouraging these outgrown divisions among the workers the capitalists carefully adjust themselves to the new conditions. They wipe out all differences among themselves and present a united front in their war upon labor. Through employers' associations, they seek to crush, with brutal force, by the injunctions of the judiciary, and the use of military power, all efforts at resistance. Or when the other policy seems more profitable, they conceal their daggers beneath the Civic Federation [local vigilante group] and hoodwink and betray those whom they would rule and exploit. Both methods depend for success upon the blindness and internal dissensions of the working class. The employers' line of battle and methods of warfare correspond to the solidarity of the mechanical and industrial concentration, while laborers still form their fighting organizations on lines of long-gone trade divisions. The battles of the past emphasize this lesson. The *textile* workers of Lowell, Philadelphia, and Fall River; the *butchers* of Chicago, weakened by the disintegrating effects of trade divisions; the *machinists* on the Santa Fe [Railroad], unsupported by their fellow-workers subject to the same masters; the long-struggling *miners* of Colorado, hampered by lack of unity and solidarity upon the industrial battle-field, all bear witness to the helplessness and impotency of labor as at present organized.

This worn-out and corrupt system offers no promise of improvement and adaptation. There is no silver lining to the clouds of darkness and despair setting down upon the world of labor.

This system offers only a perpetual struggle for slight relief within wage slavery. It is blind to the possibility of establishing an industrial democracy, wherein there shall be no wage slavery, but where the workers will own the tools which they operate, and the product of which they alone will enjoy.

It shatters the ranks of the workers into fragments, rendering them helpless and impotent on the industrial battle-field.

Separation of craft from craft renders industrial and financial solidarity impossible.

Union men scab upon union men; hatred of worker for worker is engendered, and the workers are delivered helpless and disintegrated into the hands of the capitalists.

Craft jealousy leads to the attempt to create trade monopolies.

Prohibitive initiation fees are established that force men to become scabs against their will. Men whom manliness or circumstances have driven from one trade are thereby fined when they seek to transfer membership to the union of a new craft.

Craft divisions foster political ignorance among the workers, thus dividing their class at the ballot box, as well as in the shop, mine and factory.

Craft unions may be and have been used to assist employers in the establishment of monopolies and the raising of prices. One set of workers are thus used to make harder the conditions of life of another body of laborers.

Craft divisions hinder the growth of class consciousness of the workers, foster the idea of harmony of interests between employing exploiter and employed slave. They permit the association of the misleaders of the workers with the capitalists in the Civic Federations, where plans are made for the perpetuation of capitalism, and the permanent enslavement of the workers through the wage system.

Previous efforts for the betterment of the working class have proven abortive because limited in scope and disconnected in action.

Universal economic evils afflicting the working class can be eradicated only by a universal working-class movement. Such a movement of the working class is impossible while separate craft and wage agreements are made favoring the employer against other crafts in the same industry, and while energies are wasted in fruitless jurisdiction struggles which serve only to further the personal aggrandizement of union officials.

A movement to fulfill these conditions must consist of one great industrial union embracing all industries—providing for craft autonomy locally, industrial autonomy internationally, and working-class unity generally.

It must be founded on the class struggle, and its general administration must be conducted in harmony with the recognition of the irrepressible conflict between the capitalist class and the working class.

It should be established as the economic organization of the working class, without affiliation with any political party.

All power should rest in a collective membership.

Local, national, and general administration, including union labels, buttons, badges, transfer cards, initiation fee, and per capita tax should be uniform throughout.

All members must hold membership in the local, national or international union covering the industry in which they are employed, but transfers of membership between unions, local, national, or international, should be universal.

Workingmen bringing union cards from industrial unions in foreign countries should be freely admitted into the organization.

The general administration should issue a publication representing the entire union and its principles which should reach all members in every industry at regular intervals.

A *central defense fund,* to which all members contribute equally, should be established and maintained.

All workers, therefore, who agree with the principles herein set forth, will meet in convention at Chicago the 27th day of June, 1905, for the purpose of forming an economic organization of the working class along lines marked out in this Manifesto.

Adopted at Chicago, January 2, 3 and 4, 1905.

CHAPTER 5

THE IRON HORSE

The Railroad in the American West

⚜

FOR A community to prosper, it must have population, easily available commodities, and an economy producing a surplus that can be moved, at low cost, to markets. In the vast, largely arid expanses of the American West the only practicable transportation solution was the railroad. Without this crucial link in the development of the region, the mining, agricultural, and cattle frontiers would have remained unprofitable, withering enterprises.

The Iron Horse carried a cargo of distinctive romance as well. In the later nineteenth century, with the Machine Age the wave of the future, the railroad provided both industrial interest and the excitement of westering. Trains also brought greed, corruption, and displacement of Native American populations. This chapter examines the construction, uses, and problems of this formidable force in western expansionism. It starts with the building of the transcontinental railroad during the 1860s.

⁓

READING 1

THE PACIFIC RAILWAY ACT, 1862

The idea of a transcontinental railroad spanning the American nation from Atlantic to Pacific was a long-held dream, but geographic and political problems kept its fulfillment in abeyance for many years. In the 1850s, however, there came to be general acceptance that the railway was necessary and should be partly financed by the federal government. The question then became which route was the most desirable. In 1853 the Congress authorized surveys of various possibilities, but political squabbling between the competing regions led to congressional inaction. With the onset of the Civil War, however, southern routes were abandoned, and a northern route was selected. On July 1, 1862, the first Pacific Railway Act, excerpted here, authorized the construction of a transcontinental railroad and provided extensive government financing. In 1864 a second act *doubled the land grants and rearranged financial agreements. All told, the federal government granted more than 45 million acres of land to the railroad companies involved and approximately $60 million in aid. The railroad would be completed in 1869.*

An Act to aid in the Construction of a Railroad and Telegraph Line from the Missouri River to the Pacific Ocean . . .

Be it enacted, That [a list of the names of the Corporation officers]; together with five commissioners to be appointed by the Secretary of the Interior . . . are hereby created and erected into a body corporate . . . by the name . . . of "The Union Pacific Railroad Company"; . . . and the said corporation is hereby authorized and empowered to lay out, locate, construct, furnish, maintain and enjoy a continuous railroad and telegraph line . . . from a point on the one hundredth meridian of longitude west from Greenwich, between the south margin of the valley of the Republican River and the north margin of the valley of the Platte River, to the western boundary of Nevada Territory, upon the route and terms hereinafter provided. . . .

Sec. 2. That the right of way through the public lands be . . . granted to said company for the construction of said railroad and telegraph line; and the right . . . is hereby given to said company to take from the public lands adjacent to the line of said road, earth, stone, timber, and other materials for the construction thereof; said right of way is granted to said railroad to the extent of two hundred feet in width on each side of said railroad when it may pass over the public lands, including all necessary grounds for stations, buildings, workshops, and depots, machine shops, switches, side tracks, turn tables, and water stations. The United States shall extinguish as rapidly as may be the Indian titles to all lands falling under the operation of this act. . . .

Sec. 3. That there be . . . granted to the said company, for the purpose of aiding in the construction of said railroad and telegraph line, and to secure the safe and speedy transportation of mails, troops, munitions of war, and public stores thereon, every alternate section of public land, designated by odd numbers, to the amount of five alternate sections per mile on each side of the said railroad, on the line thereof, and within the limits of ten miles on each side of said road. . . . *Provided* That all mineral lands shall be excepted from the operation of this act; but where the same shall contain timber, the timber thereon is hereby granted to said company. . . .

Sec. 5. That for the purposes herein mentioned the Secretary of the Treasury shall . . . in accordance with the provisions of this act, issue to said company bonds of the United States of one thousand dollars each, payable in thirty years after date, paying six per centum per annum interest . . . to the amount of sixteen of said bonds per mile for each section of forty miles; and to secure the repayment to the United States . . . of the amount of said bonds . . . the issue of said bonds . . . shall ipso facto constitute a first mortgage on the whole line of the railroad and telegraph. . . .

Sec. 9. That the Leavenworth, Pawnee, and Western Railroad Company of Kansas are hereby authorized to construct a railroad and telegraph line . . . upon the same terms and conditions in all respects as are provided [for the construction of the Union Pacific Railroad listed above]. . . . The Central Pacific Railroad Company of California are hereby authorized to construct a railroad and telegraph line from the Pacific coast . . . to the eastern boundaries of California, upon the same terms and conditions in all respects [as provided for the Union Pacific Railroad].

Sec. 10. . . . And the Central Pacific Railroad Company of California after completing its road across said State, is authorized to continue the construction of said railroad and telegraph through the Territories of the United States to the Missouri River . . . upon the terms and conditions provided in this act in relation to the Union Pacific Railroad Company, until said roads shall meet and connect. . . .

Sec. 11. That for three hundred miles of said road most mountainous and difficult of construction, to wit: one hundred and fifty miles westerly from the eastern base of the Rocky Mountains, and one hundred and fifty miles eastwardly from the western base of the Sierra Nevada mountains . . . the bonds to be issued to aid in the construction thereof shall be treble the number per mile hereinbefore provided; . . . and between the sections last named of one hundred and fifty miles each, the bonds to be issued to aid in the construction thereof shall be doubled the number per mile first mentioned.

READING 2

THE AMERICAN RAILWAY SYSTEM, SAMUEL MORTON PETO, 1865

In 1865 Sir Samuel Morton Peto, a prominent English railway builder and commentator, visited the United States and formulated his views on the American railway system for British readers. Many in England had invested in American railroad development, and Peto's expert views were much sought after. His 1865 observations, excerpted here, come from his 1866 book, Resources and Prospects of America.

The system . . . on which railroads have been permitted to be constructed in America has been one of great simplicity. . . . In America . . . every one in the country has felt, from the first . . . that the construction of a railroad through his property, or to the city, town, or village he inhabited, was a source of prosperity and wealth, not only to the district in which he resided, but to himself personally. . . .

As a rule, nothing has been easier than to obtain from the legislative authority of a State in America a concession, or as it is there styled, a "charter," to lay down a road. The land in many cases, especially where it belonged to the public, has been freely given for the line; in other cases, where landed proprietors were affected, comparatively small compensation have sufficed to satisfy their claims. The citizens residing in the towns and populous places of the different districts, have hailed the approach of a railroad as a blessing. Under certain regulations, lines have been permitted to be laid down in the main streets and thoroughfares of the cities, so that the trains may traverse them at prescribed speeds, and so that goods may be put upon trucks at the very doors of the warehouses and shops. . . .

The influence of railroads on the value of real estates along their lines, and in the cities in which they terminate, is so well understood in America, as to have afforded important financial facilities to their construction. It is not the public who are invited in America to take railway shares; they are subscribed for in a wholly different manner. In order to promote the construction of a line, not only does the State which it traverses frequently afford it facilities with respect to land, but pecuniary facilities are often given by the cities and towns giving securities for certain amounts on the Municipal Bonds. The cities in which it is to have its termini also agree to subscribe for portions of its share capital, and so do the inhabitants of the towns and villages through which it is to pass. This is a very important feature of the American railway system, inasmuch as it gives the inhabitants of each district which a railway traverses, a direct local and individual interest in the promotion and well-working of the line. Every one, in fact, is interested in contributing traffic to his own railway.

Not only the whole cost of maintaining the roads, but a very considerable proportion of the cost of the construction, has, in the case of the majority of the lines in America, been thrown *upon revenue*. I am afraid that the consequence of this has been injurious to public confidence in the American railways as commercial securities. Where lines are imperfectly constructed in the first instance—where they have to bear all the effects of climate and of wear and tear, whilst in indifferent condition, it is quite obvious that the cost of reparations, even in the very early stages of their working, must be a serious burden. And where all this is thrown, at once, on revenue, adequate dividends cannot be expected. . . .

Most of the American lines were originally made in short lengths, as lines of communication between different towns in the same State; and without regard to any general system of communication for the nation. It follows, that even in cases of lines which are now united and brought under a single management, much diversity of construction, and a great want of unity of system is observable. One of the great deficiencies of the American railroad system is, in fact, the absence of a general policy of management. Scarcely any attempts are made to render the working of lines convenient to travellers, by working the trains of one company in conjunction with another; and this gives rise to complaints on the part of the public, which may, some day or other, be made to afford a ground of excuse for governmental interference. Nothing can be more desirable for the success of American railroad enterprises than well-considered general arrangements for the working and interchange of traffic.

Remarkable as has been the rapidity with which the American railroads have been constructed, and great as is the total mileage already made, the railroad accommodation of the United States is not to be regarded as by any means meeting the requirements of the country. The rapid growth of the system has only been co-equal with the rapid growth of the population: the extent of mileage is attributable to the vast extent of territory settled, and the great distances between the seats of population.

In many parts of the States, indeed, the existing railways are quite insufficient. In the South, the system is very imperfectly developed. Whilst slaves existed, there was a determined hostility in the Southern States to the expansion of any general railway system, arising from the apprehension that it would be used for the escape of slaves. . . .

From West to East, also, the present railways are quite insufficient for the growing traffic. The lines of communication from the West by canals, &c., which existed previously to railways, have not been affected by their construction. The produce of the Western States has, in fact, increased faster than the means of transport, and additional facilities for the conveyance of goods are urgently required. It is of the utmost importance to the development of the West that no time should be lost in making this additional provision.

READING 3
"New Tracks in North America," W. A. Bell, 1869

Not all foreign observers were as clinically critical as Sir Samuel Peto (reading 2). A more enthusiastic commentator was W. A. Bell, an English traveler who observed the construction of the Union Pacific Railroad during the late 1860s and described the heated activities of its builders in heroic terms.

One can see all along the line of the now completed road the evidences of ingenious self-protection and defence which our men learned during the war. The same curious huts and underground dwellings which were a common sight along our army lines then, may now be seen burrowed into the sides of the hills, or built up with ready adaptability in sheltered spots. The whole organisation of the force engaged in the construction of the road is, in fact, semi-military. The men who go ahead, locating the road, are the advance guard. Following these is the second line, cutting through the gorges, grading the road, and building bridges. Then comes the main line of the army, placing the sleepers [railroad ties], laying the tracks, spiking down the rails, perfecting the alignment, ballasting the rail, and dressing up and completing the road for immediate use. This army of workers has its base, to continue the figure, at Omaha, Chicago, and still farther eastward, from whose markets are collected the material for constructing the road. Along the line of the completed road are construction trains constantly "pushing forward to the front" with supplies. The company's grounds and workshops at Omaha are the arsenal, where these purchases, amounting to millions of dollars in value, are collected and held ready to be sent forward. The advanced limit of the rail is occupied by a train of long box cars, with hammocks swung under them, bunks built within them, in which the sturdy, broad-shouldered pioneers of the great iron highway sleep at night and take their meals. Close behind this train come loads of ties and rail and spikes, &c., which are being thundered off upon the roadside, to be ready for the track-layers. The road is graded a hundred miles in advance. The ties are laid roughly in place, then adjusted, graded, and levelled. Then the track is laid.

Track-laying on the Union Pacific is a science, and we pundits of the Far East stood upon that embankment, only about a thousand miles this side of sunset, and backed westward before that hurrying corps of sturdy operatives with mingled feelings of amusement, curiosity, and profound respect. On they came. A light car, drawn by a single horse, gallops up to the front with its load of rails. Two men seize the end of the rail and start forward, the rest of the gang taking hold by twos until it is clear of the car. They come forward at a run. At the word of command the rail is dropped in its place, right side up, with care, while the same process goes on at the other side of the car. Less than thirty seconds to a rail for each gang, and so four rails go down in a minute! Quick work, you say, but the fellows on the U.P. are tremendously in earnest. The moment the car is empty it is tipped over on the side of the track to let the next loaded car pass it, and then it is tipped back again; and it is a sight to see it go flying back for another load, propelled by a horse at full gallop at the end of 60 to 80 feet of rope, ridden by a young Jehu, who drives furiously. Close behind the first gang comes the gaugers, spikers, and bolters, and a lively time they make of it. It is a grand Anvil Chorus that those sturdy sledges are playing across the plains. It is in triple time, three strokes to a spike. There are ten spikes to a rail, four hundred rails to a mile, eighteen hundred miles to San Francisco. That's the sum, what is the quotient? Twenty-one million times are those sledges to be swung—twenty-one million times are they to come down with their sharp punctuation, before the great work of modern America is complete!

READING 4

LABOR TROUBLES ALONG THE LINE, GRENVILLE DODGE, 1869

The idyllic labor picture painted by W. A. Bell (reading 3) was often far from realistic. General Grenville Dodge, the chief engineer in the construction of the Union Pacific, describes a very different situation in this excerpt from his book How We Built the Union Pacific Railway. *Dodge recounts the dangerous competition that ensued when the Central Pacific, which had started at the western terminus of the transcontinental railroad, and the Union Pacific began laying tracks side by side. The rival companies had not reached an agreement as to when, where, or even if their two lines were to be joined. Nor did the amended Pacific Railway Act clearly specify these conditions; it simply indicated that the two companies would maintain construction until they met. Hence, both railroads continued to build, each confident that its operations were to be rewarded by contractual government subsidies. This risky and foolish contest was ended only by a federally brokered compromise that established the meeting place at Promontory Point, Utah.*

Between Ogden and Promontory [in Utah] each company graded a line, running side by side, and in some places one line was right above [uphill from] the other. The laborers upon the Central Pacific were Chinamen, while ours were Irishmen, and there was much ill-feeling between them. Our Irishmen were in the habit of firing their blasts in the cuts without giving warning to the Chinamen on the Central Pacific working right above them. From this cause several Chinamen were severely hurt. Complaint was made to me by the Central Pacific people, and I endeavored to have the contractors bring all hostilities to a close, but, for some reason or other, they failed to do so. One day the Chinamen, appreciating the situation, put in what is called a "grave" on their work, and when the Irishmen right under them were all at work let go their blast and buried several of our men. This brought about a truce at once. From that time the Irish laborers showed due respect for the Chinamen, and there was no further trouble.

READING 5

LAST REPORT TO THE BOARD OF DIRECTORS, GRENVILLE DODGE, 1869

On May 10, 1869, the transcontinental railroad was completed. General Grenville Dodge soon afterward presented his final report to the board of directors of the Union Pacific Railroad. The company would be enveloped in the Crédit Mobilier financial scandal by 1872, but this was a moment of triumph. This excerpt from Dodge's report is replete with both praise for the company and thinly veiled anger and condescension toward railroad critics.

In 1863 and 1864 surveys were inaugurated, but in 1866 the country was systematically occupied; and day and night, summer and winter the explorations were pushed forward through dangers and hardships that few at this day appreciate, for every mile had to be run within range of the musket, as there was not a moment's security. In making the surveys numbers of our men, some of the ablest and most promising, were killed; and during the construction our stock was run off by the hundred, I might say by the thousand, and as one difficulty after another arose and was overcome, both in the engineering, running, and construction departments, a new era in railroad building was inaugurated.

Each day taught us lessons by which we profited for the next, and our advances and improvements in the art of railway construction were marked by the progress of the work, forty miles of track having been laid in 1865, 260 in 1866, 240 in 1867, including the ascent to the summit of the Rocky Mountains, at an elevation of 8235 feet above the ocean; and during 1868 and to May 10, 1869, 555 miles all exclusive of side and temporary tracks, of which over 180 miles were built in addition.

The first grading was done in the autumn of 1864, and the first rail laid in July, 1865. When you look back to the beginning at the Missouri river, with no railroad communication from the east, and 500 miles of the country in advance without timber, fuel, or any material whatever from which to build or maintain a road, except the sand for the bare roadbed itself with everything to be transported, and that by teams or at best by steamboats, for hundreds and thousands of miles; everything to be created, with labor scarce and high, you can all look back upon the work with satisfaction and ask, under the circumstances, could we have done more or better?

The country is evidently satisfied that you accomplished wonders and have achieved a work that will be a monument to your energy, your ability, and to your devotion to the enterprise through all its gloomy as well as its bright periods; for it is notorious that, notwithstanding the aid of the Government, there was so little faith in the enterprise that its dark days—when your private fortunes and your all was staked on the success of the project—far exceeded those of sunshine, faith, and confidence.

This lack of confidence in the project, even in the West, in those localities where the benefits of construction was manifest, was excessive, and it will be remembered that laborers even demanded their pay before they would perform their day's work, so little faith had they in the payment of their wages, or in the ability of the company to succeed in their efforts. Probably no enterprise in the world has been so maligned, misrepresented, and criticized as this; but now, after the calm judgment of the American people is brought to bear upon it, unprejudiced and biased, it is almost without exception pronounced the best new road in the United States. . . .

Its future is fraught with great good. It will develop [land that has been] a waste, will bind together the two extremes of the nation as one, will stimulate intercourse and trade, and bring harmony, prosperity and wealth to the two coasts. A proper policy, systematically and persistently followed, will bring to the road the trade of two oceans, and will give it all the business it can accommodate; while the local trade will increase gradually until the mining, grazing, and agricultural regions which it passes will build up and create a business that will be a lasting and permanent support to the country.

READING 6

THE GOLDEN SPIKE

On May 10, 1869, representatives of the Central Pacific Railroad and the Union Pacific Railroad met at Promontory Point, Utah, to formalize the completion of the transcontinental railroad. The ceremony became known as the Golden Spike Celebration. Eyewitness accounts include those of Alexander Toponce and General Grenville Dodge.

READING 6A

"A GREAT ABUNDANCE OF CHAMPAGNE," ALEXANDER TOPONCE, 1869

I saw the Golden Spike driven at Promontory, Utah, on May 10, 1869. . . .

On the last day, only about 100 feet were laid, and everybody tried to have a hand in the work. I took a shovel from an Irishman, and threw a shovel full of dirt on the ties just to tell about it afterward.

A special train from the west brought Sidney Dillon, General Dodge, T. C. Durant, John R. Duff, S. A. Seymour, a lot of newspaper men, and plenty of the best brands of champagne.

Another train made up at Ogden carried the band from Fort Douglas, the leading men of the Utah Territory, and a small but efficient supply of Valley Tan.

It was a very hilarious occasion; everybody had all they wanted to drink all the time. Some of the participants got "sloppy," and these were not all Irish and Chinese by any means.

California furnished the Golden Spike. Governor Tuttle of Nevada furnished one of silver. General Stanford [Governor Stafford] presented one of gold, silver, and iron from Arizona. The last tie was of California laurel.

When they came to drive the last spike, Governor Stanford [of California], president of the Central Pacific, took the sledge, and the first time he struck he missed the spike and hit the rail.

What a howl went up! Irish, Chinese, Mexicans, and everybody yelled with delight. "He missed it. Yee." The engineers blew the whistles and rang their bells. Then Stanford tried it again and tapped the spike and the telegraph operators had fixed their instruments so that the tap was reported in all the offices east and west, and set bells to tapping in hundreds of towns and cities.... Then Vice President T. C. Durant of the Union Pacific took up the sledge and he missed the spike the first time. Then everybody slapped everybody else again and yelled, "He missed it too, yow!"

It was a great occasion, every one carried off souvenirs and there are enough splinters of the last tie in museums to make a good bonfire.

When the connection was finally made the Union Pacific and the Central Pacific engineers ran their engines up until the pilots [the front sections] touched. Then the engineers shook hands and had their pictures taken and each broke a bottle of champagne on the pilot of the other's engine and had their picture taken again.

The Union Pacific engine, the "Jupiter," was driven by my good friend, George Lashus, who still lives in Ogden.

Both before and after the spike driving ceremony there were speeches, which were cheered heartily. I do not remember what any of the speakers said now, but I do remember there was a great abundance of champagne.

READING 6B
"THE ATLANTIC AND PACIFIC WERE
JOINED," GRENVILLE DODGE, 1869

On the morning of May 10, 1869, Hon. Leland Stanford, Governor of California and President of the Central Pacific, accompanied by Messrs. Huntington, Hopkins, Crocker and trainloads of California's distinguished citizens, arrived from the west. During the forenoon Vice President T. C. Durant and Directors John R. Duff and Sidney Dillon and Consulting Engineer Silas A. Seymour of the Union Pacific, with other prominent men, including a delegation of Mormons from Salt Lake City, came in on a train from the east. The National Government was represented by a detachment of "regulars" from Fort Douglass, Utah, accompanied by a band, and 600 others, including Chinese, Mexicans, Indians, half-breeds, negroes and laborers, suggesting an air of cosmopolitanism, all gathered around the open space where the tracks were to be joined. The Chinese laid the rails from the west end, and the Irish laborers laid them from the east end, until they met and joined.

Telegraphic wires were so connected that each blow of the descending sledge could be reported instantly to all parts of the United States. Corresponding blows were struck on the bell of the City Hall in San Francisco, and with the last blow of the sledge a cannon was fired at Fort Point. General Stafford presented a spike of gold, silver and iron as the offering of the Territory of Arizona. Governor Tuttle of Nevada presented a spike of silver from his state. The connecting tie was of California laurel, and California presented the last spike of gold in behalf of that state. A silver sledge had also been presented for the occasion. A prayer was offered. Governor Stanford of California made a few appropriate remarks on behalf of the Central Pacific and the chief engineer responded for the Union Pacific. Then the telegraphic inquiry from the Omaha office, from which the circuit was to be started, was answered: "To everybody: Keep quiet. When the last spike is driven at Promontory Point we will say 'Done.' Don't break the circuit, but watch for the signals of the blows of the hammer. The spike will soon be driven. The signal will be three dots for the commencement of the blows." The magnet tapped one—two—three—then paused—"Done." The spike was given its first blow by President Stanford and Vice President Durant followed. Neither hit the spike the first time, but hit the rail, and were greeted by the lusty cheers of the onlookers, accompanied by the screams of the locomotives and the music of the military band. Many other spikes were driven on the last rail by some of the distinguished persons present, but it was seldom that they first hit the spike. The original spike, after being tapped by the officials of the companies, was driven home by the chief engineers of the two roads. Then the two trains were run together, the two locomotives touching at the point of junction, and the engineers of the two locomotives each broke a bottle of champagne on the other's engine. Then it was declared that the connection was made and the Atlantic and Pacific were joined together never to be parted.

COMPLETION OF THE PACIFIC RAILROAD, HENRY VARNUM POOR, 1869

The completion of the transcontinental railroad in 1869 brought forth a significant amount of learned comment on its socioeconomic and cultural effects. One of the most respected ruminations came from Henry Varnum Poor, the publisher of Poor's Manual of Railroads *and a leading American authority on railroad affairs. This excerpt is from his* Manual of the Railroads of the United States, 1869–1870.

The present year witnesses the completion of the most important enterprise of the kind ever executed in any country—a line of railroad from the Missouri River across the Continent, and with connecting lines from the Atlantic to Pacific Ocean, a distance of 3,250 miles. This great undertaking was commenced in the latter part of 1863, but no considerable amount of work was made until 1865, in which year only about 100 miles were constructed; in 1866, about 300 miles were opened; in 1867, about the same number; in 1868, about 800 miles; and in the present year, about 300: the whole distance from the Missouri to Sacramento being 1,800 miles. . . .

The influence of these works . . . upon the commerce and welfare of the country, must be immense. A vast commerce, yet in its infancy, already exists between the two shores of the Continent. With the advantage and stimulus of the railroad this commerce must soon assume colossal proportions. Fronting the Pacific slope are hundreds of millions of people in Eastern Asia, who are rapidly taking part in the commerce of the world, and who will have the most intimate relations with our own Continent, which produces the gold and silver which at present forms one of the chief staples of commerce with them. It is hardly possible to estimate the magnitude of the commerce which will eventually exist between the Pacific coast and China and Japan. It is a commerce in which the world is to engage, and in which the Pacific Railroad is to be one of the most important instruments.

This road, too, will open up to settlement vast tracts of hitherto inaccessible territory, either fertile in soil, or rich in the more valuable minerals which are likely amply to compensate for the want of agricultural wealth. The main line will serve as the trunk from which lateral roads, constructed by private enterprise, will branch off in every direction. Already several important branches are in progress—one to Denver, Colorado; one to Salt Lake City;

and one to connect it with the Columbia River. These branches will open up wide sections and add largely to the traffic of the trunk line.

The construction of this, and of similar works, by the aid of the Federal Government, has excited great interest, and although at present public opinion seems to be against any further grants of money, there can be no doubt that Government has been largely the gainer by the aid it has extended to the Pacific Railroad and its branches. The public taxes equal, at the present time, ten dollars per head of our population. These works have been instrumental in adding more than 500,000 to our population, whose contributions to the National treasury have far exceeded the interest on the bonds issued to them. They have certainly been instrumental in securing the construction of an equal extent of line which, but for them, would not have been built.... The gain to the Federal Government from the creation [of the railroad] ... will, in a very short time, more than equal the principal sum of the bonds issued. Equally beneficent results will follow the construction of similar works. The people of the United States cannot afford to have extensive portions of their wide domain remain without means of access. In cases where such means have not been supplied by navigable water-courses they must be by a railway, or vast territories must remain, what they are now, deserts. The argument in favor of Government aid is as conclusive as it is simple....

There can be no doubt, if the railroads of the United States could have been secured in no other way, it would have been the soundest policy for Government to have assumed their construction, even without the expectation of realizing a dollar of direct income from them. The actual cost of these works have been about $1,200,000,000. The interest of this sum is $72,000,000. They have created a commerce worth $10,000,000,000 annually. Such a commerce has enabled the people to pay $400,000,000 into the public treasury with far greater ease than they could have paid $100,000,000 without them. No line of greater importance was ever constructed that did not, from the wealth it created, speedily repay its cost, although it may never have returned a dollar to its share or bondholders. If this be true of local and unimportant works, how much more so must it be of great lines, which will open vast sections of our public domain, now a desert, but abounding in all the elements of wealth.

While, therefore, there are but few cases which would justify the Government in extending aid to railroads, there are some in which its interposition becomes an imperative duty. In addition to the Central line now constructed, nothing could be more promotive of the general welfare than the opening, by its aid, both the Northern and Southern routes. Upon each of these are immense extents of territory, full of natural wealth, but which, without a railroad, are utterly beyond the reach of settlement or commerce. Aid extended to both lines, instead of weakening the public credit, would greatly strengthen it.

READING 8

"ACROSS THE PLAINS," ROBERT LOUIS STEVENSON, 1879

The completion of the transcontinental railroad in 1869 was a spur to western development. Population began to stream in, thanks largely to the new ease of transportation. Historians believe that between 1870 and 1900 more land was settled in the American West than in the entire previous history of American frontier development. The importance of the railroad in this process was recognized by many—among them, Robert Louis Stevenson, who made the transcontinental trip in 1879 and wrote of it in his 1892 book, Across the Plains.

And yet when day came, it was to shine upon the same broken and unsightly quarter of the world. Mile upon mile, and not a tree, a bird, or a river. Only down the long, sterile canons, the train shot hooting and awoke the resting echo. That train was the one piece of life in all the deadly land; it was the one actor, the one spectacle fit to be observed in this paralysis of man and nature. And when I think how the railroad had been pushed through this unwatered wilderness and haunt of savage tribes, and now will bear an emigrant for some £12 [English pounds] from the Atlantic to the Golden Gates; how at each stage of the construction, roaring, impromptu cities, full of gold and lust and death, sprang up and then died away again, and are now but wayside stations in the desert; how in these uncouth places pigtailed Chinese pirates worked side by side with border ruffians and broken men from Europe, talking together in a mixed dialect, mostly oaths, gambling, drinking, quarrelling and murdering like wolves; how the plumed hereditary lord of all America heard, in this last fastness, the scream of the "bad medicine waggon" charioting his foes; and then when I go on to remember that all this epical turmoil was conducted by gentlemen in frock coats, and with a view to nothing more extraordinary than a fortune and a subsequent visit to Paris, it seems to me, I own, as if this railway were the one typical achievement of the age in which we live, as if it brought together into one plot all the ends of the world and all the degrees of social rank, and offered to some great writer the busiest, most extended, and the most varied subject for an enduring literary work. If it be romance, if it be contrast, if it be heroism that we require, what was Troy town to this? But, alas! it is not these things that are necessary—it is only Homer.

Here also we are grateful to the train, as to some god who conducts us swiftly through these shades and by so many hidden perils. Thirst, hunger, the sleight and ferocity of Indians are all no more feared, so lightly do we skim these horrible lands; as the gull, who wings safely through the hurricane and past the shark. . . .

The rest [of the passengers] were all American born, but they came from almost every quarter of the Continent. All the States of the North had sent a fugitive to cross the plains with me. From Virginia, from Pennsylvania, from New York, from far western Iowa and Kansas, from Maine that borders on the Canadas, and from the Canadas themselves—some one or two were fleeing in quest of a better land and better wages. The talk in the train, like the talk I heard on the steamer, ran upon hard times, short commons, and hope that ever moves westward. I thought of my shipful from Great Britain with a feeling of despair. They had come 3000 miles, and yet not far enough. Hard times bowed them out of the Clyde, and stood to welcome them at Sandy Hook. Where were they to go? Pennsylvania, Maine, Iowa, Kansas? These were not places for immigration, but for emigration, it appeared; not one of them, but I knew a man who had lifted up his heel and left it for an ungrateful country. And it was still westward that they ran. Hunger, you would have thought, came out of the east like the sun, and the evening was made of edible gold. And, meantime, in the car in front of me, were there not half a hundred emigrants from the opposite quarter? Hungry Europe and hungry China, each pouring from their gates in search of provender, had here come face to face. The two waves had met; east and west had alike failed; the whole round world had been prospected and condemned; there was no El Dorado anywhere; and till one could emigrate to the moon, it seemed as well to stay patiently at home. Nor was there wanting another sign, at once more picturesque and disheartening; for, as we continued to steam westward toward the land of gold, we were continually passing other emigrant trains upon the journey east; and these were as crowded as our own. Had all these return voyagers made a fortune in the mines? Were they all bound for Paris, and to be in Rome by Easter? It would seem not, for, whenever we met them, the passengers ran on the platform and cried to us through the windows, in a kind of wailing chorus, to "Come back!" On the plains of Nebraska, in the mountains of Wyoming, it was still the same cry, and dismal to my heart, "Come back!" That was what we heard by the way "about the good country we were going to." And at that very hour the Sandlot of San Francisco was crowded with the unemployed, and the echo from the other side of Market Street was repeating the rant of demagogues.

If, in truth, it were only for the sake of wages that men emigrate, how many thousands would regret the bargain! But wages, indeed, are only one consideration out of many; for we are a race of gipsies, and love change and travel for themselves.

READING 9

THE ALTERNATIVE—THE STAGECOACH, RAPHAEL PUMPELLY, 1860

For comfort and convenience, the railroad far surpassed all other contemporary modes of travel. Considering the alternative of a stagecoach over rough, dusty roads is instructive. In 1870 Raphael Pumpelly, a geologist and adventurer, recalled his stagecoach journey of a decade earlier. His colorful description shows the romance of stagecoaches but also the contrast to the comfort of trains.

In the autumn of 1860 I reached the westernmost end of the railroad in Missouri, finishing the first, and, in point of time, the shortest stage in a journey, the end of which I had not even attempted to foresee. My immediate destination was the silver mines of the Santa Rita, in Arizona, of which I was to take charge, as mining engineer, for a year, under the resident superintendent.

Having secured the right to a back seat in the overland coach as far as Tucson, I looked forward, with comparatively little dread, to sixteen days and nights of continuous travel. But the arrival of a woman and her brother, dashed, at the very outset, my hopes of an easy journey, and obliged me to take the front seat, where, with my back to the horses, I began to foresee the coming discomfort. The coach was fitted with three seats, and these were occupied by nine passengers. As the occupants of the front and middle seats faced each other, it was necessary for these six people to interlock their knees; and there being room inside for only ten of the twelve legs, each side of the coach was graced by a foot, now dangling near the wheel, now trying in vain to find a place of support. An unusually heavy mail in the boot [the trunk], by weighing down the rear, kept those of us who were on the front seat constantly bent forward, thus, by taking away all support from our backs, rendering rest at all times out of the question.

My immediate neighbors were a tall Missourian, with his wife and two young daughters; and from this family arose a large part of the discomfort of the journey. The man was a border bully, armed with revolver, knife, and rifle; the woman, a very hag, ever following the disgusting habit of dipping [snuff]—filling the air, and covering her clothes with snuff; the girls, for several days overcome by sea-sickness, and in this regard having no regard for the clothes of their neighbors;—these were the circumstances which offered slight promise of comfort on a journey which, at best, could only be tedious and difficult.

For several days our road lay through the more barren and uninteresting parts of Missouri and Arkansas; but when we entered the Indian territory, and the fertile valley of the Red river, the scenery changed, and we seemed to have come into one of the Edens of the earth. Indeed, one of the scenes, still bright in my memory, embraced the finest and most extensive of natural park.

Before reaching Fort Smith [Arkansas] every male passenger in the stage had lost his hat, and most of the time allowed for breakfast at that town was used in getting new head-coverings. It turned out to be a useless expense, however, for in less than two days we were all again bareheaded. As this happens to the passengers of every stage, we estimated that not less than fifteen hundred hats were lost yearly by travellers, for the benefit of the population along the road.

After passing the Arkansas river, and travelling two or three days through the cultivated region of northeastern Texas, we came gradually to the outposts of population. The rivers became fewer, and deeper below the surface; the rolling prairie-land covered with grass gave way to dry gravelly plains, on which the increasing preponderance of species of cacti, and of the yucca, warned us of our approach to the great American desert. Soon after our entrance into this region we were one morning all started from a deep sleep by the noise of a party coming up at full gallop, and ordering the driver to halt. They were a rough-looking set of men, and we took them for robbers until their leader told us that they were "regulators," and were in search of a man who had committed a murder the previous day at a town we had passed through.

"He is a tall fellow, with blue eyes, and red beard," said the leader. "So if you have got him in there, you needn't tote him any further, for the branch of a mesquit tree is strong enough for his neck." As I was tall, and had blue eyes and a red beard, I did not feel perfectly easy until the party left us, convinced that the object of their search was not in the stage.

One can scarcely picture a more desolate and barren region than the southern part of the Llano Estacado between the Brazos and Pecos rivers. Lying about 4,500 feet above the sea, it is a desert incapable of supporting other plant or animal life than scattered cacti, rattlesnakes, and lizards. Our route winding along the southern border of this region, kept on the out-skirts of the Camanche country.

Here we are constantly exposed to the raids of this fierce tribe, which has steadily refused to be tamed by the usual process of treaties and pres-ents. They were committing serious depredations along the route, and had murdered the keepers at several stations. We consequently approached the stockade station houses with considerable anxiety, not knowing whether we should find either keepers or horses. Over this part of the road no lights were used at night, and we were thus exposed to the additional danger of having our necks broken by being upset.

The fatigue of uninterrupted travelling by day and night in a crowded coach, and in the most uncomfortable positions, was beginning to tell seri-ously upon all the passengers, and was producing a condition bordering upon insanity. This was increased by the constant anxiety caused by the dan-ger from Camanches. Every jolt of the stage, indeed any occurrence which started a passenger out of the state of drowsiness, was instantly magnified into an attack, and the nearest fellow-passenger was as likely to be taken for an Indian as for a friend. In some persons, this temporary mania developed itself to such a degree that their own safety and that of their fellow-travellers made it necessary to leave them at the nearest station, where sleep usually restored them before the arrival of the next stage on the following week. Instances have occurred of travellers jumping in this condition from the coach and wandering off to a death from starvation upon the desert.

Over the hard surface of this country, which is everywhere a natural road, we frequently travelled at great speed, with only half-broken teams. At several stations, six wild horses were hitched blindfolded into their places. When everything was ready, the blinds were removed at a signal from the driver, and the animals started off at a run-away speed, which they kept up without slackening till the next station, generally twelve miles distant. In these cases the driver had no further control over his animals than the ability to guide them; to stop, or even check them, was entirely beyond his power; the frightened horses fairly flying over the ground, and never stopping till they drew up exhausted at the next station. Nothing but the most perfect presence of mind on the part of the driver could prevent accidents. Even this was not always enough, as was proved by a stage which we met, in which every passenger had either a bandaged head or an arm in a sling.

At El Paso we had hoped to find a larger stage. Being disappointed in this, I took a place outside, between the driver and conductor. The impossibility of sleeping had made me half delirious, and we had gone but a few miles before I nearly unseated the driver by starting suddenly out of a dream.

I was told that the safety of all passengers demanded that I should keep awake; and as the only means of effecting this, my neighbors beat a constant tatoo with their elbows upon my ribs. During the journey from the Rio Grande to Tucson my delirium increased, and the only thing I have ever remembered of that part of the route was the sight of a large number of Indian campfires at Apache pass. My first recollection after this, is of being awakened by the report of a pistol, and of starting up to find myself in a crowded room, where a score or more of people were quarrelling at a gaming table. I had reached Tucson and had thrown myself on the floor of the first room I could enter. A sound sleep of twelve hours had fully restored me, both in mind and body.

READING 10

"TERRIBLE ANTIPATHY," A. C. BUELL, 1877

The development of the railroad was not an isolated phenomenon affecting only the West. Its growth was part of a much larger transformation. Industrialization had brought profound changes to the economic realm of American life—great wealth and prestige but also associated labor unhappiness and violence—and the railroad became a symbol of corporate industrialism in all its negative and positive aspects. Americans admired the incredible accomplishment of the transcontinental railroad but were uneasy about its management practices. The uneasiness grew, and by the mid-1870s the railroads had come to be the most hated and feared corporations in America. In 1877 the distrust burst into labor violence. The Great Railroad Strike of 1877, as it came to be called, began in West Virginia and quickly spread throughout the nation. Its direct cause was a management decision to cut wages; its underlying cause was the growing antagonism between labor and employer. Federal troops were sent to break the strike (the first time this had occurred since the 1830s), and sympathy strikes spread like wildfire. Protest meetings were staged in many large cities; even in small communities, strikers and their supporters filled the streets. There were pitched battles, many arrests, and a few deaths. The federal troops dispatched from firestorm to firestorm quelled the outbreaks a few weeks after the strike began, but its significance lasted much longer. For some, the strike was a harbinger of things to come as the railroad arrogantly consolidated its power; for others, it was a hopeful sign that labor could through concerted action bring even the greatest economic powers to their knees; for a few, the strike was an alarm warning of cultural disintegration and social disaster.

A. C. Buell, a special correspondent for the New Orleans Daily Democrat, *here comments on the attitudes of the strikers and provides fodder for those who saw evil intentions in this labor movement.*

The most striking fact developed by this movement is the terrible antipathy which has grown up among the poor and laboring classes against those who possess great wealth. . . . John Jones and William Smith, laborers, regard William H. Vanderbilt, Jay Gould, and Tom Scott, capitalists, as their natural enemies, whose welfare means their loss and whose downfall would redound to their gain. . . . Today, Tom Scott would not get through Pittsburgh, or Vanderbilt through Buffalo, alive! . . . You may call it whatsoever name you please—Communism, Agrarianism, Socialism, or anything else— . . . in the estimation of the vast majority of the American people the millionaire has come to be looked upon as a public enemy! . . . We have just now had a foretaste of real Civil War; of that conflict of classes, which is the most terrible of all species of war. . . . The inadequacy of the present governmental system to combat servile insurrections has been forced home upon the capitalistic classes as a fact that can no longer be evaded. . . . The average citizen may forget the danger as soon as it is past, but not the man of millions. He has seen the ghost of the Commune, and it will stalk his dreams every night until he can feel with his prototype of the old world the security of mercenary bayonets enough to garrison every considerable town.

READING II
"THE CHAMPION BUFFALO HUNTER OF THE
PLAINS," BUFFALO BILL CODY, 1920

On occasion in the American West, policies of the dominant culture might intertwine: what was good for the railroads could also be seen as benefiting military tactics and influencing societal development. Such was the case with the buffalo extermination policy instituted by the railroads in the 1860s and 1870s.

As the rails pushed westward, the workers needed food. Since the most readily available source was the vast herds of buffalo that roamed the plains, railroad companies hired professional buffalo hunters to provide meat for their labor force. The buffalo, however, constituted the main commissary of the Plains Indians as well—and they, in turn, were becoming the primary target of military action during these years. The commander of the Western Division, General Philip Sheridan, seeing buffalo killing as a way to disrupt the lifestyle and fighting capacity of the Indians, ordered the slaughter to be intensified. Moreover, hundreds of thousands of dead buffalo became a source of revenue: within a few years buffalo bones were being shipped back east by the carload to be processed into garden fertilizer; buffalo tongue became a delicacy demanded in the finer restaurants; and the discovery that buffalo hide could be transformed into a useful leather only increased the killing. All told, historians believe that before the practice of hunting for food escalated to a policy of extermination, there may have been nearly ten million free-roaming buffalo on the plains. By 1890, only about a thousand of the animals remained.

Among the most famous of the buffalo hunters was William F. Cody, better known by his nickname Buffalo Bill, who parlayed his frontier experiences as scout, guide, hunter, and explorer into a lucrative career as a showman. Buffalo Bill's Wild West and Congress of Rough Riders of the World was equal parts entertainment and mythology, but Cody's western experiences were real. In his 1920 autobiography he describes his days as a buffalo hunter for the railroad. Cody's recollections must be taken with a gigantic grain of salt, for his reputation as a flamboyant showman and promoter precedes him, but the account has enough authentic flavor to provide insight into an important activity in the development of the American West.

The western end of the Kansas Pacific was at this time in the heart of buffalo country. Twelve hundred men were employed in the construction of the [rail]road. The Indians were very troublesome, and it was difficult to engage expert hunters to kill buffaloes.

Having heard of my experience and success as a buffalo hunter, Goddard Brothers, who had the contract for feeding the men, made me a good offer to become their hunter. They said they would require about twelve buffaloes a day—twenty-four hams and twelve humps, as only the hump and hind-quarters were utilized. The work was dangerous. Indians were riding all over that section of the country, and my duties would require me to journey from five to ten miles from the railroad every day in order to secure the game, accompanied by only one man with a light wagon to haul the meat back to camp. I demanded a large salary, which they could well afford to pay, as the meat itself would cost them nothing. Under the terms of the contract which I signed with them, I was to receive five hundred dollars a month, agreeing on my part to supply them with all the meat they wanted.

I at once began my career as a buffalo hunter for the Kansas Pacific. It was not long before I acquired a considerable reputation, and it was at this time that the title "Buffalo Bill" was conferred upon me by the railroad hands. Of this title, which has stuck to me through life, I have never been ashamed. . . .

. . . I had my celebrated shooting contest with Billy Comstock, a well-known guide, scout, and interpreter. Comstock, who was chief of scouts at Fort Wallace, had a reputation of being a successful buffalo hunter, and his friends at the fort—the officers in particular—were anxious to back him against me.

It was arranged that I should shoot a match with him, and the preliminaries were easily and satisfactorily arranged. We were to hunt one day of eight hours, beginning at eight o'clock in the morning. The wager was five hundred dollars a side [a considerable sum in those days; $1,000 was an average middle-class *annual* income for a family of four], and the man who should kill the greater number of buffaloes was to be declared the winner. Incidentally my title of "Buffalo Bill" was at stake.

The hunt took place twenty miles east of Sheridan [Wyoming]. . . . Buffaloes were plentiful. It had been agreed that we should go into the herd at the same distance and make our runs, each man killing as many animals as possible. A referee followed each of us, horseback, and counted the buffaloes killed by each man. . . .

For the first run we were fortunate in getting good ground. Comstock was mounted on his favorite horse. I rode [my horse] old Brigham. I felt confident that I had the advantage in two things: first, I had the best buffalo horse in the country; second, I was using what was known at the time as a needlegun, a breech-loading Springfield rifle, caliber .50. This was a "Lucretia Borgia" [model]. . . . Comstock's Henry rifle, though it could fire more rapidly than mine, did not, I felt certain, carry powder and lead enough to equal my weapon in execution. [Most buffalo hunters favored big-caliber, single-shot rifles like Cody's; smaller-caliber weapons such as the Henry were considered significantly underpowered. By the end of this period, however, the preferred weapon was the Winchester '73, a smaller-caliber but much more reliable rifle with a much higher rate of fire.]

When the time came to go into the herd, Comstock and I dashed forward, followed by the referees. The animals separated. Comstock took the left bunch, I the right. My great forte in killing buffaloes was to get them circling by riding my horse at the head of the herd and shooting their leaders. Thus the brutes were crowded to the left, so that they were soon going round and round.

This particular morning the animals were very accommodating, I soon had them running in a beautiful circle. I dropped them thick and fast till I had killed thirty-eight, which finished my run.

Comstock began shooting at the rear of the buffaloes he was chasing and kept on a straight line. He succeeded in killing twenty-three, but they were scattered over a distance of three miles. The animals I had shot lay close together. . . .

While we were resting we espied another herd approaching. It was a small drove, but we prepared to make it serve our purpose. The buffaloes were cows and calves, quicker in their movements than the bulls. We charged in among them, and I got eighteen to Comstock's fourteen. . . .

After luncheon we resumed the hunt. Three miles distant we saw another herd. I was so far ahead of my competitor now that I thought I could afford an exhibition of my skill. Leaving my saddle and bridle behind, I rode [bareback], with my competitor, to windward of the buffaloes.

I soon had thirteen down, the last one of which I had driven close to the wagons, where the ladies were watching the contest. It frightened some of the tender creatures to see a buffalo coming at full speed directly toward them, but I dropped him in his tracks before he got within fifty yards of the wagon. This finished my run with a score of sixty-nine buffaloes for the day. Comstock had killed forty-six.

It was now late in the afternoon. Comstock and his backers gave up the idea of beating me. The referee declared me the winner of the match, and the champion buffalo hunter of the Plains.

READING 12

The Battle of Mussel Slough

The expansion of the railroad spurred western settlement but also significantly muddied the waters of land and homestead rights. The huge federal land grants to the railroad corporations opened a corridor for railroad rights-of-way and set the price of land sales to potential settlers. The conflict between corporate control of these land grants and what the historian Richard Maxwell Brown has called "the homestead ethic" led to violence and tragedy in the Mussel Slough incident of May 11, 1880.

The agricultural district of Mussel Slough, in the southern section of California's Central Valley, was part of a land grant controlled by the powerful Southern Pacific Railroad. Early in the 1870s the company's owners—Leland Stanford, Charles Crocker, Mark Hopkins, and Collis P. Huntington—had published pamphlets inviting settlement on their grant. The railroad had not yet secured full legal title to the lands, but the Southern Pacific assured the settlers that once it did have title, the occupants would be allowed to purchase the lands. Years later, in 1878, when the railroad finally did achieve legal ownership, it announced that the lands were now available for sale to anyone, not just to the settlers already there, as had been promised. The settlers felt they had been duped, but federal courts upheld the railroad's actions on the grounds that no legally binding contract existed. When the settlers attempted to negotiate a compromise, Southern Pacific refused. A confrontation seemed imminent.

When two individuals, Walter Crow and Mills Hart, purchased from the railroad lands that were already occupied, the settlers claimed that these buyers were agents of the Southern Pacific. From all accounts, this claim seems to have been erroneous, but anger can often overtake reason in heated situations. On May 11, 1880, United States Marshal Alonzo Poole—acting under federal court order—rode out with Crow and Hart (and W. H. Clark, a representative of the railroad) to take possession of the acreage the two had purchased and to evict the occupants. Near the town of Hanford, in the Mussel Slough district, a group of twenty or more settlers confronted Poole, Crow, and Hart. Angry words flew, and then gunfire erupted. When the smoke cleared, five of the settlers were dead, and Crow and Hart had also been killed (Marshal Poole had not participated in the gunfight). Later, five surviving settlers were convicted of resisting federal legal authority and sentenced to jail terms.

The Mussel Slough tragedy represented the single largest death toll of any civilian gunfight in the history of the American West—even the fabled gunfight at the O.K. Corral—and reinforced public resentment against the power, influence, and perceived political and moral corruption of the railroad corporations. Overlooking the illegality of the settlers' actions, public opinion strongly viewed their resistance as a morally justifiable response to the cruel and heartless Southern Pacific and the event as a clear example of a bloodthirsty corporation's willingness to murder peaceful, law-abiding farmers to advance its aims.

Mussel Slough received national and international attention. In London, observer Karl Marx cited the incident as evidence of the insidious influence of entrepreneurial capitalism. Five novels used the tragedy as a focal point, the most famous being The Octopus *by Frank Norris (reading 12B).*

READING 12A

"THE MOST INTENSE FEELING," *SAN FRANCISCO CHRONICLE,* 1880

On May 13, 1880, the San Francisco Chronicle *published one of the first accounts of the Mussel Slough incident.*

STORY OF THE FIGHT. . . .

For many weeks a suppressed apprehension has prevailed in Tulare county that we were on the eve of an outbreak between the settlers and the railroad. This fear has, with good reason, increased as the time drew near when, in the event of the settlers failing to comply with certain conditions, they would be dispossessed of their homes by the railroad company. Whispers that the United States Marshal was to be sent to take possession of and hold the disputed lands for the railroad company only made the crisis more certain in the opinion of those who knew the stern determination and purposes of the settlers. . . . On Monday it was reported that several parties, supposed either to be in league with the railroad company or opposed to the interests of the settlers, had received anonymous warning to leave the country. Among those said to have been thus forewarned were M. D. Hart and Walter J. Crow, who were looked upon as tools of the railroad company, and who, in consideration of their services in dispossessing the settlers, and thereby providing a test case, were to receive their land. . . . United States Marshal Poole and W. H. Clark, grader of railroad lands in the Mussel Slough region, arrived at Hanford Monday night. . . . Early Tuesday morning they drove out of town in a buggy. The settlers' meeting had called together

A LARGE CONCOURSE OF PEOPLE

From all parts of the Mussel Slough country, who began to arrive early in the morning, and when the news went around that the United States Marshal and W. H. Clark had arrived the night before, and had early that morning ridden away in company with Hart and Crow, many settlers, gathered for the meeting, were prepared for prompt and united action in whatever course they might dictate or pursue in the matter. . . . [Poole and Clark dispossessed farmers Braden, Brewer, and Storer.] Meantime, various squads of mounted men, as the presence and purposes of the Marshal became known, had followed the officer with a party from Hanford. Some of these men were armed, but many had no weapons. . . . When about half a mile from the place [Brewer's farm], they saw the two buggies . . . [containing Poole, Clark, Hart, and Crow] passing through the yard near the house and into the field, some 200 yards west of the residence, where they stopped. The settlers passed through the fence . . . and rode directly across toward the buggies. When the advance squad of some fifteen settlers came up within fifty or one hundred yards of the Marshal, he alighted, advanced, meeting them half way, and saluted them in a gentlemanly manner, saying that in his official capacity as United States Marshal, he was compelled to perform his duties in the matter, although against his desire.

A FORMAL DEMAND TO SURRENDER

Was then made to the Marshal by the leader. This he did, but refused to give up his pistol, and, with the understanding that he should not use it, was allowed to retain his revolver. . . . While the party was still going on, one man rode alongside Hartt and Crow, and commenced conversation with the latter. Crow and Hartt seemed to be watching the actions of the party around the Marshal. Once Hartt grasped his gun, when Crow said: "Don't shoot yet; it is not time." Whether Hartt and Crow were at this time ordered to surrender, according to one account, or whether a settler drew his revolver on the latter, as has been reported, we are not able to state, but they both at the same time leaped from the wagon, grasping their weapons, and Crow discharged the contents of his shotgun into the breast and face of Harris, who fell to the ground dead. The fight now commenced in earnest, and shot followed shot. Henderson, who was guarding the Marshal, ran forward, firing as he went . . . but before he was killed by Crow one shot from his pistol wounded Hartt in the abdomen. McGregor, who with Henderson had been guarding the Marshal, and who was unarmed, was shot twice in the breast, and crying "My God!" started off for the pool of water near, . . . and was shot again in the back.

KNUTSON FELL, RIDDLED WITH BUCKSHOT,

Grasping his loaded revolver, before he had fired a shot. Dan Kelly, with three shots in his back, fell from his horse near the barn. Crow, who had now run some distance from the wagon, sung out to Hartt: " —— —— it, bring the rifle." Hartt ran toward him with it, and Crow commenced reloading, when J. M. Patterson said: "This thing has gone far enough, and better stop." T. J. McQuiddy now rode up with thirty or forty settlers and handed Marshal Poole a written demand that he desist from dispossessing the settlers, and that he leave the county forthwith, which he consented to do, and with Clark was sent away under guard of four men. During this parley and the excitement Crow ran along the fence, . . . in a stooping position, holding his rifle. He was heard to say he was wounded. While the dead and dying were being cared for, bands of armed men scoured the country in quest of Crow, whom it was feared would offer a desperate resistance. . . . [Sixty minutes later, news of the incident reached Hanford. A newspaper reporter hurried to the scene, and arrived forty minutes later. There . . .]

A SICKENING SPECTACLE

Met his gaze. Stretched on the porch of Brewer's house were the bloody and lifeless remains of . . . [settlers Harris, Knutson, and Henderson] . . . while the fourth form was that of D. M. Hartt, writhing and groaning from a mortal wound in the abdomen. Inside the house was a no less ghastly spectacle. On one bed was Dan Kelly, terribly wounded with three holes in his back, and, on another couch, Archibald McGregor lay groaning with three wounds through his body. The wives, children and friends soon began to arrive, and their piercing shrieks and heartrending cries filled the air. Surgical skill, in the persons of Drs. Lovelace and Davidson, soon came to hand, and all that possibly could be was done to relieve the sufferers. It was the opinion of the surgeons that the wounds would all prove fatal, except those of Haymaker, who is slightly wounded in the head by glancing buck-shot. On his return the reporter met a squad of men, who informed him of the discovery of the body of Crow . . . lying on his face, . . . with his loaded double-barrel shotgun by his side. His face presented a sickening spectacle. The blood was oozing from the nostrils and mouth, and the black discoloration of his countenance hardly presented the semblance of a human fac[e]. Crow seems to have done

THE PRINCIPAL SHOOTING.

It is doubtful whether Hartt fired a shot, and it is further questioned whether Crow was wounded at all in the conflict. Subsequent developments seem to indicate that he pretended to have been badly wounded only to facilitate his escape. He left the scene and struck out through the fields for his home, about two miles distant. When he had gone about one and a half miles, followed by an armed man, he is said to have raised up the gun to fire at George Hackett, who was passing a few rods from where he stood. He did not fire, but a musket report from a near thicket was heard and he pitched headlong to the ground, where he apparently died without a struggle. Great excitement prevails. At the time of the arrival of the first messenger Hanford was full of people, and the excitement knew no bounds. Men hurried to and fro, women cried, while everywhere were evidences of THE MOST INTENSE FEELING.

READING 12B

"I CAN SEE THE OUTCOME. THE RAILROAD
WILL PREVAIL," FRANK NORRIS, 1901

> *In 1901 Frank Norris wrote a fictionalized account of the Mussel Slough events in his novel* The Octopus. *The title, adopting a common sobriquet for the Southern Pacific Railroad, suggested the influence in California's political, economic, and social affairs of the corporate "octopus" with tentacles reaching into every crucial aspect of California's present and future.*

In this selection the character Presley, protégé of the proprietor of the fictional rancho that represents the Mussel Slough district, reacts to the tragic and fatal events. The "S. Behrman" he refers to is a character representing the "Pacific and Southwestern Railroad," the fictional equivalent of the Southern Pacific. The passage is a powerful expression of emotions that the actual settler-participants at Mussel Slough must have felt.

Dabney dead, Hooven dead, Harran dead, Annixter dead, Broderson dead, Osterman dying, S. Behrman alive, successful; the Railroad in possession of Quien Sabe. I saw them shot. Not twelve hours since I stood there at the irrigating ditch. Ah, that terrible moment of horror and confusion! powder smoke—flashing pistol barrels—blood stains—rearing horses—men staggering to their death—Christian in a horrible posture, one rigid leg high in the air across his saddle—Broderson falling sideways into the ditch—Osterman laying himself down, his head in his arms, as if tired, tired out. These things, I have seen them. The picture of this day's work is henceforth part of my mind, part of me. They have done it, S. Behrman and the owners of the Railroad have done it, while all the world looked on, while the people of these United States looked on. Oh, come now and try your theories upon us, us of the ranchos, us who have suffered, us who *know*. Oh, talk to *us* now of the "rights of Capital," talk to *us* of the Trust, talk to us of the "equilibrium between the classes." Try your ingenious ideas upon us. *We know.* I cannot tell whether or not your theories are excellent. I do not know if your ideas are plausible. I do not know how practical is your scheme of society. I do not know if the Railroad has a right to our lands, but I *do* know that Harran is dead, that Annixter is dead, that Broderson is dead, that Hooven is dead, that Osterman is dying, and that S. Behrman is alive, successful, triumphant; that he has ridden into possession of a principality over the dead bodies of five men shot down by his hired associates.

I can see the outcome. The Railroad will prevail. The Trust will overpower us. Here in this corner of a great nation, here, on the edge of the continent, here, in this valley of the West, far from the great centres, isolated, remote, lost, the great iron hand crushes life from us, crushes liberty and the pursuit of happiness from us, and our little struggles, our moment's convulsion of death agony causes not one jar in the vast, clashing machinery of the nation's life; a fleck of grit in the wheels, perhaps, a grain of sand in the cogs—the momentary creak of the axle is the mother's wail of bereavement, the wife's cry of anguish—and the great wheel turns, spinning smoothly again, even again, and the tiny impediment of a second, scarce noticed, is forgotten. Make the people believe that the faint tremor in their great engine is a menace to its function? what a folly to think of it. Tell them of the danger and they will laugh at you. Tell them, five years from now, the story of the fight between the League of the San Joaquin and the Railroad and it will not be believed. What! a pitched battle between Farmer and Railroad, a battle that cost the lives of seven men? Impossible, it could not have happened. Your story is fiction—is exaggerated.

Yet it is Lexington—God help us, God enlighten us. God rouse us from our lethargy—it is Lexington; farmers with guns in their hands fighting for Liberty. Is our State of California the only one that has its ancient and hereditary foe? Are there no other Trusts between the oceans than this of the Pacific and Southwestern Railroad? Ask yourselves, you of the Middle West, ask yourselves, you of the North, ask yourselves, you of the East, ask yourselves, you of the South—ask yourselves, every citizen of every State from Maine to Mexico, from the Dakotas to the Carolinas, have you not the monster in your boundaries? If it is not a Trust of transportation, it is only another head of the same Hydra. Is not our death struggle typical? Is it not one of many, is it not symbolical of the great and terrible conflict that is going on everywhere in these United States? Ah, you people, blind, bound, tricked, betrayed, can you not see? Can you not see how the monsters have plundered your treasures and holding them in the grip of their iron claws, dole them out to you only at the price of your blood, at the price of the lives of your wives and your little children?

CHAPTER 6

THE PEOPLE AND THE RESPONSE

Native Americans and the Dominant Culture

AN ONGOING theme in the history of the American West has been the relationship between the native populations and the dominant culture. That relationship has combined respect and brutality, wonderment and hostility, and kindness and cruelty on both sides. The Native American groups—called Indians by the dominant culture and routinely "the People" by many tribes in naming their own population—varied dramatically throughout the West in culture, economic activity, lifestyle, religion, and attitudes toward the dominant culture. As well, the dominant culture varied over time—at some points the Spanish were dominant, or the French or Russians or British—but through much of the nineteenth century the dominant culture was the English-speaking Euro-American. To understand the American West, one must always consider the interactions among these groups.

In this chapter the readings present the viewpoints of the native cultures—primarily with regard to white encroachment on their lands—and the responses of the United States government during the nineteenth century.

THE PEOPLE

READING I

THE NATIONAL COUNCIL OF THE CHEROKEES, 1838

For many in nineteenth-century white communities, Indians presented an obstacle to progress as whites defined it. Removing the Indians from their lands or neutralizing the threat they allegedly posed often became government policy. This was best exemplified in the 1830s when the state of Georgia and the federal government succeeded in nullifying all federal Indian laws and seized the land of the Cherokee nation. Despite the 1832 Supreme Court decision in Worcester v. Georgia, *which stated that Indian nations were sovereign foreign nations, the*

federal government under President Andrew Jackson's leadership systematically
stripped the Cherokees of political and economic sovereignty. In 1838 the
Cherokees and other southeastern Indian groups were forced westward to Indian
Territory (today's Oklahoma) in the event known as "the Trail of Tears." From
the Aquohee District Camp in Tennessee the National Council of the Cherokees
issued a statement in response to the detention and imminent removal of its
people. (For President Jackson's point of view, see reading 16 below.)

Aquohee Camp
August 1, 1838
Whereas, the title of the Cherokee people to their lands, is the most ancient, pure, and absolute known to man; its date is beyond the reach of
human record; its validity confirmed and illustrated by possession and enjoyment antecedent to all pretence of claim by any other portion of the
human race;

And whereas, the free consent of the Cherokee people is indispensable to
a valid transfer of the Cherokee title; and whereas, the said Cherokee people
have neither by themselves, nor their representatives, given such consent; it
follows that the original title and ownership of said lands still vest in the
Cherokee nation unimpaired and absolute:

Resolved, therefore, By the national committee and council, and people of
the Cherokee nation, in general council assembled, That the whole Cherokee territory, as described in the first article of the treaty of 1819, between
the United States and the Cherokee nation, still remains the rightful and
undoubted property of the said Cherokee nation. And that all damages and
losses, direct or incidental, resulting from the enforcement of the alleged
stipulations of the pretended treaty of New Echota [see reading 15], are in
justice and equity chargeable to the account of the United States.

And whereas, the Cherokee people have existed as a distinct national
community, in the possession and exercise of the appropriate and essential
attributes of sovereignty, for a period extending into antiquity beyond the
dates and records and memory of man:

And whereas, these attributes, with the rights and franchises which they
involve, have never been relinquished by the Cherokee people, but are now
in full force and virtue.

And whereas, the natural, political, and moral relations subsisting among
the citizens of the Cherokee nation towards each other, and towards the

body politic, cannot in reason and justice be dissolved by the expulsion of the nation from its own territory by the power of the United States' Government:

Resolved, therefore, By the national committee and council, and people of the Cherokee nation, in general council assembled, That the inherent sovereignty of the Cherokee nation, together with the constitution, laws, and usages of the same, is, and by the authority aforesaid, is hereby declared in full force and virtue, and shall continue so to be, in perpetuity, subject to such modifications as the general welfare may render expedient.

Resolved, further, That the Cherokee people, in consenting to an investigation of their individual claims, and receiving payment upon them, and for their improvements, do not intend that it shall be so construed as yielding or giving their sanction or approval to the pretended treaty [Treaty of New Echota] of 1835: nor as compromitting, in any manner, their just claim against the United States hereafter, for a full and satisfactory indemnification for their country, and for all individual losses and injuries.

And be it further Resolved, That the principal chief be, and he is hereby authorized to select and appoint such persons as he may deem necessary and suitable for the purpose of collecting and registering all individual claims against the United States, with the proofs, and to report to him their proceedings as they progress.

Richard Taylor
    President National Council
Going Snake
    Speaker of Council

Stephen Foreman, Clerk Nat. Committee; Capt. Brown, Richard Foreman, Samuel Christee, Toonowee, William, Kotaquaskee, Katelah, Howestee, Yoh-natsee, Ooyah Kee, Beaver Carrier, Samuel Foreman. Signed by a Committee on behalf of the people.

READING 2
SEATTLE, 1855

In 1855, with the Point Elliott Treaty, Chief Seattle surrendered his lands. Seattle was chief of the Dwamish tribe of the Pacific Northwest in the Puget Sound area, and his lands were located where the present city of Seattle now stands. In the chief's statement to Governor Isaac Stevens at the signing ceremony for the treaty, his sadness and resignation are apparent.

My people are few. They resemble the scattering trees of a storm-swept plain. . . . There was a time when our people covered the land as the waves of a wind-ruffled sea cover its shell-paved floor, but that time long since passed away with the greatness of tribes that are now but a mournful memory. . . .

To us the ashes of our ancestors are sacred and their resting place is hallowed ground. You wander far from the graves of your ancestors and seemingly without regret. Your religion was written on tables of stone by the iron finger of your God so that you could not forget. The Red Man could never comprehend nor remember it. Our religion is the traditions of our ancestors—the dreams of our old men, given them in the solemn hours of night by the Great Spirit; and the visions of our sachems, and is written in the hearts of our people.

Your dead cease to love you and the land of their nativity as soon as they pass the portals of the tomb and wander away beyond the stars. They are soon forgotten and never return. Our dead never forget the beautiful world that gave them being. . . .

When the last Red Man shall have perished, and the memory of my tribe shall have become a myth among the white man, these shores will swarm with the invisible dead of my tribe, and when your children's children think themselves alone in the field, the store, the shop, or in the silence of the pathless woods, they will not be alone. . . . At night when the streets of your cities and villages are silent and you think them deserted, they will throng with the returning hosts that once filled them and still love this beautiful land. The White Man will never be alone.

Let him be just and deal kindly with my people, for the dead are not powerless. Dead—I say? There is no death. Only a change of worlds.

READING 3
MENINOCK, 1915

In 1855 the federal government reached an agreement with the Yakima Indians at Walla Walla, Washington. The treaty provided for the retention of some lands by the Yakimas and ceded the remainder to the U.S. government. When the Supreme Court later rejected the treaty and sided with the Indians, the govern-

ment filed another suit. In testimony for this new case, Chief Meninock of the Yakimas made the following statement. The court decision ruled that the Yakimas should be allowed unlimited fishing rights at their traditional fishing grounds.

God created the Indian country and it was like He spread out a big blanket. He put the Indians on it. They were created here in this country, truly honest, and that was the time this river [most likely the Walla Walla] started to run. Then God created fish in this river and put deer in the mountains and made laws through which has come the increase of fish and game. Then the Creator gave us Indians Life; we walked, and as soon as we saw the game and fish we knew they were made for us. For the women God made roots and berries to gather, and the Indians grew and multiplied as a people.

When we were created we were given our ground to live on and from this time these were our rights. This is all true. We had the fish before the Missionaries came, before the white man came. We were put here by the Creator and these were our rights as far as my memory to my grandfather. This was the food on which we lived. My mother gathered berries; my father fished and killed the game. These words are mine and they are true. My strength is from the fish; my blood is from the fish, from the roots and berries. The fish and game are the essence of my life. I was not brought from a foreign country and did not come here. I was put here by the Creator.

We had no cattle, no hogs, no grain, only berries and roots and game and fish. We never thought that we would be troubled about these things, and I tell you my people, and I believe it, it is not wrong for us to get this food. Whenever the seasons open I raise my heart in thanks to the Creator of His bounty that this food has come.

I want this treaty to show the officers what our fishing rights were. I was at the Council at Walla Walla with my father, who was one of the Chiefs who signed the treaty. I well remember hearing the talk about the [1855] treaty. There were more Indians there at Walla Walla than ever came together at any one place in this country. Besides the women and children, there were two thousand Indian Warriors, and they were there for about one moon, during the same part of the year as now, in May and June.

The Indians and Commissioners were many days talking about making the treaty. One day Governor Stevens read what he had written down and had one of the interpreters explain it to the Indians. After everybody had talked and Pu-Pu-Mox-Mox had talked, Governor Stevens wanted to hear from the head Chief of the Yakimas. He said, "Kamiaken, the great Chief of the Yakimas, has not spoken at all. His people have had no voice here today. He is not afraid to speak—let him speak out."

Something has been said about more and more whites coming into the Indian Country and then the Indians would be driven away from their hunting grounds and fishing places. Then Governor Stevens told the Indians that when the white man came here the rights of the Indians would be protected.

Then Chief Kamiaken said, "I am afraid that the white men are not speaking straight; that their children will not do what is right by our children; that they will not do what you have promised for them."

READING 4
OKUTE, 1911

> One of the most contentious issues in the relationship between Indians and the
> dominant culture was their divergent views of natural resource use. For many
> Euro-Americans nature was an exploitable resource, whereas for many Native
> Americans nature was a mysterious element that should be deeply respected and
> used with care. Here Okute, a Teton Sioux, expresses the Indian view of nature.

All living creatures and all plants derive their life from the sun. If it were not for the sun, there would be darkness and nothing could grow—the earth would be without life. Yet the sun must have the help of the earth. If the sun alone were to act upon animals and plants, the heat would be so great that they would die, but there are clouds that bring rain, and the action of the sun and earth together supply the moisture that is needed for life. The roots of a plant go down, and the deeper they go the more moisture they find. This is according to the laws of nature and is one of the evidences of the wisdom of Wakan tanka [a Teton deity]. Plants are sent by Wakan tanka and come from the ground at his command, the part to be affected by the sun and rain appearing above the ground and the roots pressing downward to find the moisture which is supplied for them. Animals and plants are taught by Wakan tanka what they are to do. Wakan tanka gives them merely the outline. Some make better nests than others. In the same way some animals are satisfied with very rough dwellings, while others make attractive places in which to live. Some animals also take better care of their young than others. The forest is the home of many birds and other animals, and the water is the home of fish and reptiles. All birds, even those of the same species, are not alike, and it is the same with animals and with human beings. The reason Wakan tanka does not make two birds, or animals, or human beings exactly alike is because each is placed here by Wakan tanka to be an independent individuality and to rely on itself. Some animals are made to live in the ground. The stones and the minerals are placed in the ground by Wakan tanka, some stones being more exposed than others. When a medicine man says that he talks with the sacred stones, it is because of all the substance in the ground these are the ones which most often appear in dreams and are able to communicate with men.

From my boyhood I have observed leaves, trees, and grass, and I have never found two alike. They may have a general likeness, but on examination I have found that they differ slightly. Plants are of different families. . . . It is the same with animals. . . . It is the same with human beings; there is some place which is best adapted to each. The seeds of the plants are blown about by the wind until they reach the place where they will grow best—where the action of the sun and the presence of moisture are most favorable to them, and there they take root and grow. All living creatures and all plants are a benefit to something. Certain animals fulfill their purpose by definite acts. The crows, buzzards and flies are somewhat similar in their use, and even the snakes have purpose in being. In the early days the animals probably roamed over a very wide country until they found a proper place. An animal depends a great deal on the natural conditions around it. If the buffalo were here today, I think they would be different from the buffalo of the old days because all the natural conditions have changed. They would not find the same food, nor the same surroundings. We see the change in our ponies. In the old days they could stand great hardship and travel long distance without water. They lived on certain kinds of food and drank pure water. Now our horses require a mixture of food; they have less endurance and must have constant care. It is the same with the Indians; they have less freedom and they fall an easy prey to disease. In the old days they were rugged and healthy, drinking pure water and eating the meat of the buffalo, which had a wide range, not being shut up like cattle of the present day. The water of the Missouri River is not pure, as it used to be, and many creeks are no longer good for us to drink.

A man ought to desire that which is genuine instead of that which is artificial. Long ago there was no such thing as a mixture of earths to make paint. There were only three colors of native earth paint—red, white, and black. These could be obtained only in certain places. When other colors were desired, the Indians mixed the juices of plants, but it was found that these mixed colors faded and it could always be told when the red was genuine—the red made of burned clay.

READING 5

JOSEPH, 1871 AND 1879

Joseph was a chief of the Nez Percé Indians, a tribe located in the Pacific Northwest. In 1863 Joseph was one among chiefs who peacefully resisted a fraudulent land cession treaty negotiated with the U.S. government. When fighting occurred in 1877, Joseph and several hundred Nez Percés undertook a dramatic thousand-mile retreat from the U.S. Army. Their goal was to reach Canada, but they were captured just thirty miles from the Canadian border and exiled to Indian Territory. Joseph was one of the most eloquent advocates for Indian land rights in their native regions. In the first passage here he explains his version of land ownership. In the second, addressing a large gathering of cabinet members and congressional representatives, his appeal is to let some of his people return to their traditional homeland in eastern Oregon (a few were allowed to relocate in Idaho). In both selections the theme is similar: a plea that Native American populations be allowed to live peacefully on their lands.

1871

The Earth was created by the assistance of the sun, and it should be left as it was. . . . The country was made without lines of demarcation, and it is no man's business to divide it. . . . I see the whites all over the country gaining wealth, and see their desire to give us lands which are worthless. . . . The earth and myself are of one mind. The measure of the land and the measure of our bodies are the same. Say to us if you can say it, that you were sent by the Creative Power to talk to us. Perhaps you think the Creator sent you here to dispose of us as you see fit. If I thought you were sent by the Creator I might be induced to think you had a right to dispose of me. Do not misunderstand me, but understand me fully with reference to my affection for the land. I never said the land was mine to do with it as I chose. The one who has the right to dispose of it is the one who has created it. I claim a right to live on my land, and accord you the privilege to live on yours.

January 14, 1879

I have shaken hands with a great many friends, but there are some things I want to know which no one seems able to explain. I cannot understand how the Government sends a man out to fight us, as it did General Miles, and then breaks his word. Such a Government has something wrong about it. . . . I do not understand why nothing is done for my people. I have heard talk and talk, but nothing is done. Good words do not last long until they amount to something. Words do not pay for my dead people. They do not pay for my country, now overrun by white men. They do not protect my father's grave. They do not pay for my horses and cattle.

Good words do not give me back my children. Good words will not make good the promise of your war chief, General Miles. Good words will not give my people good health and stop them from dying. Good words will not get my people a home where they can live in peace and take care of themselves.

I am tired of talk that comes to nothing. It makes my heart sick when I remember all the good words and all the broken promises. There has been too much talking by men who had no right to talk. Too many misinterpretations have been made; too many misunderstandings have come up between the white men about the Indians.

If the white man wants to live in peace with the Indian he can live in peace. There need be no trouble. Treat all men alike. Give them all the same law. Give them all an even chance to live and grow. . . . You might as well expect the rivers to run backward as that any man who was born free should be contented penned up and denied liberty to go where he pleases. If you tie a horse to a stake, do you expect he will grow fat? If you pen an Indian up on a small spot of earth and compel him to stay there, he will not be contented nor will he grow and prosper.

I have asked some of the Great White Chiefs where they get their authority to say to the Indian that he will stay in one place, while he sees white men going where they please. They cannot tell me.

I only ask of the government to be treated as all other men are treated. If I cannot go to my own home, let me have a home in a country where my people will not die so fast. . . .

I know that my race must change. We cannot hold our own with the white men as we are. We only ask an even chance to live as other men live. We ask to be recognized as men. We ask that the same law shall work alike on all men. If an Indian breaks the law, punish him by the law. If a white man breaks the law, punish him also.

Let me be a free man—free to travel, free to stop, free to work, free to trade where I choose, free to choose my own teachers, free to follow the religion of my fathers, free to think and talk and act for myself—and I will obey every law or submit to the penalty.

READING 6

LUTHER STANDING BEAR, 1933

Among the policies adopted by state and federal governments concerning the "Indian problem" was the education of young Indian children in schools operated by whites, where the children were generally instructed that their clothing, culture, and language were backward and uncivilized. The experience was offensive to a significant proportion of the young Indian population. In these excerpts from his autobiography, Land of the Spotted Eagle, *an Oglala Sioux (Lakota) named Luther Standing Bear describes his reaction to his tenure at the Carlisle (Pennsylvania) School, the best known of the Indian schools. His comments offer instructive insight into the Indian view of the cultural changes that such an education forced them to make.*

We did not think of the great open plains, the beautiful rolling hills, and winding streams with tangled growth as "wild." Only to the white man was nature a "wilderness" and only to him was the land "infested" with "wild" animals and "savage" people. To us it was tame. Earth was bountiful and we were surrounded with the blessings of the Great Mystery. Not until the hairy man from the east came and with brutal frenzy heaped injustices upon us and the families we loved was it "wild" for us. When the very animals of the forest began fleeing from his approach, then it was that for us the "Wild West" began. . . .

The clothing of the white man, adopted by the Lakota, had much to do with the physical welfare of the tribe, and at Carlisle School where the change from tribal to white man's clothing was sudden and direct, the effect on the health and comfort of the children was considerable. Our first resentment was in having our hair cut. It has ever been the custom of Lakota men to wear long hair, and old tribal members still wear the hair in this manner. On first hearing the rule, some of the older boys talked of resisting, but realizing the uselessness of doing so, submitted. But for days after being shorn we felt strange and uncomfortable. If the argument that has been advanced is true, that the children needed delousing, then why were not girls as well as boys put through the same process? The fact is that we were to be transformed, and short hair being the mark of gentility with the white man, he put upon us the mark, though he still retained his own custom of keeping the hair-covering on his face.

Our second resentment was against trousers, based upon what we considered the best of hygienic reasons. Our bodies were used to constant bathing in the sun, air, and rain, and the function of the pores of our skin, which were in reality a highly developed breathing apparatus, was at once stopped by trousers of heavy, sweat-absorbing material aided by that worst of all torments—red flannel underwear. For the stiff collars, stiff-front shirts, and derby hats no word of praise is due, and the heavy, squeaky, leather boots were positive tormentors which we endured because we thought that when we wore them we were "dressed up." Many times we have been laughed at for our native way of dressing, but could anything we ever wore compare in utter foolishness to the steel-ribbed corset and the huge bustle which our girls adopted after a few years in school?

Certain small ways and observances sometimes have connection with larger and more profound ideas, and for reasons of this sort the Lakota disliked the pocket handkerchief and found the white man's use of this toilet article very distasteful. The Indian, essentially an outdoor person, had no use for the handkerchief; he was practically immune to colds, and like the animal, not addicted to spitting. The white man, essentially an indoor person, was subject to colds, catarrh, bronchitis, and kindred diseases. He was a cougher and a spitter, and his constant use of tobacco aggravated the habit. With him the handkerchief was a toilet necessity. So it is easy to see why the Indian considered the carrying of a handkerchief an uncleanly habit.

According to the white man, the Indian, choosing to return to his tribal manners and dress, "goes back to the blanket." True, but "going back to the blanket" is the factor that has saved him from, or at least stayed, his final destruction. Had the Indian been as completely subdued in spirit as he was in body he would have perished within the century of his subjection. But it is the unquenchable spirit that has saved him—his clinging to Indian ways, Indian thought, and tradition, that has kept him and is keeping him today. The white man's ways were not his ways and many things that he has tried to adopt have proven disastrous and to his utter shame. Could the Indian have forestalled the flattery and deceit of his European subjector and retained his native truth and honesty; could he have shunned whiskey and disease and remained the paragon of health and strength he was, he might today be a recognized man instead of a hostage on a reservation. But many an Indian has accomplished his own personal salvation by "going back to the blanket." The Indian blanket or buffalo robe, a true American garment, and worn with the significance of language, covered beneath it, in the prototype of the American Indian, one of the bravest attempts ever made by man on this continent to rise to heights of true humanity.

To clothe a man falsely is only to distress his spirit and to make him incongruous and ridiculous, and my entreaty to the American Indian is to retain his tribal dress.

READING 7

BLACK ELK ON FETTERMAN'S MASSACRE, 1932

As quoted in the classic Black Elk Speaks, *the Lakota Sioux chief Black Elk, nearing the end of his life, reflected on the period from 1863 to 1890. Here he comments on the whites' encroachment into Sioux lands and on the dominant culture's treatment of the buffalo. The "Winter of the Hundred Slain" to which Black Elk refers is more commonly known as the "Fetterman Massacre": Captain William J. Fetterman and eighty of his men were killed by a combined force of two thousand Sioux, Cheyenne, and Arapaho warriors on December 21, 1866, near Fort Phil Kearny, Wyoming Territory.*

I can remember that Winter of the Hundred Slain (1866) as a man can remember some bad dream he dreamed when he was little, but I can not tell just how much I heard when I was bigger and how much I understood when I was little. It is like some fearful thing in a fog, for it was a time when everything seemed troubled and afraid.

I had never seen a Wasichu [white man] then, and did not know what one looked like; but everyone was saying that the Wasichus were coming and that they were going to take our country and rub us all out and that we should all have to die fighting.

Once we were happy in our own country and we were seldom hungry, for then the two-leggeds and the four-leggeds lived together like relatives, and there was plenty for them and for us. But the Wasichus came, and they made little islands for us [reservations] and other little islands for the four-leggeds, and always these islands are becoming smaller, for around them surges the gnawing flood of the Wasichu; and it is dirty with lies and greed.

I was ten years old that winter, and that was the first time I ever saw a Wasichu. At first I thought they all looked sick, and I was afraid they might just begin to fight us any time, but I got used to them.

I can remember when the bison were so many that they could not be counted, but more and more Wasichus came to kill them until there were only heaps of bones scattered where they used to be. The Wasichus did not kill them to eat; they killed them for the metal that makes them crazy [gold], and they took only the hides to sell. Sometimes they did not even take the hides, only the tongues; and I have heard that fire-boats [steamships] came down the Missouri River loaded with dried bison tongues. You can see that the men who did this were crazy. Sometimes they did not even take the tongues; they just killed and killed because they liked to do that. When we hunted bison, we killed only what we needed.

READING 8
SITTING BULL, C. 1870

Perhaps the best known Indian of the American West was Sitting Bull, Sioux spiritual leader and victor over Colonel George Custer at the Battle of Little Bighorn in 1876. Following this greatest of Indian victories during the Indian Wars, Sitting Bull and his followers fled to Canada. Promised a pardon, they returned in 1881 to a reservation. Sitting Bull appeared briefly in the 1885 version of Buffalo Bill's Wild West Show. Afterward, Sitting Bull urged the Sioux not to sell their lands and advocated the Ghost Dance religion (see reading 11). In 1890, having refused to try to stop the Ghost Dance, he was killed on the reservation by Sioux police officers while allegedly resisting arrest. Here is Sitting Bull's eloquent testimonial to his people's positive character and the negative attributes of the whites he encountered. It is a sentiment he expressed many times in various forums.

What treaty that the whites have kept has the Red Man broken? Not one. What treaty that the white man ever made with us have they kept? Not one.

When I was a boy the Sioux owned the world; the sun rose and set on their land; they sent ten thousand men to battle. Where are the warriors today? Who slew them? Where are our lands? Who owns them? What white man can say I ever stole his land or a penny of his money? Yet, they say I am a thief. What white woman, however lonely, was ever captive or insulted by me? Yet they say I am a bad Indian. What white man has ever seen me drunk? Who has ever come to me hungry and unfed? Who has ever seen me beat my wives or abuse my children? What law have I broken? Is it wrong for me to love my own? Is it wicked for me because my skin is red? Because I am a Sioux; because I was born where my father lived; because I would die for my people and my country?

READING 9

GERONIMO, C. 1905

Among symbols of Indian resistance, Geronimo is at the top of the list. Geronimo, or Goyathlay in his tribal tongue, was a leader of the Chiricahua Apache tribe for many years. After his reservation was abolished in 1876, he led a long-term and successful guerrilla effort against the U.S. Army. He was repeatedly captured but escaped each time to lead further resistance. When he finally surrendered in 1886, upon assurances that he and his band would be treated fairly, Geronimo and his followers were deported to a Florida prison—in violation of the government's promises. He was later transferred to a reservation at Fort Sill, Oklahoma. It was from this location that Geronimo made a plea, excerpted here, to the president of the United States to let him return to his home territory before he died. His request was denied, and he died at Fort Sill in 1909.

There is a great question between the Apaches and the Government. For twenty years we have been held prisoners of war under a treaty which was made with General Miles, on the part of the United States Government, and myself as the representative of the Apaches. That treaty has not at all times been properly observed by the government, although at the present time it is being more nearly fulfilled on their part than heretofore. In the treaty with General Miles we agreed to go to a place outside of Arizona and learn to live as the white people do. I think that my people are now capable of living in accordance with the laws of the United States, and we would, of course, like to have the liberty to return to that land which is ours by divine right. We are reduced in numbers, and having learned how to cultivate the soil would not require so much ground as was formerly necessary. We do not ask all of the land which the Almighty gave us in the beginning, but that we may have sufficient lands there to cultivate. What we do not need we are glad for the white men to cultivate.

We are now held on Comanche and Kiowa lands, which are not suited to our needs. . . . Our people are decreasing in numbers here, and will continue to decrease unless they are allowed to return to their native land. . . .

There is no climate or soil which, to my mind, is equal to that of Arizona. We could have plenty of good cultivating land, plenty of grass, plenty of timber and plenty of minerals in that land which the Almighty created for the Apaches. It is my land, my home, my father's land, to which I now ask to be allowed to return. I want to spend my last days there, and be buried among those mountains. If this could be I might die in peace, feeling that my people, placed in their native homes, would increase in numbers, rather than diminish as at present, and that our name would not become extinct.

I know that if my people were placed in that mountainous region lying around the headwaters of the Gila River [New Mexico] they would live in peace and act according to the will of the President. They would be prosperous and happy in tilling the soil and learning the civilization of the white men, whom they now respect. Could I but see this accomplished, I think I could forget all the wrongs that I have ever received, and die a contented and happy old man. But we can do nothing in this matter ourselves—we must wait until those in authority choose to act. If this cannot be done during my lifetime—if I must die in bondage—I hope that the remnant of the Apache tribe may, when I am gone, be granted the one privilege which they request—to return to Arizona.

READING 10

TEN BEARS AND QUANAH PARKER, 1867 AND 1875

The struggle for control of the Great Plains was not only a military one but often an internal conflict within the Native American populations over the best strategic path for the Indian nations to take. The two viewpoints presented here exemplify this divergence.

In 1867 the federal government formed a peace commission to negotiate treaties with tribes successfully resisting white encroachment into the Great Plains. The

*resulting Medicine Lodge Treaty of 1867 granted the Sioux a reservation in the
northern plains, and the Fort Laramie Treaty of 1868 granted a combined
reservation in the Indian Territory to the Cheyennes and Arapahos, with
additional reservation lands for the Comanches, Kiowas, and Kiowa-Apaches.*

*Among the Comanches there was obvious disagreement on how to proceed. Ten
Bears, an older Comanche who had visited Washington, encouraged an accommo-
dationist approach in the hope of engendering a better relationship with the
government and a brighter, more peaceful future. He urged the tribal leaders to
sign any reasonable settlement, provided that it recognized native territorial rights
and dignity. In contrast, the young subchief of the Quohadas (and future chief
of the Comanches), Quanah Parker, distrusted the government and refused
to negotiate or have any dealings whatsoever with the Congressional Peace
Commission—though he did lobby among tribal representatives, attempting to
persuade them to his viewpoint.*

Here is the October 10, 1867, speech of Ten Bears to the commission.

My heart is filled with joy, when I see you here, as the brooks fill with water,
when the snows melt in the spring, and I feel glad, as the ponies do when the
fresh grass starts in the beginning of the year. I heard of your coming, when
I was many sleeps away, and I made but few camps before I met you. I knew
that you had come to do good to me and to my people. I looked for the
benefits, which would last forever, and so my face shines with joy, as I look
upon you. My people have never first drawn a bow or fired a gun against the
whites. There has been trouble on the line between us, and my young men
have danced the war dance. But it has not been begun by us.

It was you who sent out the first soldier, and it was we who sent out the
second. Two years ago, I came up upon this road, following the buffalo, that
my wives and children might have their cheeks plump, and their bodies
warm. But the soldiers fired on us, and since that time there has been a
noise, like that of a thunderstorm, and we have not known which way to
go. . . . Nor have we been made to cry once alone. The blue-dressed soldiers
and the Utes came from out of the night, when it was dark and still, and for
campfires, they lit our lodges. Instead of hunting game, they killed my braves
and the warriors of the tribe cut short their hair for the dead. So it was in
Texas. They made sorrow come into our camps, and we went out like the
buffalo bulls, when the cows are attacked. When we found them we killed
them, and their scalps hang in our lodges.

The Comanches are not weak and blind, like the pups of a dog when seven sleeps old. They are strong and farsighted, like grown horses. We took their road and we went on it. The white women cried, and our women laughed. But there are things which you have said to me which I did not like. They were not sweet like sugar, but bitter like gourds. You said that you wanted to put us upon a reservation, to build us houses and to make us Medicine lodges. I do not want them.

I was born upon the prairie, where the wind blew free, and there was nothing to break the light of the sun. I was born where there were no enclosures, and where everything drew a free breath. I want to die there, and not within walls. I know every stream and every wood between the Rio Grande and the Arkansas. I have hunted and lived over the country. I lived like my fathers before me, and like them, I lived happily.

When I was at Washington, the Great Father told me that all the Comanche land was ours, and that no one should hinder us living upon it. So why do you ask us to leave the rivers, and the sun, and the wind, and live in houses? Do not ask us to give up the buffalo for the sheep. The young men have heard talk of this, and it has made them sad and angry. Do not speak of it more. I love to carry out the talk I get from the Great Father. When I get goods and presents, I and my people feel glad, since it shows that he holds us in his eye. If the Texans had kept out of my country, there might have been peace. But that which you now say we must live on is too small.

The Texans have taken away the places where the grass grew the thickest and the timber was the best. Had we kept that, we might have done the thing you ask. But it is too late. The white man has the country which we loved and we only wish to wander on the prairie until we die. Any good thing you say to me shall not be forgotten. I shall carry it as near to my heart as my children, and it shall be as often on my tongue as the name of the Great Spirit. I want no blood upon my land to stain the grass. I want it all clear and pure, and I wish it so, that all who go through among my people may find peace when they come in, and leave it when they go out.

Quanah Parker, about twenty-two years old in 1867, disagreed that the "Great Father . . . holds us in his eye," as Ten Bears stated. He had reason to be wary. Quanah Parker was of mixed blood. His white mother, Cynthia Parker, had been captured as a nine-year-old by the Caddo tribe and then sold to the Comanches. As a teenager she became the wife of a Nocona Comanche chief,

Peta Nocona, and Quanah was one of their three children. Cynthia Parker was recaptured in 1860 by white soldiers and, though always hoping to return to the Comanches, died four years later. Also in 1860, Peta Nocona died as the result of an infected wound incurred in battle with the whites, and one of Quanah's brothers died in the same period from a disease carried by the white population.

Following the treaty signing in 1867, Quanah Parker resisted placement on the reservation. He and other Indian militants staged raids at Forts Richardson, Belknap, Bliss, Stockton, and Griffin. In 1871–72 he fought pitched battles against Colonel Ranald Mackenzie in Texas at Rock Station. In 1872 the army seemingly gained the upper hand, capturing about a thousand horses and much ammunition, burning tepees and possessions. But Quanah Parker and other militants were still at large. In the Red River War of 1874–75 (also called the Buffalo War, because of the government policy of slaughtering buffalo), Parker led a party of seven hundred warriors from four different tribes. On June 26, 1874, they attacked twenty-eight buffalo hunters at Adobe Walls, Texas (the site of an 1864 battle between Kit Carson and Comanche and Kiowa warriors), but the hunters, with adequate cover and high-powered rifles, inflicted heavy casualties on the war party, leaving fifteen dead.

The frustrated Indians next began a campaign of violence against white settlement, and the U.S. Army intensified its response, sending waves of troops from Kansas, Texas, and New Mexico to converge on the center of Indian resistance in the Texas Panhandle. They kept the native war party unsettled, and on September 28, 1874, General Mackenzie struck a decisive blow at Palo Duro Canyon, an Indian stronghold. Only three warriors were killed, but the army managed to capture or destroy an estimated 1,500 horses and burn much property. By this time, fourteen heated battles had occurred between the war parties and the U.S. Army. In October the warriors and their families began to surrender to federal authority. On June 2, 1875, the last band to surrender, under the leadership of Quanah Parker, was led into the reservation at Fort Sill. Until then, unlike many of the other militant war chiefs, he had never signed any treaty or agreement with the federal government.

In an 1875 interview, Quanah Parker reflected on this campaign:

I came into Fort Sill, no ride me in like horse or lead me by halter like cow. Me had big war; I fought General Mackenzie. He brave man, good soldier, but uses two thousand men; many wagons, horses, and mules. Me, I only had 450 braves, no supply train, ammunition, and guns like him. I used this knife. Me see eight miles perhaps, lots of soldiers coming. I say, Hold on, no go over there. Maybe we go at night, maybe stampede troops' horses first. I stand by my men around in circle. Me tell them to holler, shoot and run. I gather 350 horses in one night. They find my trail the next morning. I ready to fight, my men hide behind hill, shoot and run. Mackenzie no catch me.

Quanah Parker never abandoned his native identity, but, adapting to his tribe's situation on the reservation, he studied aspects of land leasing, law, and rights-of-way in order to improve the treatment and future of the Comanches. He also became a leader in the pan-Indian religion that centered on a peyote ritual and came to be known as the Native American Church. In 1905, Quanah Parker attended the inauguration of President Theodore Roosevelt. He died in 1911 in Cache, Oklahoma. In recognition of his efforts, the Comanches decreed that from that time onward no one else could use the title "Chief."

READING 11

THE GHOST DANCE VISION OF WOVOKA, 1890

In 1890 a Paiute shaman named Wovoka had a vision that he shared with many tribes throughout the West. In his dream he saw that the Native Americans must participate in a ritual "Ghost Dance," which would bring all Indian ancestors back to life and restore the abundance of buffalo and game that had been lost by the encroachment of the dominant culture. Since its adherents believed it would also end white westward expansion, the dance was considered a threat to frontier security by the United States government, which responded with the military action that led to the Wounded Knee Massacre in December 1890. Wovoka's vision was a catalyst for both Indian and soldier. For the soldier, it was a military motivation—for the Native American, it was the act of a desperate people.

All Indians must dance, everywhere, keep on dancing. Pretty soon in next spring Great Spirit come. He bring back all game of every kind. The game be thick everywhere. All dead Indians come back and live again. They all be strong just like young men, be young again. Old blind Indian see again and get young and have fine time. When Great Spirit comes this way, then all Indians go to mountains, high up away from whites. Whites can't hurt Indians then. Then while Indians way up high, big flood comes like water and all white people die, get drowned. After that, water go away and then nobody but Indians everywhere and game all kinds thick. Then medicine man tell Indians to send word to all Indians to keep up dancing and the good time will come. Indians who don't dance, who don't believe in this word, will grow little, just about a foot high, and stay that way. Some of them will be turned into wood and be burned in fire.

READING 12

BLACK ELK AND WOUNDED KNEE, 1932

From the early 1860s through 1890 the longest continuous period of warfare in American history raged across the American West. Although it comprised separate and distinct conflicts, they are known collectively as the Indian Wars. Considered the final confrontation of these wars was the so-called Battle of Wounded Knee in December 1890. Far from a battle, it was a massacre of 153 Sioux men, women, and children in response to the fear of the Ghost Dance religion on the Pine Ridge Reservation. In his memoir, Black Elk recounts his experience of the event that marked the end of armed resistance to government encroachment on Indian lands.

That evening before it happened, I went in to Pine Ridge and heard these things, and while I was there, soldiers started for where the Big Foots [a band of Lakota Sioux] were. . . . That night I could hardly sleep at all. I walked around most of the night.

In the morning I went out after my horses, and while I was out I heard shooting off toward the east, and I knew from the sound that it must be wagon-guns (cannon) going off. The sounds went right through my body, and I felt something terrible would happen. . . .

I saddled up my buckskin . . . I painted my face all red, and in my hair I put one eagle feather for the One Above.

It did not take me long to get ready, for I could still hear the shooting over there.

I started out alone on the old road that ran across the hills to Wounded Knee. I had no gun. . . . I had gone only a little way when a band of young men came galloping after me. . . . I asked what they were going to do, and they said they were just coming to see where the shooting was. Then others were coming up, and some older men.

We rode fast, and there were about twenty of us now. The shooting was getting louder. A horseback from over there came galloping very fast toward us, and he said: "Hey-hey-hey! They have murdered them!" Then he whipped his horse and rode away faster toward Pine Ridge.

In a little while we had come to the top of the ridge where, looking to the east you can see . . . where the terrible thing started. Just south . . . a deep dry gulch runs about east and west, very crooked, and it rises westward to nearly the top of the ridge where we were. . . . We stopped on the ridge not far from the head of the dry gulch. Wagon-guns were still going off over there on the little hill, and they were going off again where they hit along the gulch. There was much shooting down yonder, and there were many cries, and we could see cavalrymen scattered over the hills ahead of us. Cavalrymen were riding along the gulch and shooting into it, where the women and children were running away and trying to hide in the gullies and the stunted pines.

A little way ahead of us, just below the head of the dry gulch, there were some women and children who were huddled under a clay bank, and some cavalrymen were there pointing guns at them.

We stopped back behind the ridge, and I said to the others: "Take courage. These are our relatives. We will try to get them back." . . .

Then I rode over the ridge and the others after me, and we were crying: "Take courage! It is the time to fight!" The soldiers who were guarding our relatives shot at us and then ran away fast, and some more cavalrymen on the other side of the gulch did too. We got our relatives and sent them across the ridge to the northwest where they would be safe.

I had no gun, and when we were charging, . . . the bullets did not hit us at all. . . .

The soldiers had run eastward over the hills where there were some more soldiers, and they were off their horses and lying down. I told the others to stay back, and I charged upon them. . . . They all shot at me, and I could hear the bullets all around me, but I ran my horse right close to them, and then swung around. Some soldiers across the gulch began shooting at me too, but I got back to the others and was not hurt at all.

By now other Lakotas, who had heard the shooting, were coming up from Pine Ridge, and we all charged on the soldiers. They all charged eastward toward where the trouble began. We followed down along the dry gulch, and what we saw was terrible. Dead and wounded women and children and little babies were scattered all along there where they had been trying to run away. The soldiers had followed along the gulch, as they ran, and murdered them in there. Sometimes they were in heaps because they had huddled together, and some were scattered all along. Sometimes bunches of them had been killed and torn to pieces where the wagon-guns hit them. I saw a little baby trying to suck its mother, but she was bloody and dead. . . .

When we drove the soldiers back, they dug themselves in, and we were not enough people to drive them out from there. In the evening they marched off up Wounded Knee Creek, and then we saw all that they had done there.

Men and women and children were heaped and scattered all over the flat at the bottom of the little hill where the soldiers had their wagon-guns, and westward up the dry gulch all the way to the high ridge, the dead women and children were scattered.

When I saw this I wished that I had died too, but I was not sorry for the women and children. It was better for them to be happy in the other world, and I wanted to be there too. But before I went there I wanted to have revenge. I thought there might be a day, and we should have revenge. . . .

It was a good winter day when all this happened. The sun was shining. But after the soldiers marched away from their dirty work, a heavy snow began to fall. The wind came up in the night. There was a big blizzard, and it grew very cold. The snow drifted deep in the crooked gulch, and it was one long grave of butchered women and children and babies, who had never done any harm and were only trying to run away.

READING 13

RESPONSE TO THE DAWES COMMISSION, CHOCTAW
AND CHICKASAW NATION, C. 1895

In the 1890s the Dawes Commission was established by the U.S. government to investigate conditions among the Choctaw and Chickasaw people in Indian Territory (now Oklahoma). The commission recommended that the tribal governments be abolished, tribal land redistributed, a territorial government established, and the Indian people made citizens of the United States—all provisions largely in line with the intent of the Dawes Severalty Act of 1887 (see reading 20). The reasons given ranged from the assertion that the tribal governments afforded no protection for basic human life to the claim that white children being raised on the Indian lands were receiving inferior education. The

Indians responded in a letter addressed to the president of the United States and the Congress by delegates of the Choctaw and Chickasaw Nation in Indian Territory.

We desire to recall a little history of our people. The Choctaw and Chickasaw people have never cost the United States a cent for support. They have always and are now self-sustaining. It will be admitted that but little over a half a century ago the Choctaws and Chickasaws were happily located east of the Mississippi River. Their possessions were large and rich and valuable. The whites began to crowd around and among us in the east, as they are now in the west. The Government of the United States urged us to relinquish our valuable possessions there to make homes for their own people and to accept new reservations west of the great river Mississippi, assuring us that there we would be secure from the invasion of the white man. Upon condition that the Government would protect us from such renewed invasion and would give us the lands in fee and convey them to us by patent, and would, by solemn treaty guarantee that no Territorial or State Government should ever be extended over us without consent, and as it was to yield up and surrender our old homes, we consented, and with heavy hearts we turned our backs upon the graves of our fathers and took up the dismal march for our new western home, in a wilderness west of the Mississippi River. After long and tedious marches, after suffering great exposure and much loss of life, we reached the new reservation, with but one consolation to revive our drooping spirits, which was that we were never again to be molested. There, in the jungle and wilds, with nothing but wild animals and beasts for neighbors, we went to work in our crude way to build homes and Governments suited to our people.

In 1855, at the request of the United States we leased and sold the entire west part of our reservation amounting to over 12 million acres, for the purpose of homes for the white man and of locating thereon other friendly Indians. Again in 1866, at the urgent request of the Government we gave up all that part leased for the occupancy of friendly Indians, and ceded it absolutely for the same purpose. Again, in 1890 and 1891, we relinquished . . . 3 million acres . . . to be occupied by the whites. Now in less than five years we are asked to surrender completely our tribal governments and to accept a Territorial Government in lieu thereof; to allot our lands in severalty, and to become citizens of the United States and what is worse, an effort is being made to force us to do so against our consent. Such a radical change would, in our judgement, in a few years annihilate the Indian. . . .

We ask every lover of justice, is it right that a great and powerful government should, year by year, continue to demand cessions of land from weaker and dependent people, under the plea of securing homes for the homeless. While the great government of the United States, our guardian, is year by year admitting foreign paupers into the Union, at the rate of 250,000 per annum, must we sacrifice our homes and children for this pauper element?

We have lived with our people all our lives and believe that we know more about them than any Commission, however good and intelligent, could know from a few visits . . . on the railroads and towns, where but a few Indians are to be seen and where but few live. . . . They [the white people] care nothing for the fate of the Indian, so that their own greed can be gratified.

<hr>

THE RESPONSE

READING 14
"THESE HAPPY PEOPLE," GEORGE CATLIN, 1841

For most of the nineteenth century the United States government viewed the Native American population as an obstacle to progress, a barrier to the fulfillment of Manifest Destiny. Some white Americans, particularly on the Atlantic seaboard, saw the Indian as a "noble savage" whose culture should be maintained and protected at least as a curiosity, but most regarded the Native American simply as a "savage savage." A few voices of protest, however, called for tolerance and forbearance, among them that of Helen Hunt Jackson (see chapter 8). An even earlier voice was that of George Catlin, whose Letters and Notes on the Manners, Customs, and Conditions of the North American Indians—*a compilation of drawings and writings based on his eight years of living with and observing the culture of the Native American West—is among the best descriptions of Indian culture prior to the greatest influx of the dominant culture, beginning in the 1840s. Although Catlin's depiction of the Indian culture as a human and admirable one that should not be subject to continued harassment is clearly a minority viewpoint, it does demonstrate that not all white Americans agreed with the government's policies toward the Native American population.*

In traversing the immense regions of the *classic* West, the mind of a philanthropist is filled to the brim with feelings of admiration; but to reach this country, one is obliged to descend from the light and glow of civilized atmosphere, through the different grades of civilization, which gradually sink to the most deplorable condition along the extreme frontier, thence through the most pitiable misery and wretchedness of savage degradation; where the genius of natural liberty and independence have been blasted and destroyed by the contaminating vices and dissipations introduced by the immoral part of *civilized* society. Through this dark and sunken vale of wretchedness one hurries, as through a pestilence, until he gradually rises again into the proud and chivalrous pale of savage society, in its state of original nature, beyond the reach of civilized contamination; here he finds much to fix his enthusiasm upon, and much to admire. Even here, the predominant passions of the savage breast, of ferocity and cruelty, are often found; yet *restrained,* and frequently *subdued,* by the noblest traits of honour and magnanimity,—a race of men who live and enjoy life and its luxuries, and practice its virtues, very far beyond the usual estimation of the world, who are apt to judge the savage and his virtues from the poor, degraded, and humbled specimens which alone can be seen along our frontiers. From the first settlements of our Atlantic coast to the present day, the bane of this *blasting frontier* has regularly crowded upon them, from the northern to the southern extremities of our country; and, like the fire in a prairie, which destroys everything where it passes, it has blasted and sunk them, all but their names, into oblivion, wherever it has travelled. It is to this tainted class alone that the epithet of "poor, drunken, and naked savage," can be, with propriety, applied; for all those numerous tribes which I have visited, and are yet uncorrupted by the vices of civilized acquaintance, are well clad, in many instances cleanly, and in the full enjoyment of life and its luxuries. It is for the character and preservation of these noble fellows that I am an enthusiast; and it is for these uncontaminated people that I would be willing to devote the energies of my life. It is a sad and melancholy truth to contemplate, that all the numerous tribes who inhabited our vast Atlantic States *have not* "fled to the West";—that they are not to be found here—that they have been blasted by the fire which passed over them—have sunk into their graves, and everything but their names travelled into oblivion. . . .

It is for these inoffensive and unoffending people, yet unvisited by the vices of civilized society, that I would proclaim to the world, that it is time, for the honour of our country—for the honour of every citizen of the republic—and for the sake of humanity, that our government should raise her strong arm to save the remainder of them from the pestilence which is rapidly advancing upon them. We have gotten from them territory enough, and the country which they now inhabit is most of it too barren of timber for the use of civilized man; it affords them, however, the means and luxuries of savage life; and it is to be hoped that our government will not acquiesce in the continued wilful destruction of these happy people.

READING 15

INDIAN REMOVAL, CHARLES EATON HAYNES, 1836

The United States government's response to Native Americans generally fell into three categories: accommodation, removal, or elimination. Through most of the nineteenth century the latter two were predominant. The removal aspect was never more clearly defined than with the Cherokee nation in the 1830s. In 1835 a small faction, less than one sixteenth of the tribe, signed the Treaty of New Echota. Ratified by the U.S. Congress, the treaty resulted in the removal of the Cherokees (and others) across the Mississippi River to Indian Territory. In this 1836 speech Congressman Charles Eaton Haynes of Georgia, whose district encompassed much of the Cherokee nation's territory, reviews previous Indian policy and enthusiastically supports the removal policy.

When the administration [of President Andrew Jackson] came into power, seven years ago, it found a partial system of Indian colonization west of the Mississippi in operation; partial, not in withholding its benefits from any tribe which might desire to enjoy them, but only inasmuch as it embraced but a portion of the tribes then residing east of the Mississippi. The principal of these were a portion of the Creeks and Cherokees, to which have been since added the Choctaws and Chickasaws, with numerous smaller bands, together with a treaty in 1832 contemplating the removal of the remaining and greater portion of the Creeks; and, lately, the treaty with the Cherokees, to provide for the fulfillment of which the present appropriation is asked at our hands. Within the last six or seven years, the policy of removing and colonizing the Indians in the States east of the Mississippi, to the westward of that river, in a region remote from the habitation of the white man, has been among the topics of universal and bitter discussion from one end of the Union to the other. Nor on any other subject has the course of General

Jackson's administration been more violently or unjustly assailed. And here I take leave to say, that so far from Indian hostilities having been provoked, either by the negligence or injustice of that administration, they may, with much greater justice, be ascribed to the political philanthropy, so loudly and pharisaically displayed by its political opponents; and I will further say, that should war arise on the part of the Cherokees, the sin of it lies not at the door of this administration, or its supporters. It may not be amiss to inquire, briefly, into the history of Indian emigration west of the Mississippi. If I am not greatly mistaken, one of the motives which induced Mr. Jefferson to desire the annexation of Louisiana to the United States was the prospective removal of the eastern Indians to its remote and uninhabited regions.

Certain it is, that in January 1809, when addressed by a Cherokee delegation on that subject, he encouraged their examination of the country high up on the Arkansas and White rivers, and promised to aid them in their emigration to it, if they should desire to remove after having explored it. It is believed that a portion of the tribe did emigrate to that country not long afterwards. Within the first year of Mr. Monroe's administration, the year 1819, a treaty was made with the whole tribe, providing for the emigration of such portion as might wish to join their brethren west of the Mississippi; and if the terms of that treaty had not been materially changed by another entered into in the year 1819, there can be little doubt that a much larger number would have done so. But it may be answered, that, so far, the Government had not entered upon any general system upon this subject; and that, in the partial emigrations which had then taken place, it rather followed, than attempted to lead, the inclination of the Indians. However this may have been, the whole aspect of the question was changed by the especial message communicated to Congress by Mr. [President James] Monroe, on the 27th of January, 1825, in which he stated that it had long occupied the attention of the Government, and recommended a general plan of Indian emigration and colonization west of the Mississippi, accompanied by an elaborate report of the Secretary of War on the subject. But a short period of Mr. Monroe's term of service then remained unexpired; but he did not go out of office until he had communicated to the Senate the treaty of the Indian Spring, of February of the same year, which provided, among other things, for an exchange of territory, and the removal of such of the Creek Indians as might desire it, beyond the Mississippi, and the operation of which treaty was arrested by his successor, in the manner I have already stated.

In 1826, an arrangement was made by the then Chief Magistrate for the removal of a portion of the Creeks to the west of the Mississippi; and in 1828, a treaty with the Cherokees of the west, which looked to the same object. Thus it appears, that, although by the act of Congress passed in May, 1830, and the treaties concluded with the Choctaws in 1830, with the Creeks in 1832, the Seminoles in 1834, and more recently with the Cherokees, and within the same period with many smaller bands, the scheme of Indian emigration and colonization west of the States and Territories beyond the Mississippi has been enlarged and systematized, its germe has a much earlier date, and the whole was recommended by Mr. Monroe in 1825. . . . It might, therefore, on the score of time and authority of high names, be considered worse than useless to explain or defend it. But as this is the last time that I propose ever to discuss this subject, I hope I may be permitted to present a few considerations, derived from experience and the nature of things, why this system is best, for both the whites and the Indians, and especially for the latter. The races are separate and distinct as color, character, and general condition, could well make them; the one possessing the arts and knowledge of cultivated life—the other the rude, unpolished nature of the savage. The consequence might, therefore, be naturally expected, that it is impossible that they should constitute one community with any thing like practical equality between them. Nor has experience in the slightest degree disappointed the deductions which a sound logic would have disposed to doubt it, that for many years past the remnants of Indian tribes still lingering in most of the old States of this Union have been treated with kindness and humanity. But of what avail have been all the efforts of ages to elevate their character and improve their condition? Alas! that character has continued to descend to the lowest depths of degradation, and that condition to unmitigated misery. Thus has it always been with the Indians, when surrounded by a white population; and thus it must always be, until the laws of nature and society shall undergo such change as can only be produced by the impress of the Deity. Nor can there be difficulty in explaining it. The poor Indian, (and in such condition he is indeed poor,) of inferior and degraded cast, associates with none of the white race, but such as are qualified to sink him into still deeper degradation. What, then, should be done to save the remnant from the moral pestilence which would inevitably await them, if relief and salvation shall be delayed until these causes shall be bought to operate upon them? There is no remedy but to remove them beyond the reach of the contamination which will surely come over them, if permitted to remain until they shall be surrounded by the causes to which I have adverted.

READING 16

ANDREW JACKSON ON INDIAN REMOVAL, 1835

It was during the administration of President Andrew Jackson (1829–37) that the removal of the southeastern Indians became a domestic priority. In 1830 the Congress had passed, with Jackson's approval, the Indian Removal Act. In an 1832 decision, Worcester v. Georgia, *the Supreme Court declared the bill unconstitutional. Despite this judicial opinion, state and national harassment intensified, and subsequent "treaties" resulted in the concentration and removal of the Cherokees by the army in the winter of 1838–39. On the forced march, known as "the Trail of Tears," approximately 25 percent (about 4,000 people) of the Cherokee nation died of starvation and exposure.*

In this speech, Andrew Jackson presents his justification for Indian removal. His theme that it was in the Indians' best interest would be repeated for years to come by supporters of the policy.

The plan of removing the aboriginal people who yet remain within the settled portions of the United States to the country west of the Mississippi River approaches its consummation. It was adopted on the most mature consideration of the condition of this race, and ought to be persisted in till the object is accomplished, and prosecuted with as much vigor as a just regard to their circumstances will permit, and as fast as their consent can be obtained. All preceding experiments for the improvement of the Indians have failed. It seems now to be an established fact that they can not live in contact with a civilized community and prosper. Ages of fruitless endeavors have at length brought us to a knowledge of this principle of intercommunication with them. The past we can not recall, but the future we can provide for. Independently of the treaty for the usufructuary rights they have ceded to us, no one can doubt the moral duty of the Government of the United States to protect and if possible to preserve and perpetuate the scattered remnants of this race which are left within our borders. In the discharge of this duty an extensive region in the West has been assigned for their permanent residence. It has been divided into districts and allotted among them. Many have already removed and others are preparing to go, and with the exception of two small bands living in Ohio and Indiana, not exceeding 1,500 persons, and of the Cherokees, all the tribes on the east side of the Mississippi, and extending from Lake Michigan to Florida, have entered into engagements which will lead to their transplantation.

The plan for removal and reestablishment is founded upon the knowledge we have gained of their character and habits, and has been dictated by a spirit of enlarged liberality. A territory exceeding in extent that relinquished has been granted to each tribe. Of its climate, fertility, and capacity to support an Indian population the representations are highly favorable. To these districts the Indians are removed at the expense of the United States, and with certain supplies of clothing, arms, ammunition, and other indispensable articles; they are also furnished gratuitously with provisions for the period of a year after their arrival at their homes. In that time, from the nature of the country and of the products raised by them, they can subsist themselves by agricultural labor, if they choose to resort to that mode of life; if they do not they are upon the skirts of the great prairies, where countless herds of buffalo roam, and a short time suffices to adapt their own habits to the changes which a change of the animals destined for their food may require. Ample arrangements have also been made for the support of schools; in some instances council houses and churches are to be erected, dwellings constructed for the chiefs, and mills for common use. Funds have been set apart for the maintenance of the poor; the most necessary mechanical arts have been introduced, and blacksmiths, gunsmiths, wheelwrights, millwrights, etc., are supported among them. Steel and iron, and sometimes salt, are purchased for them, and plows and other farming utensils, domestic animals, looms, spinning wheels, cards, etc., are presented to them. And besides these beneficial arrangements, annuities are in all cases paid, amounting in some instances to more than $30 for each individual of the tribe, and in all cases sufficiently great, if justly divided and prudently expended, to enable them, in addition to their own exertions, to live comfortably. And as a stimulus for exertion, it is now provided by law that "in all cases of the appointment of interpreters or other persons employed for the benefit of the Indians a preference shall be given to persons of Indian descent, if such can be found who are properly qualified for the discharge of the duties."

Such are the arrangements for the physical comfort and for the moral improvement of the Indians. The necessary measures for their political advancement and for their separation from our citizens have not been neglected. The pledge of the United States has been given by Congress that the country destined for the residence of this people shall be forever "secured and guaranteed to them." A country west of Missouri and Arkansas has been assigned to them, into which the white settlements are not to be pushed. No political communities can be formed in that extensive region, except those which are established by the Indians themselves or by the United States for them and their concurrence. A barrier has thus been raised for their protection against the encroachment of our citizens, and guarding the Indians as far as possible from those evils which have brought them to their present condition. Summary authority has been given by law to destroy all ardent spirits found in their country, without waiting the doubtful result and slow process of a legal seizure. I consider the absolute and unconditional interdiction of this article among these people as the first and great step in their melioration. Halfway measures will answer no purpose. These can not successfully contend against the cupidity of the seller and the overpowering appetite of the buyer. And the destructive effects of the traffic are marked in every page of the history of our Indian intercourse.

Some general legislation seems necessary for the regulation of the relations which will exist in this new state of things between the Government and people of the United States and these transplanted Indian tribes, and for the establishment among the latter, and with their own consent, of some principles of intercommunication which their juxtaposition will call for; that moral may be substituted for physical force, the authority of a few and simple laws for the tomahawk, and that an end may be put to those bloody wars whose prosecution seems to have made part of the social system.

After the further details of this arrangement are completed, with a very general supervision over them, they ought to be left to the progress of events. These, I indulge the hope, will secure their prosperity and improvement, and a large portion of the moral debt we owe them will then be paid.

READING 17

"THE FOLLY OF MAKING INDIAN TREATIES," *HARPER'S WEEKLY*, 1876

Given our contemporary attitudes toward the treatment of the Indians during the nineteenth century, it is often difficult for us to accept that liberal, reformist elements in nineteenth-century America frequently supported removal and concentration policies. Reform publications such as Harper's Weekly *agreed—*

as would we—with President Rutherford Hayes's 1877 declaration that "many, if not most, of our Indian wars have had their origin in broken promises and acts of injustice on our part." The modern-day American diverges from the nineteenth-century citizen, however, in the solution: where most twentieth-century observers would argue for justice and territorial integrity for the Indian, many nineteenth-century commentators argued for a decent reservation policy and fulfillment of treaties that would tend to isolate the Indian from contact with the dominant culture. This selection from Harper's Weekly, *August 5, 1876, was written a few weeks after the great Indian victory at the Battle of Little Bighorn. The defeat of Custer was a shock to the white culture, and soon afterward there appeared a number of reconsiderations of Indian policy, of which this is one.*

The fate of the brave and gallant Custer has deeply touched the public heart, which sees only a fearless soldier leading a charge against an ambushed [hiding, devious] foe, and falling at the head of his men and in the thick of the fray. A monument is proposed and subscriptions have been made. But a truer monument, more enduring than brass or marble, would be an Indian policy intelligent, moral, and efficient. Custer would not have fallen in vain if such a policy should be the result of his death.

It is a permanent accusation of our humanity and ability that over the Canadian line the relations between Indians and whites are so tranquil, while on our side they are summed up in perpetual treachery, waste, and war. When he was a young lieutenant on the frontier, General [Ulysses] Grant saw this, and watching attentively, he came to the conclusion that the reason of the difference was that the English respected the rights of the Indians and kept faith with them, while we make solemn treaties with them as if they were civilized and powerful nations, and then practically regard them as vermin to be exterminated.

The folly of making treaties with the Indian tribes may be as great as treating with a herd of buffaloes. But the infamy of violating treaties when we have made them is undeniable, and we are guilty both of the folly and the infamy.

We make treaties—that is, we pledge our faith—and then leave swindlers and knaves of all kinds to execute them. We maintain and breed pauper colonies. The savages, who know us, and who will neither be pauperized nor trust our word, we pursue, and slay if we can, at an incredible expense. The flower of our young officers is lost in inglorious forays, and one of the intelligent students of the whole subject rises in Congress and says, "The fact is that these Indians, with whom we have made a solemn treaty that their territory should not be invaded, and that they should receive supplies upon their reservations, have seen from one thousand to fifteen hundred miners during the present season entering and occupying their territory, while the Indians, owing to the failure of this and the last Congress to make adequate appropriations for their subsistence, instead of being fattened, as the gentlemen says, by the support of the government, have simply been starved."

It is plain that so long as we undertake to support the Indians as paupers, and then fail to supply the food; to respect their rights to reservations, and then permit the reservations to be overrun; to give them the best weapons and ammunition, and then furnish the pretense of using them against us; to treat with them as men, and then hunt them like skunks—so long we shall have the most costly and bloody Indian wars, and the most tragical ambuscades, slaughters, and assassinations.

The Indian is undoubtedly a savage, and a savage greatly spoiled by the kind of contact with civilization which he gets at the West. There is no romance, there is generally no interest whatever, in him or his fate. But there should be some interest in our own good faith and humanity, in the lives of our soldiers and frontier settlers, and in the taxation to support our Indian policy. All this should certainly be enough to arouse a public demand for a thorough consideration of the subject, and the adoption of a system which should neither be puerile nor disgraceful, and which would tend to spare us the constant repetition of such sorrowful events as the slaughter of Custer and his brave men.

READING 18
"THE INDIAN QUESTION," THOMAS MORGAN, 1891

Historians generally consider the Wounded Knee Massacre of 1890 to be the end of the Indian Wars of the nineteenth century. This engagement between the U.S. Army and Sioux adherents of the Ghost Dance religion ended with the deaths of approximately 150 Sioux men, women, and children near Wounded Knee Creek. The following year, Commissioner of Indian Affairs Thomas Morgan issued recommendations for improved treatment of the native populations, and many of his suggestions were adopted. But although his call for improvements in Indian policy is admirable, under the surface it is primarily a restatement of centuries-old misunderstandings and miscalculations, putting the onus on the Indian population for their condition. Morgan asserts not that "Americans" should respect treaties and the basic human rights of the native population but that the solution is for the Indian to become "Americanized."

There are certain things which the people of the United States will do well to remember.

First.—The people of this country during the past hundred years have spent enormous sums of money in Indian wars. These wars have cost us vast quantities of treasure and multitudes of valuable lives (besides greatly hindering the development of the country), have destroyed great numbers of Indians, and have wrought upon them incalculable disaster. The record which the nation has made for itself in this sanguinary conflict is not one to be proud of.

Second.—So long as the Indians remain in their present condition, the possibility of other wars, costly and dreadful, hangs over us as a perpetual menace. The recent [Ghost Dance] events have shown us how easy it is to spread alarm throughout our entire borders, and what fearful possibilities there are in store for us.

Third.—Indian wars are unnecessary, and if we will take proper precautions, they may be entirely avoided in the future. Justice, firmness, kindness, and wisdom will not only prevent future wars, but will promote the prosperity and welfare of the Indians, as well as of the entire commonwealth.

Fourth.—We should remember that the circumstances surrounding the Indians are constantly, in many cases, aggravating the difficulties in the way of their procuring a proper supply of food; and that unless wise precautions are taken at once to assist them in the development of the resources of the lands upon which they are compelled to live, they will be confronted more and more with the dread spectre of hunger, and we with that of war. We are called upon not so much to feed them, as we are to make it possible for them to feed themselves.

Fifth.—The only possible solution of our Indian troubles lies in the suitable education of the rising generation. So long as the Indians remain among us aliens, speaking foreign languages, unable to communicate with us except through the uncertain and often misleading medium of interpreters, so long as they are ignorant of our ways, are superstitious and fanatical, they will remain handicapped in the struggle for existence, will be an easy prey to the medicine man and the false prophet, and will be easily induced, by reason of real or imaginary wrongs, to go upon the warpath. An education that will give them the mastery of the English language, train their hands to useful industries, awaken within them ambition for civilized ways, and develop a consciousness of power to achieve honorable places for themselves, and that arouses within them an earnest and abiding patriotism, will make them American citizens, and render future conflicts between them and the government impossible.

Sixth.—Let it be especially remembered that the recent troubles [at Wounded Knee], deplorable as they have been, have been very small and insignificant compared to what they might have been; and that this has been brought about largely by the influence exerted upon the Indians through the schools of learning that have been established, and have already accomplished so much for their enlightenment and elevation. The influence for good exerted by the great school at Carlisle [Pennsylvania] alone, throughout the whole country, has been beyond estimate, and has repaid the government many times over every dollar that has been put into that institution.

Seventh.—It should be remembered that the time for making provision for the education of the entire body of Indian youth is now, and that any delay or postponement in the matter is hazardous and unwise.

Eighth.—In our judgment of the Indians and of the difficulties of the Indian question, we should remember that the most perplexing element in the problem is not the Indian, but the white man. The white man furnishes the Indians with arms and ammunition; the white man provides him with whiskey; the white man encroaches upon his reservation, robs him of his stock, defrauds him of his property, invades the sanctity of his home, and treats him with contempt, thus arousing within the Indian's breast those feelings of a sense of wrong, and dishonor, and wounded manhood that prepare him to vindicate his honor and avenge his wrongs.

In the late troubles in Dakota, the wrongs and outrages inflicted upon the Indians have vastly exceeded those inflicted by them upon the whites.

Ninth.—We should not forget that the prime object to be aimed at is the civilization of the Indians and their absorption into our national life, and that the agencies for the accomplishment of this work are not bayonets, but books. A schoolhouse will do vastly more for the Indians than a fort. It is better to teach the Indian to farm than to teach him to fight. Civil policemen are in every way to be preferred to Indian scouts, and we can much better afford to spend money in the employment of the Indians in useful industries, than to enroll them as soldiers in the army.

Tenth.—Finally, let us not forget what progress has already been made in this work of civilization; how potent are the forces now at work in preparing them for citizenship; how hopeful is the outlook if we, as a people, simply do our duty. Let us keep our faith with the Indian; protect him in his rights to life, liberty, and the pursuit of happiness; provide for all his children a suitable English and industrial education; throw upon them the responsibilities of citizenship, and welcome them to all the privileges of American freemen.

The end at which we aim is that the American Indians shall become as speedily as possible Indian-Americans; that the savage shall become a citizen; that the nomad shall cease to wander, and become a resident in a fixed habitation; that hunting shall cease to be a necessity, and become a pastime; that the smouldering fires of war shall become extinguished; that tribal animosities shall end; that the Indians, no longer joining in the "Sun Dance," or the "Ghost Dance," or other ceremonies in which they recount their wrongs and glory in the deeds of blood of their ancestors, shall gather at their firesides to talk of the memory of their days in school, and assemble in their places of worship to thank the Great Father above for the blessings of a Christian civilization vouchsafed to them in common with us all.

READING 19
"The Cost of Justice," Theodore Roosevelt, 1885

During the 1880s Theodore Roosevelt, future president of the United States, invested more than $50,000 in ranchland in Dakota Territory. Although he lost most of his investment, Roosevelt gained great respect for the demands and glories of the American western experience—but that respect did not extend to the Native American populations. This passage from one of his early books, Hunting Trips of a Ranchman, *recounts his experiences with and attitudes toward the Indians. His views were shared by many. In particular, his suggestion that Congress provide Indian individual land allotments was later adopted in the Dawes Act of 1887.*

There are now no Indians left in my immediate neighborhood, though a small party of harmless Grosventres [the Gros Ventre Indians of Montana] occasionally passes through. Yet it is but six years since the Sioux surprised and killed five men in a log station just south of me, where the Fort Keogh trail crosses the river; and, two years ago, when I went down on the prairies toward the Black Hills, there was still danger from Indians. That summer the buffalo hunters had killed a couple of Crows, and while we were on the prairie a long-range skirmish occurred near us between some Cheyennes and a number of cowboys. In fact, we ourselves were one day scared by what we thought to be a party of Sioux; but on riding toward them they proved to be half-breed Crees, who were more afraid of us than we were of them.

During the past century a good deal of sentimental nonsense has been talked about our taking the Indians' land. Now, I do not mean to say for a moment that gross wrong has not been done the Indians, both by government and individuals, again and again. The government makes promises impossible to perform, and then fails to do even what it might toward their fulfillment; and where brutal and reckless frontiersmen are brought into contact with a set of treacherous, revengeful, and fiendishly cruel savages a long series of outrages by both sides is sure to follow.

But as regards taking the land, at least from the Western Indians, the simple truth is that the latter never had any real ownership in it at all. Where the game was plenty, there they hunted; they followed it when it moved away to new hunting-grounds, unless they were prevented by stronger rivals; and to most of the land on which we found them they had no stronger claim than that of having a few years previously butchered the original occupants.

When my cattle came to the Little Missouri the region was only inhabited by a score or so of white hunters; their title to it was quite as good as that of most Indian tribes to the lands they claim; yet nobody dreamed of saying that these hunters owned the country. Each could eventually have kept his own claim of 160 acres, and no more.

The Indians should be treated in just the same way that we treat the white settlers. Give each his little claim; if, as would generally happen, he declined this, why then let him share the fate of the thousands of white hunters and trappers who have lived on the game that the settlement of the country has exterminated, and let him, like these whites, who will not work, perish from the face of the earth which he cumbers.

The doctrine seems merciless, and so it is; but it is just and rational for all that. It does not do to be merciful to a few, at the cost of justice to the many. The cattlemen at least keep herds and build houses on the land; yet I would not for a moment debar settlers from the right of entry to the cattle country, though their coming in means in the end the destruction of us and our industry.

The Dawes Act, 1887

The 1887 Dawes Act is often considered the prime example of the United States government's response to the "Indian problem." Promoted by reformers as a solution to the ongoing poor treatment of the Indian populations, the act converted all tribal lands to individual ownership in an effort to assimilate the Indians into the dominant culture. As shown in this excerpt, the law was specifically designed to address a central facet of native life: communal ownership of tribal lands. The belief was that altering this fundamental aspect of Indian life could accelerate the assimilation process and thereby end the isolation of Indians from white culture. Historians generally agree that the Dawes Act did significantly alter Indian social patterns but did little, if anything, to enhance their acceptance into the dominant culture.

An act to provide for the allotment of lands in severalty to Indians on the various reservations, and to extend the protection of the laws of the United States and the Territories over the Indians, and for other purposes.

Be it enacted, That in all cases where any tribe or band of Indians has been, or shall hereafter be, located upon any reservation created for their use, either by treaty stipulation or by virtue of an act of Congress or executive order setting apart the same for their use, the President of the United States be, and he hereby is; authorized, whenever in his opinion any reservation or any part thereof of such Indians is advantageous for agriculture and grazing purposes to cause said reservation, or any part thereof, to be surveyed, or resurveyed if necessary, and to allot the lands in said reservation in severalty to any Indian located thereon in quantities as follows:

To each head of a family, one-quarter of a section;

To each single person over eighteen years of age, one-eighth of a section;

To each orphan child under eighteen years of age, one-eighth of a section; and,

To each other single person under eighteen years now living, or who may be born prior to the date of the order of the President directing an allotment of the lands embraced in any reservation, one-sixteenth of a section. . . .

Sec. 5. That upon the approval of the allotments provided for in this act by the Secretary of the Interior, he shall . . . declare that the United States does and will hold the land thus allotted, for the period of twenty-five years, in trust for the sole use and benefit of the Indian to whom such allotment shall have been made, . . . and that at the expiration of said period the United States will convey the same by patent to said Indian, or his heirs as aforesaid, in fee, discharged of such trust and free of all charge or incumbrance whatsoever. . . .

Sec. 6. That upon the completion of said allotments and the patenting of the lands to said allottees, each and every member of the respective bands or tribes of Indians to whom allotments have been made shall have the benefit of and be subject to the laws, both civil and criminal, of the State or Territory in which they may reside. . . . And every Indian born within the territorial limits of the United States to whom allotments shall have been made under the provisions of this act, or under any law or treaty, and every Indian born within the territorial limits of the United States who has voluntarily taken up, within said limits, his residence separate and apart from any tribe of Indians therein, and has adopted the habits of civilized life, is hereby declared to be a citizen of the United States, and is entitled to all the rights, privileges, and immunities of such citizens, whether said Indian has been or not, by birth or otherwise, a member of any tribe of Indians within the territorial limits of the United States without in any manner impairing or otherwise affecting the right of any such Indian to tribal or other property.

CHAPTER 7

ON BOTH SIDES OF THE TIN BADGE

IN THE American West the line between law-abiding and law-breaking was not only very thin but often crossed. Many times criminals and the law were represented by the same person. Consider the case of Henry Brown. During the 1880s Brown was a bank robber and a compatriot of the famous outlaw Billy the Kid. But in 1884 the town of Caldwell, Kansas, hired him as marshal—knowing full well his previous misdeeds. Towns would overlook a man's unsavory past if he had a reputation for being tough and fearsome; in fact, some towns counted on that reputation as a deterrent to crime. In Brown's case, the outlaw-turned-lawman turned outlaw again: while out of town, Brown robbed a bank and was captured. When a lynch mob arrived to hang him, he attempted to escape and was shot dead.

The fluid line between legal and illegal activity, the individualistic dichotomy between the sacred and the profane, provides spice to the history of law enforcement in the American West. In this chapter the readings examine the historical applications of this curious brew of good and evil.

READING 1
CALIFORNIA VIGILANTES, 1851

The difference between legal and illegal often comes down to definition. To some the efforts of vigilantes are grossly illegal; for others they are simple self-defense and necessary reform. In gold rush California vigilantes were the most visible examples of law enforcement in many communities. Vigilantes are defined as unauthorized citizen groups organized to carry out a summary execution of the law. Execution was often the operative word, as justice was frequently meted out at the end of a rope. By the turn of the twentieth century, historians estimate, about seven hundred alleged criminals had been put to death by vigilantes. San Francisco had a most active vigilance committee, as these contemporary accounts, statements to the grand jury, and comments attest.

California Courier, June 10, 1851

It is clear to every man that San Francisco is partially in the hands of criminals, and that crime has reached a crisis where the fate of life and property are in imminent jeopardy. There is no alternative now left but to lay aside business and direct our whole energies as a people to seek out the abodes of these villains and execute summary vengeance upon them. . . . What now shall be done? Are we to continue to threaten, and nothing more? . . . Why stop, under the present unsafe and uncertain state of affairs, to have a thief, or one who attempts to fire [set fire to] the city, placed in the hands of law officers, from whose clutches they can, with ease, be relieved by false swearing, and the ingenuity of lawyers? or what is equally as certain, their escape from prison? Where the guilt of the criminal is clear and unquestionable, the first law of nature demands that they be instantly shot, hung, or burned alive. . . . We must strike terror into their hearts. . . .

No man, since we became a city, has been hung in San Francisco. Some fifty murders have been committed, but no murderer has suffered death for his crimes.

We ask again, what shall be done? We are in the midst of a revolution, and we should meet the emergencies with firm hearts and well-braced nerves. We have no time to talk about the defects of the laws—of the dangers which beset us: but we must act, and act at once—act as men do in revolutionary times. . . .

Statement of James Neall Jr.

On Sunday [June 8, 1851] . . . George [Oakes] . . . in conversation with me, upon the perilous condition of society at that time, said we ought to take some steps to see if we could not change these things, and suggested that we should go up and have a talk with Sam Brannan [former clerk at Sutter's Fort, the individual who announced the gold discovery at Sutter's Mill to San Francisco, merchant and real estate magnate, and California's first millionaire], and we went up to Brannan's office. . . . We there found Mr. Brannan and his clerk, and sat down and talked the matter [over]. . . . We . . . concluded that something must be done, and it was suggested that each one of us should give Mr. Brannan's clerk, Mr. Wardwell, the names of such men as we could mention, whom we knew to be reliable, to invite them to meet us at 12 o'clock noon the next day, at the California Engine House . . . to devise some means of protecting ourselves from the depredations of this hoard of ruffians, who seemed to have possession of the city. There was no such thing as doing anything with them before the courts; that had been tried in vain. Notices were sent out to parties to the effect that they were nominated, each as chairman of a committee for his neighborhood, to invite their fellow citizens, good reliable men, to meet . . . as above indicated.

Statement of *William T. Coleman*

I was early at the building, and found a number of gentlemen there, probably thirty or forty already. An organization was formed, and the objects of the meeting stated, with a brief discussion. Articles had been already prepared for the mode of organization, and some thirty or forty names were enrolled, and it was styled the *Committee of Vigilance of San Francisco,* the avowed objects of the Committee being to vigilantly watch and pursue the outlaws and criminals who were infesting the city, and bring them to justice, through the regularly constituted courts, if that could be, through more summary and direct process, if must be. Each member pledged his word of honor, his life and fortune if need be, for the protection of his fellow members, for the protection of life and property of the citizens and of the community, and for purging the city of bad characters who were making themselves odious in it. After arranging for a concert of action, watchwords, and a signal to be used to call the members to the rendezvous . . . and detailing officers for immediate duty, enrolling a number of members, all among the most respectable, substantial and well-known citizens of the place, and the disposition of some needed business,—the Committee adjourned for the evening.

Statement of *G. W. Ryckman*

When any men were arrested and turned over to the Committee, they were tried by the Executive and such trials were as honest and impartial as ever a man had, and no man was convicted without an abundance of testimony, such as would convict any human being in any court of justice; only we could not allow any alibis to come in to screen these fellows. After the trial and conviction of the prisoner, the case was referred to the General Committee for its action, and the testimony was sent to them. They invariably confirmed the decisions of the Executive Committee, and it was impossible for them to do otherwise, in the face of such proofs as were offered.

The Committee was composed mostly of our best men; the salt of San Francisco joined us. Everything was organized in a proper and unmistakable shape, so that every man had his duty to perform, and he had to report daily to the Committee, and if anything had transpired it was properly noted. Every man had his place, and there was a place for every man; there were no drones there.

Not all agreed with the activities of the Committee of Vigilance; some hoped that the rule of law would prevail. When a grand jury investigated the 1851 hanging of James Stuart and the actions of the vigilantes, Judge Alexander Campbell offered his opinions in this statement.

Charge of Judge Alexander Campbell to the Grand Jury
The question has now arisen, whether the laws made by the constitutional authorities of the State are to be obeyed and executed, or whether secret societies are to frame and execute laws for the government of this county, and to exercise supreme power over the lives, liberty, and property of our citizens. . . . Are the people willing to throw away the safeguards which the experience of ages has proved necessary . . . and to place life, liberty, property, and reputation at the mercy of a secret society? If such be the disposition of the people . . . it is time for every man who values his life, safety, and honor, to shake the dust from his feet and seek out some new home, where he may hope to enjoy the blessings of liberty under the law. But if, on the other hand, we have not quite forgotten the principles upon which our government is formed— . . . if we believe that persons accused of crime should have an open, public and impartial trial by a fair jury of unprejudiced citizens, and should have a reasonable opportunity of making their defense, of employing counsel and summoning witnesses; if we believe that the good name and reputation of our citizens is to be protected from a secret scrutiny, where accusations are made under the influence of fear, by persons of questionable character;—if we believe that our houses are to be protected from unreasonable searches without color of authority, it is our solemn and bounden duty to take immediate and energetic measures for the suppression of the spirit of reckless violence which overrules the laws and sets the Constitution at defiance.

When you [the Grand Jury] first assembled, the Court called your attention to the unlawful execution of a man named Jenkins by an association of citizens. We considered that act was greatly palliated by the circumstances, . . . that the laws had been defective, and that perhaps there had been some laxity in their administration; that the county had no sufficient jail for the detention of prisoners; that crime had increased to a fearful extent, and that a portion of our citizens, deeming that the law afforded them no protection, had in that instance undertaken to execute what they conceived to be summary justice, in violation of the law, but with a sincere desire to advance the public interest. We further stated that the law had been amended in many respects, so as to secure the speedy trial and conviction of offenders . . . [and] that the county jail had been put in a proper condition for the safe keeping of prisoners, and we expressed the hope that no further attempt would be made to interfere with the legally organized tribunals of justice. . . . From the time of your assembling, the Court, the Grand Jury, and all the officers have been actively and constantly engaged in the performance of their duties. At the time when they were making every possible effort to dispose of the criminal business of the county, and when the Court was in actual session and in the performance of its duties, an association of persons, of armed and organized men, have undertaken to trample on the Constitution, defy the laws, and assume unlimited power over the lives of the community. There is no excuse or palliation for the deed. . . . Every person who in any manner acted, aided, abetted or assisted in taking [James] Stuart's life, or counseled or encouraged his death is undoubtedly GUILTY OF MURDER. It is your sworn and solemn duty, which you cannot evade without perjuring yourselves, carefully and fully to investigate this matter, and to do your share towards bringing the guilty to punishment. Upon your fearless and faithful discharge of the trust confided to you, depends, in a great measure, the future peace, order, and tranquility of the community.

Response to Judge Campbell in the California Courier, *July 14, 1851*
No such committee could exist in any form in this city, if the whole body of the community did not consider that necessity and policy demanded it. The committee is composed of peace loving and orderly citizens—many of them elders, deacons and conspicuous members of the church. They are not composed of rowdies or blood thirsty men. . . . We are not going to complain of Judge Campbell's charge—but we can tell him that the men who hung Stuart cannot be indicted, convicted and executed in California, while the records of the Court show that some of our best citizens have been shot down in cold blood, and that murderers have been permitted entirely to run at large or to slip through their hands, unwhipped and unavenged of justice.

The Vigilantes of Bannack, Montana, 1864

Vigilantism was not an isolated phenomenon; it occurred throughout the American West. In 1863 the citizens of Bannack, Montana, elected new town officials. Most were well-known, respectable citizens of the community. But the citizenry did not know that Sheriff Henry Plummer, newly arrived in town, was the leader of an outlaw band of horse thieves and murderers. Soon after taking office Plummer instituted a reign of terror. As robberies and murders became commonplace, the citizens began to realize that their sheriff was behind it all, and vigilante organizations sprang up in response. Some of the criminals they captured implicated Plummer, who fled. In January 1864 the vigilantes caught up with Plummer and hanged him and more than thirty others in retribution. Here is an 1866 account of Plummer's capture and execution.

At dusk, three horses were brought into town, belonging severally and respectively to the three marauders, . . . Plummer, Stinson, and Ray. It was truly conjectured that they had determined to leave the country, and it was at once settled that they should be arrested that night. Parties were detailed for the work. Those entrusted with the duty performed it admirably. Plummer was undressing when taken at his house. His pistol . . . was broken and useless. Had he been armed, resistance would have been futile; for he was seized the moment the door was opened in answer to the knocking from without. Stinson was arrested at Toland's, where he was spending the evening. He would willingly have done a little firing, but his captors were too quick for him. Ray was lying on a gambling table when seized. The three details marched their men to a given point, en route to the gallows. Here a halt was made. The leader of the Vigilantes, and some others, who wished to save all unnecessary hard feeling, were sitting in a cabin, designing not to speak to Plummer, with whom they were so well acquainted. A halt was made, however, and at the door appeared Plummer. The light was extinguished; when the party moved on, but soon halted. The crisis had come. Seeing that the circumstances were such as admitted of neither vacillation nor delay, the citizen leader, summoning his friends, went up to the party and gave the military command, "Company! forward—march!" This at once was obeyed. A rope taken from a noted functionary's bed had been mislaid and could not be found. [A young] boy was sent off for some of that highly necessary but unpleasant remedy for crime and the bearer made such good time that some hundreds of feet of hempen necktie were on the ground before the arrival of the party at the gallows. On the road Plummer heard the voice and recognized the person of the leader. He came to him and begged for his life; but was told, "It is useless for you to beg for your life; that affair is settled and cannot be altered. You are to be hanged. You cannot feel harder than I do; but I cannot help it if I would." Ned Ray, clothed with curses as with a garment, actually tried fighting, but found that he was in the wrong company for such demonstrations; and Buck Stinson made the air ring with the blasphemous and filthy expletives which he used in addressing his captors. Plummer exhausted every argument and plea that his imagination could suggest, in order to induce his captors to spare his life. He begged to be chained down in the meanest cabin; offered to leave the country forever; wanted a jury trial; implored time to settle his affairs; asked to see his sister-in-law; and, falling on his knees, with tears and sighs declared to God that he was too wicked to die. He confessed his numerous murders and crimes, and seemed almost frantic at the prospect of death.

The first rope being thrown over the cross-beam, and the noose being rove, the order was given to "Bring up Ned Ray." This desperado was run up with curses on his lips. Being loosely pinioned, he got his fingers between the rope and his neck, and thus prolonged his misery.

Buck Stinson saw his comrade robber in the death agony, and blubbered out, "There goes poor Ned Ray." Scant mercy had he shown to his numerous victims. By a sudden twist of his head at the moment of his elevation, the knot slipped under his chin, and he was some minutes dying.

The order to "Bring up Plummer" was then passed and repeated; but no one stirred. The leader went over to this "perfect gentleman" as his friends called him, and was met by a request to "Give a man time to pray." Well knowing that Plummer relied for a rescue upon other than Divine aid, he said briefly and decidedly, "Certainly; but let him say his prayers up here." Finding all efforts to avoid death were useless, Plummer rose and said no more prayers. Standing under the gallows which he had erected for the execution of [an earlier criminal named] Horan, this second Haman [an allusion to a treacherous courtier in the biblical Book of Esther] slipped off his necktie and threw it over his shoulder to a young friend who had boarded at his house, and who believed him innocent of crime, saying as he tossed it to him, "Here is something to remember me by." In the extremity of his grief, the young man threw himself weeping and wailing upon the ground. Plummer requested that the men should give him a good drop, which was done, as high as circumstances permitted, by hoisting him up as far as possible in the arms, and letting him fall suddenly. He died quickly and without much struggle.

It was necessary to seize Ned Ray's hand, and by a violent effort to draw his fingers from between the noose and his neck before he died. Probably he was the last to expire of the guilty trio.

The news of a man's being hanged flies faster than any other intelligence in a Western country, and several had gathered round the gallows on that fatal Sabbath evening—many of them friends of the road agents [outlaws]. The spectators were allowed to come up to a certain point, and were then halted by the guard, who refused permission either to depart or to approach nearer that the "dead line," on pain of their being instantly shot.

The weather was intensely cold, but the party stood for a long time round the bodies of the suspended malefactors, determined that rescue should be impossible.

Loud groans and cries uttered in the vicinity attracted their attention, and a small squad started in the direction from which the sound proceeded. The detachment soon met Madam Hall, a noted courtezan—the mistress of Ned Ray—who was "making the night hideous" with her doleful wailings. Being at once stopped, she began inquiring for her paramour, and was thus informed of his fate, "Well, if you must know, he is hung." A volcanic eruption of oaths and abuse was her reply to this information; but the men were on "short time," and escorted her towards her dwelling without superfluous display of courtesy. Having arrived at the brow of a short descent, at the foot of which stood her cabin, stern necessity compelled a rapid and final progress in that direction.

Soon after, the party formed and returned to town, leaving the corpses stiffening in the icy blast. The bodies were eventually cut down by the friends of the road agents and buried. The "Reign of Terror" in Bannack was over.

READING 3
THE DRAW, EUGENE CUNNINGHAM, 1971

In the American West, skill with a gun could be a lifesaver—not only from rampaging animals or outlaws but in the classic western showdown of the gunfight as well. Many recent historical studies indicate that such confrontations were much less frequent than the popular culture would lead us to believe, but they did happen, and skill with the gun is a factor in all the readings that follow in this chapter.

For the gunfighter, technique was a paramount consideration. Eugene Cunningham, who collected the reminiscences and lore of old gunfighters in his book Triggernometry, *here explains the skill involved in "the draw."*

For the most part, when two men got "on the prod" and came hunting each other, they depended on speed on the draw, though neither was apt to overlook an opportunity to get the edge on his opponent by some trick or ferocious acting. And since the straight draw from a belt holster was the chief method of getting a pistol into action, right here is a good place to look at its technique.

There are two methods of drawing, whether from a waistband, belt, or shoulder holster. You can play safe with Method One, in which you drop gun hand to pistol butt, draw the pistol from the holster and, when it is pointing generally at the target, cock it. But this is not the fast way—not the gunman's way! For any one wishing to become fast on the draw, Method Two is the thing.

Belt on the pistol and, whether it be on the left side with butt front for a cross draw (the proper method of carrying a pistol while riding) or on the right side, butt to rear, check the height of it to be sure that the hand falls naturally to the butt, with elbow only slightly bent. A gun too high-hung means a muzzle caught on the holster top and—what flowers are your favorites?

Now, load the gun with exploded shells. Let your hands fall loosely to the sides. At a mental word of command, or a mark on a watch, whip the gun hand up to the pistol butt, catching the hammer of the single-action under the thumb and sliding the forefinger into the trigger-guard. Draw the gun, pulling back the hammer as it comes. Tighten the fingers on the butt as the gun clears the holster. Accustom yourself to whang away as the muzzle comes to level. But not until you have developed skill should the pistol be loaded, for the practiser will be clumsy at first.

This is the old gunfighter's method. . . . To mention the list of those who were like sleight-of-hand artists in its use is to call the roll of the Gallery of Gunfighters. Out of the Colt-smoked past, what a procession comes—Wild Bill Hickok, with the hawk's nose and cold blue eyes and shoulder-long golden hair; tall Clay Allison of the Washita, Allison the Wolf-Killer, another blood type with a slight limp; John Wesley Hardin and Ben Thompson, dark-haired and blue-eyed, both men of middle height, powerfully muscled but with hands as supple-fingered as any pianist's; Big Bill Longley; Mellish and Comstock; little Bass Outlaw; Billy the Kid, with his perpetual grin; John Ringo; John Slaughter; Long-Haired Jim Courtright, and many another.

These men were all quick-draw artists such as an Eastern target shot will hardly become, because he has no such impelling motive for practise and experiment. And whatever he could do on an orthodox pistol range, in a battle with such as they he would be killed before he knew exactly what was happening!

Long-Haired Jim Courtright rarely gets the credit due him as expert with the Colts, as I have commented before in these pages. But the old-timers do not forget him! They still puzzle over the mystery of Luke Short killing him.

"Short?" Jim Gillett once said, in answer to a question. "Oh, yes, Luke was pretty fast with a six-shooter. But Jim Courtright—Short just wasn't in his class."

. . . [T]here was no backing down to Short [by Courtright]. This dapper, smooth-faced little friend of Bat Masterson and Doc Holliday and Charley Bassett and the brothers Earp had run gambling houses in the tough trail-herd towns like Dodge City. Leadville, Colorado, too, had heard the staccato bark of his guns. He was salty!

But when Jim Courtright . . . tangled ropes with Luke Short, Fort Worth nodded: Short would pay—or else. On that evening of February 8, 1887, when Courtright met Short outside the White Elephant [Saloon], they came to shooting very quickly, and a lucky bullet from Short's double action tore off Courtright's hammer thumb.

Lightning fast, Courtright tried desperately to perform that evolution known as the "border shift" [transferring the gun from hand to hand by tossing it across your body]; but before the pistol could hurtle from right hand to left hand and explode, Courtright was shot to pieces. The border shift had failed Courtright!

Pink Simms of Lewistown, Montana, old Lincoln County cowboy who worked all over the West and served his time as peace officer, was yarning with me not long ago, about old-time gunfighters. We came to mention Courtright and Luke Short and Simms was reminded of hearing a contemporary of Short's tell how the little gambler always crowded in close during a shooting scrape.

"That way, he got the effect of the muzzle blast. It knocked the other man off balance. The .45 burned terribly at close range. It was impossible to face it—as I once discovered for myself! It will even set your clothes on fire. So, the man who got to shooting first when only a few feet away, he had a big advantage even if he missed his first shot."

READING 4

THE GUNFIGHT AT THE O.K. CORRAL, WYATT EARP, 1881

The most famous gunfight in the American West occurred October 26, 1881, in the streets of Tombstone, Arizona—the battle known as the Gunfight at the O.K. Corral. A central figure in that fight was Wyatt Earp, professional gambler, saloonkeeper, possible stage robber, alleged murderer, and former peace officer in Dodge City, Kansas, and other locales. Wyatt, his brothers, and Doc Holliday fought the Clanton brothers and the McLaury family as a result of either a feud or a political struggle over control of Tombstone. The full facts remain uncertain, and, as with most historical events, there are many versions of what happened, some of which have become western myth. This is Wyatt Earp's own account as recorded in the town newspaper, the Tombstone Epitaph.

I was tired of being threatened by Ike Clanton and his gang. I believed from what they had said to others and to me, and from their movements, that they intended to assassinate me the first chance they had, and I thought if I had to fight for my life against them I had better make them face me in an open fight. So I said to Ike Clanton, who was then sitting about eight feet away from me, "you d——d dirty cur thief, you have been threatening our lives and I know it. I think I should be justified in shooting you down any place I should meet you, but if you are anxious to make a fight, I will go anywhere on earth to make a fight with you, even over to the San Simon [a saloon] among your own crowd." He replied, "All right, I'll see you after I get through here. I only want four feet of ground to fight on." I walked out just then and outside the court room, near the Justice's office, I met Tom Mc-Lowry [McLaury]. He came up to me and said to me, "If you want to make a fight I will make a fight with you anywhere." . . . I felt just as I did about Ike Clanton, that if the fight had to come I had better have it come when I had an even show to defend myself, so I said to him, "all right, make a fight right here." And at the same time I slapped him in the face with my left hand, and drew my pistol with my right. He had a pistol in plain sight on his hip, but made no move to draw it. I said to him, "jerk your gun and use it." He made no reply, and I hit him on the head with my six-shooter, and walked away, down to Hafford's corner. I went into Hafford's and got a cigar, and came out and stood by the door. Pretty soon I saw Tom McLowry, Frank McLowry [McLaury], and Wm. Clanton. They passed me and went down Fourth Street to the gunsmith shop. I followed them to see what they were going to do. . . . Ike Clanton came up about that time and they all charged into the gunsmith's shop. I saw them in the shop changing cartridges into their belts. . . .

Virgil Earp was then city marshal; Morgan Earp was a special policeman for six weeks, wore a badge and drew pay. I had been sworn in in Virgil's place to act for him while Virgil had gone to Tucson on Stilwell's trial. Virgil had been back several days but I was still acting. I knew it was Virgil's duty to disarm these men. I expected he would have trouble doing so and I followed up to give assistance if necessary especially as they had been threatening us, as I have already stated. About ten minutes afterwards, and while Virgil, Morgan, Doc Holliday and myself were standing on the corner of Fourth and Allen Streets, several people said, "There is going to be trouble with those fellows," and one man named Coleman, said to Virgil Earp, "They mean trouble. They have just gone from Dunbar's corral into the O.K. Corral, all armed. I think you had better go and disarm them." Virgil turned around to Doc Holliday, Morgan Earp and myself and told us to come assist him in disarming them. Morgan Earp said to me, "They have horses, had we not better get some horses ourselves, so that if they make a running fight we can catch them?" I said, "no, if they try to make a running fight we can kill their horses and then capture them." We four then started through Fourth to Fremont Street. When we turned the corner of Fourth and Fremont we could see them. . . . We came up on them close—Frank McLowry, Tom McLowry and Bill Clanton standing all in a row against the east side of the building on the opposite side of the vacant space west of Fly's photograph gallery. Ike Clanton and Billy Claiborne and a man I did not know were standing in the vacant space about half way between the photograph gallery and the next building west. I saw that Billy Clanton and Fred McLowry and Tom McLowry had their hands by their sides, and Frank McLowry's and

Billy Clanton's six-shooters were in plain sight. Virgil said, "Throw up your hands I have come to disarm you." Billy Clanton and Frank McLowry laid their hands on their six-shooters. Virgil said, "Hold, I don't mean that; I have come to disarm you."

They—Billy Clanton and Frank McLowry—commenced to draw their pistols, at the same time Tom McLowry threw his hand to his right hip and jumped behind a horse. . . . When I saw Billy and Frank draw their pistols I drew my pistol. Billy Clanton leveled his pistol at me but I did not aim at him. I knew that Frank McLowry had the reputation of being a good shot and a dangerous man and I aimed at Frank McLowry. The first two shots which were fired were fired by Billy Clanton and myself; he shot at me and I shot at Frank McLowry. I do not know which shot was first; we fired almost together.

The fight then became general. After about four shots were fired Ike Clanton ran up and grabbed my right arm. I could see no weapon in his hand and thought at the time he had none and I said to him, "The fight has now commenced; go to shooting or get away"; at the same time I pushed him off with my left hand. He started and ran down the side of the building and disappeared between the lodging house and the photograph gallery. My first shot struck Frank McLowry in the belly. He staggered off on the sidewalk but first fired a shot at me. When we told them to throw up their hands Claiborne held up his left hand and then broke and ran. I never drew my pistol or made a motion to shoot until after Billy Clanton and Frank Mc-Lowry drew their pistols.

If Tom McLowry was unarmed I did not know it. I believe he was armed and that he fired two shots at our party before Holliday, who had the shotgun, fired at and killed him. . . . I never fired at Ike Clanton, even after the shooting commenced because I thought he was unarmed. I believed then and believe now from the acts I have stated and the threats I have related and other threats communicated to me by different persons, as having been made by Tom McLowry, Frank McLowry and Isaac Clanton, that these men last named had formed a conspiracy to murder my brothers Morgan and Virgil and Doc Holliday and myself. I believe I would have been legally and morally justifiable in shooting any of them on sight, but I did not do so or attempt to do so; I sought no advantage. When I went as deputy marshal to disarm them and arrest them, I went as part of my duty and under the direction of my brother the marshal. I did not intend to fight unless it became necessary in self defense and in the performance of official duty. When Billy Clanton and Frank McLowry drew their pistols I knew it was a fight for life and I drew and fired in defense of my own life, and lives of my brothers and Doc Holliday.

Earp's version does not recount the bloody aftermath. The shootout left Billy Clanton and Frank and Tom McLaury dead, and Morgan, Virgil, and Doc Holliday wounded. Wyatt Earp escaped injury. Weeks later the other Clantons and their friends exacted revenge on the Earps: Virgil, shot on a Tombstone street, was left with a permanent crippling in his left arm; Morgan was killed by a shot in the back while playing pool in a Tombstone saloon. Wyatt lived until 1929.

READING 5

A CHRONICLE OF BILLY THE KID, 1879–1881

One of the most famous outlaws in the American West was Billy the Kid. Born Henry McCarty in New York City, he moved with his widowed mother and brother to New Mexico Territory and led a normal existence until 1874, when his mother died. At that time the "Kid," as he was already commonly called, committed a petty theft, then killed a man in Arizona and became a fugitive. Back in New Mexico he adopted the alias William H. Bonney and became a cowboy on the Tunstall Lincoln County Cattle Ranch. As a participant in the bloody 1877 Lincoln County War between two rival factions vying for political and economic control of the county, the Kid gained a reputation for ruthlessness. He is said to have killed twenty-one men in his life, but historians now generally believe that his record was a more modest, but still gruesome, four to ten murders. Bonney next led a gang of outlaws and cattle rustlers known as the Regulators. Because he threatened the established interests in Lincoln County, his arrest was sought by local officials and the governor of New Mexico Territory, Lew Wallace (Civil War general and future author of Ben Hur).*

Starting in 1879 an all-out effort was made to apprehend the Kid. The governor offered him a pardon if he would surrender but then reneged on his promise when Billy complied. On June 17, 1879, Billy escaped from the Lincoln jail and for the next eighteen months remained on the run, now the most wanted criminal in the Southwest. Pat Garrett, Billy's erstwhile friend, had been elected sheriff during this time and captured him in December 1880. In April 1881 the Kid was tried for murder, convicted, and sentenced to hang on May 13. But on April 28 he made another dramatic jailbreak, killing two guards in the process. Governor Wallace, apparently unaware of the escape, signed Billy's death warrant on April 30. Billy eluded capture for weeks but was finally cornered and shot by the sheriff on July 13, 1881. He was twenty-one years old. The attention of the national press had focused on this character, and now the legend of Billy the Kid exploded into public consciousness.

These documents from the last two years of his life include letters between the Kid and Governor Wallace, a contemporary account of his murder trial, instructions to the jury at his trial, and Billy's death warrant.

Letter from Billy the Kid to Governor Wallace, March 10, 1879
Governor Lew Wallace

Dear Sir:

I have heard that you will give 1000 dollars for my body which as I understand it, it means alive as a witness. I know it is a witness against those that murdered Mr. Chapman [a victim of the Lincoln County War]. If it was so as I could appear in court, I would give the desired information, but I have indictments against me for things that happened in the Lincoln County War, and am afraid to give myself up because my enemys would kill me.

The night Mr. Chapman was murdered I was in Lincoln at the request of some good citizens to meet Mr. J. J. Dolan, to meet as friends so as to be able to lay aside our arms and go to work.

I was present when Mr. Chapman was murdered and know who did it and if it wasn't for those indictments I would have made it clear before now.

Please send me an answer telling me what you can do. You can send answer by bearer. I do not wish to fight any more and I have not raised an arm since your proclamation. As to my character I can refer you to any of the good citizens as a majority of them are my friends and have been helping me all they can.

Sometimes I am called Kid Antrim but Antrim is my stepfather's name.

Waiting your reply, I am,

Your obt. servant

W. H. BONNEY

Letter from Governor Wallace to Billy the Kid, March 15, 1879
W. H. Bonney

Come to the house of old Squire Wilson (not the lawyer) at nine (9) o'clock next Monday night alone. I don't mean his office, but his residence. Follow along the foot of the mountain south of the town, come in on that side, and knock at the east door. I have authority to exempt you from prosecution, if you will testify to what you say you know.

The object of the meeting at Squire Wilson's is to arrange the matter in a way to make your life safe. To do that the utmost secrecy is to be used. So *come alone.* Don't tell anybody—not a living soul—where you are coming or the object. If you could trust Jesse Evans, you can trust me.

LEW WALLACE

Letter from Billy the Kid to Squire Wilson, March 20, 1879
Friend Wilson.
Please tell You know who [Governor Wallace] that I do not know what to do, now as those prisoners [Billy's enemies] have escaped, to send word by bearer, a note through You it may be that he has made different arra[n]gements if not and he still wants it the same to send William Hudgins, as Deputy, to the Junction tomorrow at three o'clock with some men you know to be all right. Send a note telling me what to do.

W. H. BONNEY

P.S. do not send soldiers

Letter from Governor Wallace to Billy the Kid, March 20, 1879
W. H. BONNEY
The escape makes no difference in arrangements. . . .

To remove all suspicion of understanding, I think it better to put the arresting party in charge of Sheriff Kimbrell, who will be instructed to see that no violence is used.

This will go to you tonight. . . . If I don't get other words from you, the party (all citizens) will be at the junction by 3 o'clock tomorrow.

Lew Wallace

Letter from Billy the Kid to Governor Wallace, March 20, 1879
General Lew Wallace
Sir:
I will keep the appointment I made, but be Sure and have men come that You can depend on. I am not afraid to die like a man fighting but I would not like to be killed like a dog unarmed. tell Kimbal to let his men be placed around the house, and for him to come in alone; and he can arrest us. All I am afraid of is that in the Fort we might be poisoned or killed through a

Window at night, but You can arrange that all right. Tell the Commanding Officer to Watch Lt. Goodwin. [H]e would not hesitate to do anything. there Will be danger on the road of Somebody Waylaying us to kill us on the road to the Fort.

On the Pecos, all that I can remember are the so called Dolan outfit but they are all up here now; and on Rio Grande this man Cris Moten I believe his name is, he drove a herd of (80) head one year ago last December in Company with Frank Wheeler, Frank Baker, deceased, Jesse Evans, George Davis alias Tom Jones, Tom Hill, his name in Texas being Tom Chelson, also deceased. they drove the cattle to the Indian reservation and sold them to John Riley and J. J. Dolan, and the cattle were turned in for Beef for the Indians. the Beckwith family made their boasts that they Came to Seven Rivers a little over four years ago with one Milch Cow borrowed from John Chisum. they had when I was there [a] Year ago one thousand six hundred head of cattle. The male members of the family are Henry Beckwith and John Beckwith, Robert Beckwith was killed the time McSween's house was burned. Charles Robert Olinger and Wallace Olinger are of the same gang. Their cattle ranch is situated at Rock Corral twelve miles below forty miles from Seven Rivers. there are four of them: Paxton, Pierce, Jim Raymer, and Brick Powel. They had when I seen them last about one thousand head of cattle. at Rocky Arroya there is another Ranch belonging to Smith who Operated on the Penaco last year with the Jesse Evans gang. those and the places I mentioned are all I know of. this man Cris Moten, at the time they stole those cattle was in the employ of J. J. Dolan and Co. I afterwards seen Some of the cattle at the Rinconada Bonita on the reservation. those were the men we were in search of when we went to the Agency. the Beckwith family were attending to their own business when this War Started but G. W. Peppin told them that this was John Chisum's War and so they took a hand thinking they would lose their cattle in case that he—Chisum—won the fight. this is all the information I can give you on this point.

Yours Respectfully
Billie

You will Never Catch those fellows on the road. Watch Fritzes, Captain Bacas ranch and the Brewery. they Will either go to Seven Rivers or to the Jicarillo Mountains. they will stay around close until the Scouting parties come in. Give a Spy a pair of glasses and let him get on the mountain back of

Fritzes and watch and if they are there, there will be provisions carried to them. it is not my place to advise you, but I am anxious to have them caught, and perhaps know how men hide from Soldiers, better than you. please excuse me for having so much to say. Tell Kimball not to come before 3 o'clock for I may not be there before.

And I still remain Yours Truly,

W. H. BONNEY

P.S.

I have changed my mind. Send Kimbal to Gutieres just below San Patricio one mile because Sanger and Ballard are or were great friends of Comels. Ballard told me yesterday to leave for you were doing everything to catch me. It was a blind to get me to leave.

An account of the trial of Billy the Kid from the Fort Worth Star, *April 14, 1881*
The prosecution obtained a change of venue, claiming a fair trial in Lincoln County would be impossible. The case was transferred to the Dona Ana County docket and tried at La Mesilla, Judge Warren Bristol presiding.

In the little, squalid courthouse the trial was begun. The court was packed with a motley crowd of spectators; blanketed Indians, swarthy Mexicans, and cowpunchers, rough and unshaven, from the wind-swept mesas of New Mexico.

At the back of the room sat the Judge behind an old-fashioned, flat-topped desk, which was on a platform raised slightly from the floor. In front of the desk was a small space reserved for the lawyers. Only rough wooden benches were provided for the spectators. Sitting at one side of the Judge's desk was Billy the Kid. Rather pleasant was Billy. Wavy, light hair, expressive eyes, seeming just a little defiant now, but looking as though they were made for laughter. There was the mark of keen intellect on his forehead and the clean-cut sweep of his jaw. All around him sat men with guns on their hips. It looked almost ridiculous; all those armed men sitting about a helpless-looking youth, with only the suspicion of down beginning to appear upon his chin.

As a further precaution Billy was kept handcuffed and in leg irons all during his trial. There was drama when the jury filed back into the court-room to report its verdict.

Silent and contemptuous he stood before the Judge and heard his sentence pronounced—"TO BE HANGED BY THE NECK UNTIL YOU ARE DEAD."

Instructions to the jury as requested by the defense

Territory of New Mexico vs. William Bonney, Alias Kid, Alias William Antrim in the District Court of Dona Ana County, March 1881 term.

Instructions asked for by Defendant's Counsel. The court is asked to instruct the Jury as follows: to-wit:

1st Instruction asked: Under the evidence the Jury must either find the defendant guilty of murder in the 1st degree or acquit him.

2nd Instruction asked: The Jury will not be justified in finding the defendant guilty of murder in the 1st degree unless they are satisfied from the evidence, to the exclusion of all reasonable doubt, that the defendant actually fired the shot that caused the death of the deceased [William] Brady [former sheriff of Lincoln County], and that such shot was fired by the defendant with a premeditated design to effect the death of the deceased, or that the defendant was present and actually assisted in firing the fatal shot or shots that caused the death of the deceased, and that he was present and in a position to render such assistance and actually rendered such assistance from a premeditated design the death of the deceased.

3rd Instruction asked: If the Jury are satisfied from the evidence to the exclusion of all reasonable doubt that the defendant was present at the time of the firing of the shot or shots that caused the death of the deceased Brady, yet, before they will be justified in finding the defendant guilty, they must be further satisfied from the evidence and the evidence alone, to the exclusion of all reasonable doubt, that the defendant either fired the shot or shots that killed the deceased, or some one of them, or that he assisted in firing the same, either by his advice, encouragement, or procurement or command, from a premeditated design to effect the death of Brady. If the Jury entertain any reasonable doubt upon any of these points they must find a verdict of acquittal.

    A. J. Fountain

    J. B. Bail

    Attorney for Defendant

Death Warrant for Billy the Kid

To the sheriff of Lincoln county, New Mexico—

Greetings:

At the March term. A.D. 1881, of the District Court for the Third Judicial District of New Mexico, held at La Mesilla in the county of Dona Ana,

William Bonney, *alias* Kid, *alias* William Antrim; was duly convicted of the crime of Murder in the First Degree; and on the fifteenth day of said term, the same being the thirteenth day of April, A.D., 1881, the judgment and sentence of said court were pronounced against the said William Bonney, *alias* Kid, *alias* William Antrim, upon said conviction according to law; whereby the said William Bonney, *alias* Kid, *alias* William Antrim, was adjudged and sentenced to be hanged by the neck until dead by the Sheriff of the said country of Lincoln, within said county.

Therefore, you, the Sheriff of the said county of Lincoln, are hereby commanded that, on Friday, the thirteenth day of May, A.D., 1881, pursuant to the said judgment and sentence of the said court, you take the said William Bonney, *alias* Kid, *alias* William Antrim, from the county jail of the county of Lincoln where he is now confined, to some safe and convenient place within the said country, and there, between the hours of ten o'clock, A.M., and three o'clock, P.M., of said day, you hang the said William Bonney, *alias* Kid, *alias* William Antrim by the neck until he is dead. And make return of your acts hereunder.

Done at Santa Fe in the Territory
of New Mexico, this 30th day
of April, A.D., 1881.
Witness my hand and the great seal
of the Territory.

Lew Wallace
Governor, New Mexico

READING 6
THE LEGEND OF JESSE JAMES, 1882

Jesse James (1847–82) is America's equivalent of Robin Hood: he supposedly stole from the rich and gave to the poor. He and his brother Frank headed a gang that swept through the Midwest, committing robberies and murders. In 1882 Jesse assumed the alias Mr. Howard and allegedly retired from his life of crime. He was at home when Robert Ford, a former member of Jesse's gang, shot him in the back of the head for a reward. That same year James was immortalized in this familiar ballad (author unknown).

It was on a Wednesday night, the moon was shining bright,
    They robbed the Danville train,

And the people they did say, for many miles away,
 'Twas the outlaws Frank and Jesse James.

Chorus:
Jesse had a wife to mourn for his life,
 The children they were brave.
'Twas a dirty little coward that shot Mister Howard,
 And laid poor Jesse in his grave.

Jesse was a man was a friend to the poor,
 He never left a friend in pain.
And with his brother Frank he robbed the Chicago bank
 And they held up the Glendale train.

It was Robert Ford, the dirty little coward,
 I wonder how he does feel,
For he ate of Jesse's bread and he slept in Jesse's bed,
 Then he laid Jesse James in his grave.

It was his brother Frank that robbed the Gallatin bank,
 And carried the money from the town.
It was in this very place that they had a little race,
 For they shot Captain Sheets to the ground.

They went to the crossing not very far from there,
 And there they did the same;
And the agent on his knees he delivered up the keys
 To the outlaws Frank and Jesse James.

It was on a Saturday night, Jesse was at home
 Talking to his family brave,
'Twas one of the gang, dirty Robert Ford,
 That shot Jesse James on the sly.

Jesse went to rest with his hand on his breast;
 He died with a smile on his face.
He was born one day in the county of Clay,
 And came from a solitary race.

When Jesse James was buried in 1882, his family insisted on very specific wording on his tombstone near Kearney, Missouri.

In Loving Memory of My Beloved Son
Jesse W. James
Died April 3, 1882
Aged 34 Years, 6 Months, 28 Days

Murdered by a Traitor and Coward Whose
Name is Not Worthy to Appear Here

READING 7
"WILD BILL," GEORGE ARMSTRONG CUSTER, 1874

A classic example of the mixture of myth and reality that surrounded the lawman of the American West is one of the most famous, James Butler Hickok, best known by the nickname "Wild Bill." Like so many others who wore the tin badge, Hickok had a varied career. He earned his nickname during the Civil War as part of the Union-supporting guerrilla army from Kansas that raided Confederate strongholds in Missouri. Thereafter, he served briefly as a scout for Custer, then resigned to become the law in Hays City, Kansas, but garnered his greatest fame as the marshal of Abilene, Kansas. Hickok also performed on the stage back east and ultimately moved to Deadwood, South Dakota, where he was gunned down while playing poker in 1876 at the age of thirty-nine. Forever afterward the hand he was holding—a pair of aces, and a pair of eights—has been referred to as "the dead man's hand."

In this reading Wild Bill Hickok is described by his admirer and friend, George Armstrong Custer, as he was during the 1860s when he served as marshal of Hays City. Here Hickok, a man of violent mores and changeable sympathies, becomes a frontier nobleman with both feet planted firmly on the bedrock of honesty, moral fortitude, and fair play. Although Custer sketches the violent world of brute survival in the frontier town, he shows nothing of the volatile mixture of politics, personal animosities, and fleeting loyalties that often animated the life of the lawman. Rather, this description reads more like the stage characterization for the lead actor in a melodrama. For Wild Bill in action, see reading 8.

The most prominent man among [the white scouts of the Plains] was "Wild Bill," whose highly varied career was made the subject of an illustrated sketch in one of the popular periodicals a few years ago. Wild Bill was a strange character, just the one which a novelist might gloat over. He was a Plainsman in every sense of the word, yet unlike any other of his class.

In person he was about six feet one in height, straight as the straightest of the warriors whose implacable foe he was; broad shoulders, well-formed chest and limbs, and a face strikingly handsome; a sharp, clear, blue eye, which stared straight in the face when in conversation; a finely-shaped nose, inclined to be aquiline; a well-turned mouth, with lips only partially concealed by a handsome moustache. His hair and complexion were those of the perfect blond. The former was worn in uncut ringlets falling carelessly over his powerfully formed shoulders. Add to this figure a costume blending the immaculate neatness of the dandy with the extravagant taste and style of the frontiersman, and you have Wild Bill, then as now the most famous scout on the Plains. Whether on foot or horseback, he was one of the most perfect types of physical manhood I ever saw. Of his courage there could be no question; it had been brought to the test on too many occasions to admit a doubt. His skill in the use of the rifle and pistol was unerring; while his deportment was exactly opposite of what might be expected from a man of his surroundings. It was entirely free from all bluster or bravado. He seldom spoke of himself unless requested to do so. His conversation, strange to say, never bordered either on the vulgar or blasphemous. His influence among the frontiersmen was unbounded, his word was law; and many are the personal quarrels and disturbances which he had checked among his comrades by his simple announcement that "this had gone far enough," if need be followed by the ominous warning that when persisted in or renewed the quarreller "must settle it with me."

Wild Bill is anything but a quarrelsome man; yet no one but himself can enumerate the many conflicts in which he has been engaged, and which have almost invariably resulted in the death of his adversary. I have a personal knowledge of at least half a dozen men whom he has at various times killed, one of these being at the time a member of my command. Others have been severely wounded, yet he always escapes unhurt. On the Plains every man openly carries his belt with its invariable appendages, knife and revolver, often two of the latter. Wild Bill always carried two handsome ivory-handled revolvers of large size; he was never seen without them.

Where this is the common custom, brawls and personal differences are seldom if ever settled by blows. The quarrel is not from a word to a blow, but from a word to the revolver, and he who can draw and fire first is the best man. No civil law reaches him; none is applied for. In fact there is no law recognized beyond the frontier but that of "might makes right." Should death result from the quarrel, as it usually does, no coroner's jury is impaneled to learn the cause of the death, and the survivor is not arrested. But instead of these old-fashioned proceedings, a meeting of citizens takes place, the survivor is *requested* to be present when the circumstances of the homicide are inquired into, and the unfailing verdict of "justifiable," "self-defense," etc., is pronounced, and the law stands vindicated. That justice is often deprived to a victim there is not a doubt. Yet in all the many affairs of this kind in which Wild Bill has performed a part, and which have come to my knowledge, there is not a single instance in which the verdict of twelve fair-minded men would not be pronounced in his favor.

That the even tenor of his way continues to be disturbed by little events of this description may be inferred from an item which has been floating lately through the columns of the press, and which states that "the funeral of Jim Bludso, who was killed the other day by Wild Bill, took place today." It then adds: "The funeral expenses were borne by Wild Bill." What could be more thoughtful than this? Not only to send a fellow mortal out of the world, but to pay the expenses of the transit.

READING 8

WILD BILL HICKOK, ABILENE, AND JOHN WESLEY HARDIN, 1871

One of the most notorious figures of the American West was John Wesley Hardin, infamous gunman and quintessential frontier badman. Born in Texas and nicknamed "Little Arkansas," Hardin was a loyal Confederate who was outraged that former slaves had gained the right to vote following the Civil War. Sometimes in concert with the Ku Klux Klan, he fought and suppressed blacks and soon earned a reputation as a cold-blooded killer. He was not a thief or robber; he killed for political and racist reasons—the first time at the age of fifteen, his victim being a freed slave. Before his career as a gunman ended, Hardin had dispatched at least thirty-nine persons. The thirty-ninth was a deputy sheriff of Comanche, Texas, by the name of Charles Webb. That murder took place in 1874, and Hardin was captured and convicted in 1877. After serving fifteen years of a twenty-five-year sentence, he was paroled and moved to El Paso, where, ironically, he opened a law office. Three years later, in 1895, he was himself killed by a local constable with whom he had been arguing earlier in the day. The constable sneaked up behind Hardin as he was drinking at a saloon and shot him in the back of the head.

Hardin's posthumously published autobiography describes his encounter with Wild Bill Hickok on the mean streets of Abilene, Kansas, in 1871, the zenith of Abilene's time as a cattle town and railhead to the East. An undercurrent of this excerpt is the politics of the day. Civil War emotions still ran high. It was not uncommon in the rough-and-tumble cattle towns for former Yankees and Johnny Rebs—such as Hickok, a Union supporter and Republican, and Hardin, a Confederate loyalist and Democrat—to draw on each other. Additionally, the American West was witnessing an incorporation boom: cattle towns and mining communities were becoming cities. Pitched battles—both political and physical— would be fought over this issue. Some former Confederates saw in such a civic change lost independence, black suffrage, Republicanism, and an end to the freedom of the plains. Hickok was an incorporation lawman, Hardin an anti-incorporation hired gun. Add to this mix that cattle towns such as Abilene were briefly populated during the cattle drive season by cowboys who jealously guarded their independence and resented authority of any kind, and an explosive brew existed.

I have seen many fast towns, but I think Abilene beats them all. The town was filled with sporting men and women, gamblers, cowboys, desperadoes, and the like. It was well supplied with bar rooms, hotels, barber shops, and gambling houses, and everything was open.

Before I got to Abilene, I had heard much talk of Wild Bill [Hickok], who was then marshal of Abilene. He had a reputation as a killer. I knew Ben Thompson and Phil Coe [two acquaintances from Texas] were there. . . . Besides these, I learned that there were many other Texans there and so, although there was a reward offered for me, I concluded to stay some time there. . . .

Phil Coe and Ben Thompson at that time were running the Bull's Head saloon and gambling hall. They had a big bull painted outside the saloon as a sign, and the city council objected to this for some special reason [actually because the bull featured a very prominent erect penis]. Wild Bill, the marshal, notified Ben Thompson and Phil Coe to take the sign down or change it somewhat. Phil Coe thought the ordinance all right, but it made Thompson mad. Wild Bill, however, sent up some painters and materially changed the offending bovine.

For a long time everybody expected trouble between Thompson and Wild Bill, and I soon found they were deadly enemies. Thompson tried to prejudice me in every way he could against Bill, and told me how Bill, being a Yankee, always picked out Southern men to kill, and especially Texans. I told him: "I am not doing anybody's fighting just now except my own, but I know how to stick to a friend. If Bill needs killing why don't you kill him yourself?"

He said: "I would rather get someone else to do it."

I told him then he had struck the wrong man. I had not yet met Bill Hickok, but really wished for a chance to have a set-to with him just to try my luck.

One night in the wine room he [Hickok] was drinking with some friends of mine when he remarked that he would like to have an introduction with me. George Johnson introduced us, and we had several glasses of wine together. He . . . showed me a proclamation from Texas offering a reward for my arrest.

He said: "Young man [Hardin was eighteen years old at the time; Hickok was thirty-four], I am favorably impressed with you, but don't let Ben Thompson influence you. You are in enough trouble now, and if I can do you a favor, I will do it." I was charmed by his liberal views, and told him so. We parted friends.

I spent most of my time in Abilene in the saloons and gambling houses, playing poker, faro, and seven-up. One day I was rolling ten pins [some gambling halls had a bowling alley] and my best horse was hitched outside in front of the saloon. I had two six-shooters on and of course I knew the saloon people would raise a row if I did not pull them off. [Although most cattle towns required the cowboys to check their guns and pick them up when they left town, Hickok had given Hardin a waiver.] Several Texans were there rolling ten pins and drinking. I suppose we were pretty noisy. Wild Bill came in and said we were making too much noise and told me to pull off my pistols until I was ready to go out of town. I told him I was ready to go now, but did not propose to put up my pistols, go or no go. He went out and I followed him. I started up the street when someone behind me [probably one of the Texans who were bowling] shouted out: "Set up. All down but nine."

Wild Bill whirled around and met me. He said: "What are you howling about, and what are you doing with those pistols on?"

I said: "I am just taking in the town."

He pulled his pistol and said: "Take those pistols off. I arrest you."

I said all right and pulled them out of the scabbards, but while he was reaching for them I reversed them and whirled them over on him with the muzzles in his face, springing back at the same time. I told him to put his pistol up, which he did. I cursed him for a long-haired scoundrel that would shoot a boy with his back to him (as I had been told he intended to do me). He said, "Little Arkansas, you have been wrongly informed."

By this time a big crowd had gathered with pistols and arms. They kept urging me to kill him. Down the street a squad of policemen were coming, but Wild Bill motioned them to go back and at the same time asked me not to let the mob shoot him.

I shouted: "This is my fight and I'll kill the first man that fires a gun."

Bill said: "You are the gamest and quickest boy I ever saw. Let us compromise this matter and I will be your friend. Let us go in here and take a drink, as I want to talk to you and give you some advice."

At first I thought he might be trying to get the drop on me, but he finally convinced me of his good intentions and we went in and took a drink. We went into a private room and I had a long talk with him and we came out friends.

Hardin was still allowed to carry his guns, but Wild Bill's patience and hospitality did not last long. Annoyed by snoring in an adjoining hotel room, Hardin fired two shots into the wall. The second shot killed the snoring man. As Hickok and four policemen came to investigate, Hardin jumped out a window and escaped, wearing only an undershirt. He would later declare, "I believed that if Wild Bill found me in a defenseless condition, he would take no explanation, but would kill me to add to his reputation." Hickok did kill Phil Coe shortly after Hardin skipped Abilene, and the outraged Texas contingent called for Hickok's head. He would finish out the year as marshal, then quit to become a scout and later a stage performer.

READING 9

SHERIFF FRANK CANTON AND TETON JACKSON, 1880s

A key factor in law enforcement in the American West was the all-important question, who are you working for? For some lawmen, perhaps more than we know, the answer was an easy one: the most powerful figures in the community. In mining towns it would be the mine owners; in the cowtown railheads, the business community or the "better citizens"; in cattle country, the cattle barons or stockmen's associations. These last figured in the career of Frank Canton, who was not unusual among western lawmen in having a checkered past. Canton, whose given name was Joe Horner, had been both an outlaw and a cowboy in Texas before moving to Wyoming in 1880. There he first worked as a detective for the Wyoming Stockgrowers' Association and then was elected sheriff of Johnson County in 1882.

Wyoming in the 1880s was a center for outlaws. The Hole-in-the-Wall area of the Big Horn Mountains was a hiding place for many, whether unrepentant desperadoes or third-rate horse thieves and criminal wannabes. Since Johnson County was cattle country, the cattle rustler was Public Enemy Number One, with the horse thief a very close second. The cattle barons (many of whom were English absentee owners) recruited lawmen (often hired guns) to support a local vigilance committee and to hunt down and eliminate the rustlers. The barons were also playing power politics at its bloodiest, however, by eliminating as well anyone they viewed as opposition—often small ranchers and homesteaders who threatened their control of the open range.

It was in this atmosphere that Frank Canton became sheriff. Since he had worked for the stockgrowers' association, his 1930 autobiography presents a highly biased account of his legal activities. Nevertheless, his tales of searching for cattle rustlers, horse thieves, and stage robbers provide valuable insight into the nature of law enforcement in those days. As the agent of government institutions in a region that clung to its independence from government intrusion, the lawman administered a rough-and-ready justice, equal parts courage, coercion, and bluff. In this excerpt Canton describes the methods of the horse rustlers and narrates his encounter with Teton Jackson, notorious leader of a cleverly organized ring of horse thieves.

The system this band adopted was to steal ten or fifteen head from each herd on the range scattered over a large area of country, and drive them into Jackson's Hole, which was a basin of country covering several square miles, and was almost walled in by mountains; this was the most talked-of outlaw rendezvous in the world. The owners would probably not miss their stock for months, and even then would think the little bunch had strayed off.

When the thieves had secured eight hundred or a thousand head, they would then doctor the brands and as soon as the new brands healed over they would put the herd on the trail and drive them over through Johnson County, Wyoming, to Deadwood and other mining towns in the Black Hills [of South Dakota] where they would find a good market for them. This systematic stealing continued for several years. One day I received a telegram . . . saying that Teton Jackson had recently stolen about fifty head of fine horses from two ranchmen by the names of High and Stout, and that he was seen by two Snake Indians heading toward the Big Horn mountains.

There was an old trapper and hunter by the name of Lucas, who had a cabin at the mouth of Paint Rock Creek Canyon in the Basin, whom I suspected of being in league with this band of horse thieves. His cabin was forty miles from Buffalo over the Big Horn Mountains. I selected Chris Gross and Ed Loyd, two of my best deputies, and left Buffalo about dark, and by hard riding through pine timber and windfalls, reached the cabin about two hours before daylight. We tied our horses to some trees and got positions in good shooting distance of the cabin, which had only one door and one window. Of course, we did not know that Teton was there and only suspected that he was in the cabin. But I did not intend to take any more chances than I would have done had I been sure that he was there.

Just before daybreak a candle was lighted in the cabin and in a few minutes sparks began to come out of the chimney. I gave my Winchester to Gross and Loyd and gave orders for them to watch the window and door and stop anyone who might try to escape. I then drew my six-shooter and stepped quickly into the cabin. I recognized Teton Jackson instantly by the description I had of him. He was squatting down in front of the fireplace trying to light his pipe with a splinter. He was only half dressed and had not yet buckled on his six-shooter, although it was lying within his reach with a belt full of cartridges. I covered him at once with my revolver, and ordered him to throw up his hands, and at the same time called for my deputies to come in and handcuff him. Lucas was slicing up venison for breakfast. . . . After we had breakfast I sent Lucas out with my two deputies and told him that if he did not round up and bring in every horse that Teton had driven into the canyon I would arrest him too and take him to Buffalo. . . .

After they left I was in the cabin alone with Teton. He was not a pleasant companion. I have never seen a man of his description before or since. He was about forty-five, over six feet in height, weighed a hundred and ninety, stubby beard, raw-boned, coarse features, flaming red hair, red face, and eyes that were as black as a snake's. . . . I had taken a seat about six feet from him with my revolver in my hand. He began to complain that the handcuffs were so tight that the blood could not circulate and that he was in great pain, and that if I would take them off he would be quiet and promise not to hurt me. I told him that I was not the least bit uneasy about his hurting me, and that I had no objection to granting his request, but that he was the one taking all the chances, for if he made the slightest move I would kill him. He said he understood the situation. I then threw the keys over to him, and he unlocked the handcuffs and pitched the keys and cuffs back to me.

After he had removed the cuffs he began rubbing his wrists and said that I would never take him to Buffalo and that he wanted to serve notice on me right there and then that he was a better man than I was, even without a six-shooter. He began to talk very abusive. I told him that I would take him to Buffalo and that he was worth as much to me dead as alive. I told him I would prefer to take his dead body as it would be less trouble to handle than a live one. I then threw the open handcuffs on the floor at his feet and told him that if he did not snap them on his wrists in ten seconds, he could take his medicine. I think he put them on in less time than I had given him.

My deputies returned in about an hour with the stolen horses, which proved to be the property of High and Stout. We put Teton on one of the horses, tied his feet together under the horse's body, and landed him in jail in Buffalo that night. . . .

With Teton Jackson out of the way, the backbone of the band was broken. Red Anderson and Black Tom, two members of the band, were shot and killed near the Yellowstone Park. George Stevens, alias Big George, was shot and killed on the Big Horn Mountains by Chris Gross, who also captured Frank Lamb. The rest of the gang left the Teton Mountains and most of them were picked up by officers in adjoining territories and sent to the penitentiary.

Canton left his position as sheriff in 1886 and returned to work as a detective for the Wyoming Stockgrowers' Association. In this post he recruited some fifty gunmen to hunt down opponents (primarily rustlers but also homesteaders) of the cattle barons. Two of these "opponents" had been killed in this Johnson County War, as it came to be called, before the U.S. Cavalry intervened to cool down the situation.

CHAPTER 8

WOMEN OF THE AMERICAN WEST

THE WOMEN of the American West lived lives that were normally extraordinary or extraordinarily normal, depending upon whom you consult. According to one interpretive school, these women were content for the most part to conform to expected feminine roles; even if given the opportunity to reach out to new societal goals, they chose not to but determinedly remained housewives, cooks, and mothers. And yet other interpretations, using the same fact base, chronicle the courage, independence, and groundbreaking tendencies of American western women. Which one is correct? Probably, as with most historical controversies, the answer lies somewhere in the middle—and depends on the circumstances. One thing is certain: western women, regardless of age, race, culture, economic status, religion, or politics, had to be adaptable. The conditions they faced—harsh geography, cultural restrictions, economic hardships, social misconceptions, sexual repressions—would have tried the gumption and guile of anyone. It was tough out there, and a delicate flower was sure to wilt; survival required nerves of steel and a resilient psyche.

Selections throughout this book present the activities, contributions, and accomplishments of women in the American West. This chapter focuses on women not because they were separate and distinct from the sweep of American western history but because they have been the subject of historical neglect over the years. The readings here highlight the experiences of women of the wagon train, women of color, women as leaders of the reform impulse, and, most notably, women who adapted to and survived in the difficult and generally male-dominated world of the American West.

READING I

"THEY ARE SHARP AS NAILS," ANTHONY TROLLOPE, 1862

What impressed observers of all stripes about women of the American West was their resilience and adaptability. The comments of the British novelist Anthony

Trollope (1815–82) are infused with an obvious upper-crust snootiness and chauvinism, but his characterization of the American woman is still an apt jumping-off point. In a society that demonstrated little regard or respect for the accomplishments of women, the independent nature of American women in the West, as Trollope presents it, both impressed and terrified the average male. Many American western women would break all the rules and lead the country toward a more equitable future.

All native American women are intelligent. It seems to be their birthright. In the eastern cities they have, in their upper classes, superadded womanly grace to this intelligence, and consequently they are charming as companions. They are beautiful also, and, as I believe, lack nothing that a lover can desire in his love. But I cannot fancy myself much in love with a western lady, or rather with a lady of the West. They are sharp as nails, but then they are also as hard. They know, doubtless, all that they ought to know, but then they know so much more than they ought to know. They are tyrants to their parents, and never practise the virtue of obedience till they have half-grown daughters of their own. They have faith in the destiny of their country, if in nothing else; but they believe that that destiny is to be worked out by the spirit and talent of the young women. I confess that for me Eve would have no charms had she not recognized Adam as her lord. I can forgive her in that she tempted him to eat the apple. Had she come from the West country she would have ordered him to make his meal, and then I could not have forgiven her.

READING 2

SUSAN MAGOFFIN, 1846

Setting out on the overland journey westward was an occasion for a mixture of romantic speculation and serious apprehension. Such was the case for Susan Magoffin, the eighteen-year-old wife of James Magoffin, who was a wealthy trader along the Santa Fe Trail and a controversial figure during the Mexican-American War of 1846–48. Susan's diary reveals the motivations and hopes of the women who traveled west and the realities they faced. Susan Magoffin would have two children and die at the age of twenty-eight.

June [1846]

From the city of New York to the Plains of Mexico is a stride that I myself can scarcely realize. Tuesday evening we went into Independence [Missouri]; there we stayed one night only at Mr. Noland's Hotel.

11th

Now the Prairie life begins! We left "the settlements" this morning. Our mules travel well and we joged on at a rapid pace till 10 o'clock when we came up with the waggons.

We crossed the branch and stretched our tent. It is a grand affair indeed. 'Twas made in Philadelphia by a regular tent-maker of the army, and every thing is complete. Our bed is as good as many houses have; sheets, blankets, counterpanes, pillows &c. We have a carpet made of sail duck, have portable stools.

Well after a supper at *my own table* and in *my own house* I can say what few women in civilized life ever could, that the first house of his own to which my husband took me to after our marriage was a *tent;* and the first table of my own at which I ever sat was a cedar one, made with only *one leg* and that was a tent pole.

12th

At night we struck camp at "Black Jack," fourteen miles from the last, & 49 from Independence. Being tired of the carriage I got out and took a ramble.

I picked numberless flowers with which the plains are covered, and as *mi alma* [her affectionate term for her husband] told me before we started, I threw them away to gather more. I wearied myself out at this, and as the tent was now up, I returned "*home.*"

There before supper I had a little piece of work to attend to, I mean the feeding of my chickens. It is quite a farm house this; poultry, dogs, cattle, mules, horses &c. Altogether my home is one not to be objected to.

13th

This A.M. about 10 o'clock we met an Indian trader returning from "Bent's Fort" up the big Arkansas River. He is returning with his cargo of skins; we stoped and had half hour's conversation with him respecting the road, war news &c. It is all pretty good. Says the Indians are pretty bad about Pawnee Fork, which is 298 miles from Independence. His wagons are met about half a mile back; they are loaded with skins.

14th

This is my first sabbath on the plains!

A very quiet one it has been too, something I had not looked for. But all the men seem to recollect it and hitch in their teams with half the trouble, and I have scarcely heard an oath the whole day.

Camp No. 7. Wednesday, 17th.
Last night I had a wolfish kind of a serenade!

Ring, my dear, good dog! was lying under my side of the bed, which was next to the wolves, the instant they came up, he had been listening, he flew out with a firce bark, and drove them away. I felt like caressing him for his kindness.

It was solitude indeed. The howling of ravinus beasts, and the screech of not less ravinus birds. I lay perfectly still with *mi alma* breathing a sweet sleep by my side. I could not waken him, just to keep me company, when he was so well engaged. So I remained quiet occasionally knocking off a musquito and listening to the confused sounds without and wishing that my faithful Ring would not sleep so soundly.

Just then, he gave one spring from his hiding place, and in a twinkling had driven them off entirely.

Council Grove, 145 miles from Independence. Friday, 19th. Camp No. 9
In our travels today we stoped two miles the other side of Council Grove at what is called Big John's Spring.

The scenery around is very wild and rather awing. While I stood apparently very calm and bold as *mi alma* bent down to fix a little *toddy* with water from the clear flowing stream, I could not suppress the fear, or rather the thought of some wily savage or hungry wolf lurking in the thick grape vines, ready the first advantageous moment to bounce upon my shoulders. I would not tell *mi alma* these foolish fears, for I knew he would ridicule them, and this was torture to me, but Ring, my faithful Ring, came by me just then and I commenced to patting his head which made him lie at my feet and I felt *safe* with this trusty soldier near me.

Thursday, 25th. Camp 15. Cotton wood creek. 12 miles.
While Jane [Susan's maid] and I were on a little stroll after dinner, I carelessly walking along steped almost onto a large snake; it moved and frightened me very much. Of course I screamed and ran off.

Noon. No. 20. Little Arkansas River. June 30th.
Now, about dark, we came into the musquito regions, and I found to my great *horror* that I have been complaining all this time for nothing, yes absolutely for *nothing;* for some two or hundred or even thousands are nothing compared with what we now encountered. The carriage mules

became so restless that they passed all the wagons and swishing their tails from side to side, as fast as they could, and slaping their ears, required some strength of our Mexican driver to hold them in.

About 10 o'clock the mules became perfectly frantic, and nothing could make them stand. They turned out to shift for themselves, and Magoffin seeing no other alternative than to remain there all night, tied his head and neck up with pocket handkerchiefs and set about having the tent stretched.

I drew my feet up under me, wraped my shawl over my head, till I almost smothered with heat, and listened to the din without. And such a noise as it was, I shall pray ever to be preserved. Millions upon millions were swarming around me, and their knocking against the carriage *reminded me of a hard rain.* It was equal to any of the plagues of Egypt.

I lay almost in a perfect stupor, the heat and stings made me perfectly sick, till Magoffin came to the carriage and told me *to run if I could,* with my shawl, bonnet and shoes on (and without opening my mouth Jane said, for they would *choke* me) straight to bed.

When I got there they pushed me straight in under the musquito bar, which had been tied up in some kind of a fashion, and oh, dear, what a relief it was to breathe again. There I sat in my cage, like an imprisoned creature frightened half to death.

Magoffin now rolled himself up some how with all his clothes on, and lay down at my side, he dare not raise the bar to get in. I tried to sleep and towards daylight succeeded. On awakening this morning I found my forehead, arms and feet covered with knots as large as a pea.

Camp No. 23

A thunder storm at sunset on the Prairie is a sublime and awing scene indeed. The vivid and forked lightning quickly succeeded by the hoarse growling thunder impresses one most deeply of his own weakness and the magnanimity of his God.

July 4 Pawnee Fort.

What a disasterous *celebration* I have today. It is certainly the greatest miracle that I have my head on my shoulders. I think I can never forget it if I live to be as old as my grandfather.

The wagons left Pawnee Rock some time before us—for I was anxious to see this wonderful curiosity. We went up, and while *mi alma* with his gun and pistol kept watch, for the wily Indian may always be apprehended here; it is a good lurking place and they are ever ready to fall upon any unfortunate trader behind his company—and it is necessary to be careful, so while *mi alma* watched on the rock above, and Jane stood by to watch if any should come up on the front side of me, I cut my name, among the many hundreds inscribed on the rock and many of whom I knew. It was not done well, for fear of Indians made me tremble all over and I hurried it over in any way.

The wagons being some distance ahead we rode on quite briskly to overtake them. In an hour's time we had driven some six miles, and at *Ash creek* we came up with them. No water in the creek and the crossing pretty good only a tolerably steep bank on the first side of it; all but two had passed over, and as these were not up we drove on ahead of them to cross first.

The bank though a little steep was smooth and there could be no difficulty in riding down it. However, we had made up our minds always to walk down such places in case of accident, and before we got to it *mi alma* hallowed "Woe" as he always does when he wishes to stop, but as there was no motion made by the driver to that effect, he repeated it several times and with much vehemence.

We had now reached the very verge of the cliff and seeing it a good way and apparently less dangerous than jumping out as we were, he said, "Go on." The word was scarcely from his lips, ere we were whirled completely over with a perfect crash. One to see the wreck of that carriage now with the top and sides entirely broken to pieces, could never believe that people had come out of it alive. But strange, wonderful to say, we are almost entirely unhurt!

I was considerably stunned at first and could not stand on my feet. *Mi alma* forgetting himself and entirely enlisted for my safety carried me in his arms to a shade tree, almost entirely without my knowledge, and rubbing my face and hands with whiskey soon brought me entire to myself. My back and side are a little hurt, but is very small compared with what it might have been.

Mi alma has his left hip and arm on which he fell both bruised and strained, but not seriously. Dear creature, 'twas for me he received this, for had he not caught me in his arms as we fell he could have saved himself entirely. And then I should perhaps have been killed or much crushed for the top fell over me, and it was only his hands that kept it off of me. It is better as it is, for we can sympathise more fully with each other.

[July] 6th. Camp No. 26.

It is a rich sight indeed to look at the fine fat [buffalo] meat stretched out on ropes to dry for our sustinence when we are no longer in the regions of the living animal. Such soup as we have made of the hump ribs, one of the most choice parts of the buffalo. I never eat its equal in the best hotels of N.Y. and Philad[elphi]a. And the sweetest butter and most delicate oil I ever tasted, 'tis not surpassed by the marrow taken from the thigh bones.

Mi alma was out this morning on a hunt, but I sincerely hope he will never go again. I am so uneasy from the start till he returns. There is danger attached to it that the excited hunter seldom thinks of till it overtake him. His horse may fall and kill him; the buffalo is apt too, to whirl suddenly on his persuer, and often serious if not fatal accidents occur. It is a painful situation to be placed in, to know that the being dearest to you on earth is in momentary danger of losing his life, or receiving for the remainder of his days, whether long or short, a tormenting wound.

11th. Camp 31st

I am sick, rather sad feelings and everything around corresponds with them.

We have never had such a perfectly dead level before us as now. The little hillocks which formerly broke the perfectly even view have entirely disappeared. The grass is perfectly short, a real buffalo and Prairie dog and rattle snake region.

Road to Bent's Fort. Saturday, 18th. Camp 38, Bank of the Arkansas

The idea of being sick on the Plains is not at all pleasant to me; it is rather terrifying than otherwise, although I have a good nurse in my servant woman Jane, and one of the kindest husbands in the world, all gentleness and affection.

Bent's Fort, July 28th

Dctr. [Doctor] Mesure brought me medicine, and advises *mi alma* to travel me through Europ. The advice is rather better to take than the medicine, anything though to restore my health. I never should have consented to take the trip on the plains had it not been with that view and a hope that it would prove beneficial; but so far my hopes have been blasted, for I am rather going down hill than up, and it is so bad to be sick and under a physician all the time.

July 30th

Well this is my nineteenth birthday! And what? Why I feel rather strange, not surprised at its coming, nor to think that I am growing rather older, for that is the way of the human family, but this is it, I am sick! strange sensations in my head, my back and hips. I am obliged to lie down most of the time, and when I get up to hold my hand over my eyes.

There is the greatest possible noise in the *patio* [of Bent's Fort]. The shoeing of horses, neighing, and braying of mules, the crying of children, the scolding and fighting of men, are all enough to turn my head. And to add to the scene, like some of our neighbours we have our own private troubles. The servants are all quarreling and fighting among themselves, running to us to settle their difficulties; they are gambling off their cloths till some of them are next to nudity, and though each of them are in debt to *mi alma* for advancement of their wages, they are coming to him to get them out of their scrapes.

August, 1846. Thursday 6th.

The mysteries of a new world have been shown to me since last Thursday. In a few short months I should have been a happy mother and made the heart of a father glad, but the ruling hand of a mighty Providence has interposed and by an abortion deprived us of the hope.

My pains commenced and continued until 12 o'c. at night, when after much agony and severest of pains, which were relieved a little at times by medicine given by Dctr. Mesure, *all was over*. I sunk off into a kind of lethargy, in *mi alma*'s arms. Since that time I have been in my bed till yesterday a little while, and a part of today.

My situation was very different from that of an Indian woman in the room below me. She gave birth to a fine healthy baby, about the same time, *and in half an hour after she went to the River and bathed herself and it,* and this she has continued every day since. Never could I have believed such a thing, if I had not been here, and *mi alma*'s own eyes had not seen her coming from the River. And some gentlemen here tells him, he has often seen them immediately after the birth of a child go to the water and *break the ice* to bathe themselves!

It is truly astonishing to see what customs will do. No doubt many ladies in civilized life are ruined by too careful treatments during childbirth.

The Fort is quite desolate. Most who are here now of the soldiers are sick. Two have died, and have been buried in the sand hills, the common fate of man.

Camp No. 1. Saturday, 8th. Second start.
The crossing of the Arkansas was an event in my life, I have never met with before; the separating me from my dear native land. Perhaps I have left it for not only the first, but the last time.

Saturday, 15. Camp No. 9
We have an abundance of game, fine turkies, one of which we had roasted for dinner today, prairie chickens, hares, and they say we are to have bear meat soon. Three were seen this morning by the teamsters, and we passed in the road the carcass of one seeming to have been killed yesterday. I must look sharp when I ramble about through these woods, or I will get myself into a nice hugging scrape.

24th. Camp No. 18. Olla de Galinas
Traveled late tonight and it has been so dark too, it was almost necessary to feel our way—with [my husband's] careful driving though, I felt little fear.

How cheering it is to one when groping their way in the dark, over roads and through country he knew nothing about, all bewildered, and not knowing whether he is about pitching over a precipice, or driving into some deep ravine, whole &c., to have the light of the camp fires of those ahead of them, to break suddenly before the eye. It is like drink to a thirsty traveler, or a straw [sic] to a drowning man.

27. Near San Miguel
We have passed through some two or three little settlements today and I am glad to think that much is accomplished of my task. It is truly shocking to my modesty to pass such places with gentlemen.

The woman slap about with their arms and necks bare, perhaps their bosoms exposed (and they are none of the prettiest or whitest). If they are about to cross the little creek that is near all the villages, regardless of those about them, they pull their dresses, which in the first place but little more than cover their calves—up about their knees and paddle through the water like ducks, sloshing and spattering every thing about them.

Some of them wear leather shoes, from the States, but most have buckskin mockersins, Indian style.

And it is repulsive to see the children running about perfectly naked, or if they have on a chemise it is in such ribbands it had better be off at once. I am constrained to keep my veil drawn closely over my face all the time to protect my blushes.

Santa Fe. August 31st, 1846.

It is really hard to realize it, that I am here in my own house, in a place too where I once would have thought it folly to think of visiting. I have entered the city in a year that will always be remembered by my countrymen; and under the "Star-Spangled banner" too, the first American lady, who has come under such auspices, and some of our company seem disposed to make me the first under any circumstances that ever crossed the Plains.

READING 3
ELIZABETH DIXON SMITH GEER, 1848

Unlike the effusive Susan Magoffin, Elizabeth Geer recounted her experiences—on the Oregon Trail in 1848—in a terse, almost laconic style.

June 3. Passed through St. Joseph on the bank of the Missouri. Laid in our flour, cheese, and crackers and medicine, for no one should travel this road without medicine, for they are almost sure to have the summer complaint. Each family should have a box of physicking pills, a quart of castor oil, a quart of the best rum, and a large vial of peppermint essence. We traveled 4 miles by the river and encamped. Here we found nine wagons bound for Oregon.

June 5. Made 9 miles. At present 22 wagons.

June 6. Made 18 miles. Passed 70 Oregon wagons as they were encamped.

June 12. Laid by to wash. Had 2 horses stolen by the Indians last night out of the company.

June 23. Made 18 miles. At present there is one hundred and forty persons in our company. We see thousands of buffalo and have to use their dung for fuel. A man will gather a bushel in a minute; three bushels make a good fire. We call the stuff "buffalo chips."

Aug. 1. Passed over the Rocky Mountains, the backbone of America . . . made 18 miles. Had rain and hail today which made it disagreeably cold.

Aug. 29. Made 16 miles. Camped on Snake River. Plenty of grass and willows. Very dusty roads. You in "The States" know nothing about dust. It will fly so that you can hardly see the horns of your tongue yoke of oxen. It often seems that the cattle must die for the want of breath, and then in our wagons, such a spectacle—beds, clothes, victuals and children, all completely covered.

Sept. 16. Saw a boiling hot spring. Clear and good tasting water. Made 18 miles. Camped at Barrel Camp. Good grass by driving up the stream a mile or so where two cattle were shot with arrows by Indians, but not mortally wounded.

Sept. 24. Laid by to dry our things which got wet crossing the river. Mr. Kimball's oldest son died of typhus fever.

Oct. 9. Doubled teams on another mountain. Made 15 miles. Camped at Pine Camp. Good feed and water. My husband and I are both sick with the summer complaint.

Oct. 17. Cold and windy. We made a fire of a little wood that we carried all day yesterday. Made a bite to eat. Our cattle ran off in search of water which hindered us till late. Made 4 miles. Camped without wood, except a small shrub called greasewood. It burns like greased weeds. I used to wonder why it was said that men must be dressed in buckskin to come to this country, but now I know. Everything we travel through is thorny and rough. There is no chance of saving your clothes. Here we found a great hole of water 12 or 15 feet across. Had to water a hundred and fifty head of cattle with pails. Had to stand out all night in the rain to keep the cattle from drowning each other—after water in this hole.

Oct. 28. (On the Columbia River). Here are a great many immigrants encamped, some making rafts, others going down in boats which have been sent up by speculators.

READING 4
CATHERINE HAUN, 1849

In 1849 Catherine Haun and her husband, a lawyer, left Iowa for the goldfields of California. Years later Catherine dictated her reminiscences of the journey to her daughter. Her memories are washed with the softening effect of time, and she tends to romanticize the events. Moreover, Haun was a middle-class woman, and the wagon train she traveled with was large, well financed and organized; most wagon trains were not so fortunate. Even so, her narrative discloses the fear that accompanied the group and the disasters that befell others, if not herself.

During the day we womenfolk visited from wagon to wagon or congenial friends spent an hour walking, ever westward, and talking over our home life back in "the states" telling of loved ones left behind; voicing our hopes for the future in the far west and even whispering a little friendly gossip of emigrant life.

High teas were not popular but tatting, knitting, crocheting, exchanging recepes for cooking beans or dried apples or swapping food for the sake of variety kept us in practice of feminine occupations and diversions.

We did not keep late hours but when not too engrossed with fear of the red enemy or dread of impending danger we enjoyed the hour around the campfire. The menfolk lolling and smoking their pipes and guessing or maybe betting how many miles we had covered the day. We listened to readings, story telling, music and songs and the day often ended in laughter and merrymaking.

It was the fourth of July when we reached the beautiful Laramie River. Its sparkling, pure waters were full of myriads of fish that could be caught with scarcely an effort. It was necessary to build barges to cross the river and during the enforced delay our animals rested and we had one of our periodical "house cleanings." This general systematic re-adjustment always freshened up our wagon train very much, for after a few weeks of travel things got mixed up and untidy and often wagons had to be abandoned if too worn for repairs, and generally one or more animals had died or been stolen.

After dinner that night it was proposed that we celebrate the day and we all heartily join[ed] in. America West was the Goddess of Liberty, Charles Wheeler was Orator and Ralph Cushing acted as master of ceremonies. We sang patriotic songs, repeated what little we could of the Declaration of Independence, fired off a gun or two, and gave three cheers for the United States and California Territory in particular!

The young folks decorated themselves in all manner of fanciful and grotesque costumes—Indian characters being the most popular. To the rollicking music of violin and Jew's harp we danced until midnight. There were Indian spectators, all bewildered by the weird dance of the Pale Face and possibly they deemed it advisable to sharpen up their arrow heads. During the frolic when the sport was at its height a strange white woman with a little girl in her sheltering embrace rushed into the corral. She was trembling with terror, tottering with hunger. Her clothing was badly torn and her hair disheveled. The child crouched in fear and hid her face within the folds of her mother's tattered skirt. The woman could give no account of her forlorn condition but was only to sob: "Indians." and "I have nobody nor place to go to." After she had partaken of food and was refreshed by a safe night's rest she recovered and the next day told us that her husband and sister had contracted cholera on account of which her family consisting of husband, brother, sister, herself and two children had stayed behind their train. The sick ones' died and while burying the sister the survivors were attacked by Indians, who, as she supposed, killed her brother and little son. She was obliged to flee for her life dragging with her the little five year old daughter.

She had been three days walking back to meet a train. It had been necessary, in order to avoid Indians, to conceal herself behind trees or bowlders much of the time and although she had seen a train in the distance before ours she feared passing the Indians that were between the emigrants and herself. She had been obliged to go miles up the Laramie to find a place where she could get across by wading from rock to rock and the swift current had lamed her and bruised her body.

Raw fish that she had caught with her hands and a squirrel that she killed with a stone had been their only food. Our noise and campfire had attracted her and in desperation she braved the Indians around us and trusting to the darkness ventured to enter our camp. Martha, for that was her name, had emigrated from Wisconsin and pleaded with us to send her home; but we had now gone too far on the road to meet returning emigrants so there was no alternative for her but to accept our protection and continue on to California. When she became calm and somewhat reconciled to so long and uncertain a journey with strangers she made herself useful and loyally cast her lot with us. She assisted me with the cooking for her board; found lodgings with the woman whose husband was a cripple and in return helped the brave woman drive the ox team. Mr. & Mrs. Lamore kept her little girl with their own. . . .

Upon the second day of our resumed travel, still following up the North Platte, Martha spied a deserted wagon some little distance off the road which she recognized as her own. Mr. Bowen went with her to investigate, hoping to find her brother and son. The grave of her sister was still open and her clothing as well as that of her husband, who was in the wagon where he had died, were missing. The grewsome sight drove her almost mad. Mr. Bowen and she did not bury the bodies lest they might contagion back to us.

No trace of either brother or son could be found. All supplies and the horses had been stolen by the Indians.

Cholera was prevalent on the plains at this time; the train preceding as well as the one following ours had one or more deaths, but fortunately we had not a single case of the disease. Often several graves together stood as silent proof of smallpox or cholera epidemic. The Indians spread the disease among themselves by digging up the bodies of the victims for the clothing. The majority of the Indians were badly pock-marked. . . .

Turning in a southwesterly direction we came to Fort Bridger, named for the celebrated scout [Jim Bridger]. It was simply a trading post for the white and Indian fur trappers. We saw a renegade white man here who having lived for years among the Indians had forgotten his native language and dressing and eating as they did, his long unkept hair and uncouth appearance was loathsome in the extreme; it being hard to distinguish him from his brother Indians. We regarded him with more fear and abhorance than we did a manly buck, and his squaw and family of half-breeds as unfortunates.

It was with considerable apprehension that we started to traverse the treeless, alkali region of the Great Basin or Sink of the Humboldt. Our wagons were badly worn, the animals much the worse for wear, food and stock feed was getting low with no chance of replenishing the supply. During the month of transit we, like other trains, experienced the greatest privations of the whole trip. It was no unusual sight to see graves, carcasses of animals and abandoned wagons. In fact the latter furnished us with wood for the campfires as the sagebrush was scarce and unsatisfactory and buffalo chips were not as plentiful as on the plains east of the Rocky Mountains.

The alkali dust of this territory was suffocating, irritating our throats and clouds of it often blinded us. The mirages tantalized us; the water was unfit to drink or to use in any way; animals often perished or were so overcome by heat and exhaustion that they had to be abandoned, or in case of human hunger, the poor jaded creatures were killed and eaten. . . .

One of our dogs was so emaciated and exhausted that we were obliged to leave him on this desert and it was said that the train following us used him for food.

Before leaving Bear River, knowing of the utter lack of fresh water, we cooked large quantities of bread to be used on the desert. We gave a half loaf each day to each horse until the flour gave out. This was a substitute for grain.

Across this drear country I used to ride horseback several hours of the day which was a great relief from the continual jolting of even our spring wagon. I also walked a great deal and this lightened the wagon. One day I walked fourteen miles and was not very fatigued.

. . . The men seemed more tired and hungry than were the women.

Our only death on the journey occurred in this desert. The Canadian woman, Mrs. Lamore, suddenly sickened and died [a contemporary euphemism for death in childbirth], leaving her two little girls and grief stricken husband. We halted a day to bury her and the infant that had lived but an hour, in this weird, lonely spot on God's footstool away apparently from everywhere and everybody.

The bodies were wrapped together in a bedcomforter and wound, quite mummyfied with a few yards of string that we made by tying together torn strips of a cotton dress skirt. A passage of the Bible (my own) was read; a prayer offered and "Nearer My God to Thee" sung. Owing to the unusual surroundings the ceremony was very impressive. Every heart was touched and eyes full of tears as we lowered the body, coffinless, into the grave. There was no tombstone—why should there be—the poor husband and orphans could never hope to revisit the grave and to the world it was just one of the many hundreds that marked the trail of the argonaut.

The burial and one I witnessed at sea some years later made a lasting impression upon me and I always think of them when I attend a funeral; such a grewsome sensation was caused by the desolation. The immense, lonesome plain; the great fathomless ocean—how insignificant seems the human body when consigned to their cold embrace! . . . Martha and the lamented Canadian wife had formed a fast friendship while on the plains and the former was a faithful nurse during the latter's illness. What more natural than that the dying mother should ask her friend to continue to care for her orphan girls and to make [them] the sisters of her own daughter?

Years afterward when prosperity crowned Mr. Lamore's efforts the three girls were sent "back to the states" to school and Martha's daughter became the wife of a prominent United States Congressman. . . .

. . . [W]e reached Sacramento on November 4, 1849, just six months and ten days after leaving Clinton, Iowa, we were all in pretty good condition. . . .

Although very tired of tent life many of us spent Thanksgiving and Christmas in our canvas houses. I do not remember ever having had happier holiday times. For Christmas dinner we had a grizzly bear steak for which we paid $2.50, one cabbage for $1.00 and—oh horrors—some *more* dried apples! And for a Christmas present the Sacramento river rose very high and flooded the whole town! . . . It was past the middle of January before we . . . reached Marysville—there were only half dozen houses; all occupied at exorbitant prices. Some one was calling for the services of a lawyer to draw up a will and my husband offered to do it for which he charged $150.00.

This seemed a happy omen for success and he hung out his shingle, abandoning all thought of going to the mines. As we had lived in a tent and had been on the move for nine months, traveling 2400 miles we were glad to settle down and go housekeeping in a shed that was built in a day of lumber purchased with the first fee. The ground was given us by some gamblers who lived next door and upon the other side, for neighbors, we had a real live saloon. I never have received more respectful attention than I did from these neighbors.

Upon the whole I enjoyed the trip, spite of its hardships and dangers and the fear and dread that hung as a pall over every hour. Although not so thrilling as were the experiences of many who suffered in reality what we feared, but escaped, I like every other pioneer, love to live again, in memory those romantic months, and revisit, in fancy, the scenes of the journey.

READING 5
SARAH WINNEMUCCA, 1883

Women's history in the American West cuts across racial strata, economic conditions, and political viewpoints. One of the most celebrated and eloquent commentators on Native American culture and particularly the Indian woman was Sarah Winnemucca, granddaughter of Chief Truckee of the Paiutes of northern Nevada. As Sarah and her family were shuttled from one reservation to another, she was able to acquire an excellent command of English and served as a translator for the U.S. Army. Later she became a well-known lecturer, lionized by easterners for her descriptions of injustices done to her tribe and the Indian culture in general. This selection from Winnemucca's book Life among the Piutes *(the conventional spelling of Paiute in 1883) describes Native American homelife and the role of women in the culture. (Note that her characterization of the coyote is at odds with the mythologies of other tribes in which Coyote is a mischievous trickster but not necessarily mean or loathsome.)*

I was born somewhere near 1844, but am not sure of the precise time. I was a very small child when the first white people came into our country. They came like a lion, yes, like a roaring lion, and have continued so ever since, and I have never forgotten their first coming.

My people were scattered at that time over nearly all of the territory now known as Nevada. My grandfather was chief of the entire Piute nation, and was camped near Humboldt Lake, with a small portion of his tribe. . . .

Our children are very carefully taught to be good. Their parents tell them stories, traditions of old times, even of the first mother of the human race; and love stories, stories of giants, and fables; and when they ask if these last stories are true, they answer, "Oh, it is only coyote," which means that they are make-believe stories. Coyote is the name of a mean, crafty little animal, half wolf, half dog, and stands for everything low. It is the greatest term of reproach one Indian has for another. Indians do not swear—they have no words for swearing till they learn them of white men. The worst they call each other is "bad" or "coyote," but they are very sincere with one another, and if they think each other in the wrong, they say so.

We are taught to love everybody. We don't need to be taught to love our fathers and mothers. We love them without being told to. Our tenth cousin is as near to us as our first cousin, and we don't marry into our relations. Our young women are not allowed to talk to any young man that is not their cousin, except at festive dances, when both are dressed in their best clothes, adorned with beads, feathers or shells, and stand alternately in the ring and take hold of hands. These are very pleasant occasions to all the young people. . . .

My people have been so unhappy for a long time they wish now to disincrease, instead of multiply. The mothers are afraid to have more children, for fear they shall have daughters, who are not safe even in their mother's presence.

The grandmothers have the special care of the daughters just before and after they come to womanhood. The girls are not allowed to get married until they have come to womanhood; and that period is recognized as a very sacred thing, and is the subject of a festival, and has peculiar customs. The young woman is set apart under the care of two of her friends, somewhat older, and a little wigwam, called a teepee, just big enough for the three, is made for them, to which they retire. She goes through certain labors which are thought to be strengthening, and these last twenty-five days. Every day, three times a day, she must gather, and pile as high as she can, five stacks of wood. This makes fifteen stacks of wood a day. At the end of every five days the attendants take her to a river to bathe. She fasts from all flesh-meat during these twenty-five days, and continues to do this for five days in every month all her life. At the end of twenty-five days she returns to the family lodge, and gives all her clothing to the attendants in payment for their care. Sometimes the wardrobe is quite extensive.

It is thus publicly known that there is another marriageable woman, and any young man interested in her, or wishing to form an alliance, comes forward. But the courting is very different from the courting of white people. He never speaks to her, or visits the family, but endeavors to attract her attention by showing his horsemanship, etc. As he knows that she sleeps next to her grandmother, in the lodge, he enters in full dress after the family has retired for the night, and seats himself at her feet. If she is not awake, the grandmother wakes her. He does not speak to either young woman or grandmother, but when the young woman wishes him to go away, she rises and goes and lies down by the side of her mother. He then leaves as silently as he came in.

This goes on sometimes for a year or longer, if the young woman has not made up her mind. She is never forced by her parents to marry against her wishes. When she knows her own mind, she makes a confidant of her grandmother, and then the young man is summoned by the father of the girl, who asks him in her presence, if he really loves his daughter, and reminds him, if he says he does, of all the duties of a husband. He then asks his daughter the same question, and sets before her minutely all her duties. And these duties are not slight.

She is to dress the game, prepare the food, clean the buckskins, make his moccasins, dress his hair, bring all the wood—in short, do all the household work. She promises to "be himself" [probably meaning that the woman promises her father to "become one" with her husband and not consider herself any longer a part of her father's family], and she fulfills her promise. . . . They faithfully keep with them in all the dangers they can share. They not only take care of the children together, but they do everything together; and when they grow blind, which, I am sorry to say is very common, for the smoke they live in destroys their eyes at last, they take sweet care of one another. Marriage is a sweet thing when people love each other.

At the wedding feast, all the food is prepared in baskets. The young woman sits by the young man, and hands him the basket of food prepared for him with her own hands. He does not take it with his right hand; but seizes her wrist, and takes it with the left hand. This constitutes the marriage ceremony, and the father pronounces them man and wife. They go to a wigwam of their own, where they live until the first child is born. This event also is celebrated. Both father and mother fast from all flesh, and the father goes through the labor of piling the wood for twenty-five days, and assumes all his wife's household work during that time.

If he does not do his part in the care of the child, he is considered an outcast. Every five days his child's basket is changed for a new one, and the five are all carefully put away at the end of the days, the last one containing the navel-string, carefully wrapped up, and all are put up into a tree, and the child put into a new and ornamented basket. All this respect shown to the mother and child makes the parents feel their responsibility, and makes the tie between parents and children very strong.

The young mothers often get together and exchange their experiences about the attentions of their husbands; and inquire of each other if the fathers did their duty to their children, and were careful of their wives' health. When they are married they give away all the clothing they have . . . and dress themselves anew. . . .

My people teach their children never to make fun of anyone, no matter how they look. If you see your brother or sister doing something wrong, look away, or go away from them. If you make fun of bad persons, you make yourself beneath them. Be kind to all, both poor and rich, and feed all that come to your wigwam, and your name can be spoken of by every one far and near. In this way you will make many friends for yourself. Be kind both to bad and good, for you don't know your own heart. This is the way my people teach their children. It was handed down from father to son for many generations. I never in my life saw our children rude as I have seen white children and grown people in the streets.

READING 6

The Lives of Native American Women, Meriwether Lewis, 1805

For another perspective on the lives of Native American women, consider this selection from Meriwether Lewis, whose journals of the epic Lewis and Clark Expedition extensively describe the habits and mores of the Indian nations he encountered. His depiction of Native American homelife is far more grim than the account of Sarah Winnemucca. Of course, the two writers refer to different native cultures and tribal groupings—Lewis is speaking of the Shoshone tribe throughout this passage—and are presented from highly conflicting cultural perspectives.

The man is the sole propryetor of his wives and daughters, and can barter and dispose of either as he thinks proper. a plurality of wives is common among them, but these are not generally sisters as with the Minnitares & Mandans but are purchased of different fathers. The father frequently disposes of his infant daughters in marriage to men who are grown or to men who have sons for whom they think proper to provide wives. the compensation given in such cases usually consists of horses or mules which the father receives at the same time of contract and converts to his own uce, the girl remains with her parents untill she is conceived to have obtained the age of puberty which with them is considered to be about the age of 13 or 14 years. the female at this age is surrendered to her sovereign lord and husband agreeably to contract, and with her is frequently restored by the father quite as much as he received in the first instance of payment for his daughter, but this is discretionary with the father. . . .

They seldom correct their children particularly the boys who soon become masters of their own acts. they give as a reason that it cows and breaks the sperit of the boy to whip him, and that he never recovers his independence of mind after he is grown. They treat their women but with little rispect, and compel them to perform every species of drudgery. they collect the wild fruits and roots, attend to the horses or assist in that duty, cook, dress the skins and make all their apparel, collect wood and make their fires, arrange and form their lodges, and when they travel pack the horses and take charge of all the baggage; in short the man dose little else except attend his horses hunt and fish. the man considers himself degraded if he is compelled to walk any distance; and if he is so unfortunately poor as only to possess two horses he rides the best himself and leavs the woman or women if he has more than one, to transport their baggage and children on the other, and to walk if the horse is unable to carry the additional weight of their persons. the chastity of their women is not held in high estimation, and the husband will for a trifle barter the companion of his bead for a night or longer if he conceives the reward adiquate.

Black women in the west faced two difficult barriers: race prejudice and gender discrimination. Pauline Lyons Williamson came from a middle-class family and had some nursing skills. As a widow with a young son she journeyed to Oakland, California, in the 1880s and stayed with her aunt and uncle, the Thomas family. Pauline looked for a school for her son and hoped to enter a hospital training program as well as care for her ill Aunt Thomas. Then she discovered that her aunt was already planning an arranged marriage for her without Pauline's knowledge or consent. Additionally, her uncle found her claims of financial difficulty unbelievable and became increasingly unwilling to help her. As a result, Pauline's hopes of a brighter future were dashed in the sunshine of California. This is one of a series of letters describing her experiences to her sister May.

Oakland, Nov. 10th, 1885.

May dear May,

Now my dear . . . it seems that before I came to California a friend of Mrs. Thomas'—a gentleman, saw my picture and being desireous of getting a wife questioned Ms. T. concerning me, the gentleman being a West Indian by birth is very wealthy, but has refrained from marrying because he could not meet any lady who came up to his ideas of what a wife ought to be.

The gentleman, who was a perfect stranger to me but a friend of Ms. T. agreed with Ms. T. that I was the one suited to be a good wife. The name of the West Indian gentleman I do not know so I will call him Mr. H. Ms. T's accomplice in this business I shall call Mr. B. Mrs. T. and Mr. B put their heads together to make me marry Mr. H, they both saw Mr. H [and] set forth my charms, and they agreed that it would be all right as soon as I came, so Mr. H. said he would marry me.

Mrs. T told him the only obstacle in the way [was] the child but he promised her that he would fix that all right, he would send the child away to boarding school, so it was settled. Ms. T was to receive a diamond ring for her trouble and Mr. B was to receive a diamond scarf [pin?] for his trouble from Mr. H as soon as the marriage took place.

October was the time fixed for it so as to give him time to arrange for his going into business for himself. He opened a perfumery store in Panama during the holiday week, [and] we were to sail immediately for Panama which was to be my future home.

Behold the sequel: neither party told me anything of what was going on [when] I came. Mr. B was the first one to broach the subject to me, then he did not tell me about Mr. H, but simply hoped I would like California and he knew I would become so much attached that I never would want to leave, and finally, I would marry some one here.

I told him I did not care to marry, but he assured me I would marry out here, [since] every one that came to make a living ended by marrying, and in a few days he would show me some thing that would bind me forever to California. But still I did not suspect anything because I thought he was only showing off. But he kept it up so much that I finally told [him] I did not see why people worried so about my getting married. I came to earn a living and not to hunt a husband, and I intended to remain single . . . not a word about Mr. H did [Aunt Thomas] say.

So one day in talking I told [her] I had a friend in New York that I thought I would marry if he did what I wanted him to do, [which] was to come out to California. And if he came I would marry him.

So whenever the California gentlemen were mentioned I would bring up New York gentlemen, and in fun on my part lauded them up to the skies, my own in particular being lord over all.

Now in the mean time Uncle comes home, and we are invited to take tea at Mr. B's. That was the time fixed for me to meet Mr. H for the first time, but before the day arrived Uncle, Mr. B, Ms. T and myself were in Frisco and it seems Mr. H passed us on the street, and she steps up to him and tells him the game is all up, I am engaged to be married. He says he is very sorry, and thanks her kindly for the interest she has shown, and refuses to be introduced to me, as he does not wish to place himself in any ones way and unless he can have the lady to himself, he will not even call on her or be introduced.

I remember that she stopped in the street and spoke to some one, but as I was ignorant of all this, I did not pay any attention to what went on, but walked along with Mr. B. . . .

Mr. H would not come to the party as he felt much disappointed at the way the affair had turned out. Mr. B has told me since that if I had only said I would marry that he would have gone right after Mr. H and in ten minutes time it would have been all fixed.

A little while after I received a letter from my friend in New York saying he had changed his mind and would [not come] to California, so I told [Mrs. T]. Well, then the storm broke over my head, and she was furious. For it seems she had been around telling people I was engaged to be married, [and] that the gentleman was a coming out from New York. Then she up and told me about Mr. H. and what she had planned for me, but that since I would have my own way she was done with me. And she did not care what happened, and a whole lot of stuff.

She had even gone so far as to make out who she intended to send cake [to]. She intended to make New York and Brooklyn jealous of my good fortune, and all was to be done at her expense—cake and all. Then as soon as I was safely in Panama, she was going to arrange her affairs and come to Panama and pay me a visit, but sure as I preferred a New York nigger I was served just right.

She would love to set my ass in a butter firkin and I would have had servants to wait on me and plenty of money, but I would not, so then she thought I had better go home, that I was not happy, and she didn't want any one around that was not contented.

I was always fretting because I was not at work, and she did not see why I was in such a hurry to work. Then I said, I missed father and mother so much, I had better go back to them. When Uncle came home he would pay my fare back home, that is why she wrote to you as she did, for she was dreadfully put out on account of my fulfilling her wishes, when she bragged and boasted of me to him.

Well, I can't repeat all that was said, but finally I told her if Mr. H would come and see me I would accept his attentions, so she said she would see Mr. B and see what could be done.

Mr. B came to see us and the matter was talked over, he said he was afraid it was too late now to do anything as Mr. H had gone to Panama, so he wrote to him, and two weeks ago he received an answer saying that Mr. H would think the matter over and would let him know in a short time what he would do.

So there the matter rests. There will be a steamer in from Panama about the 1st of this month, and then I suppose he will send his answers. He is a Roman Catholic but I dont think he will come back as he is a very high tone.

You may rest assured I will never consent to have my boy sent away from me for any man, and I think the whole transaction was crazy to go so far and without my knowledge.

My dear sister, Ms. T is a very uncertain person. What pleases her one day tries her the next. [To her] sometimes Harry [Pauline's son] is a perfect devil and sometime he is an angel, just as the notion takes her. You see, she does not enjoy good health, and about every other day is very miserable. She has a nervous neuralgia in the head, and it is very irritating. . . .

By the way, those letters she sends she does not write herself, as she can not read as well as Harry does. I think some white person writes them for her, that much I have found out. She can not read a newspaper correctly. She told me one day that Harry was a little devil, that he wanted to destroy everything in the house, that she did not love him at all, then she told Uncle that Harry was such a good child, [and] was so respectful to her, and she really loved him and liked to have him about. . . .

You see, Uncle does not know anything about the match she had on hand, and she dont want him to know either.

[She also] said she wanted me to go to work in the Palace hotel as a chambermaid, but he said the idea of such a thing, that if he had come home and found me in the Palace he would walk me right out of it. She made him think I wanted to go there, when it was her own proposition, and after he went away, she told me that I was very foolish to mind what he said, that he had no right to control me, and that if she was me, she would go to the Palace any way.

You see, she is a good woman in her way, but she is old and cranky. I try to steer clear of all the unpleasant things I can, because I know she means well, and she thinks she never says or does any thing wrong, and she will fight all the children in the neighborhood for Harry. . . . I would never have written all this stuff, but you have asked for an explanation and of course I had to give it to you. But use your own judgement about telling father and mother.

I made up my mind when I came to . . . write only the pleasant things home. I shall never leave the field until I am thoroughly convinced that I cant get a living here.

As for my plans, I got along nicely with my case and got $20 for the two weeks, but I have found that the one great obstacle is, I have no certificate to prove I am a trained nurse and [without one] I shall have a hard time to get established. People and Doctors both require some proofs of ones proficiency, so I have been trying to get into the only training school there is in Frisco. I can not enter now, but I have a promise from the board of directors that in the spring they will admit me on probation, and if the term is passed satisfactorily, that they will give me [permission] to take the [course].

They were willing to take me this month, but the nurses, of whom there are eight, would not work with a colored person. As their accommodations

are small, they could not . . . accommodate me under the existing unpleas-
antness of the nurses. But in the the spring, their new building will be
complete, and there will be other changes made which will [be] to my
advantage. . . .

Hope my explanation is satisfactory. I shall let you know if Mr. H comes
in time, but I shall not be sorry if he does not.

Love,

Pauline

READING 8

ELINORE PRUITT STEWART, 1909

*Elinore Pruitt was born in 1876 in Arkansas. She had eight brothers and sisters
and was so poor she did not own a pair of shoes until she was six years old. Her
parents died when she was fourteen, and Elinore assumed responsibility for
raising her siblings, working on the railroad while the others were going to school.
At age twenty-two she married a Mr. Rupert, who supported her desire to write
and read. Rupert died when Elinore was twenty-six and left her widowed with a
small daughter. She went to work stoking the coal furnace for a Mrs. Coney, to
whom the following letter is written. At age thirty-three Elinore answered an ad
placed by Wyoming sheep rancher Clyde Stewart, and they were married six
weeks later. Elinore Pruitt Stewart made it quite clear to him, however, that her
goal was to own her own land and homestead it herself; she was not about to let a
husband interfere with this dream.*

Burnt Fork, Wyoming

May 24, 1909

Dear, Dear Mrs. Coney,

Well, I have filed on my land and am now a bloated landowner. I waited a
long time to even *see* land in the reserve, and the snow is yet too deep, so I
thought that as they have but three months of summer and spring together
and as I wanted the land for a ranch anyway, perhaps I had better stay in the
valley. So I have filed adjoining Mr. Stewart and I am well pleased. I have a
grove of twelve swamp pines on my place, and I am going to build my house
there. I thought it would be very romantic to live on the peaks amid the
whispering pines, but I reckon it would be powerfully uncomfortable also,
and I guess my twelve can whisper enough for me; and a dandy thing is, I

have all the nice snow-water I want; a small stream runs right through the center of my land and I am quite near wood.

A neighbor and his daughter were going to Green River [Wyoming], the county-seat, and said I might go along, so I did, as I could file there as well as at the land office; and oh, that trip! I had more fun to the square inch than Mark Twain . . . *ever* provoked. It took us a whole week to go and come. We camped out, of course, for in the whole sixty miles there was but one house, and going in that direction there is not a tree to be seen, nothing but sage, sand, and sheep. About noon the first day out we came near a sheepwagon, and stalking along ahead of us was a lanky fellow, a herder, going home for dinner. Suddenly it seemed to me I should starve if I had to wait until we got where we had planned to stop for dinner, so I called out to the man, "Little Bo-Peep, have you anything to eat? If you have, we'd like to find it." And he answered, "As soon as I am able it shall be on the table, if you'll but trouble to get behind it." Shades of Shakespeare! Songs of David, the Shepherd Poet! What do you think of us? Well, we got behind it, and a more delicious "it" I never tasted. Such coffee! And out of *such* a pot! I promised Bo-Peep that I would send him a crook with pink ribbons on it, but I suspect he thinks I am a crook without the pink ribbons.

The sagebrush is so short in some places that it is not large enough to make a fire, so we had to drive until quite late before we camped that night. After driving all day over what seemed a level desert of sand, we came about sundown to a beautiful cañon [canyon], down which we had to drive for a couple of miles before we could cross. In the cañon the shadows had already fallen, but when we looked up we could see the last shafts of sunlight on the tops of the great bare buttes. Suddenly a great wolf started from somewhere and galloped along the edge of the cañon, outlined black and clear by the setting sun. His curiosity overcame him at last, so he sat down and waited to see what manner of beast we were. I reckon he was disappointed for he howled most dismally. I thought of Jack London's "The Wolf."

After we quitted the cañon I saw the most beautiful sight. It seemed as if we were driving through a golden haze. The violet shadows were creeping up between the hills, while away back of us the snow-capped peaks were catching the sun's last rays. On every side of us stretched the poor, hopeless desert, the sage, grim and determined to live in spite of starvation, and the great, bare, desolate buttes. The beautiful colors turned to amber and rose, and then to the general tone, dull gray.

Then we stopped to camp, and such a scurrying around to gather brush for the fire and to get supper! Everything tasted so good! Jerrine ate like a man. Then we raised the wagon tongue and spread the wagon sheet over it and made a bedroom for us women. We made our beds on the warm, soft sand and went to bed.

It was too beautiful a night to sleep, so I put my head out to look and think. I saw the moon come up and hang for a while over the mountains as if it were discouraged with the prospect, and the big white stars flirted shamelessly with the hills.

At length a cloud came up and I went to sleep, and next morning was covered several inches with snow. It didn't hurt us a bit, but while I was struggling with stubborn corsets and shoes I communed with myself after the manner of prodigals, and said; "How much better that I were down in Denver, even at Mrs. Coney's, digging with a skewer into the corners seeking dirt which *might* be there, yea, even eating codfish, than that I should perish on this desert—of imagination." So I turned the current of my imagination and fancied that I was at home before the fireplace, and that the backlog was about to roll down. My fancy was in such good working trim that before I knew it I kicked the wagon wheel, and I certainly got as warm as the most "sot" Scientist that ever read Mrs. Eddy [Mary Baker Eddy, founder of the Christian Science movement] could possibly wish.

After two more such days I "arrived." When I went up to the office where I was to file, the door was open and the most taciturn old man sat before a desk. I hesitated at the door, but he never let on. I coughed, yet no sign but a deeper scowl. I stepped in and modestly kicked over a chair. He whirled around like I had shot him. "Well?" he interrogated. I said, "I am powerful glad of it. I was afraid you were sick, you looked in such pain." He looked at me a minute, then grinned and said he thought I was a bookagent. Fancy me, a fat, comfortable widow, trying to sell books!

Well, I filed and came home. If you will believe me, the Scot [Mr. Stewart] was glad to see me and didn't herald the Campbells for two hours after I got home. I'll tell you, it is mighty seldom any one's so much appreciated.

No, we have no rural delivery. It is two miles to the [post] office, but I go whenever I like. It is really the jolliest kind of fun to gallop down. We are sixty miles from the railroad, but when we want anything we send by the mail-carrier for it, only there is nothing to get.

I know this is an inexcusably long letter, but it is snowing hard and you know how I like to talk.

Baby has the rabbit you gave her last Easter a year ago. In Denver I was afraid my baby would grow up devoid of imagination. Like all the kindergartners, she depended upon others to amuse her. I was very sorry about it, for my castles in Spain have been real homes to me. But there is no fear. She has a block of wood she found in the blacksmith shop which she calls her "dear baby." A spoke out of a wagon wheel is "little Margaret," and a barrel stave is "bad little Johnny."

Well, I must quit writing before you vote me a nuisance. With lots of love to you,

Your sincere friend,

Elinore Rupert

READING 9
WOMEN AS REFORMERS

A Victorian truism was that women possessed greater virtue than men and therefore should rightly lead efforts toward societal improvement. This attitude existed in the American West as well, and women there did lead crusades for education, woman suffrage, temperance and prohibition, and rescue homes and safe houses for prostitutes, Mormon polygamist women, and unwed mothers. Although men too organized societies to promote and provide structure for such efforts, women were often the first in a community to call for the building of such institutions as churches, schools, and libraries. Their efforts expanded the conventional roles of women in the home and promoted some reforms benefiting women in business, politics, and law as well. They met the resistance of long-held beliefs, and the changes they hoped for were often dreams deferred, but change did occur. Not all reform movements were positive: some were tinged with racial intolerance and ignorance; others harbored animosities left over from the recent Civil War. Most, however, began at least with positive goals, motivations, and the vision of a better world.

The readings that follow concern various women-led reform efforts and the Oregon court case that changed legal practice forever and the lives of women industrial workers as well.

"A Century of Dishonor," Helen Hunt Jackson, 1881

In 1881 Helen Hunt Jackson (1830–85) published A Century of Dishonor, *an exposé of the U.S. government's mistreatment of Native American popula-tions, and sent a copy to every member of Congress. Her wide-ranging research re-vealed that the government had deliberately followed policies designed to eliminate or severely limit the culture and activities of the Indian nations. Jackson's crusade led to reforms that were seen as humane and progressive at the time, such as the* Dawes Act of 1887 *(see chapter 6). Here is the conclusion to her study.*

There is not among these three hundred bands of Indians [within United States jurisdiction] one which has not suffered cruelty at the hands either of the Government or of white settlers. The poorer, the more insignificant, the more helpless the band, the more certain the cruelty and outrage to which they have been subjected. This is especially true of the bands on the Pacific slopes. These Indians found themselves of a sudden surrounded by and caught up in the great influx of gold-seeking settlers, as helpless creatures on a shore are caught up in a tidal wave. There was not time for the Govern-ment to make laws. The tales of the wrongs, the oppressions, the murders of the Pacific-slope Indians in the last thirty years would be a volume by itself, and is too monstrous to be believed.

It makes little difference, however, where one opens the record of the history of the Indians; every page and every year has its dark stain. The story of one tribe is the story of all, varied only by differences of time and place, but neither time nor place makes any difference in the main facts. Colorado is as greedy and unjust in 1880 as was Georgia in 1830, and Ohio in 1795; and the United States Government breaks promises now as deftly as then, and with added ingenuity from long practice.

One of the strongest supports in doing so is the wide-spread sentiment among the people of dislike to the Indian, of impatience with his presence as a "barrier to civilization," and distrust of it as a possible danger. The old tales of the frontier life, with its horrors of Indian warfare, have gradually, by two or three generations' telling, produced in the average mind something like an hereditary instinct of unquestioning and unreasoning aversion which it is almost impossible to dislodge or soften.

There are hundreds of pages of unimpeachable testimony on the side of the Indian; but it goes for nothing, is set down as sentimentalism or partisanship, tossed aside and forgotten.

President after president has appointed commission after commission to inquire into and report upon Indian affairs, and to make suggestions as to the best methods of managing them. The reports are filled with eloquent statements of wrongs done to the Indians, of perfidies on the part of the Government; they counsel, as earnestly as words can, a trial of the simple and unperplexing expedients of telling truth, keeping promises, making fair bargains, dealing justly in all ways and all things. These reports are bound up with the Government's Annual Reports, and that is the end of them. It would probably be no exaggeration to say that not one American citizen out of ten thousand ever sees them or knows that they exist, and yet any one of them, circulated throughout the country, read by the right-thinking, right-feeling men and women of this land, would be of itself a "campaign document" that would initiate a revolution which would not subside until the Indians' wrongs were, so far as is now left possible, righted. . . .

To assume that it would be easy, or by any one sudden stroke of legislative policy possible, to undo the mischief and hurt of the long past, set the Indian policy of the country right for the future, and make the Indians at once safe and happy, is the blunder of a hasty and uninformed judgment. The notion which seems to be growing more prevalent, that simply to make all Indians at once citizens of the United States would be a sovereign and instantaneous panacea for all their ills and all the Government's perplexities, is a very inconsiderate one. To administer complete citizenship of a sudden, all round, to all Indians, . . . would be as grotesque a blunder as to dose them all round with any one medicine, irrespective of the symptoms and needs of their diseases. It would kill more than it would cure. Nevertheless, it is true, as was well stated by one of the superintendents of Indian Affairs in 1857, that, "so long as they are not citizens of the United States, their rights of property must remain insecure against invasion. The doors of the federal tribunals being barred against them while wards and dependents, they can only partially exercise the rights of free government, or give to those who make, execute, and construe the few laws they are allowed to enact, dignity, sufficient to make them respectable. While they continue individually to gather the crumbs that fall from the table of the United States, idleness, improvidence, and indebtedness will be the rule, and industry, thrift, and freedom from debt the exception. The utter absence of individual title to particular lands deprives every one among them of the chief incentive to labor and exertion—the very mainspring on which the prosperity of a people depends."

All judicious plans and measures for their safety and salvation must embody provisions for their becoming citizens as fast as they are fit, and must protect them till then in every right and particular in which our laws protect other "persons" who are not citizens.

There is a disposition in a certain class of minds to be impatient with any protestation against wrong which is unaccompanied or unprepared with a quick and exact scheme of remedy. This is illogical. When pioneers in a new country find a tract of poisonous and swampy wilderness to be reclaimed, they do not withhold their hands from fire and axe till they see clearly which way roads should run, where good water will spring, and what crops will best grow on the redeemed land. They first clear the swamp. So with this poisonous and baffling part of the domain of our national affairs—let us first "clear the swamp."

However great perplexity and difficulty there may be in the details of any and every plan possible for doing at this late day anything like justice to the Indian, however hard it may be for good statesmen and good men to agree upon the things that ought to be done, there certainly is, or ought to be, no perplexity whatever, no difficulty whatever, in agreeing upon certain things that ought not to be done, and which must cease to be done before the first steps can be taken toward righting the wrongs, curing the ills, and wiping out the disgrace to us of the present condition of our Indians.

Cheating, robbing, breaking promises—these three are clearly things which must cease to be done. One more thing, also, and that is the refusal of the protection of the law to the Indian's rights of property, "of life, liberty, and the pursuit of happiness."

When these four things have ceased to be done, time, statesmanship, philanthropy, and Christianity can slowly and surely do the rest. Till these four things have ceased to be done, statesmanship and philanthropy alike must work in vain, and Christianity can reap but small harvest.

READING 9B

"THE OBJECT OF THE ALLIANCE," BETTIE GAY, 1891

In the 1880s farmers in the agrarian South and West, finding it increasingly difficult to survive economically, banded together in political reform organizations.

These Farmers' Alliances focused on breaking the power of the establishment's economic and political interests, which they felt were denying farmers an opportunity to advance. They called for government control of transportation and communications networks and for reforms in currency, land ownership, and income taxes. Their greatest accomplishment, however, was to forge a common sense of their members' identity as besieged farmers, a common interest in improving their lot, and a common enemy in corporate capitalism. The Farmers' Alliances were beset with the same social and racial prejudices that bedeviled other organizations of the time, but they significantly influenced the politics and tenor of nineteenth-century society. Although their primary goals would not be achieved until the twentieth century, they provided a catalyst for change in many areas of American life.

Women were involved at all levels in these organizations. Here Bettie Gay advocates better opportunities for women and describes their potential for influence through the alliance movement.

[T]his is a new era in human progress, when woman demands an equal opportunity in every department of life. She is no longer considered a tool, a mere plaything, but a human being, with a soul to save and a body to protect. Her mind must be cultivated, that she may be made more useful in the reform movement and the development of the race. It is an acknowledged principle in science that cultivated and intelligent mothers produce brainy children, and the only means by which the minds of the human race can be developed is to strengthen, by cultivation, the intellectual capacities of the mothers, by which means a mentally great race may be produced. When I look into the hard and stolid faces of many of the mothers of the present, and know that they have been deprived of the opportunities which would have improved them, I am not surprised that we are surrounded by people who are advocates of a system but little better than cannibalism. . . .

If I understand the object of the Alliance, it is organized not only to better the financial condition of the people, but to elevate them socially, and in every other way, and make them happier and better, and to make this world a fit habitation for man, by giving the people equal opportunities. Every woman who has at heart the welfare of the race should attach herself to some reform organization, and lend her help toward the removal of the causes which have filled the world with crime and sorrow, and made outcasts of so many of her sex. It is a work in which all may engage, with assurance that they are entering upon a labor of love, in the interest of the downtrodden and disinherited; a work by which all mankind will be blessed, and which will bless those who are to come after for all time. . . .

What we need, above all things else, is a better womanhood,—a womanhood with the courage of conviction, armed with intelligence and the greatest virtues of her sex, acknowledging no master and accepting no compromise. When her enemies shall have laid down their arms, and her proper position in society is recognized, she will be prepared to take upon herself the responsibilities of life, and civilization will be advanced to that point where intellect instead of brute force will rule the world. When this work is accomplished, avarice, greed, and passion will cease to control the minds of the people, and we can proclaim, "Peace on earth, good will toward men."

READING 9C
"WE URGE ALL WOMEN TO ENTER PROTEST," NATIONAL AMERICAN WOMAN SUFFRAGE ASSOCIATION, 1893

Almost from the beginning of the dominant culture's influence in the American West came the call for woman suffrage, one of the most passionate of the reform movements led by and involving women. Some states responded quite early. In Kansas, for example, women were extended the right to vote in school elections in the 1880s, making Kansas one of the most progressive states in education. Western states also elected the first women mayors and congressional representatives. By 1912 eight states, all in the West, had given women full and equal voting rights— well in advance of the nineteenth Amendment, which in 1920 provided federal constitutional guarantees of equal suffrage for women.

In 1893 the issue reached fever pitch in Colorado, which adopted woman suffrage that year. This campaign influenced other states, and woman suffrage associations, to intensify their efforts. Also in 1893 the National American Woman Suffrage Association (NAWSA), convening in Washington D.C., adopted a resolution that served as a touchstone for campaigns throughout the American West and the nation.

Resolved, That without expressing any opinion on the proper qualifications for voting, we call attention to the significant facts that in every State there are more women who can read and write than the whole number of illiterate male voters; more white women who can read and write than all negro voters; more American women who can read and write than all foreign voters; so that the enfranchisement of such women would settle the vexed question of rule by illiteracy, whether of home-grown or foreign-born production.

Resolved, That as all experience proves that the rights of the laboring man are best preserved in governments where he has possession of the ballot, we therefore demand on behalf of the laboring woman the same powerful instrument, that she may herself protect her own interests; and we urge all organized bodies of working women, whether in the field of philanthropy, education, trade, manufacture or general industry, to join our association in the endeavor to make woman legally and politically a free agent, as the best means of furthering any and every line of woman's work.

Resolved, That in all States possessing School Suffrage for women, suffragists are advised to organize in each representative district thereof, for the purpose of training and stimulating women voters to exercise regularly this right, using it as a preparatory school for the coming work of full-grown citizenship with an unlimited ballot. We also advise that women everywhere work for the election of an equal number of women and men upon school boards, that the State in taking upon itself the education of children may provide them with as many official mothers as fathers.

WHEREAS, Many forms of woman suffrage may be granted by State Legislatures without change in existing constitutions; therefore,

Resolved, That the suffragists in every State should petition for Municipal, School and Presidential Suffrage by statute, and take every practicable step toward securing such legislation.

Resolved, That we urge all women to enter protest, at the time of paying taxes, at being compelled to submit to taxation without representation.

READING 9D

KANSAS WOMEN AND REFORM, 1867–1899

In 1704 the English essayist and poet Joseph Addison wrote of a military campaigner who heroically "rides in the whirlwind and directs the storm." The same words could be applied to the women of Kansas who were among the initial reformers and crusaders in the American West. The serious and complex issues they addressed were breathtaking in scope—prohibition, temperance, woman suffrage, populism, and abolition—particularly in a region that had only recently seen the influx of Euro-American settlement.

If there ever was a territory ripe for the reform impulse, it was Kansas in the mid-nineteenth century. From 1850 through 1900 Kansas endured an unprecedented series of natural and manmade disasters. There was the dress rehearsal for the Civil War called "Bleeding Kansas" in 1855–56, guerrilla raids during the Civil War, Indian "problems" following the war, twisters, drought, floods, blizzards, prairie firestorms, outlaw bands, financial scandals, and plagues of locusts. And yet Kansas survived and developed a population of tough, independent, free-thinking citizens. The understandable reluctance of most people to challenge the status quo for fear of embarrassment or failure did not seem daunting to women who had seen the green stripes eaten off their dresses by ravenous locusts or watched an entire year's farm work destroyed in an instant by a prairie fire. Women had to endure natural catastrophes, but they did not have to tolerate political and social unfairness. Addressing the social restrictions and resentments of the age, difficult in any era, was a task adopted with passion and resolve by the women of Kansas.

Lilla Day Monroe, the first woman admitted to practice before the Kansas Supreme Court and a prominent leader in the Kansas suffrage movement, interviewed Kansas women who were influential in the nineteenth-century reform movements and compiled their reminiscences. Only one selection here is not from the Monroe collection but from the autobiographical pen of radical prohibitionist Carry A. Nation.

Fanny Holsinger

Abolition! Prohibition! Suffrage! How we struggled for these issues in Kansas. How simple and natural and right these things seem now that the struggle is over. We did our best with our problems. The result is the heritage we leave our children.

Reverend Olympia Brown, 1867

Olympia Brown was the first woman ordained by the Universalist Church. Her church was in Weymouth, Massachusetts, but she was involved in many nationwide campaigns for women's rights, particularly suffrage, and acquainted with such leading feminists as Susan B. Anthony and Elizabeth Cady Stanton. The Lucy Stone she refers to in this recollection was a prominent Kansas suffragist.

[In Kansas, in 1867, an] amendment to the constitution had passed the legislature the previous winter; it was a compromise, or rather a bluff. The Republicans were then deeply interested in the Negro, and they proposed an amendment to the constitution, striking out the word "white." Then the Democrats obstructed legislation by proposing one striking out the word "male"—finally the Republicans adopted both, thus the enfranchisement of the Negro and of women were both before the people. Lucy Stone said the measure was almost sure to pass, it was only necessary to keep it before the people through the summer. The Republicans, she said, would furnish conveyance and conveniences for the speakers. They would make all the appointments and open their meetings to our cause, and she urged me to go out at once to Leavenworth [Kansas], where I would meet a member of the Central Committee who would start me on the campaign.

It is needless to say that an ardent advocate of woman's suffrage would be ready to respond to such an appeal. No difficulty was raised concerning remuneration, and no suggestions of possible failure were made. Youth is enthusiastic and hopeful but experience soon cames to warn, if not to disappoint. . . .

Kansas was then just emerging from the great struggles for freedom which culminated in the civil war. Many of her men had been killed in the conflicts with the border ruffians and in the battles of the war. The crops that season had been destroyed by grasshoppers. Many of the pioneers were suffering from malaria and other diseases incident to the settlement of a new country. There were few public conveyances, either by rail or stage route or livery, and few men owned carriages. The outlook was not encouraging. It developed that the appointments [for speeches and rallies on the suffrage issue] had been made without any knowledge of the country, and they were often fifty miles apart, necessitating starting at four in the morning to reach an appointment at two P.M., and after the lecture and a brief half hour for dinner, we would start again to reach an evening appointment.

In many places there were no roads, only a trail across the prairie and sometimes not even that. Under such circumstances, to lose our way became almost a daily experience and when now and then we chanced to meet a traveler and inquired the distance to a neighboring town we were often met by the reply that it was "right smart" or possibly "a good little bit." But on we went and the most remarkable thing about the campaign was that notwithstanding all these difficulties, the speaker did not, during the whole four months, miss one appointment. . . .

Well, the end came and the votes were counted, and Woman's Suffrage got only a little over one-third of all. But disappointment and defeat were softened by a letter from Susan B. Anthony:

Dear Olympia: Never was defeat so glorious a victory. My dear Olympia, if ever any money gets into my control, you shall have evidence that I appreciate the Herculean work you have done here in Kansas the past four long months.

I would have gone farther and done more for those words of appreciation from Susan; I was a hero worshipper then.

Stella Haines, 1875

During the year 1875, the first Literary Society was formed [in Rose Hill, Kansas], the meetings were held once a week in the homes of the members and debated different subjects. One subject which caused the greatest excitement was "Resolved That Women Should Have Equal Suffrage With Men." Four women against four men, with three judges, caused so much interest that people came for ten miles around to this debate, most of the folks asserted it was a foolish idea to think women even wanted to vote. Naturally the men judges decided for the negative. At the close of the decision, while the wild cheering was going on, one of the men debaters jumped on top of a bench, flapped his arms up and down and crowed like a rooster. Mrs. Haines, the main woman speaker, arose and said she had often heard roosters crow when they had whipped another rooster, but never when they had whipped a hen.

Julia Robinson, 1880

I well remember the struggle for state-wide prohibition. The temperance rallies held. Some of the noted speakers who came to help us out. The Good Templars' Societies. Amanda Way [temperance and suffrage crusader] was then in her prime. What a power she was for the cause. I well remember her, having entertained her in our home. . . . Many there were who shouted, "It can't be done, a state-wide prohibition amendment can't be adopted."

When the votes were counted, however, the amendment had passed narrowly, and Kansas became the first state in the nation to adopt constitutional prohibition— though local sheriffs and politicians were hesitant to enforce its provisions. A loophole that allowed druggists to dispense liquor for "medical, scientific and mechanical purposes" angered Emily Connell Biggs, the Women's Christian Temperance Union (WCTU) leader of Lincoln, Kansas. She counterattacked— but with humor, as her daughter Anna recalled.

Anna Biggs Heaney, early 1880s

A druggist by the name of Trump had secured a druggist's permit to sell liquor. All any one had to do at that time to buy liquor of any druggist having it for sale was to sign up for it with the reason therefor as cold, stomach trouble, etc. The administration of the law rested with the discretion of the druggist. And if the druggist had no discretion! So [Anna's mother, Emily Connell Biggs] wrote "A Modern Chronicle for a county convention and told in the Spiritual Chronicle style of the liquor history of the county." And when she came to the granting of the permit to Trump she said, "And the Whiskites said among themselves, 'Lo, [are] we not the lucky guys, for behold, though we have but one Trump he taketh the trick.'" That was too much for even the Whiskites. They laughed themselves hoarse.

Carrie Sain Whittaker, early 1880s

In Topeka, Kansas, in the early 1880s Carrie Sain Whittaker was elected president of a new neighborhood suffrage organization, even though she was still in school. She would eventually become one of the state's most ardent advocates of woman suffrage.

After we had lived in town for some time, Mrs. Col. Ritchie came down one evening and she and mother after talking things over decided to call a meeting of neighbors and organize a Woman's Suffrage Association. It was called to meet at Col. Ritchie's and my mother took me with her for company coming home. There were not many there, it seems to me not more than six or seven.

I was then going to school to a Mrs. Maybe. . . . We were having some lessons in Parliamentary Law, so when they were getting organized they would call on me to tell them how. After we had things planned Mrs. Ritchie said, "Let's put Carrie in as President, she is the only one who can keep us in order." I said, "Oh, you can't do that, it will be several years before I am old enough to vote." They said, "You'll be old enough long before we have the right."

Fannie Holsinger, 1887

There was no WCTU in our town until 1887. I joined the organization then and after a time became its president. We had the usual disheartening experiences. The prohibitory law was not enforced. Women came to me to beg to help save their husbands from the saloon. We besought our friends to secure evidence; we brought suits but seldom secured convictions. We went to interview the city council but were told by them "We are not a smelling committee."

One afternoon at a WCTU meeting an officer came with a summons to appear at the court immediately. I protested that court would be adjourned, as I knew it would be, but a young man, whom I knew, was waiting for me and said he was instructed to take me to his lawyer's office. The lawyer asked me to release the young man, who was under arrest for running a saloon. I told him that I could not do that. He then asked me to go with him to the county attorney.

The county attorney presented the case and said to me, "It is for you to say if he shall be released, for you are the principal witness. I have evidence enough to send him to jail." It was one of the most trying moments of my life. There sat the young man, so like my own boy, waiting for me to send him to jail or to release him. When I said aloud, "What shall I do?" the county attorney repeated, "Do as you please. You are the principal witness."

I closed my eyes and prayed for guidance. I said then, "Young man, if I thought you would go into that business again, you had better be in jail, but if you will go into some honest business I will ask that the case be dismissed." The youth answered, "Mrs. Holsinger, if you will help me this time I will promise, on my word of honor, that I will never go into the saloon business in Rosedale or anywhere else."

Now the queer part of the case was that I was not a witness. I knew nothing of the case. I was simply President of the WCTU which was fighting the traffic. . . . My WCTU friends thought my own action [not to press the case] was spineless. . . . But I have never regretted the decision made that day, for the young man became a leader in a Catholic total abstinence society and a good reliable citizen.

The reform impulse covered many issues, and they sometimes overlapped. Fanny Holsinger exhibited a tendency that characterized many women reformers: by 1894 she became involved not only in prohibition issues but woman suffrage as well.

Fanny Holsinger, 1894
When Women's Suffrage became an issue [in 1894, when Kansas resubmitted the woman's suffrage amendment to the voters], I cast my lot with the

suffragists, believing that the world was made for women too and that [God] gave them dominion. [On the day] the Suffrage Amendment was voted on I spent the day at the polls. One friend to whom I offered a ticket [a list of voting recommendations] refused to accept it. Noticing my disappointment he said, "I'll tell you, Mrs. Holsinger, I think too much of women to see them go down into the dirty pool of politics." "Perhaps," I said, "we can help to clear the pool." "Well," he said, "I'll promise not to vote against it."

I approached a well dressed, fine looking negro and offered him a ticket. "I am agin it," he said. "Why are you against it?" I asked. "I married a wife to take care of me and a woman's place is at home." "Haven't you some business that needs your attention," I asked courteously. "I'm here taking care of the polls and helping to make votes. A woman's place is at home." He went off, but I did not go home till I got ready.

Carry A. Nation, 1899

Carry A. Nation (née Moore) was the best-known radical prohibition reformer of the nineteenth century. She believed that the demon rum and the saloon culture were the root and sum of all American social evil. Other feminist leaders saw what they considered her sideshow as a distraction from their overall reform goals. For Carry A. Nation, however, the only issues were destruction of the saloon and the legal prohibition of alcohol. To those ends she embarked on the physical destruction of the already illegal drinking establishments. With her battle cry of "Smash, Smash, Smash," she swept across Kansas, wrecking saloons with hatchets, stones, and metal rods. In this excerpt from her 1908 autobiography she recounts her first foray into this militant form of protest: an 1899 raid in Kiowa, Kansas.

I got to Kiowa at half past eight, stayed all night. Next morning I had my horse hitched and drove to the first dive kept by a Mr. Dobson, whose brother was then sheriff of the county. I stacked up these smashers [rocks and bricks she had collected] on my left arm, all I could hold. They looked like packages wrapped in paper. I stood before the counter and said: "Mr. Dobson, I told you last spring to close this place, you did not do it, now I have come down with another remonstrance, get out of the way, I do not want to strike you, but I am going to break this place up." I threw as hard, and as fast as I could, smashing mirrors and bottles and glasses and it was astonishing how quickly this was done. These men seemed terrified, threw up their hands and backed up in the corner. My strength was that of a giant. I felt invincible. God was certainly with me. . . .

. . . I broke up three of these dives that day, broke the windows on the outside to prove that the man who rents his house is a partner also with the man who sells. . . . I smashed five saloons with rocks, before I ever took a hatchet.

In the last place, kept by Lewis, there was quite a young man behind the bar. I said to him: "Young man, come from behind that bar, your mother did not raise you for such a place." I threw a brick at the mirror, which was a very heavy one, and it did not break, but the brick fell and broke everything in its way. I began to look around for something that would break it. I was standing by a billiard table on which there was one ball. I said: "Thank God," and picked it up, threw it, and made a hole in the mirror.

By this time, the streets were crowded with people; most of them seemed to be puzzled. There was one boy about fifteen years old who seemed perfectly wild with joy, and he jumped, skipped and yelled with delight. I have since thought of that as being a significant sign. For to smash saloons will save the boy.

READING 9E
THE GENERAL FEDERATION OF WOMEN'S
CLUBS, MARTHA WHITE, 1904

> *Since organized efforts were crucial to the reform movements of the American West, women established networks of clubs that embraced a myriad of social concerns: some focused on prohibition, others on industrial labor issues, still others on suffrage, and so on. In 1890 many of these organizations consolidated under the banner of the General Federation of Women's Clubs. Martha White, a leader in the women's club movement, describes the formation of the federation and its goals.*

Outwardly, for twenty years, the woman's club remained an institution for the culture and pleasure of its members; but within, the desire for a larger opportunity was gradually strengthening. Parliamentary practice gave women confidence in their ability to lead larger issues to a successful conclusion. The inherent longing for power, coupled with confidence in the wisdom and beneficence of whatever woman should do, brought the leaders of the club movement to a conception of social service. To effect this, further organization was necessary. It was then, in 1890, that a union of individual clubs was formed into a chartered body, known as the General Federation of Women's Clubs. . . .

Securing the passage of laws is the extreme instance of what organized women have accomplished through the medium of public opinion. Many other concrete illustrations drawn from local conditions might be given; but they would all serve to illustrate that the woman's club is determining the mind of the community in its relation to many educational, philanthropic, and reformatory questions. . . .

The federation of one of the more enlightened states has recently undertaken to enter the field of direct politics. I quote the advice it gives to its constituents:—

"Before senators and representatives are even nominated, it is very essential that club women look up the record of the various candidates in their districts, and satisfy themselves as to their position regarding women upon boards of control of state institutions. Find out how they voted last year. Information will be gladly furnished by members of this committee. Then strive to create a sufficient public sentiment in your own locality to defeat, at the party caucus, any nominee known to oppose women representatives upon Boards of Control."

Six years ago the General Federation undertook to help the solution of certain industrial problems, notably to further organization among workingwomen; to secure and enforce child labor legislation where needed; to further attendance at school; and to secure humane conditions under which labor is performed. State federations have acted in accordance with the General Federation's plans to appoint standing industrial committees, procure investigation, circulate literature, and create a public sentiment in favor of these causes. . . . In other communities something has been accomplished by way of enacting new laws or enforcing existing ones, showing that organized women readily avail themselves of the chance for indirect service in promoting the intelligent efforts of the federations.

READING 9F
"A TREMENDOUS SPURT FORWARD," RHETA CHILDE DORR, 1905

The organization of the women's clubs into a national movement provided an impetus for increased social activism in the late nineteenth and early twentieth

*centuries. Rheta Childe Dorr, an important leader in and reporter on the
movement, here lists some of her own efforts and, particularly, the leadership of
Sarah Platt Decker of Denver, Colorado.*

[A]t the national Biennial Convention held in St. Louis in 1904, the whole club movement took a tremendous spurt forward. Not only did the program include a discussion, pro and con, of suffrage, but a woman voter was elected president of the General Federation. This was Sarah Platt Decker of Denver, a truly great woman, highly educated, widely traveled, experienced in politics, a woman whose sex alone kept her from being a United States Senator from Colorado. . . .

With all the power of her strong personality she painted a picture of the social and political problems which were troubling the world, and she made a plea to the women to drop their pleasant little essay-writing activities and to get into the struggle for a better civilization. Mrs. Decker made a clean sweep of all the committees, appointing able and energetic women to chairmanships. She created a few new committees, and to my surprise she called me from my place at the reporters' table to be chairman of the Committee on Industrial Conditions of Women and Children. She had had no direct contacts with working conditions, she told me, but she had read my articles in the *Evening Post* and she felt that the club women and the industrial workers must make common cause. Of course I accepted, and . . . I set out to enlighten the club women. With the help of my colleagues I prepared reading lists, and through letters, circular and personal, I urged on the women the duty of informing themselves of local factory conditions, and of standing by factory workers in righteous trade disputes. . . . In 1905, with leaders in the Women's Trade Union League and the Association of Social Settlements, I was instrumental in securing the first official investigation into conditions of working women in the United States.

READING 9G

THE DECISION IN *MULLER v. OREGON*, 1908

*The Progressive Era, 1900–1917, grew out of and intensified the efforts of various
reform movements to which many western women had been committed for many
years. During the Progressive Era, laws to improve the living and working
conditions of the average American were frequently passed at local, state, and*

*federal levels. A case involving one such law and western women changed the
nature of American legal practice.*

*Curt Muller, a Portland, Oregon, laundry owner, violated a 1903 Oregon law
mandating a ten-hour maximum workday for women; his female employees often
worked as long as seventeen hours per day in what amounted to a sweatshop. The
work force sued, and the case went to court. Upheld by the Oregon Supreme
Court, the law was considered in the United States Supreme Court in 1908—the
first of many cases to reach the high court involving social legislation designed to
protect children, women, and those who worked in hazardous and unhealthy
situations.*

*Defending the Oregon ten-hour law was Louis Brandeis. He presented his
argument in what came to be called the "Brandeis Brief"—the first time
sociological, medical, and other scientific evidence had been allowed in a court of
law—which became the model for later arguments for upholding social legislation.
Brandeis was named an associate justice of the United States Supreme Court in
1916.*

This excerpt is from the majority opinion in Muller v. Oregon, *penned by
Justice David J. Brewer.*

CURT MULLER, Plff. in Err., *v.* STATE OF OREGON Constitutional
law—regulating hours of women employees.

Rights under the 14th Amendment to the Federal Constitution are not in-
fringed by the limitation of the hours of labor of women employed in
laundries to ten hours daily which is made by Oregon Laws 1903, p. 148,
although like legislation affecting male employees may be invalid. . . .

That woman's physical structure and the performance of maternal functions place her at a disadvantage in the struggle for subsistence is obvious.
This is especially true when the burdens of motherhood are upon her. Even
when they are not, by abundant testimony of the medical fraternity continuance for a long time on her feet at work, repeating this from day to day,
tends to injurious effects upon the body, and, as healthy mothers are essential to vigorous offspring, the physical well-being of woman becomes an
object of public interest and care in order to preserve the strength and vigor
of the race. . . .

Though limitations upon personal and contractual rights may be removed by legislation, there is that in her disposition and habits of life which

will operate against a full assertion of those rights. She will still be where some legislation to protect her seems necessary to secure a real equality of right. Doubtless there are individual exceptions, and there are many respects in which she has an advantage over him; but looking at it from the viewpoint of the effort to maintain an independent position of life, she is not upon an equality. Differentiated by these matters from the other sex, she is properly placed in a class by herself, and legislation designed for her protection may be sustained, even when like legislation is not necessary for men, and could not be sustained. . . . The limitations which this statute places upon her right to agree with her employer as to the time she shall labor, are not imposed solely for her benefit, but also largely for the benefit of all. Many words cannot make this plainer. The two sexes differ in structure of body, in the functions performed by each, in the amount of physical strength, in the capacity for long-continued labor, particularly when done standing, the influence of vigorous health upon the future well-being of the race, the self-reliance which enables one to assert full rights, and in the capacity to maintain the struggle for subsistence. This difference justifies a difference in legislation, and upholds that which is designed to compensate for some of the burdens which rest upon her.

We have not referred in this discussion to the denial of the elective franchise in the state of Oregon, for while they may disclose a lack of political equality in all things with her brother, that is not of itself decisive. The reason runs deeper, and rests in the inherent difference between the two sexes, and in the different functions in life which they perform.

For these reasons, . . . we are of the opinion that it cannot be adjudged that the act in question is in conflict with the Federal Constitution, so far as it respects the work of a female in the laundry, and the judgment of the Supreme Court of Oregon is affirmed.

READING 9H
THE CONSUMERS' LEAGUE AND THE *MULLER*
CASE, RHETA CHILDE DORR, 1908

Even though Curt Muller paid only a $10 fine—and eventually replaced his women employees with Chinese immigrants—the impact of the decision in Muller v. Oregon *was wide ranging and significant. This case, upholding a law that originated in the West, spurred similar legislation nationwide. Women actively promoted these legislative efforts through such reform organizations as the*

*National Consumers' League, headquartered in New York City. Here Rheta
Childe Dorr describes the role of the Consumers' League in the Muller case and
how it led to the application of the "Oregon standard" to other bills throughout
the nation, particularly Illinois.*

The case was appealed, and appealed again, by the laundrymen, and finally
reached the Supreme Court of the United States. Then the Consumers'
League took a hand.

The brief for the State of Oregon . . . was prepared by Louis S. Brandeis,
of Boston, assisted by Josephine Goldmark, one of the most effective workers in the League's New York Headquarters. This brief is probably one of
the most remarkable legal documents in existence. It consists of one hundred and twelve printed pages, of which a few paragraphs were written by
the attorney for the State. All the rest was contributed, under Miss Goldmark's direction, from the Consumers' League's wonderful collection of
reasons why women workers should be protected. . . . The Consumers'
League convinced the Supreme Court of the United States, and the Oregon
ten-hour law was upheld. . . .

Waitresses' Union, Local No. 484, of Chicago, led by a remarkable young
working woman, Elizabeth Maloney, . . . drafted, and introduced into the
Illinois Legislature, a bill providing an eight-hour working day for every
woman in the State. . . .

The "Girls Bill," as it immediately became known, was the most hotly
contested measure passed by the Illinois Legislature during the session.
Over 500 manufacturers appeared at the public hearing on the bill . . .
presenting the business aspect of the questions; the girls showed the human side. . . .

"I am a waitress," said Miss Maloney, "and I work ten hours a day. In that
time a waitress who is tolerably busy *walks* ten miles, and the dishes she
carries back and forth aggregate in weight 1,500 to 2000 pounds. Don't you
think eight hours a day is enough for a girl to walk?"

Only one thing stood in the way of passage of the bill after that day. The
doubt of its constitutionality proved an obstacle too grave for the friends of
the workers to overcome. It was decided to substitute a ten-hour bill, an
exact duplicate of the "Oregon standard" established by the Supreme Court
of the United States. The principle of limitation upon the hours of women's
work once established in Illinois, the workers could proceed with their fight
for an eight-hour day.

CHAPTER 9

WESTERNERS OF COLOR

THE POPULATION of the American West is composed of many gradations in social strata, economic activity, religious values, political structure, and—perhaps most striking—ethnic complexity. Many divergent cultures have contributed to the development of the region. History, however, tends to examine minority cultures primarily as victims. It is an easy approach, as the history of the American West is rife with examples of abuse and fraud perpetrated against various ethnic groups in the name of Manifest Destiny. Less frequent are commentaries on their accomplishments, achievements, and interactions in the face of the odds arrayed against them. The greatness of the American West was in significant part built upon their sweat, blood, and sacrifice under difficult and discriminatory circumstances.

In this chapter the readings highlight primarily the relationship between the dominant white American culture and the most conspicuous of the minority groups: African American, Chinese, and Hispanic. Other selections throughout the book provide examples of the lifestyle and accomplishments of these cultures.

READING 1
"THE HEATHEN CHINEE," BRET HARTE, 1870

When the Chinese began to arrive in significant numbers during the California gold rush, sentiment against them was whipped up quickly. The Chinese brought a "foreign" culture and a "foreign" look to the gold camps and, most important from the perspective of the white miner, economic competition. The resentment grew during the 1860s, when 90 percent of the labor force constructing the Pacific end of the transcontinental railroad was Chinese.

The literature of the time reflected the various forms of this bias. The famous American western writer Bret Harte wrote this poem simply as newspaper filler.

It is believed he did not mean it as an anti-Chinese message, yet it soon became popular among those who favored discriminating against and excluding the Chinese.

Which I wish to remark—
And my language is plain—
That for ways that are dark
And for tricks that are vain,
The heathen Chinee is peculiar
Which the same I would rise to explain.

Ah Sin was his name;
And I shall not deny
In regard to the same
What his name might imply
But his smile it was pensive and childlike,
As I frequent remarked to Bill Nye.

It was August the third;
And quite soft was the skies;
Which it might be inferred
That Ah Sin was likewise;
Yet he played it that day upon William
And me in a way I despise.

Which we had a small game,
And Ah Sin took a hand;
It was Euchre, the game,
He did not understand;
But he smiled as he sat by the table,
With the smile that was childlike and bland.

Yet the cards they were stacked
In a way that I grieve,
And my feelings were shocked
At the state of Nye's sleeve;
Which was stuffed full of aces and bowers,
And the same with intent to deceive.

But the hands that were played
By that heathen Chinee,
And the points that he made,
Were quite frightful to see—
Till at last he put down a right bowers,
Which the same Nye had dealt unto me.

Then I looked up at Nye,
And he gazed upon me;
And he rose with a sigh,
And said, "Can this be?
We are ruined by Chinese cheap labor"—
And he went to that heathen Chinee.

In the scene that ensued
I did not take a hand
But the floor it was strewed
Like the leaves on the strand
With the cards that Ah Sin had been hiding,
In the game "he did not understand."

In his sleeves, which were long,
He had twenty-four packs—
Which was coming it strong,
Yet I state but the facts;
And we found on his nails, which were toper,
What is frequent in tapers—that's wax.

Which is why I remark,
And my language is plain,
That for ways that are dark,
And for tricks that are vain,
The heathen Chinee is peculiar—
Which the same I am free to maintain.

"John Chinaman," Anonymous, 1855

Much of the anti-Chinese literature had a mean-spirited bite. A good example is this song, which became popular during the California gold rush. It expresses quite clearly the white miners' distrust of Chinese culture, their fear of economic competition, and their racial prejudice.

John Chinaman, John Chinaman,
    But five short years ago,
I welcomed you from Canton, John—
    But wish I hadn't though;

For then I thought you honest, John,
    Not dreaming but you'd make
A citizen as useful, John
    As any in the state.

I thought you'd open wide your ports
    And let our merchants in
To barter for their crapes and teas,
    Their wares of wood and tin.

I thought you'd cut your queue off, John,
    And don a Yankee coat,
And a collar high you'd raise, John,
    Around your dusky throat.

I imagined that the truth, John,
    You'd speak when under oath,
But I find you'll lie and steal too—
    Yes, John, you're up to both.

I thought of rats and puppies, John,
    You'd eaten your last fill;
But on such slimy pot-pies, John,
    I'm told you dinner still.

Oh, John, I've been deceived in you,
    And all your thieving clan,
For our gold is all you're after, John,
    To get it as you can.

READING 3
A CHINESE CHRONICLE, 1848–1868

The contributions of the Chinese population of the American West centered in no small sense upon their efforts in building the Central Pacific, or westernmost, branch of the transcontinental railroad. At one point the Chinese constituted about 90 percent of the labor force. Their heroic work under extremely difficult conditions completed the greatest American engineering feat of the nineteenth century. But it was an accomplishment that meant almost constant danger and discrimination. The efforts of the Chinese during this 1860s railroad building era are chronicled here in excerpts from Oscar Lewis's The Big Four *and O. G. Villard's "Justice for the Chinese."*

When work began on the Central Pacific, Charles Crocker, head of construction, and J. H. Strobridge, superintendent of construction, were faced with a labor problem. Because white workers often left employment after the first payday, Lewis relates, and replacements were hard to find, they turned to the only alternative.

When no other recourse appeared in sight, Strobridge dubiously decided to try the experiment and fifty Chinese were hired. They were hauled to the end of the track. They disembarked, glanced around without curiosity at the surrounding forest, then tranquilly established camp, cooked a meal of rice and dried cuttlefish and went to sleep. By sunrise, they were at work with picks, shovels, and wheelbarrows. At the end of their first twelve hours of plodding industry, Crocker and his engineers viewed the results with gratified astonishment. Those who through the day had been momentarily expecting the weaklings to fall in their tracks from exhaustion permanently revised their opinion of the Chinaman's endurance.

[This performance convinced the Central Pacific to hire more Chinese, eventually more than ten thousand. They often worked in dangerous conditions.] The winter of 1865–1866 was severe as any on record. Snow fell in quantity as early as October, and the next five months saw an almost continuous succession of storms. As ground froze and the tracks and construction lines were blanketed under an icy mass fifteen feet thick, the work slowed down to a walk. . . .

Tunnels were dug beneath forty-foot drifts, and for months, three thousand workmen lived curious mole-like lives, passing from work to living quarters in dim passages far beneath the snow's surface. This eerie existence was complicated by constant danger, for as snows accumulated on the upper ridges, avalanches grew frequent, their approach heralded only by a brief thunderous roar. A second later, a work crew, a bunkhouse, sometimes an entire camp, would go hurtling at a dizzy speed down miles of frozen canyons. Not until months later were the bodies recovered; sometimes groups were found with shovels or picks still clutched in their frozen hands.

Others not directly associated with the Central Pacific also paid tribute to the heroic efforts of the Chinese labor force. O. G. Villard, in testimony before a House Committee on Chinese Exclusion, spoke of the Chinese who worked on the Northwest Pacific railroad line.

I want to remind you of the things that Chinese labor did for us in opening up the western portion of this country. I am a son of the man who drove the first transcontinental railroad across the American Northwest, the first rail link from Minnesota to Oregon and the waters of the Puget Sound. I was near him when he drove the last spike and paid an eloquent tribute to the men who had built that railroad by their manual labor for there were no road-making machines in those days.

He never forgot and never failed to praise the Chinese among them, of whom nearly 10,000 stormed the forest fastnesses, endured cold and heat and the risk of death at the hands of the hostile Indians to aid in the opening of our great northwestern empire.

I have a dispatch from the chief engineer of the Northwestern Pacific, telling how the Chinese laborers went out into eight feet of snow with the temperature far below zero to carry on the work when no American dared face the conditions.

Summer had its trials, too—and never more than in the construction of track at Cape Horn in the Sierra Nevada, as Lewis relates.

Throughout the summer of 1866, "Crocker's pets" [the derogatory nickname applied to the Chinese labor force], six thousand strong, swarmed over the upper canyon, pecking methodically at the broken rock of the cuts, trooping in long lines beneath their basket hats to pour wheelbarrow-loads of debris down the canyon-side, threading precarious paths with seventy pound kegs of black powder suspended from both ends of bamboo poles, refreshing themselves at intervals with sips of tea near at hand in whisky kegs emptied and abandoned by their white confreres. The Chinese were presently found to be adept at the backbreaking work of drilling and placing blasts, by then a major part of the work, for the upper ridges were scraped clear of soil by the winter deposits of ice.

Track-layers followed close behind the graders, and locomotives pushed strings of flatcars loaded with construction iron, lumber, explosives, food, drink and more men to the rail head. Cape Horn, a sheer granite buttress, proved the most formidable obstacle of the year; its lower sides dropped away in a thousand-foot vertical cliff that offered no vestige of a foothold. The indomitable Chinese were lowered from above on ropes, and there suspended between sky and earth, chipped away with hammer and chisel to form the precarious ledge which was then laboriously deepened to a shelf wide enough to permit the passage of cars. Three years later, when overland trains crept cautiously along this ledge, passengers gazed straight down from their windows into thin air.

The remarkable accomplishments of the Chinese did not escape the notice of other industries. In agriculture, by 1870, 10 percent of the California farm labor force was Chinese; by 1884 the figure had risen to about 50 percent. In construction, much of the marshy San Francisco shoreline was reclaimed by Chinese labor without benefit of drainage machinery, cranes, bulldozers, or trucks. It is estimated that more than five million acres of prime farm land was reclaimed by the Chinese labor force in the Sacramento–San Joaquin delta.

READING 4

A CHINESE MASSACRE, *LOS ANGELES DAILY NEWS*, 1871

A listing of accomplishments is positive and instructive, but the sad reality is that the history of an ethnic group is more often a tale of conflict. In the American

West the conflict was between the aspirations of the dominant Euro-American culture and anyone else who was seen as an obstacle to achieving its goals. In Los Angeles on October 24, 1871, for reasons that are unclear, an anti-Chinese riot swept through the area then known as Negro Alley. Since the initial trouble was internal, according to newspaper reports, the action may have begun as simple law enforcement. Or it may have been an attempt at forcibly controlling a population that was increasingly perceived as troublesome.

The difficulty which occurred yesterday at Negro Alley, between two opposition Chinese companies, in which pistols were then freely used, again broke out afresh about five o'clock last evening. The difficulty of yesterday had been taken into court where it was supposed that it would be properly disposed of. It appears, however, that after coming from Justice Gray's Court where the preliminary examination was commenced yesterday afternoon, they renewed their quarrel and again resorted to the pistol for settlement. Immediately after the first shots were fired, officers and citizens rushed to the scene, and an attempt was made to arrest the parties engaged in the melee. Instead of surrendering, these miscreants at once turned to bay, and discharged the contents of their revolvers at those attempting to arrest them. This dispersed the crowd quicker than it had collected; but two of the Chinese still stood at the door of one of their dens, and discharged their weapons at the retreating crowds. One of the officers . . . in a gallant attempt, with one or two others of the officers and some volunteers, to enter this den, was shot in the right shoulder and badly wounded. His brother, a boy about 15 years of age, received a ball in his right leg below the knee. Another man, a well known and respected citizen . . . while endeavoring to enter was confronted by a Chinaman with a loaded pistol in each hand. These he placed against [the man's] breast, and fired, one of the balls entering the right breast, the wound resulting fatally in about an hour and a half. This repeated firing was the signal for the closing of the iron shutters of neighboring stores.

Knots of men congregated at the street corners; and, in less time than it takes to be told, the entire block was surrounded, so as to permit none to escape. A string of men extended across Los Angeles Street along the east side of Negro Alley and on the western side of the block along Sanchez Street; and an unbroken line formed around the Plaza connecting with both the ends of the lines of Sanchez Street and Negro Alley. The wildest excitement prevailed. The mob was demoralized and uncontrollable. No definite organization prevailed. There seemed to be an understanding on the part of some few to drive the inmates of the blockaded houses up to the upper end of the block and allow them to escape into the Plaza where parties were stationed to receive them.

A Capture—The Captive Lynched

Shortly after the line had been formed, one of the inmates of the den in which these Chinamen had taken refuge, was observed endeavoring to escape across Los Angeles Street. The cry was raised; and he was quickly captured by one Romo Sortorel. He had evidently made up his mind to cut his way through the circle, being armed at the time with a hatchet. When arrested, someone made an attempt to stab him with a knife, cutting the hand of Sortorel. Others took him in charge, with the view of placing him in jail. The infuriated mob followed. Cries of "Hang him!" "Take him from Harris!" "Shoot him!" rose in every direction. The officers proceeded safely with their prisoner until they arrived at the junction of Temple and Spring Streets. Here they were surrounded, and the Chinaman forcibly taken from them, and dragged up Temple Street to New High Street. The frame of the sliding doors of a corral at the corner of this street afford a convenient gallows. A rope was at hand, and amid his own wailings and the hootings and imprecations of the crowd, he was elevated. The cord broke, however, but another was at hand, and he was again hoisted to the beam, and there left to swing.

The Multitude Maddened

Returning to the scene, efforts were made by the Sheriff to organize a body of men to watch the place until morning, when more efficient means would be used for capturing those remaining in the houses. But all his efforts failed. Parties then proceeded on the roofs of the Chinese dens, breaking them in with axes, and discharging their pistols into the interior, hoping thereby to succeed in driving them out. In the center of the block, behind the residences, is a corral. Last evening this contained some seven or eight horses, behind which some of the Chinamen were discovered secreting themselves, and four of them were summarily despatched. The demoniacal desire to set the block on fire and burn them out was broached, but a better spirit prevailed, and the repeated cries of "Burn the S —— of B ——s out," were answered by more numerous ones, in the negative. The dread of a conflagration was, providentially, predominant in the minds of the majority. Two attempts, nevertheless, were made by throwing fireballs into the open doorways, and through the holes in the roofs, but they were expeditiously extinguished.

For three hours, that portion of the city was a pandemonium. Yells, shouts, curses, and pistol shots rent the air in every direction. A novel idea at last suggested itself to some-one's mind, viz.: that water through the firemen's hose be brought to play upon their retreat, to try and drive them out in that manner. The effort was made, but was unsuccessful, as it was impossible to get any concert of action.

Ferreted Out

About half past nine, some person ventured to enter one of the houses, and presently emerged with a prisoner. The crowd instantly seized him, and hurried him off down to Los Angeles Street to the point south of Commercial Street. At this point were several empty wagons; and in lieu of any more convenient place, a rope was attached to his neck, and he was raised from the ground. Further search resulted in the capture, as far as we could ascertain, of fourteen others, who were similarly dealt with, four of them being taken to the place of execution on New High Street and the other ten to Los Angeles and Commercial Streets. The dwellings on Los Angeles Street, where these scenes were enacted, have an awning projecting over the sidewalk. Six of the Chinamen—one a mere child—swung from it in a row, three hanging together in a bunch. An empty wagon close by had four others hanging to its sides. So furious had the mob become, that they placed the ropes around the necks of their captives as soon as they got them into their hands, and then dragged them along the street to the places of execution, where, more dead than alive, their existence was ended. An effort to stay the proceedings, as possible innocence was sacrificed for guilt, was squelched, and the humanitarian, threatened with having a place given him among the ghastly row of victims hanging there before him. Such was the terrible vengeance that overtook these men. The bodies of those who were shot were lying on the street and sidewalk last night. . . .

As might be expected, thieves were not idle. Upon breaking open the Chinese establishment, and obtaining complete mastery over the inmates, they commenced to ply their trade, helping themselves to everything they could lay their hands upon. "Help yourself, boys," was the advice boldly given by one, who was actively putting same into practice. When he proceeded to retire, however, the crowd marched him back and forced him to disgorge.

It was currently reported that during the melee about forty of the opposition party of Chinamen, or the Yo Hing Company had decamped, crossing the Los Angeles River, and going in an eastward direction.

Latest

At the time of going to press, seventeen bodies are reported at the jail, and three wounded, besides a large number of women and children in custody.

Everything is now quiet in Negro Alley and the neighborhood, and a strong special force will keep guard throughout the rest of the night.

READING 5

THE CHINESE EXCLUSION ACT, 1882

> *The Chinese Exclusion Act of 1882 was the first law of any significance to restrict immigration into the United States. The Chinese made up only about 2/1000 of the United States population, but concerns of the dominant culture in the West about Chinese economic competition and the dilution of "white racial purity" spurred the congressional act. The law suspended Chinese immigration for ten years and made the Chinese already in the United States ineligible for naturalization. The act was renewed for another ten years, and in 1902 Chinese immigration was made "permanently" illegal. Chinese were ineligible for citizenship or for further immigration (under a very small quota) until 1943.*

> *An act to execute certain treaty stipulations relating to Chinese.*

WHEREAS, in the opinion of the Government of the United States the coming of Chinese laborers to this country endangers the good order of certain localities within the territory thereof: Therefore,

Be it enacted, That from and after the expiration of ninety days next after the passage of this act, and until the expiration of ten years next after the passage of this act, the coming of Chinese laborers to the United States be . . . suspended; and during such suspension it shall not be lawful for any Chinese laborer to come, or, having so come after the expiration of said ninety days, to remain within the United States.

SEC. 2. That the master of any vessel who shall knowingly bring within the United States on such vessel, and land or permit to be landed, any Chinese laborer, from any foreign port or place, shall be deemed guilty of a misdemeanor, and on conviction thereof shall be punished by a fine of not more than five hundred dollars for each and every such laborer so brought, and may be also imprisoned for a term not exceeding one year.

SEC. 3. That the two foregoing sections shall not apply to Chinese laborers who were in the United States on the seventeenth day of November, eighteen hundred and eighty, or shall have come into the same before the expiration of ninety days next after the passage of this act. . . .

SEC. 6. That in order to the faithful execution of articles one and two of the treaty in this act before mentioned, every Chinese person other than a laborer who may be entitled by said treaty and this act to come within the United States, and who shall be about to come to the United States, shall be identified as so entitled by the Chinese Government in each case, such identity to be evidenced by a certificate issued under the authority of said government, which certificate shall be in the English language or (if not in the English language) accompanied by a translation into English, stating such right to come, and which certificate shall state the name, title, or official rank, if any, the age, height, and all physical peculiarities, former and present occupation or profession, and place of residence in China of the person to whom the certificate is issued and that such person is entitled conformably to the treaty in this act mentioned to come within the United States. . . .

SEC. 12. That no Chinese person shall be permitted to enter the United States by land without producing to the proper officer of customs the certificate in this act required of Chinese persons seeking to land from a vessel. And any Chinese person found unlawfully within the United States shall be caused to be removed therefrom to the country from whence he came, by direction of the President of the United States, after being brought before some justice, judge, or commissioner of a court of the United States and found to be one not lawfully entitled to be or remain in the United States.

SEC. 13. That this act shall not apply to diplomatic and other officers of the Chinese Government traveling upon the business of that government, whose credentials shall be taken as equivalent to the certificate in this act mentioned, and shall exempt them and their body and household servants from the provisions of this act as to other Chinese persons.

SEC. 14. That hereafter no State court or court of the United States shall admit Chinese to citizenship; and all laws in conflict with this act are hereby repealed.

SEC. 15. That the words "Chinese laborer," whenever used in this act, shall be construed to mean both skilled and unskilled laborers and Chinese employed in mining.

READING 6

"I couldn't be more surprised!" Hanayo Inouye, 1923

The violence done to a community can take various forms—physical, psychological, or emotional—or the impact may be on tradition and expectation. The "culture shock" experienced by those new to the American West was frequently profound. Hanayo Inouye, an educated, privileged Japanese woman who differed greatly from "picture brides" (those who came to the United States to marry men who had selected them from a book), describes the shock of her encounter with this brave new world. Her 1923 experiences echo those of thousands of Japanese women immigrants in the nineteenth century.

We landed in San Francisco . . . in late September. For some time I just kept wanting to go back home. I . . . was lonely for my mother. She made beautiful kimonos when I became of marriageable age, but I never got to put them on, not even once. She wanted me to wear them when I became a real bride. . . . She used to tell me, "When you become a bride, neighbors will look forward to seeing you wear new kimonos every day. . . . You have to wait until then."

Well, naturally, she was not expecting me to leave home so quickly. . . .

For quite a long time after I came here, I thought of my mother almost every moment. In fact, when I cut my finger as I was picking grapes, I called out "Mother!" quite unconsciously. However, I think I began to like it here for its vastness of land and for the fact that a day's work meant a day's wages.

When I arrived . . . my husband said, "We are going to the country. You'd better not put good clothes on." When we got to the farm, Mr. Omaye showed me around and said, "Please make yourself comfortable in here." I couldn't be more surprised! He motioned to a corner of the barn where there was hay spread in a square shape with a partition! That was all there was! I certainly did not feel like taking off my clothes and napping there. I never felt more distressed in my whole life. My husband should have told me about such conditions before I left Japan. He had shown me some pictures of himself in suits and of nothing but the best scenery. Naturally, I thought I was coming to a really nice place when I left Japan. I might have taken it differently had I been raised in a less fortunate family. . . .

When I asked my husband where the toilet was, he pointed outside. It was out in the field. He then told me to hit the toilet with a stick before going in . . . there were black spiders living in it. . . . Many people were bitten by those black spiders, and I heard someone died of a fever caused by the spider bites. I was quite scared of the place. I realized, however, that no matter how much I thought of my mother back in Japan or of anybody, it wouldn't do any good. I knew then I had to live with it and give it a try. But I told myself I was going back home as soon as I made some money here.

READING 7

LIFE IN A BLACK ARMY REGIMENT, THOMAS HIGGINSON, 1869

A striking feature of the post–Civil War American West was the development of black army units. The famous Buffalo Soldiers, or Black Cavalry, were former slaves and Civil War veterans. Most historians generally agree that the Buffalo Soldier units were among the most courageous and well-disciplined troops of the period. Since many of them had gained their first military experience during the Civil War, an account of their activities during that conflict is important in putting their history in context. Thomas Higginson, the white commander of the First South Carolina Volunteers, a black unit of the Union army, provides interesting background for later events in the West. Higginson was an ardent abolitionist who had known John Brown and is believed to have known in advance of Brown's Harpers Ferry raid of 1859. Wounded in 1864 and forced to retire, Higginson returned to New England, where he became best known for discovering the poet Emily Dickinson.

I had always had so much to do with fugitive slaves, and had studied [blacks] with such interest, that I found not much to learn or unlearn as to this point. Their courage I had seen before tested; their docile and lovable qualities I had known; and the only real surprise that experience brought me was in finding them so little demoralized. I had not allowed for the extreme re-moteness and seclusion of their lives. . . . Many of them had literally spent their whole existence on some lonely island or remote plantation, where the master never came, and the overseer only once or twice a week. With these exceptions, such persons had never seen a white face, and of the excitements or sins of larger communities they had not a conception. . . . While I had some men who were unprincipled and troublesome, there was not one whom I could call a hardened villain. I was constantly expecting to find male Topsies, with no notions of good and plenty of evil. But I never found one. Among the most ignorant there was very often a childlike absence of vices, which was rather to be classed as inexperience than as innocence, but which had some of the advantages of both.

Apart from this, they were very much like other men. General Saxton, examining with some impatience a long list of questions from some philanthropic Commission at the North, respecting the traits and habits of the freedmen, bade some staff-officer answer them all in two words—"Intensely human." We all admitted that it was a striking and comprehensive description.

For instance, as to courage. So far as I have seen, the mass of men are naturally courageous up to a certain point. A man seldom runs away from danger which he ought to face, unless others run; each is apt to keep with the mass, and colored soldiers have more than usual of this gregariousness. In almost every regiment, black or white, there are a score or two of men who are naturally daring, who really hunger after dangerous adventures, and are happiest when allowed to seek them. Every commander gradually finds out who these men are, and habitually uses them; certainly I had such, and I remember with delight their bearing, their coolness, and their dash. [Some] were neat and well-drilled soldiers, while others were slovenly, heedless fellows,—the despair of their officers at inspection, their pride on a raid. They were the natural scouts and rangers of the regiment; they had the two-o'clock-in-the-morning courage. . . . The mass of the regiment rose to the same level under excitement, and were more excitable, I think, than whites, but neither more nor less courageous.

Perhaps the best proof of a good average of courage among them was in the readiness they always showed for any special enterprise. I do not remember ever to have had the slightest difficulty in obtaining volunteers, but rather in keeping down the number. . . . There were more than a hundred men in the ranks who had voluntarily met more dangers in their escape from slavery than any of my young [white] captains had incurred in all their lives. . . . I used to think that I should not care to read "Uncle Tom's Cabin" in our camp; it would have seemed tame. Any group of men in a tent would have had more exciting tales to tell. . . .

I often asked myself why it was that, with this capacity of daring and endurance, they had not kept the land in a perpetual flame of insurrection; why, especially since the opening of the war, they had kept so still. The answer was to be found in the peculiar temperament of the races, in their religious faith, and in the habit of patience that centuries had fortified. The shrewder men all said substantially the same thing. What was the use of insurrection, where everything was against them? They had no knowledge, no money, no arms, no drill, no organization,—above all, no mutual confidence. It was the tradition among them that all insurrections were always betrayed by somebody. . . .

It always seemed to me that, had I been a slave, my life would have been one long scheme of insurrection. But I learned to respect the patient self-control of those who had waited till the course of events should open a better way. When it came they accepted it. Insurrection on their part would at once have divided the Northern sentiment; and a large part of our army would have joined with the Southern army to hunt them down. By their waiting till we needed them, their freedom was secured.

Two things chiefly surprised me in their feeling toward their former masters,—the absence of affection and the absence of revenge. . . . I never could cajole one of them, in his most discontented moment, into regretting "ole mas'r time" for a single instant. I never heard one speak of the masters except as natural enemies. Yet they were perfectly discriminating as to individuals; many of them claimed to have had kind owners, and some expressed great gratitude to them for particular favors received. It was not the individuals, but the ownership, of which they complained. That they saw to be a wrong which no special kindnesses could right. On this, as on all points connected with slavery, they understood the matter as clearly as [William Lloyd] Garrison or [Wendell] Phillips [two of the most prominent abolitionists]; the wisest philosophy could teach them nothing as to that, nor could any false philosophy befog them. After all, personal experience is the best logician.

Certainly this indifference did not proceed from any want of personal affection, for they were the most affectionate people among whom I had ever lived. They attached themselves to every officer who deserved love, and to some who did not; and if they failed to show it to their masters, it proved the wrongfulness of the mastery. On the other hand, they rarely showed one gleam of revenge. . . .

But side by side with this faculty of patience, there was a certain tropical element in the men, a sort of fiery ecstasy when aroused. . . . Their gregariousness and love of drill made them more easy to keep in hand than white American troops, who rather like to straggle or go in little squads, looking out for themselves, without being bothered with officers. The blacks prefer organization.

The point of inferiority that I always feared, though I never had occasion to prove it, was that they might show less fibre, less tough and dogged resistance, than whites, during a prolonged trial,—a long, disastrous march, for instance, or the hopeless defence of a besieged town. I should not be afraid of their mutinying or running away, but of their drooping and dying. It might not turn out so; but I mention it for the sake of fairness, and to avoid overstating the merits of these troops. As to the simple general fact of courage and reliability I think no officer in our camp ever thought of there being any difference between black and white. And certainly the opinions of these officers, who for years risked their lives every moment on the fidelity of their men, were worth more than those of all the world beside.

No doubt there were reasons why this particular war was an especially favorable test of the colored soldiers. They had more to fight for than the whites. Besides the flag and the Union, they had home and wife and child. They fought with ropes around their necks, and when orders were issued [by the War Department] that the officers of colored troops should be put to death on capture, they took a grim satisfaction. It helped their *esprit de corps* immensely. With us . . . there was to be no play-soldier. Though they had begun with a slight feeling of inferiority to the white troops, this compliment substituted a peculiar sense of self-respect. And even when the new colored regiments began to arrive from the North my men still pointed out this difference,—that in the case of ultimate defeat, the Northern troops, black or white, would go home, while the First South Carolina must fight it out or be re-enslaved. . . .

When the army was reorganized following the Civil War, four regiments made up of black enlistees were formed, and all four—the Twenty-fourth and Twenty-fifth Infantries and Ninth and Tenth Cavalries—saw significant action in the West. These units had the lowest desertion and highest reenlistment rates of any in the region.

READING 8

Causes of the Exodus, Henry Adams, 1877

After the Civil War the stream of former slaves moving westward in search of a better life eventually became a flood. In 1879 alone, some twenty thousand blacks migrated from southern states to Kansas. Many "Exodusters" faced their new lives with admirable determination (see chapter 3, reading 15), but these and earlier migrants also encountered racial discrimination and wary western residents. In the late 1870s the Congress, receiving complaints that the Exodus was out of control as the result of sinister intentions on the part of railroad companies and political parties, decided to investigate. In 1880 the congressional committee, dominated by powerful southern Democrats, issued a report blaming migration problems on Republican policies and promoters.

Among those testifying before the committee in 1877 was Henry Adams, a black Civil War veteran who became a leader in the migration to Kansas.

Q. Now tell us, Mr. Adams, what, if anything, you know about the exodus of the colored people from the Southern to the Northern and Western States; and be good enough to tell us in the first place what you know about the organization of any committee or society among the colored people themselves for the purpose of bettering their condition, and why it was organized. Just give us a history as you understand it.

A. I went into the Army in 1866 and came out last of 1869—and went right back home again where I went from, Shreveport. . . . After we have come out a parcel of we men that was in the Army and other men thought that the way our people had been treated during the time we was in the service— we heard so much talk of how they had been treated and opposed so much and there was no help for it. That caused me to go into the Army at first, the way our people was opposed. There was so much going on that I went off and left it; when I came back it was still going on, part of it, not quite so bad as at first. So a parcel of us got together and said that we would organize ourselves into a committee and look into affairs and see the true condition of our race, to see whether it was possible we could stay under a people who had held us under bondage. . . . We organized a committee.

Q. What did you call your committee?

A. We just called it a committee. . . . Some of the members of the committee was ordered by the committee to go into every State in the South where we had been slaves there, and post one another from time to time about the true condition of our race, and nothing but the truth.

Q. I want to know how many traveled in that way to get at the condition of your people in the Southern States?

A. I think about one hundred or one hundred and fifty went from one place or another.

Q. And they went from one place to another, working their way and paying their own expenses and reporting to the common center at Shreveport, do you mean?

A. Yes, sir.

Q. What was the character of the information they gave you?

A. . . . . [T]hey said in several parts where they was that the land rent was still higher there in that part of the country than it was where we first organized it, and the people was still being whipped, some of them, by the old owners, the men that had owned them as slaves, and some of them was being cheated out of their crops just the same as they was there.

Q. Was anything said about their personal and political rights in these reports, as to how they were treated about these?

A. Yes, some of them stated that in some parts of the country where they voted they would be shot. Some of them stated that if they voted the Democratic ticket they would not be injured.

Q. But they would be shot, or might be shot, if they voted the Republican ticket?

A. Yes, sir.

Q. I am speaking now of the period from 1870 to 1874, and you have given us the general character of the reports that you got from the South; what did you do in 1874?

A. Well, along in August sometime in 1874, after the white [supremacist] league sprung up, they organized and said this is a white man's government, and the colored men should not hold any offices; they were no good but to work in the fields and take what they would give them and vote the Democratic ticket. That's what they would make public speeches and say to us, and we would hear them. We then organized an organization called the colonization council.

Q. What was the difference between that organization and your committee, as to its objects?

A. Well, the committee was to investigate the condition of our race.

Q. And this organization was then to better your condition after you had found out what your condition was?

A. Yes, sir.

Q. In what way did you propose to do it?

A. We first organized and adopted a plan to appeal to the President of the United States and to Congress to help us out of our distress, or protect us in our rights and privileges.

Q. Well, what other plan had you?

A. And if that plan failed our idea was then to ask them to set apart a territory in the United States for us, somewhere where we could go and live with our families.

Q. You preferred to go off somewhere by yourselves?

A. Yes.

Q. Well, what then?

A. If that failed, our other object was to ask an appropriation of money to ship us all to Liberia, in Africa; somewhere where we could live in peace and quiet.

Q. Yes, and what after that?

A. When that failed then our idea was to appeal to other governments outside of the United States to help us get away from the United States and go there and live under their flag.

Q. Now when you organized the council what kind of people were taken into it?

A. Nobody but laboring men. . . . When we met in committee there was not any of us allowed to tell our name. . . . We first appealed to President Grant. . . . That was in September, 1874, . . . at other times we sent to Congress. . . . We told them our condition, and asked Congress to help us out of our distress and protect us in our lives and property, and pass some law or provide some way that we might get our rights in the South, and so forth. . . . After the appeal in 1874, we appealed when the time got so hot down there they stopped our churches from having meetings after nine o'clock at night. They stopped them from sitting up and singing over the dead, and so forth, right in the little town where we lived, in Shreveport. I know that to be a fact; and after they did all this, and we saw it was getting so warm—killing our people all over the whole country—there was several of them killed right down in our parish—we appealed. . . .

We had much rather stayed there [in the South] if we could have had our rights. . . . In 1877 we lost all hopes . . . [because] we found ourselves in such condition that we looked around and we seed that there was no way on earth, it seemed, that we could better our condition there, and we discussed that thoroughly in our organization along in May. We said that the whole South—every State in the South—had got into the hands of the very men that held us as slaves—from one thing to another and we thought that the men that held us as slaves was holding the reins of government over our heads in every respect almost, even the constable up to the governor. We felt we had almost as well be slaves under these men. . . .

We said there was no hope for us and we had better go. . . . Then, in 1877 we appealed to President Hayes and to Congress, to both Houses. I am certain we sent papers there; if they didn't get them that is not our fault; we sent them. . . .

Mighty few ministers would allow us to have their churches [used for meetings]; some few would in some of the parishes. . . . When we held our meetings we would not allow the politicians to speak. . . .

It is not exactly five hundred men belonging to the council, . . . they have now got at this time 98,000 names enrolled, . . . men and women, and none under twelve years old. . . .

Q. Now, Mr. Adams, you know, probably, more about the causes of your exodus from that country than any other man from your connection with it; tell us in a few words what you believe to be the causes of these people going away?

A. Well, the cause is, in my judgment, and from what information I have received, and what I have seen with my own eyes—it is because the largest majority of the people, of the white people, that held us as slaves treats our people so bad in many respects that it is impossible for them to stand it. Now, in a great many parts of that country there our people most as well as be slaves as to be free; because, in the first place, I will state this: that in some times, in times of politics, if they have any idea that the Republicans will carry a parish or ward, or something of that kind, why, they would do anything on God's earth. There ain't nothing too mean for them to do to prevent it; nothing I can make mention of is too mean for them to do.

"In consequence of abolition incendiarism," 1860

Troubled race relations, whether between whites and Indians, Hispanics and whites, blacks and whites, or any other combination, were an underlying issue in the history of the West. In Texas on the eve of the Civil War the problem was exacerbated by fear—the fear of slave insurrection fomented by "Lincolnites." On July 8, 1860, most of the downtown section of Dallas was burned, and fires broke out in seven other Texas communities. Rumors spread that the fires were the work of abolitionist agents sent to free the slaves and kill the slaveholders. When a letter was intercepted from a northern abolitionist which seemed to outline the plot, hysteria became rampant. "Slave leaders" of the "riot" were tortured and executed in retribution. Vigilance committees sprang up throughout Texas, and "trials" led to the execution of seventy-five to one hundred individuals, mostly black.

This letter written by a southern white to the editor of a northern newspaper— and reproduced in an 1860 pamphlet by John Townsend titled The Doom of Slavery in the Union; Its Safety out of It*—reflects the attitudes of some whites during this period of unrest.*

Marshall, Texas

Aug. 12, 1860

Editors of the Evening Day Book:

The wildest excitement prevails throughout the north-western, north-eastern, and the central portions of Texas, in consequence of *Abolition incendiarism*. I have no doubt but you have seen, ere this reaches you, the burning of Dallas, Denton, Black Jack Grove, and quite a large number of stores and mills. Loss estimated at between $1,500,000 and $2,000,000. Since then the *Abolitionists* have been detected in attempts to fire a number of towns South of the above, and in an extensive plan of insurrection among the negros, headed by these demons of hell. On some plantations the negros have been examined, and arms and ammunition in considerable amount have been found in their possession; they all admit they were given to them by these *Lincolnites*. Every day we hear of the burning of some town, mill, store, or farmhouse.... *Women and children* have been so frightened by these burnings and threatened rebellion of the negros, that in several instances they have *left their homes in their fright, and when found were almost confirmed maniacs!* Military companies are organized all over the state, and one-half of our citizens do constant patrol duty. But unfortunately up to this time Judge Lynch [a code reference to the practice of hanging individuals without benefit of trial] has had the honor to preside only in ten cases of white (northern Lincolnites) and about sixty-five of negros, all of whom were hung or burnt, as to the degree of their implication in the rebellion and burning. The plan was to burn all of the towns, thereby destroy the arms and ammunition. . . . [A]fter pillaging and burning those . . . cities, the negros were promised by these devils incarnate [abolitionists], that they would have in readiness a number of vessels, and would take them forthwith to Mexico. . . . The *credulity of the negro* is so great, that he can be *induced to believe almost anything,* no matter how impossible it may be, particularly when he is informed by a shrewd white man that the thing can be done, and that he will lead them on and accomplish the object. But the end is not yet. I believe that the northern churches are at the bottom of this whole affair—in fact the fanatics have already acknowledged it. They say that this Texas raid is in revenge for the expulsion of some of their brethren of the Methodist church from Texas . . . for preaching and teaching Abolition incendiarism to the negros of northern Texas. Unless the churches send out new recruits of John Browns [code for abolitionists], I fear the boys will have nothing to do this winter (as they have hung all that can be found), the school boys have become so excited by the sport of hanging Abolitionists, that the schools are completely deserted, they having formed companies, and will go seventy-five or one hundred miles on horseback to participate in a single execution of the sentence of Judge Lynch's Court. It has now become a settled conviction in the South *that this Union cannot subsist one day after Abe Lincoln has been declared President,* if God, in his infinite wisdom, should permit him to live that long, for they (the people of the South) have made up their minds that they had rather die, sword in hand, in defence of their homes, their wives, their children and slaves, in defence of the Constitution, the laws, and their sacred honor, than *tamely submit to an organized system of robbery, a degraded and loathsome scheme of amalgamation,* a breaking up of the compromises of the Constitution, and a total exclusion of the South from the common territories of the country won by their blood and treasure.

Senator Bruce and the Indians, 1880

The three groups most discriminated against in the American West were the Indians, the African Americans, and the Hispanics. And yet it is unusual to find much comment by one of these groups about another; only infrequently did Indians mention the black cavalry units whom they dubbed "Buffalo Soldiers," or black settlers refer to the Indian threat. One exception, however, is a discussion of Indian policy by U.S. Senator Blanche Bruce, a Republican from Mississippi who was elected during the first years of Reconstruction and served from 1875 to 1881—the first black to serve a full term in the Senate. In a speech of April 7, 1880, Bruce comments on one of the bills concerning Indian policy which were being debated in Congress. Bruce supported the acts, viewed as reform measures, which broke up the tribal units, divided reservation lands into 160-acre individual allotments, and provided a system for Indian citizenship. He believed that these actions would dramatically change for the better a policy that had "kept the Indian a fugitive and a vagabond . . . [and] bred discontent, suspicion, and hatred in the mind of the red man."

Our Indian policy and administration seem to me to have been inspired and controlled by a stern selfishness, with a few honorable exceptions. Indian treaties have generally been made as the condition and instrument of acquiring the valuable territory occupied by the several Indian nations and have been changed and revised from time to time as it became desirable that the steadily growing, irrepressible white races should secure more room for their growth and more lands for their occupancy; and wars, bounties and beads have been used as auxiliaries for the temporary peace and security for the whites, and as the preliminary to further aggressions upon the red man's lands, with the ultimate view of his expulsion and extinction from the continent.

No set purpose has been evinced in adequate, sufficient measure to build him up, to civilize him, and to make him part of the great community of states. Whatever of occasional and spasmodic effort has been made for his redemption from savagery and his perpetuity as a race, has been only sufficient to supply that class of exceptions to the rule necessary to prove the selfishness of the policy that we allege to have been practiced toward him. . . .

Now, sir, there must be a change in the Indian policy if beneficent practical results are expected, and any change that gives promise of solving this red-race problem must be a change based upon an idea of harmony, and not at war with our free institutions. If the Indian is expected and required to respond to federal authority; if this people are expected to grow up into organized and well-ordered society; if they are to be civilized, in that the best elements of their natures are to be developed in the exercise of their best functions, so as to produce individual character and social groups characteristic of enlightened people; if this is to be done under our system, its ultimate realization requires an adoption of a political philosophy that shall make the Indians, as an individual and as a tribe, subjects of American law and beneficiaries of American institutions, by making them first American citizens, and clothing them, as rapidly as their advancement and location will permit, with the protective and ennobling prerogatives of such citizenship.

I favor the measure pending, because it is a step in the direction that I have indicated. You propose to give the Indian not temporary but permanent residence as a tribe, and not tribal location, but by a division of lands in severalty you secure to him the individual property rights which, utilized, will sustain life for himself and family better than his nomadic career. By this location you lay the foundation for that love of country essential to the patriotism and growth of a people, and by the distribution of lands to the individual, in severalty, you appeal to and develop that essential constitutional quality of humanity, the disposition to accumulate, upon which, when healthily and justly developed, depends the wealth, the growth, the power, the comfort, the refinement and the glory of the nations of the earth. . . .

Mr. President, the red race are not a numerous people in our land, not equaling probably a half million souls, but they are the remnants of a great and multitudinous nation, and their hapless fortunes heretofore not only appeal to sympathy and to justice in any measures that we may take affecting them, but the vigor, energy, bravery and integrity of this remnant entitle them to consideration on the merits of the question. . . .

Now, sir, the Indian is a physical force; a half million vigorous, physical, intellectual agents ready for the plastic hand of Christian civilization, living in a country possessing empires of untilled and uninhabited lands. The Indian tribes, viewed from this utilitarian standpoint, are worth preservation, conservation, utilization and civilization, and I believe that we have reached a period when the public sentiment of the country demands such a modification in the Indian policy, in its purposes and in its methods, as shall save and not destroy these people. . . .

The Indian is human, and no matter what his traditions or his habits, if you will locate him and put him in contact, and hold him in contact, with the forces of our civilization, his fresh, rugged nature will respond, and the fruit of his endeavor, in his civilization and development, will be the more permanent and enduring because his nature is so strong and obdurate. When you have no longer made it necessary for him to be a vagabond and fugitive; when you have allowed him to see the lovable and attractive side of our civilization as well as the stern military phase; when you have made the law apply to him as it does to others; so that the ministers of the law shall not only be the executors of its penalties but the administrators of its saving, shielding, protecting provisions, he will become trustful and reliable; and when he is placed in position in which not only to become an industrial force—to multiply his comforts and those of his people—but the honest, full sharer of the things he produces, savage life will lose its attractions, and the hunter will become the herdsman, the herdsman in his turn the farmer, and the farmer the mechanic, and out of the industries and growth of the Indian homes will spring up commercial interests and men competent to foster and handle them.

The American people are beginning to reach the conscientious conviction that redemption and civilization are due to the Indian tribes of the United States, and the present popular purpose is not to exterminate them but to perpetuate them on this continent.

READING II

"That was courtship," Laura Black Bear Miles, c. 1960

Despite the often serious depredations visited upon the Native American (and other) cultures in the American West, family life and tradition remained strong. It is a testament to the human spirit that people enduring the greatest hardship retained that which was most dear to them—respect for family and the past. This attitude is represented by Laura Black Bear Miles, a Cheyenne woman born in Oklahoma in 1904 who was the great-granddaughter of Red Moon, a powerful Cheyenne chief. Here she describes the courtship rituals common in the Cheyenne culture at the turn of the century, customs that still mirrored age-old traditions.

I was born in 1904 along the river not far from the trading post, where there were not railroad tracks or roads of any sort. There was a camp there, where we lived, until we moved west, to an area still along the river . . . not far from the trading post. My mother built a house there, where we stayed until [she] passed away. . . .

My maiden name was Black Bear, which came from my grandfather on my father's side. My father's name was Joe White Bird, and he had gone to the Carlisle Indian School. . . .

In the old days courtship went like this.

During the daytime the young men [would not] speak or congregate with the young ladies. The way of courtship was that after dark the young man, if he liked a certain young lady, would go and wait patiently behind her tipi. In those days they wore red and blue blankets, which the men still use today, and some of the young men even wore white sheets. Then they would wait for an opportunity. If the young lady happened to have to go out for something, then he would just come up behind her and then wrap her in his blankets.

It was common to see after dark a couple in a blanket. That was court-ship. In that time the young ladies were afraid to step outside. The only time they ever went out was when it was absolutely necessary.

The way a young man asked for a hand in marriage was like this; if a young lady had a brother, he was given the greatest respect by his sister, and if someone liked the young lady, he would take some kind of gift over to the brother, and if the brother accepted the gift, then the sister was promised to the young man who presented the gift . . . even if the young lady had never talked, or so much as looked, at him.

If her brother accepted the gift, then that's the way it was. It was final, and the parents were not even involved.

The brothers and sisters hardly spoke to each other, because of the deep respect they held for one another. There was no joking around. . . . Brothers would never kid their sisters. If someone said something . . . about a sister or brother . . . [they would] have to leave the room in order not to show disrespect.

That respect is also true between a father-in-law and daughter-in-law. A father-in-law never speaks to his daughter-in-law unless absolutely neces-sary. Son-in-law to mother-in-law is the same thing.

After the [marriage] transaction is made, the bride is dressed in the finest buckskins, and goes home with the groom. The groom's relations get together these blankets, bedding materials, and many household items. On the bride's side they . . . give tipis, moccasins, tents and also food, and gather on the bride's side and make a big feast.

On the groom's side they come over with all these quilts and dry goods so all the bride's relations—usually ladies—sort out the various gifts. When they get through, the groom's side of the family—usually men—go over and eat this food that is prepared, and then go and take down the tents and the moccasins, and so forth, that's theirs to take. But of all these gifts, the bride and groom get the best of what is there—the best tipi, the most comfortable bedding, pots and pans and what they're going to need.

All are prepared to give the best. Prestige is distinguished not by how much you have, but by how much you give away. If you give away something very fine, then you are a very prestigious person. Everyone gives their finest. That's the way it is consummated. And so when all the gift giving is over . . . the bride goes home with the groom and they go and pitch their tents.

That's the way I was brought up.

READING 12
"A CONTINUAL ROUND OF PLEASURE AND JOY,"
JAMES HENRY GLEASON, 1846–1850

Before the arrival of the argonauts, California life at least for the gentility was peaceful and romantic. This charmed atmosphere did not survive the gold rush tidal wave. In these letters to his sister, however, James Henry Gleason, who arrived in Monterey in 1845, depicts the life-style of the prosperous Californio culture into which he married. They are a paean to a vanishing age.

Monterey
U. States of America
July 25, 1846
Miss Frances A. Gleason
My dear sister,
[I realize] you are very anxious for me to come home . . . but why destroy the fine prospects that are now presented to me by being absent eighteen months. . . .

[Here in Monterey] I am received into the highest society and *respected far more than I would be at home.*

The greater likelihood is that I shall go as a *married* man. I am engaged to the belle of Monterey! Miss Kate Watson. They are fine people all of them and my Kate is beyond compare. Her father James Watson is a great honest hearted man who is a friend to every one. He is quite well off being worth about 60,000$. He is very hospitable and his house at the rancho near town is the stopping place for all his friends. . . .

in haste your dear Brother James

Monterey January 28, 1847

Dear sister . . . My last letter to you was by the "Levant" [a sailing ship]. Since then I have purchased three house lots in San Francisco which will in a few years hence be valued at $8000 or $10,000. . . . I have been on this coast now ten months and have acquired a knowledge of the Spanish language and become acquainted with the people and country consequently my chance of *making a fortune* is somewhat more promising than that of thousands now arriving strangers in the country. . . . [T]here is a good society here now *far better than in Plymouth* and my beautiful little Spanish wife (that is to be) Catarina will make you happy.

Dearly your brother,

James

Pr. U.S. Ship "Prebble"

Monterey California May 2, 1847

My dear sister,

I have just finished my fourth business letter to the Sand'ch Islands [Hawaii]—lit my cigar—and now I am ready to devote my time to a dear acquaintance. I am not married yet but tomorrow I intend to ask for the hand of Catarina Watson, *we must be united,* she is one of the loveliest—a disposition that an angel might envy, her father is a merchant in this place, worth about 30,000$. I have a rival, sole heir to about 50,000$ these are large numbers. However I have hopes of success Kate tells me that she loves me—that she will wed me and no other—David Spence, my rival, has been her companion from infancy yet my happy disposition and *good looks* has removed from her all the attachments she had to him, and the charm of *Fifty thousand.* I am received into the family as a favorite. . . .

There is not a young man in California with more promising prospects before him than are now presented to me. Mr. Watson is aware of this and this encourages me to hope for success. . . . You must excuse me for a few moments my servant has just brought into the office a piece of pie. I wish I could share with you it looks so nice.

15 minutes later

Having ate my pie—smoked a cigar—walked the terrace, blowed my nose, and censured the servant for a blunder I again return to you. I am thinking of a subject to commence upon—here's one at once.

The above ten lines are filled with nonsense I must quit that for I pay 1.50 cts. postage for this letter in advance.

Sister . . . I would that your days were as happy as mine. Nearly every afternoon a pic-nic in the woods with the Senoritas and nearly every night a dance. Our music [is] the guitar and harp and for a partner, a Spanish maiden whose very existence is *Love*. I imagine myself associated with Angels while moving around with these lovely beings their very language—the Castilian— is sufficient to warm the coldest heart when they speak of *Love*. . . .

Monterey 30 May 1847
Night 11 O.Clock
My affectionate Sister, . . .

I have *popped* the question for the hand of that lovely girl Catarina Watson her parents wish me to wait for 18 months and then ask for her again as she is too young to marry only 14 years of age. She tells me that she will have me and none other we often speak of you in our *love chats* she wishes you to come to her country—to her home

Her father is worth about 40,000$ I am now enjoying the happiest days of my life nothing but Pic-nic's and dances. . . .

California April 1 1848
Dearly beloved Sister. . . .

The last two years [have] been a continual round of pleasure and joy, it has appeared to me like a dream. I am a particular favourite with the Californians and there is not a house on the Coast [where I do not enjoy the] freedom of one of the family. a Ball or *Mereanda* cannot pass off *alegre* without [my] presence. Dona Narisa de Osio is now waiting my return to Monterey to give me a splendid Ball. . . . I have often wished you could see me at times traveling up and down the coast in my California riding dress, sometimes camping out in the mountains surrounded by wild indians and bears other times at some rancho luxuriating on a bullock hide stretched out over a few sticks, at other times dressed up in a fine broad cloth at the house of a rich family as I am at present while writing this Dona Arcadia and Isadora pursuad me every few moments to [sing] while the latter is running her delicate fingers over the harp strings. . . .

I have a good prospect for the future. I . . . hope to acquire a fortune I have a house building in Monterey which ought to be finished now it will cost 1600$ to 1800$. I have besides this in Monterey about 350 yards of land in house lots. I own also in San Francisco a house lot of 50 yards which I have leased and I own in Benicia 3 more house lots. . . . I purchased this land very cheap before the Am. flag was hoisted in California the land I have in S. Fran'co cost me 200.$ and I have been offered for it 1400.$

Your very Affectionate Brother
James

Monterey Nov'r 15, '49
Dona Francesca Gleason, Plymouth
My dear sister

Well Fanny I'm married. My bonny Kate is now reclining over my shoulder & anxious to know what I am about to say, . . . she understands but few words in English. She saw "My" & "Kate" in the second line and knew what it meant at once but the "bonny" which intervenied was a damper. I told her it was saltfish and she curled her pretty lip. . . .

I was married on the 7th of Oct at 3 Oc in the morning. a large dinner party was given by my father at his house in the afternoon and a dance followed in the evening. the expenses must have been nearly $1000. . . . there are thousands [of gold seekers] now in the country seeking employment & suffering for the want of funds to support themselves with. . . .

My wife joins me in love to you all.

Your Affec't Brother James

San Francisco Mar 31, 1850
My dear sister

My wife tells me to say that as she cannot write in English. You must excuse her and as a token of her deep affection . . . she will send a pina scarf by Mrs. Paty . . . they are valued here at 125.$ each. She will also send her Deguereotype in her bridal dress and reclining on a harp as she was at a moment on the marriage eve, when my attention was called to her.

San Francisco July 1, 1850

My dear sister Fanny

I have a great desire to go home but it seems that every month I remain here plunges me still deeper in business.... I left my wife well at Monterey & should nothing occur to frustrate the workings of nature I shall be a Father in a few months, and then I am going home partly to see my old acquaintances and relations & partly to get clear of a squalling baby. I like babys very much but not untill they arrive at a certain age.

READING 13

HISPANICS IN THE AMERICAN WEST

One of the most conspicuous elements of the development of the American West was the shifting definition of the "dominant culture." From Native American it changed over time to Spanish to Mexican to Euro-American, with brief inroads by the British and Russians. Throughout most of the eighteenth and into the early nineteenth century the dominant culture was Spanish and Mexican, which strongly influenced social structure, religion, land ownership, and political organization in the vast region under its control. But all that was to change with the English-speaking Euro-American "invasion" of the American West beginning early in the nineteenth century and reaching a climax with the Mexican-American War of 1846–48. The loss of the war meant loss of political status for the Hispanic cultures. The Californios (Californians of Mexican heritage), Tejanos (Texans of Mexican descent), and Mexicanos (Americans of Mexican heritage throughout the West) saw their influence wane dramatically and their lives become studies in often not-so-peaceful coexistence. The battles over politics in this new Euro-American-dominated world frequently centered on the issues of suffrage, legal rights, and social discrimination. The conflicts would continue throughout the remainder of the nineteenth century and would still influence the politics of the twentieth.

The following selections highlight aspects of these issues in Texas, California, and New Mexico, which had the largest and most influential Hispanic populations.

"THEY COULD NOT BE CONSIDERED WHITE PERSONS; THEY WERE MEXICANS," TEXAS CONSTITUTIONAL CONVENTION, 1846

In 1836 Texas gained its independence from Mexico through revolution and established its Lone Star Republic. By 1835 there were about 30,000 Euro-American immigrants residing in Texas and approximately 5,000 Tejanos. By the mid-1840s the Tejano population was about 15,000 and the Anglo population approximately 200,000. The Tejanos, even though many had fought for independence from Mexican control, were generally distrusted and considered disloyal by the new dominant culture. When Texas was annexed by the United States in 1845 and a state constitutional convention called in 1846, one of the most contentious issues was suffrage for residents of Mexican heritage. The argument revolved around the definition of "white," the primary qualification for voting rights. Did the Tejanos qualify? Should the word "white" be stricken from the constitution? The debates on this issue, as recorded by William F. Weeks, are excerpted here.

Remarks attributed to Mr. Rusk, a wealthy Democrat who had positive relationships with many Tejanos.

[H]e hoped the word *white* would be stricken out. If, as decided by the courts of the United States, all others except Africans are white, where is the necessity of retaining it. It will be the same thing, whether it is stricken out, or remain. But if it remains, it may give rise to misunderstanding and difficulty. Every gentleman will put his own construction upon the term *white*. It may be contended that we intend to exclude the race which we found in possession of the country when we came here. This would be injurious to those people, to ourselves, and to the magnanimous character which the Americans have ever possessed.

Remarks attributed to Colonel Kinney, another wealthy Democrat who had Tejano friends and business acquaintances.

[H]e said that from the arguments of the gentleman from Brazoria, he was more inclined to believe that it was absolutely necessary that the word *white* should be stricken out. All must be aware that in closely contested elections every means is made use of to carry the election on the one side or the other. He had himself, on such occasions, seen persons known to have been in the service of the country without ever receiving one dollar of compensation, refused the privilege of voting. He had known such men to take the oath of allegiance three times, and the only objection made was that they could not be considered white persons; they were Mexicans.

Remarks attributed to opponents of the Tejano vote
Strike out the term *white,* and what will be the result? Hordes of Mexican Indians may come in here from the West and may be more formidable than the enemy you have vanquished. Silently they will come moving in; they will come back in thousands to Bexar, in thousands to Goliad, perhaps to Nagodoches, and what will be the consequence? Ten, twenty, thirty, forty, fifty thousand may come in here, and vanquish you at the ballot box though you are invincible in arms. This is no idle dream; no bugbear; it is the truth.

Talk not to me of democracy which brings the mean, grovelling yellow race of Mexico . . . upon an equality of rights and privileges with the freeborn races of Europe. The God of nature has made them inferior; he has made the African and the red man inferior to the white.

Remarks attributed to Jose Antonio Navarro, a conservative delegate believed to be proslavery.
He made no remarks with the idea that this question had any relation to the Mexican people, for they were unquestionably entitled to vote. . . . He was much opposed to giving the right of suffrage to Africans or descendants of Africans as any other gentleman. He hoped the Convention would be clearly convinced of the propriety and expediency of striking out this word. It is odious, captious, and redundant, and may be the means at elections of disqualifying persons who are legal voters, but who perhaps by arbitrary judges may not be considered as white.

In the end the Texas Constitutional Convention made the suffrage of Tejanos conditional: the word "white" was stricken from the voter qualifications, but whether a Tejano would be allowed to vote was generally left at the discretion of the local communities, which would decide primarily on the basis of character. Other results of the convention were not so nebulous. The capital would be placed in predominantly Anglo Austin, not in Tejano-dominated San Antonio. Only one Tejano would serve in the first legislature, although the Mexican population was estimated at about 7 percent.

"Those objectionable races," California
Constitutional Convention, 1849

In California the 1849 constitutional convention echoed many of the same issues debated a few years earlier in Texas—with certain differences: there was much more active participation by the Hispanic population (although most Californios had very little fluency in English, and translators were necessary), and there was a greater concern about already existing Mexican law protecting Indians, blacks, and mestizos (persons of mixed heritage). Moreover, Californio and Euro-American elites had formed an alliance. None of this stopped the most racially prejudiced of the delegates from arguing for race-based voting and social exclusions and restrictions. In fact, some Anglos argued that prominent Californio delegate and rancher Manuel Dominguez had too much Indian blood to be allowed to participate in convention debates. Samples of the convoluted arguments, reflecting the social dynamic of gold rush California, appear in this selection from the September 12, 1840, debate as recorded by J. Ross Browne.

Mr. Noriega desired that it should be perfectly understood in the first place, what is the true signification of the word "white." Many citizens of California have received from nature a very dark skin; nevertheless, there are among them men who have heretofore been allowed to vote, and not only that, but to fill the highest public offices. It would be very unjust to deprive them of the privileges of citizens merely because nature had not made them white. But if by the word "white," it was intended to exclude the African race, then it was correct and satisfactory.

Mr. Botts had no objection to color, except so far as it indicated the inferior races of mankind. He would be perfectly willing to use any words which would exclude the African and Indian races. It was in this sense the word "white" had been understood and used. His only object was to exclude those objectionable races not objectionable for their color, but for what that color indicates.

Mr. Gilbert hoped the amendments proposed by the gentleman from Monterey [Botts] would not prevail. He was confident that if the word "white" was introduced, it would produce great difficulty. The treaty [of Guadalupe Hidalgo] has said that Mexican citizens, upon becoming citizens of the United States, shall be entitled to the rights and privileges of American citizens. It does not say whether those citizens are white or black, and we have no right to make the distinction. If they be Mexican citizens, it is sufficient; they are entitled to the rights and privileges of American citizens. No act of this kind could, therefore, have any effect. The treaty is above and superior to it.

Mr. Gwin would like to know from some gentleman acquainted with Mexican law, whether Indians and negroes are entitled to the privileges of citizenship under the Mexican government.

Mr. Noriega understood the gentleman from Monterey (Mr. Botts) to say that Indians were not allowed to vote according to Mexican law.

Mr. Botts said that, on the contrary, it was because he believed they were, that he had offered the amendment. He wished to exclude them from voting. Mr. Gwin asked the gentleman from Santa Barbara (Mr. Noriega) whether Indians and Africans were entitled to vote according to Mexican law.

Mr. Noriega said that, according to Mexican law, no race of any kind is excluded from voting.

Mr. Gwin wished to know if Indians were considered Mexican citizens? Mr. Noriega said that so far were they considered citizens, that some of the first men in the Republic were of the Indian race.

The 1849 California constitution compromised on the issue: any resident who had been considered a Mexican citizen would, regardless of race, be considered a citizen of California under the new constitution; however, blacks and Indians who had not been Mexican citizens would be excluded from citizenship. The result was a muddled interpretation of race and citizenship rights with the implication that Hispanics had been provided an exemption of sorts.

READING 13C
"BEHOLD THE FRIENDSHIP EXISTING FOR THE MEXICAN VOTERS,"
BROWNSVILLE (TX) AMERICAN FLAG, 1856

When elections drew near, Hispanic voters were courted just as intensely as any others. Observers, however, often found this courting cynical, particularly in Texas, where Hispanics seemed to be especially vulnerable. On August 20, 1856, the newspaper of Brownsville, Texas, commented sarcastically on this phenomenon.

Americans have at times committed offenses which in them have been overlooked, but which, if committed by Mexicans would have been severely punished. But when election time comes, it is wonderful to behold the friendship existing for the Mexican voters, and the protection extended to them, the sympathy which until then had remained latent or concealed, suddenly reveals itself in all its plentitude, and many are astonished not to have found until then the amount of kindly feeling professed towards them by their whilom [former] friends. Promises of all kinds are made to them, but scarcely are the promises made, when they are broken. An hour before the election they are fast friends—an hour after the election, they are a "crowd of greasers."

READING 13D
"PRESUMPTIVE POSSESSORS OF THE LANDS,"
ANTONIO MARIA PICO, 1859

When most of the northern provinces of the Mexican homeland were incorporated into the United States by revolution, war, or purchase, many Hispanic residents lost not only status but land, which had a serious impact on the culture and economics of the regions involved. Part of the problem stemmed from the practices of discrimination, but a large part originated in the different methods of claiming title. Spanish and Mexican land grant laws were not dissimilar to United States homestead laws, but the process of registration was sharply different. Under the Spanish / Mexican system, the land grantee had to describe the land in detail in a petition, then erect permanent buildings or establish fences or boundary markers before title was finalized. At that point the local magistrate had to complete the boundary definition through an act called "juridical possession," a kind of survey that tended to describe boundaries as ranging from, say, an oak tree to the foothills of a mountain range—very unlike the measured property lines common to the American system. The juridical possession measurements were then to be documented and stored in the Spanish / Mexican archives. Sometimes the documents were inadequately prepared or not properly registered; additionally, portions of the archives had been destroyed by fire or war by the time the transition to United States control occurred. Thus, when American authorities demanded proof of ownership from Hispanic landholders, many could not provide it. For example, John Sutter, a Mexican land grantee in the Sacramento Valley, was unable to prove his title and lost most of his 40,000 acres to incoming gold rushers

*in the late 1840s. With the burden of proof on the original claimant, an inability
to provide documentation, the high legal costs of fighting the case, and intimidation
all played a part in the land loss Hispanics suffered.*

*In 1859 California a solution was proposed by a member of the Californio
elite, Antonio Maria Pico. His proposal was far from perfect, but it would have
been vastly preferable to the system then in place.*

It would have been better for the state, and for those newly established in it,
if all those titles to lands, the *expedientes* of which were properly registered in
the Mexican archives, had been declared valid; if those holders of titles
derived from former governments had been declared perpetual owners and
the presumptive possessors of the lands (in all civilized countries they would
have been acknowledged legitimate owners of the land); and if the government, or any private person or official who might have pretensions to the
contrary, should have been able to establish his claim only through a regular
court of justice, in accordance with customary judicial procedure. Such a
course would have increased the fame of the conquerors, won the faith and
respect of the conquered, and contributed to the material prosperity of the
nation at large.

San Francisco, February 21, 1859

Antonio Maria Pico

[The document was signed by 49 others as well.]

READING 13E

"NUESTRA PLATFORMA," LAS GORRAS BLANCAS, 1890

*By 1890, Hispanic residents in New Mexico had become frustrated by the
overwhelming encroachments on their lives, property, and personal well-being. In
response, and in anger over the fact that some Hispanics had joined with Anglos
in discriminating against other Hispanics, a semisecret organization sprang up
near Las Vegas, New Mexico, called Las Gorras Blancas, or "the White
Caps." This group comprised Hispanic former landowners, railroad and timber
workers, and some disenchanted political leaders who combined to provide armed
defense, electioneering, and union organizing. They drew their membership not
only from the disenfranchised and powerless but also from such other protest
movements as the Knights of Labor and the People's Party (the political arm of
the Populist movement). Upset with the manipulations of their community by the*

local political machine called the Santa Fe Ring, they targeted its members for action as well.

On March 12, 1890, Las Gorras Blancas issued a manifesto. The grievances and demands it expresses are a passionate testament to the loss of political status many Hispanics felt.

NUESTRA PLATAFORMA

Our purpose is to protect the rights and interests of the people in general and especially those of the helpless classes.

We want the Las Vegas Grant [New Mexico] settled to the benefit of all concerned, and this we hold is the entire community within the Grant.

We want no "land grabbers" or obstructionists of any sort to interfere. We will watch them.

We are not down on lawyers as a class, but the usual knavery and unfair treatment of the people must be stopped.

Our judiciary hereafter must understand that we will sustain it only when "justice" is its watchword.

We are down on race issues, and will watch race agitators.

We favor irrigation enterprises, but will fight any scheme that tends to monopolize the supply of water sources to the detriment of residents living on lands watered by the same streams.

The people are suffering from the effects of partisan "bossism" and these bosses had better quietly hold their peace. The people have been persecuted and hauled about in every which way to satisfy their caprices.

We must have a free ballot and fair court and the will of the Majority shall be respected.

We have no grudge against any person in particular, but we are the enemies of bulldozers and tyrants.

If the old system should continue, death would be a relief to our suffering. And for our rights our lives are the least we can pledge.

If the fact that we are law-abiding citizens is questioned, come out to our houses and see the hunger and desolation we are suffering; and "this" is the result of the deceitful and corrupt methods of "bossism."

The White Caps, 1,500 Strong and Gaining Daily

"Arrested and Hanged as Suspects," *El Clamor Publico*, 1857

The dominance of the Anglo-American culture following the period of westward expansionism and the gold rush often meant difficulty or danger for Hispanics— particularly in the geographic areas where they had once been in control, especially California. In many parts of the Golden State a double standard of justice discriminated against Hispanics but protected the whites. Vigilantism against Hispanics grew. Lynchings occurred. When citizens of Los Angeles set out to retaliate against a band of Mexican thieves, all Californios became suspect. This letter describing the result was originally written by a French correspondent to a French-language newspaper in San Francisco. It was translated into Spanish and republished by Francisco Ramirez, the multilingual editor of the Los Angeles newspaper El Clamor Publico, *who asserted that it accurately reflected conditions in 1857 Los Angeles.*

Los Angeles
February 21
Mr. Editor:

Now you must have learned through the newspapers of our city of the sad events that have occurred in the country during the present month. But these newspapers have omitted many circumstances, in spite of their being well known and of public notoriety. Under no pretext should their silence be excused. Journalism is the advanced sentinel of civilization; its life is a life of continual combat, constantly on the defense. . . .

For three months a band of thieves has run about the streets and outlying areas of this city by night, abandoning themselves to all kinds of wickedness, including the most refined highway robbery. Various persons have complained to the authorities, but the authorities respond: "Do you have witnesses? Do you want to pay to have them arrested?" And the band continued robbing and killing with all security, by the light of day and in the middle of the city under the chin of the police officials who seem to view this as a comedy. This is not strange; [they say] "the Mexicans are killing each other." . . . Four or five Americans have established a Vigilante Committee, made a call to all the population for the public security, and named captains of a company to go in pursuit of the bandits. Here is where the drama begins with all its horrors, and wrapped in a mystery so strange that one is obliged to believe that the bandits were not the persecuted ones. In a few words, a company (all Americans), its captain Sanford, headed toward the Mission of San Gabriel. All the Mexican residents in that place were arrested and treated with unequalled brutality. Two of these unfortunates had been arrested at the entrance of the Mission. They had to submit to an interrogation of the most provocative sort. Intimidated by the threats, and impelled by the instinct of self preservation, they began to run, especially when they saw the captain draw his pistol. But . . . at the first movement that they made, a general volley followed. One fell wounded from various shots. The other was able to reach a lake or marsh. He abandoned his horse and concealed himself in the rushes. Vain efforts. The American band arrived, set fire to the marsh, and very soon, among the general cries of gaiety, they discovered the head of the unfortunate above the flames. A second volley and all was done.—I deceive myself. It was not finished so quickly. The body, loaded over a horse, was transported to the Mission in the midst of cries and shouts of joy and gaiety. Here, overtaken by horror, thought stops because it is impossible to find expressions to describe the scene which took place and was related to me by many witnesses worthy of trust. The body was thrown to the ground in the midst of the mob. One being, with a human face, stepped forward with a knife in his hand. . . . With one hand he took the head of the dead man by its long hair, separated it from the body, flung it a short distance and stuck his dagger in the heart of the cadaver. Afterward, returning to the head, he made it roll with his foot into the middle of his band and the rabble, amidst the cries and hurrahs of the greater number. . . . Is it not horrible? But wait, we have not yet seen all. Another band arrived from another place with two Californios. They had been arrested as suspects, one of them going in search of some oxen, the other to his daily work. They were conducted into the middle of the mob. The cries of "To death! To death!" were heard from all sides. The cutter of heads entered his house, coming out with some ropes, and the two unfortunates were hanged— despite the protests of their countrymen and their families. Once hanged from the tree, the ropes broke and the hapless ones were finished being murdered by shots or knife thrusts. The cutter of heads was fatigued, or his knife did not now cut! Perhaps you will believe that this very cruel person was an Indian from the mountains, one of those barbarians who lives far from all civilization in the Sierra Nevada! Wrong. That barbarian, that mutilator of cadavers, is the Justice of the Peace of San Gabriel! . . . He is a citizen of the United States, an American of pure blood. . . .

Afterwards, two Mexicans were found hanging from a tree, and near there another with two bullets in the head.

On the road from Tejon another company had encountered two poor peddlers (always Mexicans) who were arrested and hanged as suspects.

The letter concludes at this point. But in another section of the same March 21, 1857, issue of El Clamor Publico *a notice informs the public that the Justice of the Peace of San Gabriel has been charged with the murder of three innocent Mexicans.*

READING 15

"A FOREIGNER IN MY NATIVE LAND," JUAN SEGUIN, 1858

In 1836, among the rebel combatants in the Texas war for independence were many Texans of Mexican heritage—and among the most prominent of these was Juan Nepomuceno Seguin, the mayor of San Antonio. Yet once Texas was independent, many Anglo Texans questioned the loyalty of the Tejanos, and life became increasingly difficult for them. Even the powerful Seguin finally realized that for his and his family's safety it would be wise to leave Texas. He moved to Mexico, the country he had fought against during the revolution. In his 1858 memoirs Seguin explains his actions.

A native of the City of San Antonio de Bexar, I embraced the cause of Texas at the report of the first cannon which foretold her liberty; filled an honorable situation in the ranks of the conquerors of San Jacinto, and was a member of the legislative body of the Republic. I now find myself, in the very land, which in other times bestowed on me such bright and repeated evidences of trust and esteem, exposed to the attacks of scribblers and personal enemies, who, to serve *political purposes,* and engender strife, falsify historical facts, with which they are but imperfectly acquainted. I owe it to myself, my children and friends, to answer with a short, but true exposition of my acts, from the beginning of my political career, to the time of the return of General [Adrian] Woll [a French soldier of fortune] from the Rio Grande, with the Mexican forces, amongst whom I was then serving. . . .

I have been the object of the hatred and passionate attacks of some few disorganizers, who, for a time, ruled, as masters, over the poor and oppressed population of San Antonio. Harpy-like, ready to pounce on every thing that attracted the notice of their rapacious avarice, I was an obstacle to the execution of their vile designs. They, therefore, leagued together to exasperate and ruin me; spread against me malignant calumnies, and made use of odious machinations to sully my honor and tarnish my well earned reputation.

A victim to the wickedness of a few men, whose imposture was favored by their origin, and recent domination over the country; a foreigner in my native land; could I be expected stoically to endure their outrages and insults? Crushed by sorrow, convinced that my death alone would satisfy my enemies, I sought for a shelter amongst whom I had fought; I separated from my country, parents, family, relatives and friends, and what was more, from the institutions, on behalf of which I had drawn my sword, with an earnest wish to see Texas free and happy. . . .

Ere the tomb closes over me and my contemporaries, I wish to lay open to publicity this stormy period of my life; I do it for friends as well as for my enemies, I challenge the latter to contest, with facts, the statements I am about to make, and I leave the decision unhesitatingly to the witnesses of the events. . . .

The jealousy evinced against me by several officers of the companies recently arrived at San Antonio, from the United States, soon spread amongst the American straggling adventurers, who were already beginning to work their dark intrigues against the native families, whose only crime was, that they owned large tracts of land and desirable property. . . .

In those evil days, San Antonio was swarming with adventurers from every quarter of the globe. Many a noble heart grasped the sword in the defence of the liberty of Texas, cheerfully pouring out their blood for our cause, and to them everlasting public gratitude is due; but there were also many bad men, fugitives from their country, who found in this land an open field for their criminal designs.

San Antonio claimed then, as it claims now, to be the first city of Texas; it was also the receptacle of the scum of society. My political and social situation brought me in continual contact with that class of people. At every hour of the day and night, my countrymen ran to me for protection against the assaults or exactions of those adventurers. Some times, by persuasion, I prevailed on them to desist; some times . . . force had to be resorted to. How could I have done otherwise? Were not the victims my own countrymen, exposed to the assaults of foreigners, who, on the pretext they were Mexicans, treated them worse than brutes. Sound reason and the dictates of humanity would have precluded a different conduct on my part. . . .

On my return to San Antonio [in 1842], several persons told me that the Mexican officers had declared that I was in their favor [and against the Texas Republic]. This rumor . . . left me but little doubt that my enemies would try to ruin me. . . .

Reports were widely spreading about my pretended treason. . . . [As a result] I remained, hiding from rancho to rancho, for over fifteen days. Every party of volunteers en route to San Antonio, declared, "they wanted to kill Seguin." I could no longer go from farm to farm, and determined to go on to my own farm and raise fortifications.

Several of my relatives and friends joined me. Hardly a day elapsed without receiving notice that a party was preparing to attack me; we were constantly kept under arms. Several parties came in sight, but, probably seeing that we were prepared to receive them, refrained from attacking. . . . In those days I could not go to San Antonio without peril of my life.

Matters being in this state, I saw that it was necessary to take some step which would place me in security, and save my family from constant wretchedness. I had to leave Texas, abandon all, for which I had fought and spent my fortune, to become a wanderer. The ingratitude of those, who had assumed themselves the right of convicting me; their credulity in declaring me a traitor, on mere rumors, when I had to plead in my favor the loyal patriotism with which I had always served Texas, wounded me deeply. . . .

Seeing that all these plans were impracticable, I resolved to seek a refuge amongst my enemies, braving all dangers. But before taking this step, I sent my resignation to the Corporation of San Antonio, as Mayor of the city, stating to them, that, unable any longer to suffer the persecutions of some ungrateful Americans, who strove to murder me, I had determined to free my family and friends from their continual misery on my account, and go and live peaceably in Mexico. That for these reasons I resigned my office, with all my privileges and honors as a Texan.

I left Bexar . . . exiled and deprived of my privileges as a Texas citizen, I was in this country a being out of the pale of society, and when she could not protect the rights of her citizens, they were privileged to seek protection elsewhere. I had been tried by a rabble, condemned without a hearing, and consequently was at liberty to provide for my own safety. . . .

. . . I did not return to Texas until the treaty of Guadalupe Hidalgo [in

1848, ending the Mexican-American War of 1846–48]. During my absence nothing appeared that could stamp me as a traitor. My enemies had accomplished their object; they had killed me politically in Texas, and the less they spoke of me, the less risk they incurred of being exposed in the infamous means they had used to accomplish my ruin.

... The rumor, that I was a traitor, was seized with avidity by my enemies in San Antonio. Some envied my military position, as held by a *Mexican;* others found in me an obstacle to the accomplishment of their villainous plans.

Following the defeat of Mexico in 1848, the Texas government granted Juan Seguin's petition to return, and he lived in the state in relative anonymity until 1867. In that year, upset over continuing discrimination against Tejanos, he returned to Mexico, where he remained for the rest of his life. He died in 1890 at the age of eighty-four.

CHAPTER 10

THE FAR-FLUNG BATTLE LINE

Soldiers in the American West

THE MILITARY presence in the American West was noticeable from the very beginning of the nineteenth century. The Lewis and Clark Expedition was organized along military lines. The military structure of the Texas revolution was important to its success. The American military victory in the Mexican-American War vastly expanded the size of the American West. Westerners provided mineral wealth and personnel to both sides in the Civil War. And army units thereafter, most notably the cavalry, were significant factors in the relationships between the United States government and the Native Americans.

But the military's role and size changed dramatically through time. Following the Civil War the United States Army reorganized and turned its attention to the "Indian problem" of the American West. Very different from the army that fought the battles of Bull Run and Gettysburg and Appomattox, the western army was tiny by comparison—reduced from a Civil War high of 1.5 million troops to about 25,000. Pay was low—$16 a month in 1866, slashed to $13 a month in 1869. Civil War field commissions were reduced; wartime generals such as George Custer became colonels out west. Poor food, dust, and isolation also awaited the western troops. Yet the army never had a problem filling its ranks. The possibility of a secure job lured thousands of newly arrived immigrants to the armed forces. Freedom, together with a chance to prove personal courage and demonstrate a commitment to the nation, was a draw for the black soldiers who formed highly effective cavalry and infantry units. Whatever their reasons, the life of soldiers on the army frontier was harsh and often unforgiving. Depending on one's viewpoint, their actions were heroic or, in the words of one commander, either "blind stupidity or criminal indifference."

In this chapter the selections provide insight into the mission and the lives of the troops, the events that touched the common soldier, and the behavior of some of the most famous (and infamous) military leaders, from the Battle of the Alamo to the Battle of Little Bighorn and beyond.

"Winning the West: The Setting and the Challenge," *American Military History*, 1969

In 1969 the United States Army commissioned a chronicle of American military history, which incorporated a section on the army of the American West in the later nineteenth century. Here are excerpts from that portion of the study.

After Appomattox the Army had to muster out over a million volunteers and reconstitute a Regular establishment that had languished during the Civil War when bounties and short enlistments made service in the volunteers more profitable. There were operational commitments to sustain during and after the transition, some an outgrowth of the war just ended, others the product of internal and external situations that could not be ignored. Whereas the prewar Army of the 1850's was essentially a frontier Army, the postwar Army became something more. To defense of the frontier were added military occupation of the southern states, neutralization of the Mexican border during Napoleon's colonial enterprise under Maximilian, elimination of a Fenian (Irish Brotherhood) threat to Canada in the Northeast, and dispersion of white marauders in the border states. But these and other later involvements were passing concerns. The conflict with the red man was the overriding consideration in the next twenty-five years until Indian power was broken.

Unfortunately, the military assets released from other tasks were lost through reductions in force instead of being diverted to frontier defense. For even though the country during the Indian campaigns could not be said to be at peace, neither Congress nor the war-weary citizens in the populous Atlantic states were prepared to consider it in a state of war. And in any case, there was strong sentiment against a large standing army as well as a widely held belief that the Indian problem could be settled by other than military means.

As the postwar Army took shape, its strength began a decade of decline, dropping from an 1867 level of about 57,000 to half that in the year that General Custer was killed [1876], then leveling off at an average of about 26,000 for the remaining years up to the War with Spain [1898]. Effective strength always lay somewhere below authorized strength, seriously impaired, for example, by high rates of sickness and desertion.

Because the Army's military responsibilities were of continental proportions, involving sweeping distances, limited resources, and far-flung operations, an administrative structure was required for command and control. The Army was, therefore, organized on a territorial basis, with geographical segments variously designated as divisions, departments, and districts. There were frequent modifications of organization, rearrangements of boundaries, and transfers of troops and posts to meet changing conditions. . . .

Development of a basic defense system in the Trans-Mississippi West had followed the course of empire; territorial acquisition and exploration succeeded by emigration and settlement brought the whites increasingly into collision with the Indians and progressively raised the need for military posts along the transcontinental trails and in settled areas.

The annexation of Texas in 1845, the settlement of the Oregon boundary dispute in 1846, and the successful conclusion of the Mexican War with the cession to the United States in 1848 of vast areas of land, all drew the outlines of the major task facing the Army in the West in the middle of the nineteenth century. During the period between the Mexican War and Civil War [1848–1861] the Army established a reasonably comprehensive system of forts to protect the arteries of white travel and areas of white settlement across the frontier. At the same time, operations were launched against the Indian tribes that represented actual or potential threats to movement and settlement.

Militarily successful in some cases, these operations nevertheless hardened Indian opposition, prompted wider red provocation, and led to the delineation of an Indian barrier to westward expansion extending down the Great Plains from the Canadian to the Mexican border. . . .

In the Southwest between the wars, Army units pursued Apaches and Utes in New Mexico Territory, clashing with the Apaches . . . in 1854 . . . and the Utes . . . in 1855. There were various expeditions against various branches of the elusive Apaches involving hard campaigning but few conclusive engagements. . . .

In the Northwest, where numerous small tribes existed, there were occasional hostilities between the late 1840's and the middle 1860's. Their general character was similar to operations elsewhere: white intrusion, Indian reaction, and white counteraction with superior force. . . . The Army, often at odds with civil authority and public opinion in the area, found it necessary on occasion to protect Indians from whites as well as the other way around.

The Regular Army's frontier mission was interrupted by the onset of the Civil War, and the task of dealing with the Indians was transferred to the volunteers. Although the red man demonstrated an awareness of what was going on and took some satisfaction from the fact that white men were fighting each other, there is little evidence that he took advantage of the transition period between removal of the Regulars and deployment of the volunteers. . . . [B]y 1865 Army strength in the frontier departments was about double what it had been at the time of Fort Sumter. The volunteers were generally able to keep pace with a continuing and gradually enlarging westward movement by developing further the system of forts begun by their predecessors.

Thus the regional defense systems established in the West in the 1850's and 60's provided a framework for the deployment of the Army as it turned from the Civil War to frontier responsibilities. In the late summer of 1866 the general command and administrative structure for frontier defense comprised the Division of the Missouri, containing the Departments of Arkansas, Missouri, Dakota, and the Platte; the Division of the Pacific, consisting of the Departments of California and the Columbia; and the independent Department of the Gulf, whose area included Texas.

The Army's challenge in the West was one of environment as well as adversary, and in the summer of 1866 General [Ulysses] Grant sent a number of senior officer inspectors across the country to observe and report on conditions. The theater of war was uninhabited or only sparsely settled, and its great distances and extreme variations of climate and geography accentuated manpower limitations, logistical and communications problems, and the difficulties of movement. The extension of the rail system only gradually eased the situation. Above all, the mounted tribes of the Plains were a different breed from the Indians the Army had dealt with previously in the forested areas of the East. Despite the fact that the Army had fought Indians in the West in the period after the Mexican War, much of the direct experience of its officers and men had been lost during the Civil War years. Until frontier proficiency could be re-established, the Army would depend upon the somewhat intangible body of knowledge that marks any institution [in that situation].

"I SHALL NEVER SURRENDER NOR RETREAT,"
WILLIAM BARRET TRAVIS, 1836

The emotional touchstone for the military history of the American West was the battle for the Alamo during the Texas revolution in 1836. "Remember the Alamo" is a potent battle cry that resonated through the Texas war for independence and has played a part in all American wars since. It really was not much of a battle, though. In 1835, Texicans (English-speaking residents of Texas) organized to achieve independence or at least a level of autonomy from Mexico. They held a convention and elected Henry Smith as governor and Sam Houston as major general of the army. Fighting began soon afterward. The Mexican forces were driven out of San Antonio de Bexar but returned a year later with a vengeance. General Santa Anna approached with a force approximating 3,000 and laid siege to the city. In the mission and barracks complex called the Alamo, 187 defenders of Texas independence had holed up to await the inevitable assault. On March 6, 1836, Santa Anna attacked, and in less than an hour the garrison was wiped out. The decision to defend the Alamo had been a mistake, but there is no denying the impact the battle had on Texan resolve. Within weeks the Texas army defeated Santa Anna at San Jacinto, and a treaty was signed granting independence to the Republic of Texas.

A few days before the March 6 attack, William Barret Travis, the commandant within the Alamo, was asked to surrender. His reply became an article of faith in Texas history and an opening statement of American commitment toward defending and developing "their country"—the American West.

Commandancy of the Alamo, Bexar, February 24, 1836.—
To the people of Texas and all Americans in the world.
Fellow citizens and compatriots: I am besieged by a thousand or more of the Mexicans under Santa Anna. I have sustained a continual bombardment and cannonade for twenty-four hours and have not lost a man. The enemy has demanded a surrender at discretion; otherwise the garrison are to be put to the sword if the fort is taken. I have answered the demand with a cannon shot, and our flag still waves proudly from the walls. *I shall never surrender nor retreat.* Then, I call on you in the name of liberty, of patriotism, and everything dear to the American character, to come to our aid with all dispatch. The enemy is receiving reinforcements daily and will no doubt increase to

three or four thousand in four or five days. If this call is neglected, I am determined to sustain myself as long as possible and die like a soldier who never forgets what is due to his own honor and that of his country, VICTORY OR DEATH.

William Barret Travis
Lieutenant Colonel Commandant

READING 3
THE MEXICAN-AMERICAN WAR

A critical turning point in U.S. western involvement occurred with the Mexican-American War of 1846–48. Some historians have simplified the conflict into a border dispute between the United States and Mexico, but as with most historical events its genesis was much more complex. Relations between the two countries had been difficult ever since Mexico gained its independence from Spain in 1821. Chronically unstable governments in Mexico had led to a series of dictators who frequently imposed their harsh will upon the residents of Texas in particular. Damage inflicted on property and persons in the northern provinces of Mexico led the governments of the United States, France, and Great Britain to demand restitution for harm done to their nationals. An agreement was reached for reparations from Mexico, but the Mexican government defaulted, leading to calls for war from the United States.

Mexican concern focused on Texas. Mexico had never accepted Texan independence and wished to regain its lost territory. Additionally, the newly annexed state of Texas had declared its southern boundary to be the Rio Grande; Mexico put the line farther north, at the Nueces River. Both sides sent troops to occupy and defend "their" territory. In early May 1846 soldiers under the command of Zachary Taylor were ambushed north of the Rio Grande (in "American territory"). When news of this engagement reached the halls of American government, President James K. Polk asked Congress to declare war.

The Mexican-American War (a training ground for participants in the Civil War) cost the United States some 13,000 deaths (most due to disease) and about $100 million. The victory greatly expanded American territory, however: the Mexican cession included lands that make up all or part of the present-day states of California, Nevada, Arizona, New Mexico, Utah, and Colorado. Perhaps most important from the American perspective, the territory gained fulfilled the American dream of Manifest Destiny, the idea that the United States was divinely destined to stretch from sea to shining sea.

"WAR . . . EXISTS BY THE ACT OF MEXICO," JAMES K. POLK, 1846

On May 11, 1846, President James K. Polk presented a message to Congress, excerpted here, asking for war with Mexico. On May 13 Congress complied.

To the Senate and House of Representatives:

The existing state of the relations between the United States and Mexico renders it proper that I should bring the subject to the consideration of Congress. . . .

In my message at the commencement of the present session I informed you that upon the earnest appeal both of the Congress and convention of Texas I had ordered an efficient military force to take a position "between the Nueces and the Del Norte." This had become necessary to meet a threatened invasion of Texas by the Mexican forces, for which extensive military preparations had been made. The invasion was threatened solely because Texas had determined . . . to annex herself to our Union and under these circumstances it was plainly our duty to extend our protection over her citizens and soil. . . .

Meantime Texas, by the final action of Congress, had become an integral part of our Union. The Congress of Texas, by its act of December 19, 1836, had declared the Rio del Norte [the commonly used alternative name for the Rio Grande] to be the boundary of that Republic. Its jurisdiction had been extended and exercised beyond the Nueces. . . . Our own Congress had, moreover, with great unanimity, by the act approved December 31, 1845, recognized the country beyond the Nueces as a part of our territory by including it within our revenue system. . . . It became, therefore, of urgent necessity to provide for the defense of that portion of our country. Accordingly, on the 13th of January last instructions were issued to the general in command of these troops to occupy the left bank of the Del Norte. The river, which is the southwestern boundary of the State of Texas, is an exposed frontier. . . .

The Mexican forces at Matamoras assumed a belligerent attitude, and on the 12th of April General Ampudia, then in command, notified General [Zachary] Taylor to break up his camp within twenty-four hours and to retire beyond the Nueces River, and in the event of his failure to comply with these demands announced that arms, and arms alone, must decide the question. But no open act of hostility was committed until the 24th of April.

On that day General Arista, who had succeeded to the command of the Mexican forces, communicated to General Taylor that "he considered hostilities commenced and should prosecute them." A party of dragoons of 63 men and officers were on the same day dispatched from the American camp up the Rio del Norte, on its left bank, to ascertain whether the Mexican troops had crossed or were preparing to cross the river, "became engaged with a large body of these troops, and after a short affair, in which some 16 were killed and wounded, appear to have been surrounded and compelled to surrender." . . .

The cup of forbearance had been exhausted even before the recent information from the frontier of the Del Norte. But now, after reiterated menaces, Mexico has passed the boundary of the United States, has invaded our territory and shed American blood upon the American soil. She has proclaimed that hostilities have commenced, and that the two nations are now at war.

As war exists, and, notwithstanding all our efforts to avoid it, exists by the act of Mexico herself, we are called upon by every consideration of duty and patriotism to vindicate with decision the honor, the rights, and the interests of our country. . . .

In further vindication of our rights and defense of our territory, I invoke the prompt action of Congress to recognize the existence of the war, and to place at the disposition of the Executive the means of prosecuting the war with vigor, and thus hastening the restoration of peace.

READING 3B
"THE ATTACK WAS MADE," ULYSSES S. GRANT, 1847

In 1847 Ulysses S. Grant, who would later achieve great fame as the commanding general of the Union forces in the Civil War, was just twenty-five years old, four years out of West Point. Grant served with distinction in the Mexican-American War under the command of Generals Winfield Scott and Zachary Taylor. This selection from his 1885 memoirs describes his experiences in the capture of Veracruz and the Battle of Cerro Gordo.

[O]n the 7th of March, 1847, the little army of ten or twelve thousand men, given [General Winfield] Scott to invade a country with a population of seven or eight millions, a mountainous country affording the greatest possible natural advantages for defence, was all assembled and ready to commence the perilous task of landing from vessels lying in the open sea.

The debarkation took place inside of the little island of Sacrificious, some three miles south of Vera Cruz. . . . [T]he Mexicans were very kind to us, however, and threw no obstacles in the way of our landing except an occasional shot from their nearest fort. . . . On the 29th, Vera Cruz [was] occupied by Scott's army. About five thousand prisoners . . . fell into the hands of the victorious force. The casualties on our side during the siege amounted to sixty-four officers and men, killed and wounded. . . .

It was very important to get the army away from Vera Cruz as soon as possible, in order to avoid the yellow fever, or vomito, which usually visits that city early in the year, and is very fatal to persons not acclimated. . . . The leading division ran against the enemy at Cerro Gordo, some fifty miles west, on the road to Jalapa, and went into camp at Plan del Rio, about three miles from the [Mexican] fortifications. . . . General Scott . . . at once commenced his preparations for the capture of the position held by [Mexican General] Santa Anna. . . .

Cerro Gordo is one of the highest spurs of the mountains some twelve to fifteen miles east of Jalapa, and Santa Anna had selected this point as the easiest to defend against an invading army. The road, said to have been built by Cortez, zigzags around the mountain-side and was defended at every turn by artillery. On either side were deep chasms or mountain walls. A direct attack along the road was an impossibility. A flank movement seemed equally impossible. After the arrival of the commanding-general upon the scene, reconnoissances were sent out . . . under the supervision of Captain Robert E. Lee, assisted by Lieutenants P. G. T. Beauregard . . . [and] George B. McClellan. . . . The reconnoissance was completed, and the labor of cutting out and making roads by the flank was . . . accomplished without the knowledge of Santa Anna or his army, and over ground where he supposed it impossible. . . . The engineers, who had directed the opening, led the way and the troops followed. Artillery was let down the steep slopes by hand. . . . In like manner the guns were drawn by hand up the opposite slopes. In this way Scott's troops reached their assigned position in rear of most of the entrenchments of the enemy, unobserved. The attack was made. . . . The surprise of the enemy was complete, the victory overwhelming; some three thousand prisoners fell into Scott's hands. . . . Santa Anna['s] . . . attack on Taylor [at Buena Vista] was disastrous to the Mexican army, but, notwithstanding this, he marched his army to Cerro Gordo, a distance not much short of one thousand miles . . . in time to entrench himself well before Scott got there. If he [Santa Anna] had been successful at Buena Vista his troops would have no doubt have made a more stubborn resistance at Cerro Gordo. Had the battle of Buena Vista not been fought Santa Anna would have had time to move leisurely to meet the invader further south and with an army not demoralized nor depleted by defeat.

READING 3C
"ABSOLUTELY NOTHING WAS SAVED, NOT EVEN
HOPE," JOSÉ FERNANDO RAMIREZ, 1847

*A Mexican perspective on the Battle of Cerro Gordo and on Mexico's conduct of
the war is provided by José Fernando Ramirez, a member of the Mexican elite. A
lawyer and a political adviser to the Mexican government, Ramirez would in 1852
be named director of the National Museum. Writing to his friend Francisco
Elorriaga in letters alternately filled with national pride, frustration, and anger,
Ramirez describes his impressions of the war effort.*

Mexico City, April 21, 1847
Senor Don Francisco Elorriaga
My dear friend:
. . . Our army has been completely routed at Cerro Gordo without any other consolation than that of having preserved its honor. . . .

Scott attacked our camp with his entire force (15,000 men) forming two columns of 4,000 each, while another of 7,000, making a flanking movement for a distance of about two leagues, got around our lines and attacked S.A. [Santa Anna] in the rear, setting fire to a dense woods that was on all sides of him. Canalizo, who was in command of the cavalry and some of the infantry in order to cover the rear guard, did little or nothing to stop the enemy. He retreated in complete disorder, leaving our troops caught between two fires. Some say that he did this because he was frightened, and others say it was because he could do nothing else. We do not yet know the facts. S.A. escaped from the midst of the defeated force by cutting through with a column of 400 men under the command of Uraga, who protected him so that he could get away. The letters [from the front] also state that S.A. then intended to reassemble the scattered troops and that he is now in La Joya with about four or five thousand man. The battle was a very bloody one, and they say it was honorably fought. They agree that the losses total from eight to nine thousand men, including killed and wounded. According to this account we probably lost only 3,000, since S.A. had no more than 8,000 men with him. At the present time 4,000 men ought to be on their way to join him; they had been sent to defend the approaches to the town, but there is nothing to fear in that quarter now. In La Joya some work has already been done on the defenses, and seven cannon are in position there. The guns brought from Perote can be used to increase this number.

It is five o'clock in the afternoon, and a friend who has just come in from the street says he saw a letter that contradicts the news contained in the others. This letter maintains that our defeat was actually a rout in which our troops scarcely fought at all. . . .

Mexico City, April 25, 1847
Senor Don Francisco Elorriaga
My dear friend:
. . . Our reverse at Cerro Gordo was a rout as complete as it was shameful. Everything was lost. Absolutely nothing was saved; not even hope, that last consolation the gods left at the bottom of the famous box. A small portion of our troops fought and died heroically; the rest surrendered their arms almost without putting up any defense, or else they ran away. We must consider the soldiers' morale. In them the instincts of race still dominate the fear inspired by the invaders. As for supplies, the less said the better. No money, no muskets, no artillery, not even a fortified place in which we could take refuge in order to have some point where we could reassemble or effect a retreat. At the time when Canalizo was abandoning the stronghold at Perote, the Government was sending him orders to the same effect, and thus the move was carried out on double authority. Some hours later contrary orders came from General S.A., who intended to make it his base of operations, but there was no longer time to carry out his orders. It is rumored that the Americans are now occupying it. All we have left to compensate us for our misfortunes are the things that have been the sources of all that we deplore: vanity, pride, and lack of cooperation—all in the highest degree. You can judge whether I am mistaken, for I shall give you a brief idea of our fundamental characteristics, as I see them expressed.

Beginning with the men who run our affairs, we find that we have a Congress without prestige, without power, and without ability. What is worse, it is undermined and disrupted by partisan hatreds which prevent it from seeing anything clearly, except when it wishes to wound its opponents. You have probably noticed that history records innumerable cases substantiating the oft-repeated saying that "a war with a foreign foe preserves a feeling of nationality and strengthens institutions." In our privileged country quite the contrary has happened on the only two occasions there have been to prove the truth of the maxim: namely, the Spanish conquest under Cortes, and the Yankee conquest under Scott. And to make the terrible comparison complete, both set foot upon the shores of Veracruz during the Holy Week. The reason for the difference is clear. A sensible, patriotic people unites and offers a solid front at the first hint of the common peril. A people that is neither sensible nor patriotic grows weak, thus smoothing out difficulties for the invader, who wins without opposition.

READING 3D

The Treaty of Guadalupe Hidalgo, 1848

In the fall of 1847 American forces occupied Mexico City, and by the end of the year Mexican resistance had practically ceased. Nicholas Trist had been empowered to negotiate a treaty with the Mexican authorities, but with war fever raging and sentiment growing that the United States should attempt to gain even more Mexican territory, he was recalled. Trist ignored the order, however, and completed his negotiations on February 2, 1848. Although the finished Treaty of Guadalupe Hidalgo vastly expanded United States territory in the American West, President James K. Polk was unhappy with it, confiding to his diary that "if the treaty was now to be made, I should demand more territory." Nevertheless, he presented the treaty to the Senate, which ratified it on May 30. One of the great ironies of this event is that less than two weeks before the treaty was signed, gold was discovered in California's Mother Lode region, on January 24, 1848. It was as a result of the Mexican-American War and the Treaty of Guadalupe Hidalgo that the gold rush would take place on American, not Mexican, soil.

Article I.

There shall be firm and universal peace between the United States of America and the Mexican Republic, and between their respective countries, territories, cities, towns, and people, without exception of place or persons. . . .

Article V.

The boundary line between the two Republics shall commence in the Gulf of Mexico, three leagues from land, opposite the mouth of the Rio Grande, otherwise called Rio Bravo del Norte, or opposite the mouth of its deepest branch, if it should have more than one branch emptying directly into the sea; from thence up the middle of that river, following the deepest channel, where it has more than one, to the point where it strikes the southern boundary of New Mexico (which runs north of the town called *Paso*) to its western termination; thence, northward, along the western line of New Mexico, until its intersects the first branch of the River Gila; (or if it should not intersect any branch of that river, then to the point on the said line nearest to such branch, and thence in a direct line to the same;) thence down the middle of the said branch and of the said river, until it empties into the Rio Colorado; thence across the Rio Colorado, following the division line between Upper and Lower California, to the Pacific Ocean. . . .

Article VII.

The River Gila, and the part of the Rio Bravo del Norte lying below the southern boundary of New Mexico, being, agreeably to the fifth article, divided in the middle between the two republics, the navigation of the Gila and of the Bravo below said boundary shall be free and common to the vessels and citizens of both countries; and neither shall, without the consent of the other, construct any work that may impede or interrupt, in whole or in part, the exercise of this right; not even for the purpose of favoring new methods of navigation. . . .

Article VIII.

Mexicans now established in territories previously belonging to Mexico, and which remains for the future within the limits of the United States, as defined by the present treaty, shall be free to continue where they now reside, or to remove at any time to the Mexican republic, retaining the property which they possess in the said territories, or disposing thereof, and removing the proceeds wherever they please, without their being subjected, on this account, to any contribution, tax, or charge whatever. . . .

Article XII.

In consideration of the extension acquired by the boundaries of the United States, as defined in the fifth article of the present treaty, the Government of the United States engages to pay to that of the Mexican Republic the sum of fifteen millions of dollars. . . .

Article XIII.

The United States engage, moreover, to assume and pay to the claimants all the amounts now due them, and those hereafter to become due, by reason of the claims already liquidated and decided against the Mexican Republic, under the conventions between the two republics severally concluded on the eleventh day of April, eighteen hundred and thirty-nine, and on the thirtieth day of January, eighteen hundred and forty-three; so that the Mexican Republic shall be absolutely exempt, for the future, from all expense whatever on account of the said claims.

Article XIV.

The United States do furthermore discharge the Mexican Republic from all claims of citizens of the United States, not heretofore decided against the Mexican Government, which may have arisen previously to the date of the signature of this treaty; which discharge shall be final and perpetual, whether the said claims be rejected or to be allowed by the board of commissioners provided for in the following article, and whatever shall be the total amount of those allowed. . . .

Article XV.

The United States, exonerating Mexico from all demands on account of the claims of their citizens mentioned in the preceding article, and considering them entirely and forever cancelled, whatever their amount may be, undertake to make satisfaction for the same, to an amount not exceeding three and one quarter millions of dollars. . . .

Article XXI.

If unhappily any disagreement should hereafter arise between the governments of the two republics, whether with respect to the interpretation of any stipulation in this treaty, or with respect to any other particular concerning the political or commercial relations of the two nations, the said governments, in the name of those nations, do promise to each other that they will endeavor, in the most sincere and earnest manner, to settle the differences so arising, and to preserve the state of peace and friendship in which the two countries are now placing themselves; using, for this end, mutual representations and pacific negotiations. And if, by these means, they should not be enabled to come to an agreement, a resort shall not, on this account, be had to reprisals, aggression, or hostility of any kind, by the one republic against the other, until the Government of that which deems itself aggrieved shall have maturely considered, in the spirit of peace and good neighborship, whether it would not be better that such difference should be settled by the arbitration of commissioners appointed on each side, or by that of a friendly nation. And should such course be proposed by either party, it shall be acceded to by the other, unless deemed by it altogether incompatible with the nature of the difference, or circumstances of the case.

READING 4

THE CIVIL WAR IN THE AMERICAN WEST

The bitter national conflagration of the Civil War, 1861–65, saw its most intense fighting and impact east of the Mississippi River, but the West played a significant role in the outcome of the conflict and suffered consequences as well.

The only western state to secede was Texas, but the loyalty to the Union of other areas was considered suspect. Secessionist conspiracies sprang up in California, particularly its capital, Sacramento, and more serious threats to federal sovereignty occurred in New Mexico, Utah, Kansas, Missouri, and, especially, Indian Territory. The Confederacy offered to reach an alliance with the Five Civilized Tribes, which had been removed to Indian Territory during the Jackson administration. The tribes split in their reaction. Native American soldiers fought on both sides of the conflict, and those who chose the Confederate side received especially harsh treatment after the war. Additionally, the internal conflict within the Indian nations led to anger and recriminations among them.

The most heated activities in the West occurred in Kansas and Missouri, where the raids of proslavery guerrillas and the retaliations of free-state sympathizers known as Jayhawkers created a violent atmosphere charged with uncertainty and fear. (Actually, the term Jayhawkers was often applied to any raiders, Union or Confederate. Those on the Union side formed many units, perhaps the most interesting of which was Jennison's Jayhawkers, whose commander was Susan B. Anthony's brother and on whose muster list John Brown Jr. appeared as a captain.)

In New Mexico the territorial government was threatened by Texas, which hoped to annex New Mexico and Arizona into the Confederacy. These efforts failed: Texas troops moving westward were repulsed by California and Colorado volunteers. California volunteers also replaced the regular Utah forces, whose loyalty under the sway of Brigham Young and the Mormon hierarchy was considered questionable. And California gold strengthened the federal treasury.

In the long run, with the notable exception of Texas, federal sovereignty continued in the West. In fact, most historians believe that the Civil War stabilized territorial governments. The federal government brought the remainder of the unorganized trans-Mississippi West under territorial control and also added two states, Kansas and Nevada, to the Union. The feared consequences of the Civil War in the American West—wholesale crumbling of governments and fearsome battles between independent westerners with their varying emotional attachments to the sections from which they came—never achieved the degree of intensity expected.

READING 4A

"THE ARSENAL WAS SURROUNDED BY A THOUSAND
SPIES," *CHICAGO TRIBUNE,* 1861

In Missouri, where war fever was particularly intense, the Confederacy hoped to exploit southern sympathies in order to gain control of important war supplies. Very inviting was the federal arsenal in St. Louis, where 60,000 weapons were stored. To keep this vital equipment from Confederate hands, Governor Richard Yates of Illinois, his representative Captain James Stokes, and Captain Nathaniel Lyon of the Union Army conspired to remove the arms to safekeeping in Illinois. This report from the Chicago Tribune *of April 29, 1861, details their exploit—only seventeen days after the assault on Fort Sumter.*

Captain James H. Stokes, of Chicago, . . . volunteered to undertake the perilous mission, and Governor Yates placed in his hands the requisition of the Secretary of War for 10,000 muskets. Captain Stokes went to St. Louis, and made his way as rapidly as possible to the arsenal. He found it surrounded by an immense mob, and the postern gates all closed. The requisition was shown. Captain Lyon doubted the possibility of executing it. He said the arsenal was surrounded by a thousand spies, every movement was watched and reported to the headquarters of the Secessionists, who could throw an overpowering force upon them at any moment. Captain Stokes represented that every hour's delay was rendering the capture of the arsenal more certain, and that the arms must be moved to Illinois now or never. . . .

About 700 men were employed in the work. He then took 500 Kentucky flint-lock muskets, which had been sent there to be altered, and sent them to be placed on a steamer as a blind to cover his real movements. The Secessionists nabbed them at once, and raised a perfect Bedlam over the capture. A large portion of the outside crowd left the arsenal when this movement was executed; and Capt. Lyon took the remainder, who were lying around as spies, and locked them in the guard-house. About 11 o'clock the steamer *City of Alton* came alongside, planks were shoved out from the windows to the main deck, and the boxes [each weighing about three hundred pounds] slid down. When the 10,000 were safely on board, Capt. Stokes went to Capt. Lyon and Major Callender, and urged them, by the most pressing appeals, to let him empty the arsenal. They told him to go ahead and take whatever he wanted. Accordingly, he took 10,000 more muskets, 500 new rifle carbines, 500 revolvers, 110,000 musket cartridges, to say nothing of the cannon and a large quantity of miscellaneous accoutrements, leaving only 7,000 muskets in the arsenal to arm the St. Louis volunteers.

When the whole were on board, about 2 o'clock on Friday morning the order was given by the captain of the steamer to cast off. Judge of the consternation of all hands when it was found that she would not move. The arms had been piled in great quantities around the engines to protect them against the battery on the levee, and the great weight had fastened the bows of the boat firmly on a rock, which was tearing a hole through the bottom at every turn of the wheels. A man of less nerve than Capt. Stokes would have gone crazy on the spot. He called the arsenal men on board, and commenced moving the boxes to the stern.

Fortunately, when about two hundred boxes had been shifted, the boat fell away from shore, and floated in deep water. "Which way?" said Captain Mitchell, of the steamer. "Straight to Alton, in the regular channel," replied Captain Stokes. "What if we are attacked?" said Captain Mitchell. "Then we will fight," said Captain Stokes. "What if we are overpowered?" said Captain Mitchell. "Run her to the deepest part of the river, and sink her," replied Captain Stokes. "I'll do it," was the heroic reply of Captain Mitchell; and away they went past the secession battery, past the entire St. Louis levee, and on to Alton, in the regular channel. . . .

When the boat touched the landing, Capt. Stokes, fearing pursuit by some two or three of the Secession military companies by which the city of St. Louis is disgraced, ran to the market-house and rang the fire-bell. The citizens came flocking pell-mell to the river, in all sorts of habiliments. Capt. Stokes informed them of the situation of things, and pointed out the freight cars. Instantly, men, women, and children boarded the steamer, seized the freight, and clambered up the levees to the cars. Rich and poor tugged together with might and main for two hours, when the cargo was all deposited in the cars, and the train moved off, amid their enthusiastic cheers, for Springfield [Illinois].

READING 4B

"A PARTY OF REBEL J H," WILLIAM GULICK, 1862

> *By 1862 Confederate guerrilla bands were harassing Union supporters throughout Missouri and Kansas. Some Confederate guerrillas were called "Jayhawkers," although the term generally applied to Union-sympathizing raiders. Whatever name they were called by, their actions were violent and indiscriminate. In a letter home, Corporal William Gulick of Iowa describes the activities of the "rebel J H," or Confederate Jayhawkers, on the Kansas-Missouri border.*

Butler, Bates Co. Mo. June 1 [1862]

Dear Sister Cynthia,

The 29th the wind blew hard & the Tents as well as every thing else was a cloud of dust. Next day I was on Guard, & yesterday I just comencd this letter when a messenger came from Johnstown with foaming stead stating that a small party with baggage train from here to Osceola had been attacked by a larger party of Rebel J H. I volunteered with two other of our Co. & as many from each of the six Cos here to go to the rescue. In less than twenty minutes we were on the raod. Our Horses were let out to Fourteen miles an hour all hands expecting for once to have some fighting. But it turned out as usual we were to late, for about Fifteen minutes after the engagement commenced a party of Co. L came up. They were on their way from Clinton to this place. The rebels took to the brush.

Our boys followed them but the brush is so thick at this season of the year that they all escaped. One or two of there men were wounded. Our loss was one horse killed. One man shot in the foot. One through his coat collar, another through the hat.

The contemptable J.H.s have the advantage of us now & they use it too. It is folly to even *attempt* to hunt them in the brush. They lay in ambush & shoot a Soldier where ever they can. Not long since Three of our men were killed & one severely wounded while out after Forage. The rebels fired at them while watering at a creek. One escaped to give the alarm, the killed were bruitaly stabed and heads nearly mashed in the ground also Robed of every thing they had even boots. . . . Last week Three men were killed at Osceola in nearly the same manner. . . . A man was also shot from Co. I. Three or Four days ago near this place, as yet we have only succeeded in killing one of the miscreants. But now a special order has been issued to shoot. Two of the prisoners we have in our prison for every soldier that is shot. I think this order will be carried out. . . . I am one of the unfortunate ones I can never get a shot or scarcely ever have an occasion to shoot. I go on nearly every scout but cannot shoot a secesh. They say we will not scout much more here. I hope then we will leave this miserable God forsaken country. . . .

Truly Yours

Wm O. Gulick

READING 4C

"THE BUSHWHACKERS ARE HERE," GURDON GROVENOR, 1863

Perhaps the most vicious Civil War participant in the American West was William Clarke Quantrill, who moved to Kansas in 1857. During the day he taught school under the name William Quantrill; at night he engaged in criminal activities as Charley Hart. When the war broke out, Quantrill organized a band of Confederate guerrillas that terrorized Kansas and Missouri. The Union declared him an outlaw, but the Confederacy commissioned him a captain. Captain Quantrill and his band—which included the outlaws Frank James, Cole Younger, and Jim Younger—are best known for their August 1863 raid on antislavery Lawrence, Kansas. Quantrill's 450 men killed some 150 men, women, and children, set the town ablaze, then celebrated by getting drunk. In October they attacked Baxter Springs, Missouri, with similar results. Despite concentrated efforts, the Union could not capture Quantrill until 1865, when he was surprised and killed in Kentucky. Because of their brutality these Confederate guerrillas were denied the amnesty offered to regular Confederate soldiers following the war.

This account of the Lawrence, Kansas, raid was penned by one of the few residents who escaped.

The raid occurred on the morning of Aug. 21st, 1863. It was a clear, warm, still morning, in the midst of one of the hot, dry, dusty spells of weather common in Kansas in the month of August. The guerrillas reached Lawrence just before sunrise after an all night's ride from the border of Missouri. Myself and family were yet in bed and asleep. They passed directly by our house, and we were awakened by their yelling and shouting.

I thought at first that the noise came from a company of colored recruits who were camped just west of our house; thought they had got to quarreling among themselves. I got up and went to the window to see what was the matter, and as I drew aside the curtain the sight that met my eyes was one of terror—one that I shall never forget. The bushwhackers were just passing by my house. There were 350 of them, all mounted and heavily armed; they were grim and dirty from their night's ride over the dusty roads and were a reckless and bloodthirsty set of men. It was a sight we had somewhat anticipated, felt that it might come, and one that we had dreaded ever since the commencement of the war. I turned to my wife and said: "The bushwhackers are here."

They first made for the main street, passing up as far as the Eldridge House to see if they were going to meet any opposition, and when they found none they scattered out all over town, killing, stealing, and burning. We hastily dressed ourselves and closed the house tightly as possible and began to talk over what was best to do. My first thought was to get away to some hiding place, but on looking out there seemed no possibility of that as the enemy were everywhere, and I had a feeling that I ought not to leave my family, a young wife and two children, one a babe of three months old, and so we sat down and awaited developments. We saw men shot down and fires shooting up in all directions.

Just on the north of our house, a half a block away and in full view was a camp of recruits twenty-two in all, not yet mustered into service and unarmed. They were awakened by the noise, got up and started to run but were all shot down but five. I saw this wholesale shooting from my window, and it was a sight to strike terror to a stouter heart than mine. But we had not long to wait before our time came. Three of the guerrillas came to the house, stepped up on our front porch, and with the butt of a musket smashed in one of the front windows; my wife opened the door and let them in. They ransacked the house, talked and swore and threatened a good deal, but offered no violence. They set the house on fire above and below, took such things as they fancied, and left. After they had gone I put the fire out below, but above it had got too strong a hold, and I could not put it out.

Not long after a single man rode up to the front gate; he was a villainous looking fellow, and was doubly villainous from too much whiskey. He saw me standing back in the hall of the house, and with a terrible oath he ordered me to come out. I stepped out on the piazza, and he leveled his pistol at me and said; "Are you union or secesh?"

It was my time of trial; my wife with her little one in her arms, and our little boy clinging to her side, was standing just a little ways from me. My life seemingly hung on my answer, my position may be imagined but it cannot be described. The thought ran through me like an electric shock, that I could not say that I was a secessionist, and deny my loyalty to my country; and so I answered that I was a union man. He snapped his pistol but it failed to fire. I stepped back into the house and he rode around the north door and met me there, and snapped his pistol at me again, and this time it failed. Was there a providence in this?

Just then a party of a half dozen of the raiders came riding towards the house from the north, and seeing my enemy, hallooed to him, "Don't shoot that man." They rode up to the gate and told me to come there; I did so and my would be murderer came up to me and placed the muzzle of his revolver in my ear. It was not a pleasant place to be in, but the leader of the new crowd told him not to shoot, but to let me alone until he could inquire about me, so he asked me if I had ever been down in Missouri stealing niggers or horses; I told him "No that I never had been in Missouri, except to cross the state going and coming from the east." This seemed to be satisfactory so he told my old enemy to let me alone and not to kill me. This seemed to make him very angry, and he cursed me terribly, but I ventured to put my hand up and push away his revolver. The leader of the party then told me if I did not expect to get killed, I must get out of sight, that they were all getting drunk, and would kill everybody they saw; I told him that that was what I wanted to do all morning, but I could not; "Well," he says, "you must hide or get killed." And they all rode away.

After they had gone I told my wife that I would go into the cellar. . . .

. . . Awhile after my wife came and said she thought the raiders were all gone, and so I came out of my prison just as the fire was eating through the floor over my head, thankful that I had passed through that dreadful ordeal and was safe.

Such was my experience during those four or five terrible hours. Our home and its contents was in ashes, but so thankful were we that my life was spared that we thought but little of our pecuniary loss. After the raiders had left and the people could get out on the street, a most desolate and sickening sight met their view. The whole business part of town, except two stores, was in ashes. The bodies of dead men, some of them partly burned away, were laying in all directions. A large number of dwellings were burned to the ground, and the moaning of the grief stricken people was heard from all sides. Gen. Lane, who was in the city at the time, told me that he had been over the battleground of Gettysburg a few days before, but the sight was not so sickening as the one which the burned and sacked city of Lawrence presented. The exact number killed was never known, but it was about 150, many of them of the best citizens.

READING 4D

THE BATTLE OF GLORIETTA PASS, W. R. SCURRY, 1862

Civil War battles west of Kansas and Missouri were scattered and few. One of the most significant occurred early in 1862 at Glorietta Pass in New Mexico Territory. In July 1861 the Confederate government had authorized an expedition to conquer New Mexico under the direction of General Henry H. Sibley. In November 1861 Sibley left Texas with a force of 3,700 soldiers. Union forces under the command of Colonel Edward R. S. Canby were stationed at Fort Defiance, New Mexico. Sibley and Canby met in combat in January 1862; Sibley's forces emerged victorious, and he went on to capture Albuquerque and Santa Fe. In response, the Union reorganized to assault the Confederate forces.

They met at Apache Canyon in Glorietta Pass. The Confederates in this battle were commanded by Colonel W. R. Scurry, the Union troops led by Colonels Canby and John Slough. The Confederates again won a victory, but at great cost: casualties were high, and they were eventually forced into a retreat across two hundred miles of desert. The Confederate foray into New Mexico ended with this campaign. General Sibley had started with 3,700 men; he returned to Confederate territory with less than 2,000. Here the Confederate commander, Colonel Scurry, describes the action at Glorietta Pass.

Santa Fe, New Mexico, March 31, 1862

To Major A. M. Jackson

A.A. General, Army New Mexico

Late on the afternoon of the 26th, while encamped at Galistoe, an express from Major Pyron arrived with the information that the major was engaged in sharp conflict with a greatly superior force of the enemy, about sixteen miles distant, and urging me to hasten to his relief. . . .

[Upon my arrival, and] as soon as daylight enabled me, I made a thorough examination of the ground, and so formed the troops as to command every approach to the position we occupied, which was naturally a very strong one. The disposition of the troops was soon completed, and by 8 o'clock were ready to receive the expected attack. In this position we remained until the next morning. The enemy still not making their appearance, I concluded to march forward and attack them. Leaving a small wagon guard, I marched in their direction with portions of nine companies of the 4th regiment. . . . From details and other cause they were soon reduced, until, all combined, they did not number over six hundred men fit for duty. At about six miles from camp the advance guard gave notice that the enemy was near, in force. I hastened in front to examine their position, and found they were about one mile west . . . in *canon Glorietta.*

The mounted men who were marching in front were ordered to retire slowly to the rear, dismount, and come into the action on foot. The artillery was pushed forward to a slight elevation in the *canon,* and immediately to open fire. The infantry were rapidly deployed into line, extending across the *canon* from a fence on our left up into the pine forest on our right.

About the time these dispositions were made, the enemy rapidly advanced in separate columns, both upon our right and left. . . .

A large body of infantry, availing themselves of a gulch that ran up the centre of an inclosed field to our left, were moving under its cover past our left flank to the rear of our position.

Crossing the fence on foot, we advanced over the clearing some two hundred yards under a heavy fire from the foe, and dashed into the gulch in their midst, pistol and knife in hand. For a few moments a most desperate and deadly hand to hand conflict raged along the gulch, when they broke before the steady courage of our men, and fled in the wildest disorder and confusion. . . .

Sending to the rear to have two of the guns brought back to the field, a pause was made to reunite our forces, which had become somewhat scattered in the last rencontre. When we were ready to advance, the enemy had taken cover, and it was impossible to tell whether their main body was stationed behind a long adobe wall that ran nearly across the *canon,* or had taken position behind a large ledge of rocks in the rear. . . .

I took command of the right and immediately attacked the enemy, who were at the ranche. Majors Ragnet and Pyron opened a galling fire upon their left from the rock on the mountain side, and the centre charging down the road, the foe was driven from the ranche to the ledge of rocks before alluded to, where they made their final and most desperate stand. At this point three batteries of eight guns opened a furious fire of grape, canister, and shell upon our advancing troops.

Our brave soldiers, heedless of the storm, pressed on, determined, if possible, to take their battery. A heavy body of infantry, twice our number, interposed to save their guns. Here the conflict was terrible. Our men and officers, alike inspired with the unalterable determination to overcome every obstacle to the attainment of their object, dashed among them. . . . Inch by inch was the ground disputed, until the artillery of the enemy had time to escape with a number of their wagons. The infantry also broke ranks and fled from the field. So precipitate was their flight, that they cut loose their teams and set fire to two of their wagons. The pursuit was kept up until forced to halt from the extreme exhaustion of the men, who had been engaged for six hours in the hardest contested fight it had ever been my lot to witness. The enemy is now known to have numbered fourteen hundred men, Pike's Peak miners and regulars, the flower of the United States army.

During the action, a part of the army succeeded in reaching our rear, surprising the wagon guard, and burning our wagons, taking at the same time some sixteen prisoners. About this time a party of prisoners, whom I had sent to the rear, reached there, and informed them how the fight was going in front, whereupon they beat a hasty retreat, not, however, until the perpetration of two acts which the most barbarous savage of the plains would blush to own. One was the shooting and dangerously wounding the Rev. L. H. Jones, chaplain of the 4th regiment, with a white flag in his hand; the other an order that the prisoners they had taken be shot in case they were attacked on the retreat. These instances go to prove that they have lost all sense of humanity, in the insane hatred they bear to citizens of the

Confederacy, who have the manliness to arm in defence of their country's independence.

W. R. Scurry

Colonel commanding A.N.M.

READING 4E

THE CONFEDERATES AND THE INDIAN
NATIONS, MATTHEW LEEPER, 1862

During the Civil War natives in the Indian Territory and elsewhere fought alongside whites, but allegiances were divided, even within tribes. Recruits from the Cherokees, Choctaws, Creeks, and Seminoles fought on both sides. Caddos, Wichitas, Osages, Shawnees, Delawares, Senecas, and Quapaws also served, primarily with the Confederacy. Some Indian nations felt they should support the Confederacy in retaliation for mistreatment by the federal government, particularly during the removal episodes of the 1830s. Other nations opposed the Confederacy because of the South's adherence to slavery and because of brutalities suffered at the hands of southerners in years past.

In order to expand its influence in the Southwest, the Confederacy made strong efforts to form alliances with the Indian Territory, sending agents to negotiate with the tribal leadership. Among these was Matthew Leeper, operating primarily out of the reservation called the Wichita Agency. The many letters and documents Leeper issued evince the remarkable efforts undertaken to reach alliances with the native population and to quiet any Indian opposition to the Confederacy. These two selections are Leeper's report of his treaty negotiations with the Kiowa Indians and a subsequent notice stipulating that the negotiations had been successful.

July 11, 1862

Washita Agency, L.D., July 11, 1862

Brig. Gen'l Albert Pike, & Act'g Superintendent, Commissioner, etc.,

Sir: In compliance with your instructions and authority, I have this day, entered into Treaty stipulations with the Kioway Indians and all the wild Comanche bands with the exception of the Kua-ha-ra-tet-sa-co-no who inhabit the western portion of the "Staked Plains," and with those I am negotiating and shall probably conclude a treaty of peace in September or October next. Those who treated in August last have also signed and adopted amendments of [the Confederate] Congress.

They retired well satisfied with themselves, and with the action of the Confederate Government, consequently peace and quietness may be expected to prevail in future upon the frontier of Texas, provided, however, that a band of fugitives from various clans who have congregated on the Pecos, numbering it is said one hundred and fifty or two hundred, governed by no law and disposed to spread desolation wherever they go are destroyed or our troops can receive aid from those bands who have treated in hunting down and destroying these "fellows." I am sir, Very respectfully, Your obt. ser't

[Matthew Leeper] Ind. Agency, C.S.A.

July 21, 1862

NOTICE

As Agent and Acting Commissioner on the part of the Confederate States of America, I have entered into Solemn Treaty stipulations of perpetual friendship and peace with the Kioway Indians and wild bands of Comanches except the Kua-ha-ra-tet-sa-co-no whose habitations are on the Western extremity of the "Staked Plains" and with those I am negotiating and will probably conclude a treaty some time in September next.

Therefore perfect peace and quietness may soon be expected to prevail on the Texas frontier.

In order to convince the Indians of our sincerity and punctuality, it is necessary to comply strictly with the Treaty, and to do that, the Government expects me to employ four or five farmers and twenty laborers which I desire to do; farmers with families would be preferred, to whom fifty dollars per month and rations will be given, and to laborers twenty-five dollars per month and rations, negro men would be preferred.

At present there is not the slightest danger there, the agency is one of the most quiet and peaceful places within the limits of the Confederate Government. . . .

READING 5

CAMP DOUGLAS, PATRICK EDWARD CONNOR, C. 1868

The backbone of the U.S. Army's frontier defenses during and after the Civil War was the string of forts spread throughout the West. One such fort, constructed in 1863 in the Utah Territory, was Camp Douglas, commanded by General

Patrick Edward Connor. His manuscript medical history of the camp, written
about 1868, includes one of the most complete descriptions extant of a frontier
army post.

The parade ground is laid out in the form of a perfect square each side of
which is 440 feet in length. A stream of water flows along three sides of it,
viz.: the northern, eastern, and southern. There is also a row of young locust
and mulberry trees on each of these three sides and a gravel walk thirty-
three and one third feet in width. The flag staff stands in the parade ground
fifty-two feet from the center of the eastern side and is one hundred feet in
height. The guard house is situated on the western or rather southwestern
side of the parade ground and is sixty by eighteen feet; height of side wall six
feet; of gable eight and one half feet. On either side of the guard house is a
stone building; the one on the right [northwest] is the magazine; the one on
the left [southeast] is the arsenal; the guard house is also built of stone.

On the right of the parade ground are five barracks; near the lower right
hand corner of the parade ground is the post trader's store; his residence
being at the rear of his store. On the left of the parade ground are five
(formerly six) barracks; near the lower left hand corner on this side is the
Commissary store house; immediately above this is the Ordnance store
house; and above this is a vacant space occupied by the sixth barracks, which
was destroyed by fire . . . on . . . August [2], 1868. The dimensions of the
barracks are eighty-five and five twelfths feet by twenty-eight and one quarter feet; height of side wall ten and three quarters; of gable sixteen and one
sixth feet. There is an open verandah in front of each sixty by nine feet. In
the center of the northeastern side of the parade ground is situated the
headquarters building, on either side of which are the officers quarters—
eight in number, four on each side. The "officers' row" consists of small
huts built of hewn logs, whitewashed. Each building consists of a double set
of quarters and is forty feet six inches long by twenty-six feet six inches
wide, and nine feet in the clear, containing eight rooms averaging twelve by
ten by nine feet in size, two of which are kitchens, so called. At the upper
right hand corner of the parade ground but outside of the square formed by
the barracks on that side and the officers' quarters, is situated the post
bakery, it might be said to be *en echelon* with the barracks on that side.

At the rear of each barracks. . . . on each side is a deep ravine, in which the
drains of the camp empty, and in which a stream of water is constantly

flowing. The married soldiers' quarters are twelve in number and are situated on a line parallel with and seventy-five yards in rear of the officers' quarters. The hospital is situated one hundred yards in rear of the married soldiers' quarters, on a line passing through the guard house, flag staff and headquarters.

There is a gravelled walk leading from the headquarters to the hospital; that portion between the married soldiers' quarters and the hospital having a row of trees and stream of water on each side. There is also a row of trees and a stream of water on each side of the building. The building is sixty-six by thirty-four feet and has an open verandah in front thirty-four by eight feet. The Commanding Officers' quarters are on the left and the Surgeon's quarters on the right of the hospital, each being twenty-five yards distant from it. . . . Back of all is the hospital garden which contains two and one quarter acres of land. At the left of the lower end of the hospital garden is the post ice house, which is capable of holding three hundred tons of ice. A building on a line with the officers' quarters, but about two hundred yards from the upper right hand corner of the parade ground is a large building originally designed for the General commanding the district [General Connor], and his staff. Religious services are held in a building still further west. There is in the same building a school room and a hall, used by the soldiers for a dance and concert hall. This building was originally designed for artillery barracks.

On the opposite side of the post and about one hundred yards to the rear of the left hand barracks are the Quartermaster store houses, stables, and barns, seven in number: the coal house, wood and hay yards on the same line but lower down, and on a line passing in front of the guard house. The Quartermaster's work shops, four in number, are on a line about fifty yards to the rear of the store houses. A line of stockade ten feet in height commences about one hundred yards in front of the guard house and runs in such a manner as to inclose the Quartermaster store houses, work shops, coal, wood and hay yards on three sides. The cemetery is outside of this stockade and about five hundred yards east, across a deep ravine which is bridged.

READING 6

AN OFFICER'S WIFE IN AN ARMY CAMP,
SARAH ELIZABETH CANFIELD, 1867–1868

*Women sometimes accompanied their husbands to western military posts, where
they faced the constant possibility of danger but very little direct violence. Women's
experiences in these army camps varied from the monotonous to the exciting, often
involving the garrison's social whirl. Libbie Custer recalled that her husband,
George Armstrong Custer, "had a very keen sense of his social responsibilities as
post commander, and believed that our house should be open at all hours."*

*Sarah Elizabeth Canfield's journal describes her journey by riverboat to the
fort in the Dakota Territory where her husband, a first lieutenant, was stationed
and relates her experiences there in the late 1860s.*

April 13, 1867

This is a worse country than I ever dreamed of, nothing but hills of dry sand
with little streaks of short shriveled grass in the hollows and on the river
bottoms.

We saw several large groves of antelopes today—I suppose several hundred in all. And just before night a large grey wolf came down to the river
bank to see us pass—We saw three Indians yesterday but nothing like a
human today.

April 25

The wild flowers are beginning to bloom, and today when the boat stopped
to cut wood, we went ashore and gathered a few. The gentlemen armed
themselves and acted as our escort, even though we did not go very far from
the boat—for wild Indians are all around us. We do not often see them, but
we know they are near, for this morning about daylight as our boat was just
starting from where it had been tied to the bank all night . . . the pilot was
shot with arrows, no one knew it until he was found. The Captain says he
will leave the body at Ft. Rice tomorrow for burial.

The Clerk of the boat has just brought me three letters from [my hus-
band] Mr. C directed to my Iowa address. . . . The date of the latest letter was
early in January, nearly four months ago, and what might not happen in four
months, for I had not had a letter for a month or more when I left home. I
had a hard cry over my letters but Capt. Oldman told me not to worry, but if

anything had happened to my husband, he would bring me back home all right which is very kind of him.

May 19
This is Sunday and a very beautiful day. I am out on deck pretending to read but my mind is not on my reading very much for the Captain has just told me he hopes to reach Ft. Bertold to-night. Is my dear Husband alive? Am I indeed to see him soon? I am very anxious but am determined to appear calm as possible.

May 20
I was delighted to recognize [my husband] in the first man to step on the gangplank when we stopped. After introductions and the congratulations of my fellow travelers on the happy termination of my journey, I said good-by to all with many thanks to the kind old captain. . . .

I am at home with my dear husband.

Our two rooms [in officers' quarters at the fort] are very neat and cosy. One is a sitting room which contains a center table, an army cot for a sofa covered with a buffalo robe which is beautifully decorated on the flesh side with bright colors, a shelf of books, three chairs, and a writing desk.

May 30
I was awakened last night by a great screeching, groaning, and a series of, to me, distressing sounds together with a great barking of dogs. Mr. C—— assured me I need not be alarmed. It is, he said, only a young warrior serenading or making love to his chosen one. The custom is for the young man to come late at night and tie some ponies in front of her tepee, then spend an hour or two on the roof reciting his own prowess as a warrior and praising the charms of his lady love. If the father of the girl thinks the number of ponies enough, he takes them and thus signifies his approval. If not, the lover will the next night bring one more and continue to do so until the father is satisfied. I do not know that they have any marriage ceremony. I think not.

June 3
The three chiefs came in today to hold a "Powwow" with the officer[s]. . . . The costume of the Chiefs seemed to be buffalo robes, beads and moccasins, though one wore a large string of bear claws for a necklace.

The robes were only held by the hands and had a way of slipping down and displaying their splendid brown shoulders. They were magnificent specimens of manhood.

June 10

Mr. C—— told me that one day last year the warriors started out, leaving the squaws and children at home. Encountering their enemy, the Sioux, having killed one, they scalped [their victim], cut him up, and coming back to their camp held a regular Pow Wow over it, singing and dancing all day. They seemed to think [this] an act of bravery or at any rate a victory over their enemies.

[This] reminds me of the way they make warriors. They take a young man, cut two slits in the skin of his back just below the shoulder blades; raising the narrow strip of skin they insert a pole strong enough to bear his weight, then raise him off the ground and leave him to struggle until he breaks the strip and is free. Then there is a great feast made for him, but if, as is sometimes the case, he faints or cannot endure the pain—he is called a squaw man and works with the women.

Dec. 26

The winter is passing away. We have had little dinner dances and card parties to help pass the time. Some of the soldiers formed a theatrical troupe [and] have an entertainment once a month. The one at Christmas was especially fine—music, dancing, and a short play.

Jan. 1, 1868

Today the ladies of the Ft. received. The officers came calling, all in full uniform. We made as much of a ceremony of it as we could.

May 4

I shall remain at the Ft. until a steamboat comes up, goes on to Ft. Benton, and returns on the way to the States. Mrs. H—— is going home too. One of the ladies, realizing how lonely she would be, offered to board me if I would stay, but if I cannot be with my husband I think I shall go home.

Lieutenant Canfield was frequently away from the camp on various assignments. His duties included escorting travelers through Sioux territory.

May 5

We have had a great excitement today. About 3 P.M. Indians in great numbers were seen coming over the hills South of the Fort . . . painted and
mounted for war. . . . They circled round three sides of the Ft. (the river
being the fourth). . . .

When we Ladies saw what might happen we held a "council of war" and
decided if the Ft. could not be held that we preferred to be shot by our own
officers rather than be taken captive. The officers promised to do so before
surrendering . . . but while it would have been done, if necessary, we are
still spared to tell about the attack of the Ft. by three thousand Indians.
Now that the scare is over I remember that they came from the direction
Mr. C—— went 24 hours ago. A new agony and nothing to do but wait
for news.

June 1, 1868

We left camp at sundown. It was a sad parting. The life at . . . camp is
so dangerous. I wanted to stay but could not, and it will be so long before I
get a letter.

READING 7

THE SAND CREEK MASSACRE, 1864

*Soldiers and their commanders in the West shared an almost universal mind-set:
their job was to protect the white settlements from attack by the "hostiles."
Rarely was the reverse true, with the army protecting the Indians from white
encroachment. Perhaps too frequently, military action was heartless with little or
no provocation. No better example can be found than the Sand Creek Massacre
of 1864. In that year Colorado militia, under the command of confirmed Indian
hater Colonel John Chivington, attacked a village of five hundred unsuspecting
Cheyennes and Arapahos on the banks of Sand Creek in southeastern Colorado.
This incident provided the catalyst for later Indian resistance and correspondingly
intensified army efforts.*

*When a congressional investigation of the Sand Creek Massacre was later
convened, a joint committee officially condemned the action. The report specifically
denounced Chivington, but since he had already left the army, he was never
punished. The testimony of two lieutenants who witnessed the massacre spells out
the gory details.*

Lieutenant James Connor First New Mexico Volunteer Infantry, . . . being duly sworn, says: That on the 28th day of November, 1864, I was ordered by Major General Scott J. Anthony to accompany him on an expedition (Indian) as his battalion adjutant; the object of that expedition was to be a thorough campaign against hostile Indians, as I was led to understand. I referred to the fact of there being a friendly camp of Indians in that immediate neighborhood and remonstrated against simply attacking that camp, as I was aware that they were resting there, in fancied security under promises held out to them of safety . . . [by the] former Commander of the post of Fort Lyon, and by Major J. S. Anthony, then in command.

Our battalion was attached to the command of Colonel J. M. Chivington, and left Fort Lyon on the night of the 28th of November, 1864; about daybreak on the morning of the 29th of November we came in sight of the camp of the friendly Indians aforementioned, and were ordered by Colonel Chivington to attack the same, which was accordingly done. The command of Colonel Chivington was composed of about one thousand men; the village consisted of from one hundred to one hundred and thirty lodges, and, as far as I am able to judge, of from five hundred to six hundred souls, the majority of which were women and children; in going over the battle-ground the next day I did not see a body of man, woman, or child but was scalped, and in many instances their bodies were mutilated in the most horrible manner—men, women, and children's privates were cut out; . . . I heard one man say that he had cut out a woman's private parts and had them for exhibition on a stick; I heard another man say that he had cut the fingers off an Indian to get the rings on the hand; according to the best of my knowledge and belief these atrocities that were committed were with knowledge of J. M. Chivington, and I do not know of his taking any measures to prevent them; I heard of one instance of a child a few months old being thrown in the feed-box of a wagon, and after being carried some distance left on the ground to perish; I also heard of numerous instances in which men had cut out the private parts of females and stretched them over the saddle-bows, and wore them over their hats while riding in the ranks. All these matters were a subject of general conversation, and could not help being known by Colonel J. M. Chivington.

Lieutenant Cramer Sworn: I am stationed at this post, First Lieutenant, Company C, veteran battalion, Colorado Cavalry. I was at this post when Colonel Chivington arrived here, and accompanied him on his expedition.

He came into the post with a few officers and men, and threw out pickets, with instructions to allow no one to go beyond the line. I was then in command of company K. He brought some eight or nine hundred men with him, and took from this post over a hundred men, all being mounted. My company was ordered along to take part. We arrived at the Indian village about daylight. On arriving in sight of the village a battalion were ordered on a charge to surround the village and the Indian herd. . . . About this time, Captain John Smith, Indian interpreter, attempting to come to our troops, was fired on by our men, at the command of some one in the rear, "To shoot the damned old son of a bitch." One of my men rode forward to save him, but was killed. To get out of the fire from the rear, we were ordered to the left. About this time Colonel Chivington moved his regiment to the front, the Indians retreating up the creek, and hiding under the banks. There seemed to be no organization among our troops; every one on his own hook, and shots flying between our own ranks. White Antelope ran towards our columns unarmed, and with both hands raised, but was killed. Several other of the warriors were killed in like manner. The women and children were huddled together, and most of the fire was concentrated on them. . . . During the fight, the battery on the opposite side of the creek kept firing at the bank while our men were in range. The Indian warriors, about one hundred in number, fought desperately; there were about five hundred all told. I estimated the loss of the Indians to be from one hundred and twenty-five to one hundred and seventy-five killed; . . . and all the dead were scalped. . . . Our force was so large that there was no necessity of firing on the Indians. . . . I told Colonel Chivington . . . that it would be murder, in every sense of the word, if he attacked those Indians. His reply was bringing his fist down close to my face, "Damn any man who sympathizes with Indians." I told him what pledges were given the Indians [that they would be safe and protected]. He replied, "That he had come to kill Indians, and believed it honorable to kill Indians under any and all circumstances." . . . Lieutenant Dunn went to Colonel Chivington and wanted to know if he could kill his [Indian] prisoner. . . . His reply was, "Don't ask me; you know my orders; I want no prisoners." Colonel Chivington was in a position where he must have seen the scalping and mutilation going on. . . . On our approach to the village I saw some one [an Indian] with a white flag approaching our lines, and the troops fired upon it.

CUSTER AND THE SIOUX, GEORGE ARMSTRONG CUSTER, 1867

Without question the most controversial figure of the Indian Wars was George Armstrong Custer. Custer's record in the Civil War led to his being named the youngest general in the Union Army—at the age of twenty-three. Following his Civil War exploits the "Boy General" accepted a peacetime reduction in rank (as did many army officers of the time) to colonel. Custer campaigned against the Sioux from 1867 to 1876, when he and his detachment of more than two hundred cavalrymen were killed by the Indians at the Battle of Little Bighorn. His attitudes toward the Native American culture and his military judgment and actions have made him the most discussed military figure of the period; his death at Little Bighorn made him the most popular military hero of the time as well.

This account from Custer's own book, My Life on the Plains, *describes a minor engagement in 1867. Custer's admiration for the horsemanship and strategic skills of the Sioux is evident, but equally clear is his determination to confront and destroy the Sioux threat—an objective that would lead to his downfall nine years later.*

Soon after arriving at camp a small party of Indians was reported in sight in a different direction. Captain Louis Hamilton, a lineal descendant of Alexander Hamilton, was immediately ordered to take his troop and learn something of their intentions. The Indians resorted to their usual tactics. There were not more than half a dozen to be seen—not enough to appear formidable. These were there as a decoy. Captain Hamilton marched his troop toward the hill on which the Indians had made their appearance, but on arriving at its crest found that they had retired to the next ridge beyond. This manoeuver was repeated several times, until the cavalry found itself several miles from camp. The Indians then separated into two parties, each going in different directions. Captain Hamilton divided his troop into two detachments, sending one detachment, under command of my brother, after one of the parties, while he with twenty-five men continued to follow the other.

When the two detachments had become so far separated as to be of no assistance to each other, the Indians developed their scheme. Suddenly dashing from a ravine, as if springing from the earth, forty-three Indian warriors burst out upon the cavalry, letting fly their arrows and filling the air with their wild war-whoops. Fortunately Captain Hamilton was an officer of great presence of mind as well as undaunted courage. The Indians began circling about the troops, throwing themselves upon the sides of their ponies and aiming their carbines and arrows over the necks of their well-trained war-steeds. Captain Hamilton formed his men in order to defend themselves against the assaults of their active enemies. The Indians displayed unusual boldness, sometimes dashing close up to the cavalry and sending in a perfect shower of bullets and arrows. Fortunately their aim, riding as they did at full speed, was necessarily inaccurate.

All this time we who had remained in camp were in ignorance of what was transpiring. Dr. Coates . . . had accompanied Captain Hamilton's command, but when the latter was divided the doctor had joined the detachment of my brother. In some unexplained manner the doctor became separated from both parties, and remained so until the sound of the firing attracted him toward Captain Hamilton's party. When within half a mile of the latter, he saw what was transpiring; saw our men in the center and the Indians charging and firing from the outside. His first impulse was to push on and endeavor to break through the line of savages, casting his lot with his struggling comrades. This impulse was suddenly nipped in the bud. The Indians, with their quick, watchful eyes, had discovered his presence, and half a dozen of their best mounted warriors at once galloped toward him.

Happily the doctor was in the direction of camp from Captain Hamilton's party, and comprehending the peril of his situation at a glance, turned his horse's head toward camp, and applying the spur freely set out on a ride for life. The Indians saw this move, but were not disposed to be deprived of their victim in this way. They were better mounted than the doctor, his only advantage being in the start and the greater object to be attained. When the race began he was fully four miles from camp, the day was hot and sultry, the country rough and broken, and his horse somewhat jaded from the effects of the ride of the morning. These must have seemed immense obstacles in the eyes of a man who was riding for dear life. A false step, a broken girth, or almost any trifle might decide his fate.

How often, if ever, the doctor looked back, I know not; his eyes more probably were strained to catch a glimpse of camp or of assistance accidentally coming to his relief. Neither the one nor the other appeared. His pursuers, knowing that their success must be gained soon, if at all, pressed their fleet ponies forward until they seemed to skim over the surface of the green plain, and their shouts of exultation falling clearer and louder upon his ear told the doctor that they were surely gaining upon him. Fortunately our domestic horses, until accustomed to their presence, are as terrified by Indians as by a huge wild beast, and will fly from them if not restrained. The yells of the approaching Indians served, no doubt, to quicken the energies of the doctor's horse and impelled him to greater efforts to escape.

So close had the Indians succeeded in approaching that they were within arrow range and would soon have sent one flying through the doctor's body, when to the great joy of the pursued and the corresponding grief of his pursuers camp suddenly appeared in full view scarcely a mile distant. The ponies of the Indians had been ridden too hard to justify their riders in venturing near enough to provoke pursuit upon fresh animals. Sending a parting volley of bullets after the flying doctor, they turned and disappeared. The doctor did not slacken his pace on this account, however; he knew that Captain Hamilton's party was in peril, and that assistance should reach him as soon as possible. Without tightening rein or sparing spur he came dashing into camp, and the first we knew of his presence he had thrown himself from his almost breathless horse and was lying on the ground, unable, from sheer exhaustion and excitement, to utter a word.

The officers and men gathered about him in astonishment, eager and anxious to hear his story, for all knew that something far from any ordinary event had transpired to place the doctor in such a condition of mind and body. As soon as he had recovered sufficiently to speak, he told us that he had left Captain Hamilton surrounded by a superior force of Indians, and that he himself had been pursued almost to the borders of camp.

This was enough. The next moment the bugle rang out the signal "To horse," and in less time than would be required to describe it, horses were saddled and arms ready. Then "there was mounting in hot haste." A moment later the command set off at a brisk trot to attempt the rescue of their beleaguered comrades.

Persons unfamiliar with the cavalry service may mentally inquire why, in such an emergency as this, the intended reinforcements were not pushed forward at a rapid gallop? But in answer to this it need only be said that we had a ride of at least five miles before us in order to arrive at the point where Captain Hamilton and his command had last been seen, and it was absolutely necessary to so husband the powers of our horses as to save them for the real work of conflict.

We had advanced in this manner probably two miles, when we discerned

in the distance the approach of Captain Hamilton's party. They were returning leisurely to camp, having succeeded in driving off their assailants in
inflicting upon them a loss of two warriors killed and several wounded. The
Indians could only boast of having wounded a horse belonging to Captain
Hamilton's party.

The Battle of Little Bighorn, 1876

*On June 25, 1876, U.S. Army forces commanded by George Custer fought an
Indian coalition led by the Sioux warrior Crazy Horse in the most famous battle
of the Indian Wars. The Battle of Little Bighorn was the greatest (and last
major) victory for Native Americans, and the biggest defeat suffered by the army.
It was here that Custer's life ended but his legend began.*

*The following newspaper accounts—the first a terse recital of the facts; the
second a more detailed (and emotional) special dispatch—are supplemented
by a portion of the official report by General Philip Sheridan, who directed the
campaign against the Plains Indians. (For the Native American perspective,
see reading 10.)*

Helena Daily Herald, July 2, 1876, by W. H. Norton, Stillwater, Montana
Territory

Muggins Taylor, scout for General [John] Gibbon, got here last night, direct
from Little Big Horn. General Custer found the Indian camp of about 2,000
lodges, on the Little Horn, and immediately attacked the camp. Custer took
five companies and charged the thickest portion of the camp. Nothing is
known of the operations of this detachment only as they trace it by the dead.
Major Reno commanded the other seven companies, and attacked at the
lower portion of the camp. The Indians poured in a murderous fire from all
directions; besides, the greater portion fought on horseback.

Custer, his two brothers, nephew and brother-in-law were all killed, and
not one of his detachment escaped. Two hundred and seven men were
buried in one place, and the killed is estimated at 300, with only 31 wounded.
The Indians surrounded [Marcus] Reno's command and held them one day
in the Hills, deprived of water, until Gibbon's command came in sight, when
they broke camp and left. The Seventh [Cavalry] fought like tigers, and were
overcome by mere brute force. The Indian loss cannot be estimated, as they

bore off and cached most of their killed. The remnant of the Seventh Cavalry and Gibbon's command are returning to the mouth of the Little Horn, where the steamboat lies. The Indians got all the arms of the killed soldiers.

Special to the St. Paul and Minneapolis (MN) Pioneer-Press and Tribune, July 6, 1876, THE TERRIBLE DETAILS:

Sioux Expedition, Mouth of the Big Horn, July 1, via Bismarck, Dakota Territory

Long before the arrival of this dispatch you will have heard of the tragedy which has been enacted here. The ghastly details would seem to court oblivion if it were in the nature of things possible to forget or cloak them.

At noon on the 22nd day of June, General Custer, at the head of his fine regiment of twelve veteran companies, left camp at the mouth of the Rosebud [River], to follow the trail of a very large band of hostile Sioux, leading up the river, and westward in the direction of the Big Horn. The signs indicated that the Indians were making for the eastern branch of the last named river, marked on the map as the Little Big Horn.

At the same time General [Alfred] Terry, with Gibbon's command of five companies of infantry, four of cavalry, and the Gatling [gun] battery, started to ascend the Big Horn, aiming to assail the enemy in the rear. The march of the two columns was so planned as to bring Gibbon's command within cooperating distance of the anticipated scene of action by the evening of the twenty-sixth. In this way only could the infantry be made available, as it would not do to encumber Custer's march with foot troops.

On the evening of the 24th, Gibbon's command was landed on the South bank of the Yellowstone, near the mouth of the Big Horn, and on the 25th was pushed twenty-three miles over a country so rugged that the endurance of the men was taxed to the uttermost. The infantry then halted for the night; but the department commander, with the cavalry, advanced twelve miles farther, to the mouth of the Little Big Horn, marching until midnight, in the hope of opening communication with Custer.

The morning of the twenty-sixth brought the intelligence communicated by three badly frightened Crow scouts of the battle of the previous day and its results. The story was not credited, because it was not expected that an attack would be made earlier than the 27th, and chiefly because no one could believe that a force such as Custer commanded could have met with disaster. Still the report was in no manner disregarded. All day long the toilsome march was plied, every eye bent upon a cloud of smoke, resting over the southern horizon, which was hailed as a sign that Custer was successful, and had fired the village. It was only when night was falling that the weary troops lay down their arms. The infantry had marched 29 miles.

The march of the next morning revealed at every step some evidence of the conflict which had taken place two days before. At an early hour the head of the column entered a plain half a mile wide, bordering the left bank of the Little Big Horn, where had recently been an immense Indian village, extending three miles long along the stream, and where were still standing two funeral lodges, with horses slaughtered around them, and containing the bodies of nine chiefs. The ground was strewn everywhere with the carcasses of horses, and cavalry equipments, besides buffalo robes, packages of dried meat, and weapons and utensils belonging to the Indians. On this part of the field was found the clothing of [two soldiers] . . . pierced with bullets, and a blood-stained gauntlet. . . . Further on were found the bodies of men. . . .

Just then a breathless scout arrived, with the intelligence that Colonel Reno, with a remnant of the Seventh Cavalry, was entrenched on a bluff near by, waiting for relief. The command was pushed rapidly on, and soon came in sight of a group surrounding a cavalry guidon [a small identification flag], upon a lofty eminence on the right bank of the river. General Terry forded the stream, accompanied by a small party, and rode to the spot. All the way the slopes were dotted with the bodies of men and horses. The General approached, the men swarmed out of the works and greeted him with hearty and repeated cheers. . . .

In the center of the enclosure was a depression in the surface, in which the wounded were sheltered, covered with canvas. Reno's command had been fighting from Sunday noon of the 25th until the night of the 26th, when General Terry arrived, which caused the Indians to retire. Up to this time Reno and those with him were in complete ignorance of the fate of the other five companies, which had been separated from them early on the 25th, to make an attack under Custer on the village at another point. While preparations were being made for the removal of the wounded, a party was sent on Custer's trail to look for traces of his command. They found awaiting them a sight fit to appall the stoutest heart. At a point about three miles down the right bank of the stream, Custer had evidently attempted to ford and attack the village from the ford. The trail was found to lead back up the bluff and to the northward, as if the troops had been repulsed and compelled to retreat, and at the same time had been cut off from regaining the forces under Reno. The bluffs along the right bank come sharply down to the water, and are interspersed by numerous ravines. All along the slopes and ridges, and in the ravines, lay the dead, arranged in order of battle, lying as they had fought, line behind line, showing where the defensive positions had been successfully taken up, and held till none were left to fight. There, huddled in a narrow compass, horses and men were piled promiscuously. At the highest point of the ridge lay Custer, surrounded by a chosen band. Here were his two brothers and his nephew, Mr. Reed, Colonels Yates and Cooke, and Captain Smith, all lying in a circle of a few yards, their horses beside them. Here, behind Yates' company, the last stand had been made, and here one after another these last survivors of Custer's five companies had met their death. The companies had successively thrown themselves across the path of the advancing enemy, and had been annihilated. Not a man had escaped to tell the tale, but it was inscribed on the surface of these barren hills in a language more eloquent than words.

General Philip Sheridan, Official Report to the U.S. Secretary of War, 1876
[After relating the events of June 25, Sheridan recounts those of June 26 and 27.] There were now many wounded, and the question of obtaining water was a vital one, for the troops had been without any from 6 o'clock the previous evening, a period of sixteen hours. A skirmish line was formed under command of Colonel [Frederick] Benteen, to protect the descent of volunteers down the hill in front of the position to reach the water. A little was obtained in canteens, but many of the men were struck while obtaining the precious fluid. The fury of the attack was now over, and the Indians were seen going off in parties to the village. . . . About two o'clock in the afternoon the grass in the bottom was extensively fired by the Indians, and behind the dense smoke thus created, the hostile village began to move away. Between six and seven o'clock in the evening the village come out from behind this cloud of smoke and dust, the troops obtaining a full view of the cavalcade as it filed away in the direction of the Big Horn Mountains, moving in almost full military order. . . .

During the night of June 26th the troops under Reno changed position as to better secure a supply of water, and prepare against another assault, should the warriors return in strong force, but early in the morning of June 27th, while preparing to resist any attack that might be attempted, the dust of the moving column was seen approaching in the distance. Soon it was discovered to be troops who were coming, and, in a little while, a scout arrived with a note from General Terry to Custer, saying that some Crow scouts had come into camp, stating that he had been whipped, but that their story was not believed. About 10:30 o'clock in the morning, General Terry rode into Reno's lines, and the fate of General Custer was ascertained.

Precisely what was done by Custer's immediate command subsequent to the moment when the rest of the regiment last saw him alive, has remained partly a matter of conjecture, no officer or soldier who rode with him into the valley of the Little Big Horn having survived to tell the tale. The only real evidence of how they came to meet their fate was the testimony of the field where it overtook them. . . .

Custer's trail . . . passed along and in the rear of the crest of bluffs on the right bank for nearly or quite three miles. Then it came down to the bank of the river, but at once diverged from it again, as though Custer had unsuccessfully attempted to cross; then turning upon itself, and almost completing a circle, the trail ceased. It was marked by the remains of officers and men, and the bodies of horses, some of them dotted along the path, others heaped in ravines and upon knolls, where halts appeared to have been made. There was abundant evidence that a gallant resistance had been offered by Custer's troops, but they were beset on all sides by overpowering numbers.

READING 10

"MANY SOLDIERS FELL," TWO MOONS, 1898

For another perspective on the Battle of Little Bighorn, consider this eyewitness account. Two Moons, a Northern Cheyenne warrior who participated in the battle, was a chief of the Fox warrior society. Members of this group were "policemen" patrolling the northern end of the Indian encampment on June 25, 1876. Two Moons told his story to the writer Hamlin Garland two decades later.

That spring [March 1876] I was camped on Powder River with fifty lodges of my people—Cheyennes. The place is near what is now Fort McKenney. One morning the soldiers charged my camp. . . . We were surprised and scattered, leaving our ponies. The soldiers ran all our horses off. That night the soldiers slept, leaving the horses on one side; so we crept up and stole them back again, and then we went away.

We traveled far, and one day we met a big camp of Sioux at Charcoal Butte. We camped with the Sioux and had a good time, plenty grass, plenty game, good water. Crazy Horse was head chief of the camp. Sitting Bull was camped a little ways below, on the Little Missouri River. Crazy Horse said to me, "I'm glad you are come. We are going to fight the white man again."

The camp was already full of wounded men, women, and children. I said to Crazy Horse, "All right, I am ready to fight. I have fought already. My people have been killed, my horses stolen. I am satisfied to fight." I believed at the time the Great Spirits had made Sioux, put them there . . . and white men and Cheyennes here . . . expecting them to fight. The Great Spirits I thought liked to see them fight; it was to them all the same like playing. . . .

About May, when the grass was tall and the horses strong, we broke camp and started across the country to the mouth of the Tongue River. Then Sitting Bull and Crazy Horse and all went up the Rosebud. There we had a big fight with General [George] Crook, and whipped him. Many soldiers were killed—few Indians. It was a great fight, much smoke and dust.

In the Battle of Rosebud, June 17, 1876, about seven hundred Sioux and Cheyennes under Crazy Horse attacked Crook's thousand-man army and its three hundred Crow and Shoshone allies. Crook's troops suffered many casualties.

From there we all went over the divide, and camped in the valley of the Little Bighorn. Everybody thought, "Now we are out of the white man's country. He can live there, we will live here." After a few days, one morning when I was in camp north of Sitting Bull, a Sioux messenger rode up and said, "Let everybody paint up, cook, and ready for a big dance."

Cheyennes then went to work to cook, cut up tobacco, and get ready. We all thought to dance all day. We were very glad to think we were far away from the white man. I went to water my horses at the creek, and washed them off with cool water, then took a swim myself. I came back to the camp afoot. When I got near my lodge, I looked up the Little Bighorn toward Sitting Bull's camp. I saw a great dust rising. It looked like a whirlwind. Soon a Sioux horseman came rushing into camp shouting, "Soldiers come! Plenty white soldiers!"

I ran into my lodge, and said to my brother-in-law, "Get your horses; the white man is coming. Everybody run for horses." Outside, far up the valley, I heard a battle cry, *Hay-ay, hay-ay!* I heard shooting, too, this way, . . . I couldn't see any Indians. Everybody was getting horses and saddles. After I had caught my horse, a Sioux warrior came again and said, "Many soldiers are coming." Then he said to the women, "Get out of the way, we are going to have a hard fight."

I said, "All right, I am ready." I got on my horse, and rode out into my camp. I called out to the people all running about, "I am Two Moons, your chief. Don't run away. Stay here and fight. You must stay and fight the white soldiers. I shall stay even if I am to be killed."

I rode swiftly toward Sitting Bull's camp. There I saw white soldiers fighting in a line [Reno's detachment, which was to attack the southern end of the village, while Custer would attack from the northern end]. Indians covered the flat. They began to drive the soldiers all mixed up—Sioux, then soldiers, then more Sioux, and all shooting. The air was full of smoke and dust. I saw the soldiers fall back and drop into the riverbed like buffalo fleeing. They had no time to look for a crossing. The Sioux chased them up a hill, where they met more soldiers in wagons [Captain Benteen's detachment], and then messengers came saying more soldiers were going to kill the women, and the Sioux turned back. Chief Gall [a Hunkpapa warrior] was there fighting. Crazy Horse also.

Reno lost fifty-three men in his retreat—forty dead and thirteen wounded. His and Benteen's surviving soldiers dug in on a hilltop.

I then rode toward my camp, and stopped squaws from carrying off lodges. When I was sitting on my horse I saw flags come up over the hill to the east like that. . . . Then the soldiers rose all at once, all on horses. . . . They formed into three bunches with a little ways between. Then a bugle sounded, and they all got off horses, and some soldiers led the horses back over the hill.

Then the Sioux rode up the ridge on all sides, riding very fast. The Cheyennes went up the left way. Then the shooting was quick, quick. Pop-pop-pop, very fast. Some of the soldiers were down on their knees, some standing. Officers all in front. The smoke was like a great cloud, and everywhere the Sioux went the dust rose like smoke. We circled all round them—

swirling like water round a stone. We shoot, we ride fast, we shoot again. Soldiers drop, and horses fall on them. Soldiers in line drop, but one man rides up and down the line—all the time shouting. He rode a sorrel horse with white face and white forelegs. I don't know who he was. He was a brave man.

Indians kept swirling round and round, but the soldiers killed only a few. Many soldiers fell. At last all horses killed but five. Once in a while some man would break out and run toward the river, but he would fall. At last about a hundred men and five horsemen stood on the hill all bunched together. All along the bugler kept blowing his commands. He was very brave, too. Then a chief was killed. I hear it was Long Hair [Custer], I don't know; and then the five horsemen and the bunch of men, maybe forty, started toward the river. The man on the sorrel horse led them, shouting all the time. He wore a buckskin shirt, and had long black hair and mustache. He fought hard with a big knife. His men were all covered with white dust. I couldn't tell whether they were officers or not. One man all alone ran far down toward the river, then round up over the hill. I thought he was going to escape, but a Sioux fired and hit him in the head. He was the last man. He wore braid on his arms.

All the soldiers were now killed, and the bodies were stripped. After that no one could tell which were the officers. The bodies were left where they fell. We had no dance that night. We were sorrowful.

Other sources, contradicting Two Moons, state that the Northern Cheyennes did have a victory dance. Two Moons may have forgotten over the years, or perhaps he did not want to admit that a celebration had occurred after Custer's death.

The next day, four Sioux chiefs and two Cheyennes and I, Two Moons, went up on the battlefield to count the dead. One man carried a little bundle of sticks. When we came to dead men, we took a little stick and gave it to another man, so we counted the dead. There were 388 dead.

The army death count officially agreed upon was about 265: 225 from Custer's command, and 40 from Reno's detachment (Reno and Benteen themselves eventually escaped). Forty-six Indian scouts died. The discrepancy may have been due to Two Moons' faltering memory or a simple counting mistake. Or perhaps the stick tally included more Indian dead.

There were thirty-nine Sioux and seven Cheyennes killed, and about a hundred wounded. Some white soldiers were cut with knives to make sure they were dead; and the war women mangled some. Most of them were left just where they fell. We came to the man with the big mustache; he lay down the hills toward the river. The Indians did not take his buckskin shirt. The Sioux said, "That is a big chief. That is Long Hair." . . .

That day as the sun was getting low our young men came up the Little Bighorn riding hard. Many white soldiers were coming in a big boat, and when we looked we could see the smoke rising. I called my people together, and we hurried up the Little Bighorn, into Greasy Grass Valley. We camped there three days, and then rode swiftly back over our old trail to the east. Sitting Bull went back into the Rosebud and down the Yellowstone, and away to the north. I did not see him again.

READING 11

BUFFALO SOLDIERS IN THE DESERT, CHARLES COOPER, 1877

> *Not all the tales of soldiers in the American West were stories of depravity and defeat; there were tales of triumph over adversity as well. Here Lieutenant Charles Cooper describes an ordeal endured by the Tenth Cavalry, a black unit among those known as the Buffalo Soldiers. For three and a half days in 1877 these men struggled in the Texas desert without water and without much hope. Their perseverance is a testament to the hardiness of many who faced the difficult conditions of the American West.*

[W]e were to make a supply camp at some convenient point, and manoeuvre from there in pursuit of depradating Indians, as also to protect settlers who are rapidly populating this region of the country. . . .

[After trailing the Indians for several days, we found ourselves] lost on the Staked Plains [of Texas], without water and no prospects of getting any, as we did not know which way to go for it, and from our experience we knew the greater part of the country was "dry as a bone."

In the meantime our men had been dropping from their horses with exhaustion, as we had been nearly two days without water, and we were retarded greatly in endeavoring to keep the men together. . . .

[The next day] the men were almost completely used up, and the captain and I were not much better. Our men had dropped back, one by one, unable to keep up with us; their tongues and throats were swollen, and they were unable even to swallow their saliva—in fact, they had no saliva to swallow, that is if I judge of their condition from my own. My tongue and throat were so dry that when I put a few morsels of brown sugar, that I found in my pocket, into my mouth, I was unable to dissolve it in order to swallow it. During this time while lying on the ground, one of my private horses showed signs of exhaustion, staggered, and fell; so, in order to relieve the men, I had his throat cut, and the blood distributed among them. The captain and I drank heartily of the steaming blood. . . .

This, our fourth day without water, was dreadful. . . . Men gasping in death around us; horses falling dead to the right and left; the crazed survivors of our men fighting each his neighbor for the blood of the horses. . . . We left camp at 8 o'clock at night, and travelled until about 3 the next morning. . . . The captain and I travelled some five miles . . . and finally reached Double Lake, completely exhausted. We found there six of the men of our company, whom we had missed, and immediately started them out with canteens of water for their suffering comrades. Our loss on the trip was four men [out of a company of 61] died from thirst. . . .

CHAPTER 11

COWBOYS AND COWMEN

CHAPTER 1 examined the cowboy as symbol of the American western experience. Like many legends, cowboy mythology was based upon equal parts romance and hard truth. The cowpoke of popular culture—the independent, laconic Knight of the Plains—was based in reality: these characters existed, but their exploits were either slightly exaggerated or grossly overstated. The cowboys (or "cowmen" as they preferred to be called) of historical fact were remarkable in their own right. Hard-working, skilled, adventurous, and self-reliant to a fault, they could also be as harsh and unforgiving as the landscape they roamed. Certainly not all cowboys were admirable—there were racists, scofflaws, goldbricks, fools, and scoundrels among them—but most were simply doing their best in an often dangerous occupation. They were, as Philip Ashton Rollins stated in his 1922 book, *The Cowboy*, "merely folks, just plain, every-day, bow-legged humans."

The cowboy culture still exists today, but the romantic Wild West, open-range legend we are most familiar with was a short-lived phenomenon, lasting only from about 1865 to 1887. By then, brutal winters had killed almost 90 percent of the cattle, and increased settlement was bringing an end to the open range. Thereafter, the cattle kingdom consisted primarily of ranch-based operations. Yet of all the individuals that populated the nineteenth-century American West, it is the cowboy that has had the greatest historical and cultural resonance.

In this chapter the readings provide some details to flesh out the myth. They were chosen in an effort to steer away from the image and present historical reality. It is an inescapable fact, however, that the descriptions and accounts of the time often intermingle actuality with legend. A culture is developed from fact, tradition, expectation, hope, imagination, and attitude, and the cowboy culture is no exception. From the beginning what people thought the cowboys represented was often as important as what the cowboys actually were—and the writings of the period reflect that viewpoint.

Thus in the contemporary historical record of the activities and attitudes of the cowboys, a conjunction between facts and myth sometimes occurs.

⌒

"Pioneers of civilization," Theodore Roosevelt, 1888

One of the most interesting lives of an American westerner was led by, of all things, an American easterner—Theodore Roosevelt. In the 1880s the young Roosevelt owned and operated a cattle ranch in the Dakota badlands. In an article for Century Magazine *he describes the methods and processes of establishing and running a western cattle ranch—including the role of the cowboy. Although Roosevelt's writing is infused with cultural biases and racial prejudices, and his view of cattle ranchers as the "pioneers of civilization" is open to argument, the thoroughness of his account is not in question.*

[T]he herds are set in motion as early in the spring as may be, so as to get on the ground in time to let the travel-worn beasts rest and gain flesh before winter sets in. Each herd is accompanied by a dozen, or a score, or a couple of score of cowboys, according to its size, and beside it rumble and jolt the heavy four-horse wagons that hold the food and bedding of the men and the few implements they will need at the end of the journey. As long as possible they follow the trails made by the herds that have already traveled in the same direction, and when these end they strike out for themselves. In the upper Missouri basin, the pioneer herds soon had to scatter out and each find its own way among the great dreary solitudes, creeping carefully along so that the cattle might not be overdriven and might have water at the halting places. An outfit might thus be months on its lonely journey, slowly making its way over melancholy, pathless plains, or down the valleys of lonely rivers. It was a tedious, harassing work, as the weary cattle had to be driven carefully and quietly during the day and strictly guarded at night, with a perpetual watch kept for Indians or white horse-thieves. Often they would skirt the edges of streams for days at a time, seeking a ford or a good swimming crossing, and if the water was up and the quicksand deep the danger to the riders was serious and the risk of loss among the cattle very great.

At last, after days of excitement and danger and after months of dreary, monotonous toil, the chosen ground is reached and the final camp pitched. The footsore animals are turned loose to shift for themselves, outlying camps of two or three men being established to hem them in. Meanwhile the primitive ranch-house, out-buildings, and corrals are built, the unhewn cottonwood logs being chinked with moss and mud, while the roofs are of branches covered with dirt, spades and axes being the only tools needed for the work. Bunks, chairs, and tables are all homemade, and as rough as the houses they are in. The supplies, of coarse, rude food are carried perhaps two or three hundred miles from the nearest town, either in the ranch-wagons or else by some regular freighting outfit, whose huge canvas-topped prairie schooners are each drawn by several yoke of oxen, or perhaps by six or eight mules. . . .

The small outlying camps are often tents, or mere dugouts in the ground. But at the main ranch there will be a cluster of log buildings, including a separate cabin for the foreman or ranchman; often another in which to cook and eat; a long house for the men to sleep in; stables, sheds, a blacksmith's shop, etc.—the whole group forming quite a little settlement, with the corrals, the stacks of natural hay, and the patches of fenced land for gardens or horse pastures. This little settlement might be situated right out in the treeless, nearly level open, but much more often is placed in the partly wooded bottom of a creek or river, sheltered by the usual background of somber brown hills.

When the northern plains began to be settled, such a ranch would at first be absolutely alone in the wilderness, but others of the same sort were sure soon to be established within twenty or thirty miles on one side or the other. The lives of the men in such places were strangely cut off from the outside world, and, indeed, the same is true to a hardly less extent at the present day [1888]. Sometimes the wagons are sent for provisions, and the beef-steers are at stated times driven off for shipment. Parties of hunters and trappers call now and then. More rarely small bands of emigrants go by in search of new homes. . . . But this is all. Civilization seems as remote as if we were living in an age long past. The whole existence is patriarchal in character; it is the life of men who live in the open, who tend their herds on horseback, who go armed and ready to guard their lives by their own prowess, whose wants are very simple, and who call no man master. . . .

All cattle are branded, usually on the hip, shoulder, and side, or on any one of them, with letters, numbers, or figures, in every combination, the outfit being known by its brand. Near me, for instance, are the Three Sevens, the Thistle, the Bellows, the ox, the vi. . . . All brands are registered, and thus protected against imitators, any man tampering with them being punished as severely as possible. Unbranded animals are called mavericks, and when found on the round-up are either branded by the owner of the range on which they are, or else are sold for the benefit of the [stockmen's or stockgrowers'] association. At every shipping point, as well as where the beef cattle are received, there are stock inspectors who jealously examine all the brands on the live animals or on the hides of the slaughtered ones, so as to determine any foul play, which is immediately reported to the association. It becomes second nature with a cowboy to inspect and note the brands of every bunch of animals he comes across. . . .

The ranching industry itself was copied from the Mexicans, of whose land and herds the Southwestern frontiersman of Texas took forcible possession; and the traveler in the Northwest will see at a glance that the terms and practices of our business are largely of Spanish origin. The cruel curb-bit and heavy stock-saddle, with its high horn and cantle, prove that we have adopted Spanish-American horse-gear; and the broad hat, huge blunt spurs, and leather *chaperajos* of the rider, as well as the corral in which the stocks are penned, all alike show the same ancestry. Throughout the cattle country east of the Rocky Mountains, from the Rio Grande to the Saskatchewan, the same terms are in use and the same system is followed. . . .

The ranchowners differ more from each other than do the cowboys; and the former certainly compare favorably with similar classes of capitalists in the East. Anything more foolish than the demagogic outcry against "cattle kings" it would be difficult to imagine. Indeed, there are very few businesses so absolutely legitimate as stock-raising and so beneficial to the nation at large. . . . Stockmen in the West are the pioneers of civilization, and their daring and adventurousness make the after settlement of the region possible. The whole country owes them a great debt. . . . Stockmen are learning more and more to act together; and certainly the meetings of their associations are conducted with a dignity and good sense that would do credit to any parliamentary body. . . .

But the cowboys resemble one another much more and outsiders much less than is the case even with their employers, the ranchmen. A town in the cattle county, when for some cause it is thronged with men from the neighborhood about, always presents a picturesque sight on the wooden sidewalks of the broad, dusty streets. The men who ply the various industries known only to frontier existence jostle one another as they saunter to and fro or lounge lazily in front of the straggling, cheap-looking board houses. . . . If the town is on the borders of the mountain country, there will also be sinewy lumbermen, rough-looking miners, and packers, whose business it is to guide the long mule trains that go where wagons cannot and whose work in packing needs special and peculiar skill. And mingled with and drawn from all these classes are desperadoes of every grade, from the gambler up through the horse-thief to the murderous professional bully, or, as he is locally called, "bad man"—now, however, a much less conspicuous object than formerly.

But everywhere among these plainsmen and mountainmen, and more important than any, are the cowboys—the men who follow the calling that has brought such towns into being. Singly, or in twos or threes, they gallop their wiry little horses down the street. . . . When drunk on the villainous whisky of the frontier towns, they cut mad antics, riding their horses into the saloons, firing their pistols right and left, from boisterous light-heartedness rather than from any viciousness, and indulging too often in deadly shooting affrays, brought on either by the accidental contact of the moment or on account of some long-standing grudge, or perhaps because of bad blood between two ranches or localities; but except while on such sprees they are quiet, rather self-contained men, perfectly frank and simple. . . .

READING 2

"A MAN SUITED FOR HIS TIMES," EMERSON HOUGH, 1898

Often, as time passes, history and legend merge into a concoction where one element cannot be distinguished from the other. Historical scholarship has done an admirable and comprehensive analysis of the realities of the cowboy culture, but there is a gnawing sense that the myth still influences the history or, perhaps, that the history still animates the myth. One can only examine the contemporary accounts and hope to draw appropriate conclusions. Whether they contain hyperbole and exaggeration or straightforward journalistic documentation, these accounts represent at least part of the evidence needed to answer a seemingly simple question but one that is actually very complete: "What was the typical cowboy like?"

Emerson Hough's attempt to answer it in his book The Story of the

Cowboy reflects the problems: his description is part fact, part romantic fiction, and part lyrical apotheosis.

What was really the life of this child of the wild region of America, and what were the conditions of the life that bore him can never be fully known by those who have not seen the West with wide eyes. Those who did not, but who looked superficially and superciliously, remembering only their own surroundings, and forgetting that in the eye of Nature one creature is as good as another if only it prevail where it stands, were content with distorted views of that which they saw about them. Having no perspective in their souls, how could they find it in their eyes? They saw color but not form in these wild men of the wild country. They saw traits but did not see the character beneath them. Seeking to tell of that which they had not seen, they became inaccurate and unjust. Dallying with the pleasant sensation of exciting themes, they became grotesque instead of strong in their handling of them.

The cowboy was simply a part of the West. He who did not understand the one could never understand the other. Never was any character more misunderstood than he; and so thorough was his misrepresentation that part of the public even today will have no other way of looking at him. They see the wide hat and not the honest face beneath it. They remember the wild momentary freaks of man, but forget his lifetime of hard work and patient faithfulness. They insist upon the distorted mask and ask not for the soul beneath it. If we care truly to see the cowboy as he was, and seek to give our wish the dignity of a real purpose, the first intention should be to study the cowboy in connection with his surroundings. Then perhaps we may not fail in our purpose, but come near to seeing him as he actually was, the product of primitive, chaotic, elemental forces, rough, barbarous, and strong. Then we shall love him because at heart each of us is a barbarian, too, and longing for that past the ictus of whose heredity we can never eliminate from out our blood. Then we shall feel him appeal to something hid deep down in our common nature. And this is the way we should look at the cowboy of the passing West; not as a curiosity, but as a product; not as an eccentric driver of horned cattle, but as a man suited to his times.

An Englishman Describes the "Cow Boy," 1887

> *The English were particularly fascinated by the American West—both its culture*
> *and its economic opportunities. Wealthy Britons established cattle ranches or*
> *invested heavily in the cattle kingdom, and there were English cowboys (see*
> *reading 4). English visitors wrote detailed accounts of their experiences. One of*
> *these, who identified himself only as "Bunny," published an exuberant narrative*
> *titled* Two Years a Cow-Boy & Life on the Prairie among the Indians
> & Back Woods of America. *Among the interesting descriptions he provides is*
> *his characterization of the "Cow Boy"—a more straightforward presentation*
> *than that of Emerson Hough (reading 2).*

Cow Boy is the name given to every man, irrespective of his age, who lives on the prairies and is engaged in the management or handling of cattle in the manner peculiar to that part of the continent of North America which forms the great stock-raising country of the United States and Canada.

The genuine specimen of a Western cow boy is beyond description and is only to be seen to be admired.

His dress generally consists of "chapps," which are a peculiar kind of leather leggings reaching to the hips and covering the whole of the legs, with a ragged fringe of thongs hanging from the outside seams, a red or blue flannel shirt, and a large slouch hat, ornamented with a dried rattlesnake or other strange band.

Add to this somewhat startling attire, a gaudy handkerchief, loosely tied round the neck, a belt, with bowie-knife and brace of pistols, not forgetting an enormous pair of Spanish spurs, and you have something of the dress....

As a rule, the cow boy proper has been nothing else from his youth, and would not be, if he had the finest opportunities.

He lives mostly in the open air, and is the most reckless, devil-may-care, light-hearted man to be met in creation; ever ready to help a friend, or resent an insult, and as free with his money as his pistol.

Unlike most boys in America, he does not aspire to be President, and the height of his ambition is to be boss cow boy, and never to be beaten at anything pertaining to his profession, the art of which is chiefly riding and throwing the lasso. In a word, his virtues are many, and his vices few, worst of the latter being the propensity for gambling and shooting.

Of course, as in every other class of society, there are exceptions. I have seen some of the best, and others of the worst, and they each excel in their respective qualities.

READING 4
THE ROUNDUP, JOHN BAUMANN, 1887

For the cowboy, the beginning of the end in raising cattle was the roundup— collecting the herd in preparation for the drive to market. Here John Baumann, another English visitor to the American West, describes his experience with a roundup.

At last we are ready; our boss gives final instructions with regard to the circle each man will have to ride, and the exact spot towards which we are to converge by midday. No, we are not off yet; look at yon dun broncho ridden by a young hand; his stride is short and jerky, he is fetching at his bridle in an ominous manner, his ears laid back, and his long tail tight between his hind quarters; should he succeed in getting his head down or detect the slightest symptom of nervousness in his rider, we shall see some fun. He stops, shies half round, and with a vicious squeal pitches high into the air; his rider is already clutching the horn of his saddle, another buck and he is hanging on by the mane, yet another, and he is sprawling on the ground. Yoicks, gone away! We all gallop after the riderless brute, swinging our lassoes exultingly round our heads, and in a few minutes he is dragged sullenly back to his crestfallen rider, who with his blood now fairly roused, remounts full of vengeful resolve, and this time succeeds in proving himself master.

But now to our work. We cross the river at a wild spot where its banks are formed by steep bluffs studded with cactus and prickly pears; cypress, cedar, and maple nestling at their base. A steep, narrow gorge leads to wide plains, bounded by a low range of flat-topped antelope hills. Up this gorge the circle-riders make their way, and dividing into couples, start at a lope for the lurking-places of the cattle. Creek, shady canon, and arroyo are searched, and after many a chase after wilful calf or sullen bull, a goodly round up of seven or eight hundred head is formed.

"So—o, so—o, so gently, lads; hold them together! Gallop round them; head back that little column led by a frightened steer. Quick! quick! or by the powers the whole herd will be off." Good! our little cow-ponies can go like the wind for a short distance; can turn and twist, and stop in the twinkling of an eye (sharper, indeed, than suits the seat of an awkward horseman); the fugitives are pressed back, bellowing loud protest the while. But now the whole mass is violently agitated; a couple of sharp-horned Texas bulls have come foul of each other. Quickly a space is cleared around them; they stand face to face glaring and snorting, with heads lowered, and defiantly tearing up clouds of dust till one or the other rushes to the attack. With a crash their heads meet; they sway about for a moment with locked horns; separate, retreat, and dash together again forehead to forehead, with all their strength and fury concentrated into that ferocious collision, until at length, after a combat lasting several minutes, the weaker turns tail and leaves his victor triumphant.

It is a wild and variegated spectacle, this mass of tangled and tossing horns. Rough, poor-looking cows, with calves as pretty as paint; savage, long-horned Texans; handsome, bald-faced Herefords; big, black, hornless Galloways; broad-browed shorthorn bulls, all thoroughbreds, intermingle with nondescript grades of all sizes and ages. They have not yet quite shed their winter coats, or the big brands on shoulder, side, and hip would stand out more distinctly. They are ear-marked in every conceivable manner, from the becoming underslope to the disfiguring grub, which leaves a mere stump in the place of an ear. All are in lean condition, not having filled out yet on the juicy and fattening grasses which will shortly ripen as the season advances, but they look bright-eyed, clean, and healthy, with the exception of a few locoed beasts, whose dull, stupid eyes, mangy coats, and clumsy, purposeless movements, prove them to have indulged in orgies of the fatal plant [locoweed]. . . .

Tom Connor, range foreman of some fifty thousand head of cattle, is for the moment our "big chief," for it is on his ground that we are working. Tall, good-looking, and somewhat of a prairie "dude" in appearance, he is now the centre of a group of men awaiting his instructions. Some half-a-dozen of these, mounted on well-trained cutting-ponies, proceed quietly to enter the herd and wind their way in and out among the cattle until they mark one of their own brands. With a smart cut from the rawhide quirt a young steer is set in motion; whichever way he twists and turns he find the relentless horseman at his heels, and is forced against his will to the outskirts of the herd. Why should he leave his companions? He makes a sudden desperate turn, and rushes among them again. Before the eager little pony has had time to follow, he has succeeded in diving well into their midst. Leave him there for the present; he is on the alert now, and will be "mean to cut"; these youngsters, be they bull, heifer, or steer, always are. Others have been more successful; animals are being separated from the main bunch on all sides, and sent trotting in the direction of the respective cuts.

It is an animated, blood-stirring scene. The cuts are "held" by cowboys, who are tearing about in their endeavours to keep the beasts together. The cutting-ponies are dodging and turning with marvellous rapidity and sagacity, appearing almost to anticipate the movements of the pursued. The air is filled with smoke-like clouds of dust and the ground trembles with the thunder of many hoofs. By the time the sun nears the horizon the big round-up has been divided into several bunches, which are being slowly moved to their respective bedding-grounds, there to be held by night guards until the following day, when they will be day-herded and driven to our next camping-place. Both men and horses are dog-tired. We have changed our mounts after the mid-day meal, it is true, but the ground is rough, the work has been fast and furious. Our wiry little ponies, standing barely over fourteen hands, have to carry saddles weighing full forty pounds, and in many cases big, strapping fellows who, riding purely by balance and with a loose seat, are all over their backs, when the clever little animals dart about after cattle. They are, besides, roughly used, getting no praise or encouragement for work willingly done, but whip, spurs, and oaths for the slightest mistake. One form of suffering so common to their kind they certainly do escape. Their riders are light of hand, the enormous Mexican spade-bit hangs loosely in their mouths, and it is rarely that they are made to realise its full power. Their heads are now turned towards camp, and they make an effort to gallop in gaily. We off-saddle and coil up our lariats to catch our night-horses out of the bunch which the horse-rustler is holding in readiness for us, saddle them, stake them out, and leave them there until our turn comes to go out on "night guard"; hobble the remainder of the bunch and let them wander off at their own sweet will. The day's work is done!

READING 5

THE TRAIL DRIVE, CLARENCE GORDON, 1883; ANDY ADAMS, 1903

After the roundup was completed, if the cattle were to be driven to a railhead shipping point, the organization of the "trail herd" was crucial. It was the

responsibility of a driver variously called the "trail boss" or "drover" to secure the
kind of cattle the buyer desired, hire the cowboys, and complete the drive as
profitably as possible. Many ranch owners drove their own cattle to the railheads
(which were primarily in Kansas), but by the 1870s professional, contracted
drovers had become more common. Here Clarence Gordon, an agricultural agent,
describes the logistics of a trail drive in 1883.

Early in the year, the drover goes to that region of the state [in this case, Texas] where he expects to find suitable stock and visits the various ranches. Having bought the cattle and arranged with the sellers to deliver his purchases on a fixed day at a certain point, he goes to some horse ranch and buys such a lot of horses as shall carry his drove through, say 40 horses for each average drove of 2,300 to 2,500 cattle. He also engages about a dozen cowboys for each drove, at the rate of $25 to $30 per month, and a "boss" drover as captain and field manager of the stock, equipment, and men, at $90 per month. Having made these engagements, and purchased a camp-wagon [chuck wagon], team [usually two yokes of oxen or four mules], cooking utensils, and other necessities of an outfit, he is ready to receive his purchases, only enough coming in at a time to make one drove, which is road-branded [in 1871 the Texas legislature passed a law that required a distinctive brand to be placed on the shoulder of cattle being driven to market], and is then started out on the trail. So the deliveries go on until all his droves are under way. When first put on the road the cattle are closely guarded and driven briskly for several days, until the danger of their breaking away for home is passed. For the first few days at sunset the drove is "rounded up" compactly, and half of the men, relieved by the other half at midnight, ride round and round the bed-ground. This labor decreases as the cattle become tractable, and two men at each watch are then sufficient to guard them through the night. The ordinary order of march is the foreman ahead, searching for camping place with grass and water, the drove drifting onward in the shape of a wedge, the strong few stretching out to a sharp point in front, then the line growing thicker and wider, until in the butt end is crowded the mass. On each side of the lead rides a man on "point," that is, to direct the column. Back where the line begins to swell ride two more at "swing," further back ride two at "flank," and the remainder are on "drag," while the cowboys experienced in driving hold the places at "point," the post of honor. These distinctions are observed at mess and bed. One man drives the horse herd apart from the line of cattle, or, with large bands, two men are employed. The distance traveled each day is 12 or 15 miles, according to grass and water. At daybreak the cattle are moved off the "bed-ground" to graze, and while the two men who were last on guard remain with them all other hands breakfast. The first to finish breakfast relieve the guards on duty and allow them to come in for their morning meal. Then, the horses being caught and saddled, and the cook having cleaned up, the drive is started and continued until about eleven, when the cattle are allowed to graze again, and lunch or dinner is eaten. Immediately after that the men who are to stand first guard at night, and who also act as horse-herders, go on ahead with the mess-wagon and the horses to the next camp, where they get supper, so that when the herd comes up they are ready to "graze," and hold it until the first relief of the night. The bed-ground is, when possible, on elevation, with space sufficient for all the stock to sleep. The men off guard roll themselves in their blankets without removing their clothing and lie down on the ground near the camp-fire to sleep.

The "Long Drives," often exercises is simple drudgery, could on occasion become eerie endurance tests. Such an event was recounted by Andy Adams in his 1903 novel The Log of a Cowboy. *As Ramon F. Adams, a leading collector and compiler of the early cowboy historical record, points out in* The Old-Time Cowhand *and elsewhere, Adams's carefully researched fiction is still one of the best descriptions of the trail drive extant.*

The first week after leaving San Antonio, our foreman scouted in quest of water a full day in advance of the herd. One evening he returned to us with the news that we were in for a dry drive, for after passing the next chain of lakes it was sixty miles to the next water, and reports regarding the water supply even after crossing this arid stretch were very conflicting.

"While I know every foot of this trail through here," said the foreman, "there's several things that look scaly. There are only five herds ahead of us, and the first three went through the old route, but the last two, after passing Indian Lakes, for some reason or other turned and went westward. These last herds may be stock cattle, pushing out west to new ranges; but I don't like the outlook. It would take me two days to ride across and back, and by that time we could be two thirds of the way through. I've made this drive before without a drop of water on the way, and wouldn't dread it now, if there was any certainty of water at the other end. I reckon there's nothing to do but tackle her; but isn't this a hell of a country? I've ridden fifty miles to-day and never saw a soul."

The Indian Lakes, some seven in number, were natural reservoirs with rocky bottoms, and about a mile apart. We watered at ten o'clock the next day, and by night camped fifteen miles on our way. There was plenty of good grazing for the cattle and horses, and no trouble was experienced the first night. McCann had filled an extra twenty gallon keg for this trip. Water was too precious an article to be lavish with, so we shook the dust from our clothing and went unwashed. This was no serious deprivation, and no one could be critical of another, for we were all equally dusty and dirty. The next morning by daybreak the cattle were thrown off the bed ground and started grazing before the sun could dry out what little moisture the grass had absorbed during the night. The heat of the past week had been very oppressive, and in order to avoid it as much as possible, we made late and early drives. Before the wagon passed the herd during the morning drive, what few canteens we had were filled with water for the men. The *remuda* [the herd of cow ponies] was kept with the [cattle] herd, and four changes of mounts were made during the day, in order not to exhaust any one horse. Several times for an hour or more, the herd was allowed to lie down and rest; but by the middle of the afternoon thirst made them impatient and restless, and the point men were compelled to ride steadily in the lead in order to hold the cattle to a walk. A number of times during the afternoon we attempted to graze them, but not until the twilight of evening was it possible.

After the fourth change of horses was made, Moneyman pushed on ahead with the saddle stock and overtook the wagon. Under Flood's orders he was to tie up all the night horses, for if the cattle could be induced to graze, we would not bed them down before ten that night, and all hands would be required with the herd. McCann had instructions to make camp on the divide, which was known to be twenty-five miles from our camp of the night before, or forty miles from the Indian Lakes. As we expected, the cattle grazed willingly after nightfall, and with a fair moon, we allowed them to scatter freely while grazing forward. The beacon of McCann's fire on the divide was in sight over an hour before the herd grazed up to camp, all hands remaining to bed the thirsty cattle. The herd was given triple the amount of space usually required for bedding, and even then for nearly an hour scarcely half of them lay down.

We were handling the cattle as humanely as possible under the circumstances. The guards for the night were doubled, six men on the first half and the same on the latter. . . . If any of us got more than an hour's sleep that night, he was lucky. . . . To those of us who could find time to eat, our cook kept open house. Our foreman knew that a well-fed man can stand an incredible amount of hardship and appreciated the fact that on the trail a good cook is a valuable asset. Our outfit therefore was cheerful to a man, and jokes and songs helped to while away the weary hours of the night.

The second guard . . . pushed the cattle off their beds an hour before dawn, and before they were relieved had urged the herd more than five miles on the third day's drive over this waterless mesa. In spite of our economy of water, after breakfast on this third morning there was scarcely enough left to fill the canteens for the day. In view of this, we could promise ourselves no midday meal—except a can of tomatoes to the man; so the wagon was ordered to drive through to the expected water ahead, while the saddle horses were held available as on the day before the middle of the forenoon, the cattle lolled their tongues in despair, while their sullen lowing surged through from rear to lead and back again in piteous yet ominous appeal. The only relief we could offer was to travel them slowly, as they spurned every opportunity offered them either to graze or to lie down.

It was nearly noon when we reached the last divide, and sighted the scattering timber of the expected watercourse. The enforced order of the day before—to hold the herd in a walk and prevent exertion and heating— now required four men in the lead [twice the usual number], while the rear followed over a mile behind, dogged and sullen. Near the middle of the afternoon, McCann returned on one of his mules with the word that it was a question if there was water enough to water even the horse stock. The preceding outfit, so he reported, had dug a shallow well in the bed of the creek, from which he had filled his kegs, but the stock water was a mere loblolly. On receipt of the news, we changed mounts for the fifth time that day, . . . and the horse wrangler, pushed on ahead with the *remuda* to the waterless stream.

The outlook was anything but encouraging. Flood and Forrest scouted the creek up and down for ten miles in a fruitless search for water. The outfit held the herd back until the twilight of evening. . . .

Holding the herd this third night required all hands. Only a few men at a time were allowed to go into camp and eat, for the herd refused even to lie down. What few cattle attempted to rest were prevented by the more rest-less ones. By spells they would mill, until riders were sent through the herd at a breakneck pace to break up the groups. During these milling efforts of the herd, we drifted over a mile from camp; but by the light of moon and stars and the number of riders, scattering was prevented. As the horses were loose for the night, we could not start them on the trail until daybreak gave us a change of mounts, so we lost the early start of the morning before.

Good cloudy weather would have saved us, but in its stead was a sultry morning without a breath of air, which bespoke another day of sizzling heat. We had not been on trail over two hours before the heat became almost unbearable to man and beast. Had it not been for the condition of the herd, all might yet have gone well; but over three days had now elapsed without water for the cattle, and they became feverish and ungovernable. The lead cattle turned back several times, wandering aimlessly in any direction, and it was with considerable difficulty that the herd could be held on the trail. The rear overtook the lead, and the cattle gradually lost all semblance of a trail herd. Our horses were fresh, however, and after about two hours' work, we once more got the herd strung out in trailing fashion; but before a mile had been covered, the leaders again turned, and the cattle congregated into a mass of unmanageable animals, milling and lowing in their fever and thirst. The milling only intensified their sufferings from the heat, and the outfit split and quartered them again and again, in the hope that this unfortunate outbreak might be checked. No sooner was the milling stopped than they would surge hither and yon, sometimes half a mile, as ungovernable as the waves of an ocean. After wasting several hours in this manner, they finally turned back over the trail, and the utmost efforts of every man in the outfit failed to check them. We threw our ropes in their faces, and when this failed, we resorted to shooting; but in defiance at the fusillade and the smoke they walked sullenly through the line of horsemen across their front. Six-shooters were discharged so close to the leaders' faces as to singe their hair, yet, under a noonday sun, they disregarded this and every other device to turn them, and passed wholly out of our control. In a number of instances wild steers deliberately walked against our horses, and then for the first time a fact dawned on us that chilled the marrow in our bones,—*the herd was going blind.*

STAMPEDE, ANONYMOUS, 1870; CHARLES J. STEEDMAN, 1904

Of all the occurrences that could make a trail drive something more than routine,
the most feared was a stampede, when the animals would break from the herd
and run uncontrollably. According to Charles Goodnight, the famous Texas
cattleman of the 1860s and 1870s after whom the Goodnight-Loving cattle trail is
partially named, "When the cattle are first started, the risk of stampedes is great.
They are nervous and easily frightened, the slightest noise may startle them into
running. Some cattle are stampeders by nature. The greatest losses occurred at
night when all was utter confusion." In the 1870s an unidentified observer (quoted
in Clarence Gordon's 1883 report) wrote about the efforts taken to forestall a
stampede.

A herd traveling with calves cannot make 12 miles per day. A "mixed"
herd—that is, one made up of various ages and of both sexes—is the easiest
to control; a beef-herd of four-year-olds is the most difficult. The slightest
disturbance at night may stampede them. The first symptom of alarm is
snorting. Then, if the guards are numerous and alert, so that the cattle
cannot easily break away, they will begin "milling," i.e., crowding together
with their heads toward a common center, their horns clashing, and the
whole body in confused rotary motion, which increases, and, unless controlled, ends in a concentrated outbreak and stampede. The most effectual
way of quieting the cattle is by the cowboys circling around and around the
terrified herd, singing loudly and steadily, while too, the guards strive to
disorder the "milling" by breaking up the common movement, separating a
bunch here and there from the mass and turning them off, so that the
sympathy of panic shall be dispersed and their attention distracted, as it is in
part, no doubt, by the singing. The somber surroundings of a wild country
at night, with the accompanying strange sounds—the tramp, the clashing of
horns, the bellowings of alarm, and the shouted song of the cowboys—are
very weird.

According to Peter Watts in his 1977 Dictionary of the Old West, *cattle*
"were known to take to their heels at the snapping of a twig, the approach or
arrival of a storm, or the sudden movement of a rabbit. Some herds stampeded a
dozen times on the trail from Texas to the railhead in Kansas, with the

unfortunate trail-boss losing animals each time he rounded them up." Charles J. Steedman's Bucking the Sagebrush; or, The Oregon Trail in the Seventies *describes a "wild night" in which three herds stampeded simultaneously in a lightning storm. Here Steedman recounts the response of the cowboys.*

A day or two after I joined the herd we had about as wild a night as I ever saw or want to see. . . .

. . . The crash of the elements and the tramping of the horses, added to the bawling of the rapidly approaching cattle, the yells and the oaths of the men, created a symphony that was calculated to raise hair on anything that lived in the particular neighborhood. . . .

The main thought was to get on to something with four legs, and either head off those bellowing brutes that were coming through a black night on a dead run, with forked lightning prodding them in the rump at every jump, or else get into a hole and pull it in after us. Just then the rain came. . . .

Men work pretty fast under pressure, and it was not long before we were in the saddle and striking out in the direction in which we thought the herd was. A flash, a series of flashes, of lightning showed me a bunch of steers stampeding and running east about two hundred yards off. The next flash revealed old Flatteau and Riley [two cowboys] going like the wind in the opposite direction. Flatteau's linen duster was about the same color as Riley, and the lightning made them look like a phantom as they disappeared.

Of all the mixed-up messes one can imagine, this was the worst. The expected had happened, and, evidently, the whole three herds had come together, making a bunch of between eight and nine thousand head. [My horse] Coalie showed his intelligence. When the ground was right he would run his best, but when we came to pitfalls he knew it and was cautious. We slid down bluffs and jumped into gullies and out, but never a misstep or stumble. I lost all track of direction or distance, but soon found myself, or, rather, felt myself in the immediate vicinity of quite a bunch of animals that had come to a halt and evidently were telling one another how foolish it was for others to be frightened about nothing. I knew their terror was over, for they were mooing, not bawling. By this time the worst of the storm had passed, and before long the stars began to show in places, although the thunder and lightning continued.

CATTLE PRICES AND QUALITY, SOLON ROBINSON, 1854

The purpose of the cattle drive was not adventure but profit. All the hard work
and danger were focused on making as much money per head as possible. Solon
Robinson, a reporter for the New York Daily Tribune, *here comments on the*
sale of Texas cattle arriving in New York City in July 1854.

Another thing is demonstrated in the yards to-day, which proves that cattle
can be brought two thousand miles with profit to the drovers, and sold at
such prices as prevail to-day. . . . From Illinois here the expense is $17 a
head. . . . The top of the drove are good quality of beef, and all are fair. A lot
of twenty-one, short 8 cwt., sold to Weeks at $80, and a good many others
sold at 10 [cents per pound]. These cattle are generally 5, 6, and 7 years old,
rather long-legged, though fine horned, with long taper horns, and something of a wild look [Robinson is describing Longhorns]. Some of them are
the descendants of a most excellent breed of cattle from the South, originally imported by the Spaniards, and generally known in all the southwestern States as Spanish cattle. It is said that the meat of this description of
stock is fine-grained and close, somewhat like venison, and apt to be a little
tough cooked in the ordinary way, and therefore not as good to eat fresh as
that of cattle of a more domestic character. This will be somewhat changed
by purchasing them young and feeding them two years as well as this drove
has been fed one year.

READING 8
COWBOY ETHNICITY AND PAY, ANONYMOUS, 1905

The ethnic mix of the cowboys was as varied as the landscape. There were Euro-
Americans, Mexicans, Hispanic Americans, African Americans, Native
Americans, and Englishmen, plus a smattering from other cultures.
It is estimated that about a third were Mexican Americans, inheritors of the
long-standing cattle tradition of the Spanish and Mexican eras of the American
West (in fact, "buckaroo" is a corruption of the Spanish word for cowboy,
vaquero). *From them many other cowboys learned skills that were especially*
useful in arid regions.
Historians believe that 15 to 25 percent of all cowboys in the American West

were African Americans, mostly former slaves who moved westward to take
advantage of job opportunities and independence in the cattle kingdom.
Unfortunately, however skillful they became with the horse and the rope, it
is indisputable that discrimination and prejudice negatively influenced the
relationship between cowboys of the dominant culture and minority cowhands.

Here an anonymous writer comments on the relationships among cowboys of
various cultures (though he does not mention black cowhands) and on the issue
of pay. This reading comes from one of the rarest of publications on the cattle
industry: a limited edition, leather-bound volume that was distributed to members
of the National Livestock Association. Its title was Prose and Poetry of the
Live Stock Industry.

Before the close of the period of the trail and the open range the western
cowboys had developed traits, manners, and practices that may have been
said to have made them a separate class of men. A large majority were
native-born Americans, but in their ranks there were many young Englishmen, Irishmen, and Scotchmen, together with some of German origin. But
the life brought all so close together that those of alien birth hardly were
distinguishable from the others after a few years. Their manner of living and
the routine of their occupation were the same from Texas to Montana;
conditions then existing in the West also were much the same over the range
country from far South to far North, and so the influence of these combined to impress upon this remarkable body of men a sort of "hallmark," a
distinctive and not unattractive class-stamp.

For some ten or fifteen years after the Civil War there was a considerable
number of Mexican cowboys on the range, most of them being from the
southern part of the country. These were skilful men in every branch of
the work and did it well, but the standing objection to them on the part of
the employers was that they were rough, abusive, and unfeeling in their
treatment of the stock, and personally untrustworthy. Between these and
the others there seldom was any of the fraternal feeling, and usually the
caste-prejudice placed the Mexicans under great disfavor from the start; a
prejudice that was stronger among the Texans than among their brothers
from the North, but with all it was sufficient soon to make the combination
a disagreeable one.

Among these old-time cowboys the Texans and those of Texas antece-
dents were the most efficient for all-around work on the range and on the

trail. Nearly all of them lived and moved as if they had been born in the saddle and had seldom been out of it since. They hesitated about doing anything outdoors on foot, and if they had to go but a few yards they would mount their horse for the journey—a habit, however, that was but a little less fixed among the entire fraternity. While all cowboys had to be good horsemen, the Texan was, it would seem, as skilful and daring a rider as he could have been were he and his pony grown together. . . .

. . . The cowboy was not what most people now look upon as a well-paid man. Around thirty years ago [the 1870s], in the times when the raucous and brawling cowtowns were mazes of snares and pitfalls for him, many of his class were working for from $20.00 to $25.00 per month, . . . though the experienced trailman was paid more for his services while on the trail. But the cowboy then required that his wages be in the form of "hard money"—a stroke of business sagacity that stood out in sharp, almost comical, contrast with the foolish recklessness that was characteristic of the brotherhood as a whole in spending the money. At that time the Mexicans in the calling were content with even less, few of these receiving more than $12.50 to $15.00 per month. . . . These also did business with their employers on a specie basis; and with many gestures of suspicion, and even of contempt, repudiated a tender of paper money for any amount. In later years the cowboy's wages moved higher notch by notch, and before railroads and wire fences had put him out of business his pay ranged from $30.00 to $40.00 by the month in the specie-basis currency of the land. . . . By this time, while he still was a generous soul, he had become much less reckless in squandering his money.

READING 9

DEADWOOD DICK, NAT LOVE, 1907

Among the best known of the black cowboys was Nat Love. Others—Cherokee Bill, Ben Hodges, Isom Hart, and Bill Pickett—may have been more influential, but none was quite as flamboyant. A few years after the Civil War ended, Nat, then fifteen years old, traveled west and entered the cowboy culture. The accounts in his 1907 autobiography are filled with exaggeration and hyperbole, but no more so than the fanciful tales spun by and about such historical figures as Daniel Boone, Davy Crockett, Buffalo Bill, and Jim Beckwourth, or such fictional characters as Pecos Bill, or mythmakers such as Ned Buntline.

In these selections Nat Love tells how he earned the nickname Deadwood Dick on July 4, 1876, in Deadwood, Dakota Territory, and how he single-handedly fought off an Indian attack on October 4, 1876.

Our trail boss was chosen to pick out the mustangs from a herd of wild horses just off the range, and he picked out twelve of the most wild and vicious horses that he could find.

The conditions of the contest were that each of us who were mounted was to rope, throw, tie, bridle and saddle, and mount the particular horse picked for us in the shortest time possible. The man accomplishing the feat in quickest time [was] to be declared the winner.

It seems to me that the horse chosen for me was the most vicious of the lot. Everything being in readiness the "45" [pistol] cracked and we all sprang forward together, each of us making for our particular mustang.

I roped, threw, tied, bridled, saddled, and mounted my mustang in exactly nine minutes from the crack of the gun. The time of the next nearest competitor was twelve minutes and thirty seconds. This gave me the record and championship of the West, which I held up to the time I quit the business in 1890 and my record has never been beaten. It is worthy of passing remark that I never had a horse pitch with me so much as that mustang, but I never stopped sticking my spurs in him and using my quirt [a riding whip] on his flanks until I proved his master. Right there the assembled crowd named me Deadwood Dick and proclaimed me champion roper of the western cattle country.

. . . I was riding alone when all at once I heard the well-known Indian war whoop and noticed not far away a large party of Indians making straight for me. They were all well mounted and they were in full war paint, which showed me that they were on the war path, and as I was alone and had no wish to be scalped by them I decided to run for it. . . . I turned in my saddle every once in a while and gave them a shot by way of greeting, and I had the satisfaction of seeing a painted brave tumble from his horse and go rolling in the dust every time my rifle spoke. . . . Reaching Yellow Horse Canyon, I had about decided to stop and make a stand when one of their bullets caught me in the leg, passing clear through it and then through my horse, killing him. Quickly falling behind him I used his dead body for a breast work and stood the Indians off for a long time, as my aim was so deadly and they [had] lost so many that they were careful to keep out of range.

But finally my ammunition gave out, and the Indians were quick to find this out, and they at once closed in on me, but I was by no means subdued, wounded as I was and almost out of my head, and fought with my empty gun until finally overpowered. When I came to my senses I was in the Indians' camp. [Nat Love concludes the episode by recounting at length how he dramatically and cleverly escaped from the Indians.]

READING 10
TOOLS OF THE TRADE, MARY J. JAQUES, 1894

Every profession has its "tools of the trade," and the cowboy's occupation, which required spending most of the day on a horse, depended upon specialized and customized gear. Ropes, saddles, hats, bridles, bits, spurs, and other paraphernalia all helped make the job safer, more efficient, and more comfortable. Mary J. Jaques, in her book Texan Ranch Life, *describes some of this crucial equipment.*

Roping is very skillful, and in the hands of an expert the rope is a very dangerous weapon. In Mexico it is called the lasso, the lariat, or *la reata,* and it is difficult to say whether the Texas cowboy or the Mexican vaquero uses it the more expertly. In the art of riding, too, the one and the other are perfect.

The cowboy would no more speak of his rope as a lasso than describe the evolution of his pony as bucking; this is always "pitching." . . . The rope measures forty feet in length, and varies in price from 45 cents to a dollar, according to its quality and the finish of its noose, either with leather or an iron ring, or more often with nothing but a simple knot at the end for the length to pass through. This running noose is swung horizontally over the head, with the elbow at the height of the crown. By this circular motion sufficient force is acquired to project the whole length of the line, the remainder of the coil being held in the left hand until the noose falls upon the object to be roped. A well-trained pony will stop dead on feeling the strain, and the rope is wound round the horn of the saddle. There is a tremendous strain from a full-grown steer; but these small ponies are strong in the shoulder, and show wonderful intelligence, throwing themselves back on their haunches to resist the pull the moment the rope tightens.

If the rider fouls [misses the steer], the pony gallops on and trots up again, until the animal is captured and ready to be branded.

The rope ought to fall, and when thrown by a skillful hand, generally does fall, upon the horns and feet, and I have been told that some of these ponies will even pass it on if it catches the neck. . . .

Mexican and Texas saddles are both extremely heavy and cumbersome, high in the cantle, with a long horn or peak in front—to which the rope is secured—sometimes being adorned with goat-skin pockets. I tried to lift one of these saddles from the ground quite in vain. Those of the Mexican ranchers are really costly, often being trimmed with gold or silver to match the rider's own highly ornamental suit of clothes. He has three rows of buttons down his legs, and his handsomely braided jacket is stitched with gold and silver thread, the whole being surmounted by the expensive sombrero, costing from thirty to three hundred dollars. The cowboys also wear a similar broad-brimmed hat, but made of plain straw with a leather band round its high crown, and occasionally with another band of gold and silver thread twisted over that. A leather strap passes under the chin to prevent the hat from falling off when the pony pitches, or in riding through thick brush.

Ordinary saddles are made of hard wood, covered with leather or parchment tightly stretched; from the peak to the cantle an open space runs down the middle, which I concluded was for ventilation in this hot climate. They are not in any way stuffed or padded, but a thick blanket, folded square, is placed beneath to protect the horse's back from the frame. They do not often gall, except after some hours' "cutting out," when very sudden swerves and stoppages at full speed become necessary to turn the cattle, causing an unavoidable wring of the saddle and consequently sore shoulders.

The Texan spurs are heavy and large, but not so enormous as those used by the Mexicans, which weigh several pounds; and whilst the rowels are two or three inches in diameter, they are never so sharp or cruel as the smaller English type. The bits are very severe, but the cowboy never rides on his reins, these generally hanging slack on the horse's neck. . . .

. . . Instead of bearing on the right or left rein, according to the desired direction, the hand, with both reins, is drawn outward and across. When you wish to go to the right, for instance, the hand is drawn out on that side, the left rein pressing against the horse's neck. . . .

A snaffle [a jointed bit] is never used, the curb being about an inch high in the crossbar or port, but short in the cheekbits or branches. . . . Both Texans and Mexicans ride with extremely long stirrup leathers.

THE END OF THE TRAIL, *WICHITA EAGLE*, 1874;
DANIEL WILDER, 1886; *WICHITA TRIBUNE*, 1871

The goal of any cattle drive was to reach one of the railroad shipping points that
flourished during the 1870s and 1880s. In Kansas alone fifteen cowtowns boomed
during the spring and summer of each year: Baxter Springs, Abilene, Waterville,
Junction City, Chetopa, Coffeyville, Newton, Salina, Solomon, Ellsworth,
Brookville, Wichita, Great Bend, Caldwell, and Dodge City. In Missouri the
main one was Sedalia.

 The cattle towns provided not only a marketplace for the drovers but a release
for the often young cowboys who had just spent weeks eating dust and smelling
steer manure. Here a reporter for the Wichita Eagle *describes the preparations*
under way for the arrival of the cattle drovers.

Broad-brimmed and spurred Texans, farmers, keen business men, real estate agents, land seekers, greasers, hungry lawyers, gamblers, women with
white sun bonnets and shoes of a certain pattern, express wagons going pell
mell, prairie schooners, farm wagons, and all rushing after the almighty
dollar. The cattle season has not fully set in, but there is a rush of gamblers
and harlots who are "lying in wait" for the game which will soon begin to
come up from the south [Texas]. There was a struggle for a while which
should run the city, the hard cases or the better people. The latter got the
mastery, and have only kept it by holding a "tight grip." Pistols are as thick as
blackberries. The taxes are paid by the money received from whiskey sellers,
gambling halls, and the *demi monde,* and thousands of dollars are obtained
besides to further the interests of the town. Wichita flourishes off the cattle
business, and these evils have to be put up with; at least that is the way a large
majority of the people see it. But notwithstanding this a man is safe in
Wichita as anywhere else if he keeps out of bad company. The purlieus of
crime there are no worse than in many eastern cities of boasted refinement
and good order. But woe to the "greeny" who falls into the hands of the
dwellers therein, especially if he carries money. From these must come most
of the stories of outrage at Wichita. They are entitled to little sympathy
because they can find plenty of good company if they desire it.

For the typical cowboy at the end of a typical cattle drive, the cowtowns offered
excitement and a veritable pot of gold at the end of the rainbow. Flushed with

The typical cowboy wears a white hat, a gilt cord and tassel, high-top boots, leather pants, a woolen shirt, a coat, and no vest. On his heels he wears a pair of jingling Mexican spurs, as large around as a tea-cup. When he feels well (and he always does when full of what he calls "Kansas sheep-dip"), the average cowboy is a bad man to handle. Armed to the teeth, well mounted, and full of their favorite beverage, the cowboys will dash through the principal streets of a town yelling like Comanches. This they call "cleaning out a town."

Plenty of rotten whiskey and everything to excite the passions was freely indulged in. . . . Rogues, gamblers, and lewd men and women run the town. I have been in a good many towns but Newton is the fastest one I have ever seen. Here you may see young girls not over sixteen drinking whisky, smoking cigars, cursing and swearing until one almost loses the respect they should have for the weaker sex. I heard one of the townsmen say he didn't believe there were a dozen virtuous women in town. This speaks well for a town claiming 1,500 inhabitants.

ON THE CATTLE RANCH

The open-range cattle drives could be dramatic, but in the long run the efforts of the cattle ranchers were probably more significant. As more and more cattle were bred and reared on privately owned ranches, which stretched from the Southwest to the Northwest, most of the cowboy's work was performed there, and the economic backbone of the cattle kingdom was found there. Contemporary commentators chose to focus on the more dashing, romantic figure of the open-range, trail-driving cowboy, but to understand the nature of the cattle industry, one must examine the ranch culture too.

By the 1880s the romance of the cowboy culture was waning. Business problems affecting the cattle range included price fluctuations, crime, overproduction, competition, and labor troubles. Moreover, the independent, self-reliant cowboys were coming to be seen as a nuisance to the settlers, often harassing the "sodbusters" (farmers) and bringing disrepute to the cattle business. Most ominously, a few cowboys and other nefarious types were becoming "rustlers" (cattle thieves) as well. The solution was twofold. First, ranches supplanted the open range, particularly after the disastrous winter of 1885–86. Costs were easier to control and so were the cowboys. Second, cattlemen's associations expanded to control marketing, employee behavior, transportation, and legal and political considerations. The romance was buried in a flurry of ledger books and association resolutions, the lyrical adventure replaced by hard business sense.

The term "ranch" generally referred to the land, cattle, and equipment but was sometimes used to mean just the buildings on the land. A poor newcomer's ranch house might consist of a one-room, dirt-floored shack; later, it might have two rooms and a few more amenities. If lumber was nearby, the ranch house could be much more elaborate. For a handful of the cattle barons, it was a mansion.

Among those who chose ranch life there were some strongly felt attitudes. Besides the traditional spirit of independence, disdain for governmental authority, and belief in laconic speech, there was a sense of agricultural and social superiority among the cattlemen and cowboys. They felt that they had opened the American West to civilization and, by rights, had the first and forever claim on the future development of the region. This feeling was particularly manifest in the cattlemen's attitudes toward sheep. Sheepherding had arrived in the West through the Spanish. And as the western grasslands became home to both cattle and sheep, prejudices developed among the cattlemen. Sheep ate the grass intended for the cattle; sheep cropped the grass too close; sheep would sweat through their hooves and poison the ground; cattle would not drink from water holes used by sheep until the rain washed away the sheep smells, they asserted. Another factor was the racial prejudice of Anglo-American cowboys toward the shepherds, who were often of Mexican or Basque heritage. These attitudes could erupt into violence. For example, some cattle ranchers arbitrarily marked open rangeland with sheep boundaries called "deadlines"; herders who brought their sheep into these areas might be met by night raiders known as "gunnysackers," who would kill sheep and valuable sheepdogs or scatter flocks. Some gunnysackers actually dynamited flocks or set them afire.

The following selections describe various aspects of cattle ranching: expenses, organization, physical structures, and the rules of the ranch cowboy culture, both written and unwritten.

READING 12A
BUSINESS CONSIDERATIONS, JAMES
BRISBIN, 1881; JOSEPH G. McCOY, 1874

James Brisbin's The Beef Bonanza; or, How to Get Rich on the Plains *specified the requirements for raising a herd of five thousand head on the Colorado ranch of General R. A. Cameron. This is not the stuff of romantic legends; it is pure economic consideration. Although Brisbin had spent years in the American West as a soldier, he had actually had little firsthand experience with the cattle culture; according to the historian David Dary, Brisbin's book borrowed heavily from an 1871 book by Hiram Latham,* Trans-Missouri Stock Raising. *He did excel, however, in promoting the potential profitability of cattle ranching and operating as a cattle and sheep broker. His descriptions (or economic propaganda) attracted significant investment from the East Coast and from Europe and changed the nature of cattle ranching in the years that followed.*

This passage is primarily designed to demonstrate the enormous profits that could be earned from a relatively small investment in the cattle business, but the numbers he presents also provide an insight into the necessary expenses of operating a cattle ranch.

[The ranch requires] about eight herders, at an expense of $900 [each] per annum for two and $600 each per annum for six, including their food; total, $5,400. Allowing $2,100 for incidental expenses, including teams, horses, saddles, and shanties for the men, the grand expense would be $7,500 or $1.50 per head. Again, allowing one year of breeding, and four years for the growth of the calf, a full-grown, four-year-old steer, worth $20.00 to $30.00 would cost the breeder $7.50. A Texas yearling can be bought for from $7.00 to $10.00; a two-year-old from $12.00 to $15.00; and a cow from $15.00 to $25.00. The difference is partly in quality but more in time and place and purchase. New stock, just driven in, is always the lowest priced. A two-year-old heifer brought from Iowa or Missouri will bring $35.00, and the same grade of cows from $45.00 to $55.00. Excellent milkers will bring even more; a two-year-old Durham bull, three-fourths thoroughbred will bring from $60.00 to $75.00, and a full-grown thoroughbred will bring from $200 to $500. In cattle-raising in Colorado, General Cameron puts the profits at 50 to 55 per cent per annum on the capital invested, over and above all expenses and losses of every kind.

In 1874, Joseph G. McCoy, who claimed credit for starting the Texas cattle drives and establishing Abilene, Kansas, as the first shipping railhead, wrote Historic Sketches of the Cattle Trade of the West and Southwest. *It brought the cattle industry to popular attention and remains one of the best sources of information about the early cattle kingdom. McCoy promoted the cattle industry not only as profitable enterprise but also as a means of transforming the plains into a wonderland of commercial utility and social improvement. Like the writings of other boosters whose primary goal was to increase business revenue, McCoy's must be considered in the spirit in which they were written, but his discussion of the nuts and bolts of the cattle trade is instructive. Here he describes practical start-up concerns.*

[L]et us look into the life of the producer, the owner, the ranchman, their manner of life and their labor—in short, how the cattle are raised. In Texas perhaps not one owner in ten lives upon his stock "ranch," but usually in some near post-office village; occasionally one is found living in a city. In choosing a location for a stock ranch a point centrally situated as to grazing lands and an abundance of living water is selected for a headquarters of the ranch. Here is erected, usually of logs, a rude house and corrals, with capacity in proportion to the herd, with a small pound or chute for branding of large cattle, such, for instance as a drove of beeves, preparatory to starting them to market.

The slight brand put on the stock at that time is called a road brand, in contradistinction to the ranch brand, which is usually put on the animal when young.

We will suppose a man to be just commencing in the stock business; after having purchased enough land to give him a footing whereon to build the above houses and corrals with sufficient water and timber for his purposes, he then decides what his "ranch brand" and ear marks shall be, and whatever device or letter or figure he selects, he is careful to have it differ from all other brands and marks in that portion of the State. Then he goes before an officer of the county or district and places upon record his brand and ear marks, filing a copy thereof, also a statement of the number of cattle and horses he has at that time bearing that brand and marks, taking from the Recorder a certificate of his action, from thenceforward all stock found bearing that brand and ear marks are his, and by him can be taken possession of by summary process, wherever found in the State. The stock laws of Texas are very complete and provide ample penalties for violation. When a stock man sells his entire cattle or horses he gives the purchaser articles of writing which are proper subjects of record, conveying all right and title to all stock bearing the brands and ear marks therein described. The conveyance is as absolute and complete as is a deed to a piece of land in the Northern States, and as has been said, like deeds should be recorded. The ownership of a stock of cattle in Texas is determined in a legal contest by the records just as we determine the ownership of a piece of land. When the stock is purchased as usual, if it be not very large, that each animal is counterbranded; i.e., the first brand burned out and the purchaser's brand burned on instead. The purchaser has the right to continue the same brand if he so chooses, not only upon those he buys but upon their increase, for he not only by his purchase becomes the owner of the stock, but of the brand also, and has all the rights thereunto pertaining to the original owner. . . .

The ownership of the young animal is determined by the brand of its mother. . . . It is a legal and universal practice to capture any unmarked and unbranded animal upon the range and mark and brand the same in their employer's brand, no matter to whom the animal may really belong, so be it is over one year old and is unbranded.

It is easy to see that any energetic, enterprising ranchman can greatly increase the number of his stock by this means; in fact, to this opportunity is the rapid increase of many stockmen's herds owing. Unbranded animals over a year old are, in the ranchman's parlance, called "Mauvrics" [mavericks], which name they got from a certain old Frenchman of that name, who began stock raising with a very few head, and in a very brief space of time had a remarkably large herd of cattle. It was found that he actually branded fifty annually for each cow he owned. Of course he captured the unbranded yearlings. To supply a ranch, whereon a stock of ten thousand head of cattle are kept, with the necessary saddle-horses, a stock of at least one hundred and fifty brood mares should be kept.

Most sources trace the common term for unbranded cattle to Samuel Maverick, a South Carolinian who moved to Texas in 1835. Around 1845, according to the most accepted version of the story, Maverick received a herd of cattle in payment of a debt. Because he was not interested in cattle raising at the time, the herd was neglected and many animals left unbranded. Consequently, an unbranded stray in the area was likely to be identified as "one of Maverick's." When he sold his herd in 1856, it was spread throughout the coastal plains south of San Antonio. By 1857 any unbranded, free-roaming cattle were referred to as mavericks.

In a later passage McCoy recounts the experiences of Charles Goodnight, who had extensive Texas holdings and was establishing a ranch in Colorado both to increase profits and, partly, to escape the financial and biological impact of tick fever, which infected Texas cattle. McCoy presents the ledger figures of Goodnight's enterprise.

As soon as the stock [of seven thousand head] could be gathered it was put upon the trail for Southeastern Colorado. But the journey was not made without danger, exposure and severe Indian fighting almost daily whilst crossing the Staked Plains, a distance of about four hundred miles. In one of these hostile attacks the Indians killed his partner and captured a large number of cattle.

With the remaining herds Mr. Goodnight sorrowfully made his way, through daily dangers and untold privation and hardships, into Colorado.

Not daunted by the bitter, sorrowful experiences of the previous year, Mr. Goodnight renewed and continued the business of droving for the three succeeding years, realizing the profit of $104,000, a part of which belonged to the heirs of his former partner. The year of 1871 he operated in connection with Mr. [Jesse] Chisholm [a Texas rancher of Cherokee ancestry], and cleared $17,000. He has retired from droving, and two years since put a stock of cattle upon his ranch amounting, in cost value, including $3,000 paid for

Durham bulls, to $26,650.00. At the end of two years, by actual record kept for business purposes, the operations stand: Value of Cattle on hand, $27,950; amount realized from sales of stock, over and above the expense of keeping the stock two years, $17,925; which, added to the present value of stock, aggregates $45,875; from which deduct the original investment, and the net profit for the two years' operation is $19,225, or $9,612.50 annually, or 36⅔ per cent. per annum—which ought to be a satisfactory per cent. profit, and an equally satisfactory exhibit in favor of Southeastern Colorado as a cattle country. For the benefit of any reader who may be looking toward Colorado and indulging thoughts of entering its borders to become stock growers, we submit a statement of Mr. Goodnight's live stock assets, as appears in an inventory upon his own books kept for business purposes:

400 Texan Cows,	$15.00 per head	$ 6,000
400 Graded Cows,	20.00 per head	8,000
150 three-year old Steers,	20.00 per head	3,000
300 two-year old Steers,	12.00 per head	3,600
550 yearlings,	9.00 per head	4,950
48 bulls,	50.00 per head	2,400
1848	Total Value	$27,950

READING 12B
THE MESS HOUSE, GALVESTON NEWS, 1886

An important component of ranch life was the mess house, where the cowboys cooked (or had cooked for them) their "grub." A mess house could be a simple, rude affair—a lean-to or a shack—or an elaborate structure. During the 1860s the pioneer Texas cattleman Charles Goodnight purchased 24,000 acres of public land for seventy-five cents an acre. On this land he built an extensive ranch community with more than fifty buildings, including two-story houses, a blacksmith shop, a tin shop, bunkhouses, and storage sheds. A Galveston News *reporter who visited Goodnight's ranch in 1886 here describes the mess house operation.*

The mess-house is a large and very substantial structure. . . . Near this house is a dairy, where the butter is made and stored during the summer in sufficient quantities to last headquarters during the entire year. . . . A short distance from this house is the poultry yard and house where the largest and finest breeds of fowls are kept. They supply eggs by the gross for the residents of this village, and the cook who takes care of them says that at least 1000 chickens a year are appropriated for table use. . . .

The size of Goodnight's mess house operation was unusual, but so was that of his ranch. Others may have owned several thousand cattle; Goodnight owned two thousand bulls alone and would eventually run more than 100,000 head of cattle. Ranch cooking, however, was similar regardless of size: the food was simple fare, hearty and filling, and it was washed down with barrels of coffee.

Ranch bunkhouses too—living quarters for the ranch hands—varied in size and quality. None would ever be accused of being four-star hotels; some were simply shacks without any creature comforts. But others included beds, or bunks, and some amenities, and a handful were more elaborate. Most provided modest sleeping arrangements for the cowboys, and such essentials as tobacco, guns and ammunition, fuel oil or kerosene, lamps, matches, a woodstove, some foodstuffs, plates, cups, utensils, frying pans, coffee, and a crude table and chairs. But bunkhouses tended to be merely functional, mostly by design. For many cowboys, the quality of their food was more important than the quality of their accommodations.

READING 12C

COWBOY RULES, DAVID DARY, 1989; RAMON ADAMS, 1969

The realities of ranch and range life and the nature of the cowboy culture led to the development of cowboy rules of behavior—mostly unwritten but familiar enough to be spelled out in later works such as David Dary's Cowboy Culture: A Saga of Five Centuries.

A cowboy was expected to be cheerful even if he was tired or sick.

A cowboy was expected to have courage. (Cowards could not be tolerated in the cowboy culture because one coward might endanger the whole outfit in time of danger.)

No real cowboy was a complainer. (Complainers were associated with quitting, and no real cowboy was a quitter.)

A cowboy always helped a friend, but if the cowhand saw a stranger or even an enemy in distress, the rule said he was to render assistance as quickly as possible. (This mutual-help principle was essential to survival on the open range where everyone helped one another, especially during roundup time.)

A cowboy did the best he could at all times.

Additional widely understood principles appear in the limited edition 1969 work by Ramon Adams titled The Cowman & His Code of Ethics.

A standing rule in the old trail days was to awaken a man by speech and not by touch. The hardships and dangers of the drive frayed his nerves and he was apt to "come alive" with a gun in his hand. No firing of guns around a cow camp unless emergency demanded it was another unwritten rule.

Rude and unlettered though he might be, and treating his companions with a rough and ready familiarity, the cowboy yet accorded his neighbor the right to live the life and go the gait which seemed most pleasing to himself. One did not intrude upon the rights of others in the cattle country, and he looked to it very promptly that no one should intrude upon his.

READING 12D
"General Rules of the xit Ranch," 1888

In rare instances the management of a ranch would spell out its rules for cowboys in lengthy and legalistic detail. In 1888 the company operating the xit *Ranch in the Texas Panhandle did so, following a month-long cowboy strike—the first in the American West. It was not much of a strike—consisting of a few fights, a lot of drinking, and drunken bravado—but it scared the ranch management into listing twenty-three regulations that a cowboy must agree to before accepting employment. This unique document reflects the changes occurring in the 1880s in the cowboy's American West.*

GENERAL RULES OF THE XIT RANCH

No. 1
Whenever a person is engaged to work on the ranch, the person so engaging him will fill out and sign a blank, giving the name of the party employed, for what purpose employed, the amount of wages he is to receive, the date he will begin work, and deliver the same to the person employed, who must

sign the counterpart of such contract, which must be forwarded to head-quarters at the first opportunity; and no one will be put upon the Company's pay roll, or receive any pay until this is complied with.

No. 2

Employees, when discharged, or on leaving the Company's service, are required to bring or send to the headquarters office, a statement from the person under whom they were at work, showing the day they quit the Company's service, and no settlement will be made with any employee, until such a statement is furnished.

No. 3

Employees discharged from or leaving the service of the Company are expected to leave the ranch at once and will not be permitted to remain more than one night in any camp.

No. 4

The wages due any employee will not be paid to any other person without a written order from the employee to whom such wages are due.

No. 5

No person in charge of any pasture, or any work on the ranch, or any contractor on the ranch, will be permitted to hire any one who has been discharged from the Company's own accord, with the intention of getting employment at some other place on the ranch, [and no one can] be so employed except by special agreement, made beforehand between the person in charge of the outfit he leaves and the one in charge of the outfit he wishes to work for.

No. 6

Private horses of employees must not be kept at any of the camps, nor will they be allowed to be fed grain belonging to the Company. No employee shall be permitted to keep more than two private horses on the ranch and all such horses must be kept in some pasture designated by the ranch manager.

No. 7

No employee shall be permitted to own any cattle or stock horses on the ranch.

No. 8

The killing of beef by any person on the ranch, except by the person in charge of the pasture, or under his instruction, is strictly forbidden. Nor is the person in charge of a pasture allowed to have beef killed, unless it can be distributed and consumed without loss. And all hides of beef killed must be taken care of and accounted for. It shall be the duty of each person having beef killed to keep a tally of the same and report the number, age and sex killed to headquarters every month.

No. 9

The abuse of horses, mules or cattle by any employee will not be tolerated, and any one who strikes a horse or mule over the head, or spurs it in the shoulder, or in any other manner abuses or neglects to care for it while in his charge, shall be dismissed from the Company's service.

No. 10

Employees are not allowed to run mustang, antelope, or any kind of game on the Company's horses.

No. 11

No employee of the Company, or of any contractor doing work for the Company, is permitted to carry on or about his person or in his saddle bags, any pistol, dirk, dagger, sling shot, knuckles, bowie knife or any similar instruments for the purpose of offense or defense. Guests of the Company, and persons not employees of the ranch temporarily staying at any of its camps, are expected to comply with this rule, which is also a State law.

No. 12

Card playing and gambling of any description, whether engaged in by employees, or by persons not in the service of the Company, is strictly forbidden on the ranch.

No. 13

In case of fire upon the ranch, or on lands bordering on the same, it shall be the duty of every employee to go to it at once and use his best endeavors to extinguish it, and any neglect to do so, without reasonable excuse, will be considered sufficient cause for dismissal.

No. 14

Each outfit of men that is furnished with a wagon and cook is required to make its own camping places, and not impose on the other camps on the ranch unnecessarily.

No. 15

Employees are strictly forbidden the use of vinous, malt, spirituous, or intoxicating liquors, during their time of service with the Company.

No. 16

It is the duty of every employee to protect the Company's interests to the best of his ability, and when he sees they are threatened in any direction to take every proper measure at his command to accomplish this end, and as soon as possible to inform his employers of the danger threatened.

No. 17

Employees of neighboring ranches on business are to be cared for at all camps, and their horses fed if desired (provided there is feed in the camp to spare); but such persons will not be expected to remain on the ranch longer than is necessary to transact their business, or continue their journey.

No. 18

Bona fide travelers may be sheltered if convenient, but they will be expected to pay for what grain and provisions they get, at prices to be fixed from time to time by the Company, and all such persons must not remain at any camp longer than one night.

No. 19

Persons not in the employment of the Company, but freighting for it, are not to be furnished with meals for themselves or feed for their teams at any of the camps on the ranch, but are expected to come on the ranch prepared to take care of themselves.

No. 20

Loafers, "sweaters" [men who sweat because they expended so much effort to *avoid* work; "slackers" or "goldbricks"], deadbeats, tramps, gamblers, or disreputable persons, must not be entertained at any camp, nor will employees be permitted to give, loan or sell such persons any grain, or provisions of any kind, nor shall such persons be permitted to remain on the Company's land anywhere under any pretext whatever.

No. 21

No person or persons, not in the employment of the Company, shall be permitted to hunt or kill game of any kind, inside the ranch inclosure, under any pretext whatsoever, and all employees are instructed to see that this rule is enforced. Employees of the Company will also not be permitted to hunt or kill game except when necessary for use for food.

No. 22

It is the aim of the owners of this ranch to conduct it on the principle of right and justice to every one; and for it to be excelled by no other in the good behavior, sterling honesty and integrity, and general high character of its employees, and to this end it is necessary that the foregoing rules be adhered to, and the violation of any of them will be considered just cause for discharge.

No. 23

Every camp will be furnished with a printed copy of these rules, which must be nailed up in a conspicuous place in the camp; and each and every rule is hereby made and considered a condition and part of the engagement between the Company and its employees, and any employee who shall tear down or destroy such printed rules, or shall cause the same to be done, shall be discharged.

By order of the Company,
Abner Taylor,
Manager.

To everything there is a beginning and an end. The end of the open-range cattle kingdom, source of the cowboy culture of legend, occurred near the end of the 1880s. The reasons included range overcrowding, the development of cheap barbed wire for fencing, the harsh winter of 1885–86, and the impact of sheepherding on available forage. Yet although the reality of the open range was ending, the mythology of the cowboy culture was just in its infancy.

SOURCES

CHAPTER I. THE SPIRIT AND THE MYTH

1. The Papers of Thomas Jefferson, Library of Congress, Washington DC. These instructions are quoted in many sources; a particularly good compilation that includes them is *The Papers of Thomas Jefferson,* ed. Julian Boyd (Princeton: Princeton University Press, 1950–).

2. John O'Sullivan, "The Great Nation of Futurity," *United States Magazine and Democratic Review* 6 (November 1839): 2–3, 6.

3. Thomas Hart Benton, speech to the U.S. Senate, *Congressional Globe,* 29th Cong., 2d sess., May 28, 1846, pp. 857–62.

4. Mary Austin Holley, *Texas* (Baltimore MD: Armstrong & Plaskitt, 1833), pp. 127–31.

5A. Walt Whitman, *Complete Prose Works* (New York: Putnam, 1902), 1: 270–71, 272–73.

5B. Walt Whitman, *Leaves of Grass,* 8th ed. (Boston: James R. Osgood, 1902), pp. 194–97. The poem first appeared in the self-published *Drum Taps* (1865).

6. W. M. Thayer, *Marvels of the New West* (Norwich, 1887), pp. 628, 630, 637–38, 640–45, 710–11.

7. Samuel L. Clemens, *Roughing It* (New York: Harper, 1899), pp. 210–15.

8. Willa Cather, *My Ántonia* (New York: Houghton Mifflin, 1918), pp. 70–75.

9. Frederick Jackson Turner, "The Significance of the Frontier," *Report of the American Historical Association* 1893: 199–227.

10. Owen Wister, *The Virginian* (New York: Grosset & Dunlap, 1902), pp. 27–30.

11. Ramon F. Adams, *The Old-Time Cowhand* (New York: Macmillan, 1961), pp. 3–4.

12. Texas Jack [John Burwell Omohundro], "The Cow-boy," *Wilkes' Spirit of the Times,* March 24, 1877.

13. "Cowboy Halloween in the Dakota Badlands," *Bismarck Daily Tribune,* November 3, 1885.

14. Joseph G. McCoy, *Sketches of the Cattle Trade of the West and Southwest* (Kansas City MO: Ramsey, Millett, & Hudson, 1874), p. 139.

15. John Baumann, "On a Western Ranche," *Fortnightly Review* 47 (1887): 516–33.

16. Theodore Roosevelt, *The Wilderness Hunter* (New York: Putnam, 1893), 1:24.

17. Charles W. Harris and Buck Rainey, eds., *The Cowboy: Six-Shooters, Songs, and Sex* (Norman: University of Oklahoma Press, 1976), pp. 23–25.

18. James Michie, *Possible Laughter* (New York: Macmillan, 1961), n.p.

1. *The Journals of Lewis and Clark* (New York: Bradford & Inskeep, 1814), June 13, 1805.

2A. Manuel Lisa to Governor General Salcedo, June 4, 1802, translated from an original Spanish document in the Archivo General de India (Sevile), Seccion Papeles de Cuba, legajo 77. The best source for primary documentation of this era is Abraham P. Nasatir, *Before Lewis and Clark: Documents Illustrating the History of the Missouri, 1785–1804,* 2 vols. (St. Louis MO: St. Louis Historical Documents Foundation, 1952).

2B. Documents of the Missouri Fur Company, Chouteau Collection, Missouri Historical Society, St. Louis. For an excellent discussion of the activities and legacy of Manuel Lisa, see Richard Edward Oglesby, *Manuel Lisa and the Opening of the Missouri Fur Trade* (Norman: University of Oklahoma Press, 1963).

2C. Documents of the St. Louis Missouri Fur Company, Chouteau Collection, Missouri Historical Society, St. Louis. These documents are cited in many sources related to the establishment of the fur trade: e.g., Hiram Chittenden, *The American Fur Trade of the Far West,* 2 vols. (Palo Alto CA: Stanford University Press, 1954); and Daniel Wishart, *The Fur Trade of the American West, 1807–1840* (Lincoln: University of Nebraska Press, 1979).

3. George F. Ruxton, *Adventures in Mexico and the Rocky Mountains* (London: John Murray, 1849), pp. 241–46.

4. Alexander Ross, *Fur Hunters of the Far West* (Norman: University of Oklahoma Press, 1956), pp. 133–39.

5. John C. Fremont, July 1, 1843, in Senate, *The Report of the Exploring Expedition to the Rocky Mountains in the year 1842, and to Oregon and North California in the years 1843–44* (S. Doc. 174, 28th Cong., 2d sess.); new ed., ed. Donald Jackson and Mary Lee Spence (Urbana: University of Illinois Press, 1970), pp. 186–88.

6. James Beckwourth, *The Life and Adventures of James Beckwourth, Mountaineer, Scout, Pioneer, and Chief of the Crow Nation of Indians* (London: Unwin, 1892), pp. 424–27.

7A. "The Testimony of Joseph Smith," prepared in 1838 and published serially in the *Nauvoo* (IL) *Times and Seasons,* beginning March 15, 1842.

7B. Horace Greeley, "Two Hours with Brigham Young," in *An Overland Journey from New York to San Francisco in the Summer of 1859* (New York: Saxton, Barker, 1860), interview of July 13, 1859.

7C. "Report of the Second Handcart Company, 1856," *Journal of Discourses,* September 26, 1856.

7D. Richard Burton, *The City of the Saints and Across the Rocky Mountains to California* (London, 1862), 426–33.

8. Jesse Applegate, *Transactions of the Fourth Annual Reunion of the Oregon Pioneer Association for 1876* (Salem OR, Oregon Pioneer Association, 1877), n.p.

9. John Minton, "Reminiscences of Experiences on the Oregon Trail in 1844," *Quarterly of the Oregon Historical Society* 2 (September 1901): 212–13.

10. *The Journals of Lewis and Clark* (New York: Bradford & Inskeep, 1814), February 11, 1805–August 17, 1806.

1. Howard Ruede, *Sod-House Days: Letters from a Kansas Homesteader, 1877–1886* (New York: Columbia University Press, 1937), pp. 27–29, 43. Copyright © 1937, Columbia University Press. Reprinted with the permission of the publisher.

2. "The Little Old Sod Shanty," in *Cowboy Lore,* ed. Jules Verne Allen (San Antonio: Naylor, 1935), pp. 104–7.

3. Seth K. Humphrey, *Following the Prairie Frontier* (Minneapolis: University of Minnesota Press, 1931), pp. 229–57. Copyright 1931 by the University of Minnesota.

4. *The Homestead Act of 1862, U.S. Statutes at Large* 12 (1863): 392–93.

5. Mary Chaffee Abell, "Hard Work Is the Watchword in Kansas," in *Victorian Women: A Documentary Account of Women's Lives in Nineteenth-Century England, France, and the United States,* ed. Erna Olafson Hellerstein et al. (Stanford CA: Stanford University Press, 1981), pp. 308–18.

6. Hamlin Garland, *A Son of the Middle Border* (New York: Macmillan, 1925), pp. 107–16.

7. Hamlin Garland, *A Son of the Middle Border* (New York: Macmillan, 1925), pp. 283–85.

8. Herbert Quick, *One Man's Life* (Indianapolis: Bobbs-Merrill, 1925), pp. 207–9, 212–17. Reprinted with the permission of Simon & Schuster. Copyright © 1925 by The Bobbs-Merrill Company, Inc., renewed 1953 by Edward Connell Quick.

9. John E. Read, *Farming for Profit: A Handbook for the American Farmer* (Philadelphia: J. C. Moody, 1881), pp. 848–50.

10. John Wesley Powell, 1878, in House, *Report on the Lands of the Arid Region of the United States* (H. Doc. 73, 45th Cong., 2d sess.). A second edition was issued in March 1879.

11. Jessie Rowland (c. 1870), quoted in Joanna Stratton, *Pioneer Women: Voices from the Kansas Frontier* (New York: Simon & Schuster, 1981), pp. 135–36. Reprinted with the permission of Simon & Schuster and International Creative Management, Inc. Copyright © 1981 by Joanna L. Stratton.

12. William Banta, from his 1893 manuscript, revised by William Banta and J. W. Campbell Jr. as *Twenty-Seven Years on the Texas Frontier* (Council Hill OK: L. G. Park, 1933), pp. 4–7.

13. "Busted in Kansas," *Emporia (KS) Gazette,* June 15, 1895.

14. J. K. Howard, *Montana: High, Wide, and Handsome* (New Haven: Yale University Press, 1943), p. 14. Copyright © 1943, 1959 by Yale University Press.

15. Henry King, "A Year of the Exodus in Kansas," *Scribner's Monthly* 8 (June 1880): 211–15.

16. Guadalupe Vallejo, "Ranch and Mission Days in California," *Century Magazine* 41 (December 1890): 183, 184, 189, 191–92.

17. Barbara Ruth Bailey, *Main Street Northeastern Oregon* (Portland: Oregon Historical Society, 1982), pp. 87–121.

18. Frederick Law Olmsted, *A Journey through Texas* (New York: Mason Brothers, 1857), chap. 3.

19. Luther A. Lawhon (c. 1865) in *The Trail Drivers of Texas,* ed. J. Marvin Hunter (San Antonio: Jackson, 1920–23), 1:176–77.

20. *The World Almanac, 1893,* pp. 83–85.

CHAPTER 4. BURY ME IN A TREE

1. James Marshall, quoted in Charles Gillepsie, "The California Gold Discovery," *Century Magazine* 19 (February 1891): 525.

2. Lithographed letter-sheet, lithographed and published by San Francisco: Britton and Rey, 1854. The original document is housed in the California State Library, Sacramento CA. This document was also reproduced in: (a) Harry T. Peters, *California on Stone* (Garden City NJ: Doubleday, Doran, 1935), pp. 28, 67–69, and (b) Rodman W. Paul, *The California Gold Discovery: Sources, Documents, Accounts, and Memoirs Relating to the Discovery of Gold at Sutter's Mill* (Georgetown CA: Talisman Press, 1967), pp. 121–24.

3. Henry David Thoreau, *Journal* (Boston: Houghton Mifflin, 1906), 3:265–67, February 1, 1852.

4. Daniel B. Woods, *Sixteen Months in the Gold Diggings* (New York: Harper, 1849), pp. 56–58.

5. Louise Amelia Knapp Smith Clappe, *The Shirley Letters* (San Francisco, 1922), pp. 213–19. First published by Ferdinand Ewer in *The Pioneer; or California Monthly Magazine,* 1854–55.

6. William Tecumseh Sherman, *Memoirs of General William T. Sherman* (New York: Appleton, 1875), 216–18.

7. Mary McNair Mathews, *Ten Years in Nevada, or Life on the Pacific Coast* (Buffalo NY: Baker, Jones, 1880; rpt. Carson City: University of Nevada Press, 1990).

8. Gary Noy, "Tommyknockers—Elves of the Hardrock Mines," *Sierra Heritage* 9 (November–December 1989): 52–53.

9. Michael Malone and Richard Etulain, *The American West* (Lincoln: University of Nebraska Press, 1989), pp. 23–26. Reprinted by permission of the University of Nebraska Press. Copyright © 1989 by the University of Nebraska Press.

10. *Woodruff v. North Bloomfield Gravel Mining Co.,* 18 F. 753–813 (Cir. Calif. 1884).

11. *Homestake Centennial 1876–1976* (Lead SD and San Francisco: Homestake Mining Company, 1976), pp. 26–27.

12. *Homestake Centennial 1876–1976* (Lead SD and San Francisco: Homestake Mining Company, 1976), pp. 54–58.

13. Antonio Franco Coronel, "Casas de California." Reprinted from David Weber, ed., *Foreigners in Their Native Land* (Albuquerque: University of New Mexico Press, 1973): 169–73, 174–76.

14. "Violence in Coeur D'Alene," *Spokane (WA) Weekly Review,* July 14, 1892.

15. Quoted in Paul F. Brissenden, *Launching of the Industrial Workers of the World* (New York: Haskell House, 1971), pp. 46–49. The main repository of IWW documents is in Archives of Labor and Urban History, Wayne State University, Detroit. Another good collection can be found at the University of Washington Library, Seattle.

CHAPTER 5. THE IRON HORSE

1. *The Pacific Railway Act of July 1, 1862, U.S. Statutes at Large* 12 (1863): 489.

2. Sir Samuel Morton Peto, *Resources and Prospects of America* (New York: A. Strahan, 1866), pp. 255–56.

3. W. A. Bell, *New Tracks in North America* (New York: Scribner, Welford, 1869), 2:253.

4. General Grenville Dodge, *How We Built the Union Pacific Railway* (Council Bluffs IA: Monarch, n.d. [c. 1870]; rpt. U.S. Senate, 61st Cong., 2d sess., March 22, 1910), p. 447.

5. General Grenville Dodge, *How We Built the Union Pacific Railway* (Council Bluffs IA: Monarch, n.d. [c. 1870]; rpt. U.S. Senate, 61st Cong., 2d sess., March 22, 1910), p. 447.

6A. "Reminiscences of Alexander Toponce, Pioneer," 1869, in *A Treasury of Railroad Folklore,* ed. B. A. Botkin et al. (New York: Crown, 1953), pp. 124–25.

6B. General Grenville Dodge, *How We Built the Union Pacific Railway* (Council Bluffs IA: Monarch, n.d. [c. 1870]; rpt. U.S. Senate, 61st Cong., 2d sess., March 22, 1910), p. 447.

7. Henry Varnum Poor, *Manual of the Railroads of the United States, 1869–1870* (New York: H. V. and H. W. Poor, 1869), xlvi–xlviii.

8. Robert Louis Stevenson, *Across the Plains* (New York: Scribner, 1892), pp. 48–50, 59–61.

9. Raphael Pumpelly, *Across America and Asia* (New York: Leypoldt & Holt, 1870), pp. 1–5.

10. A. C. Buell, dispatch of July 30, 1877, *New Orleans Daily Democrat,* August 4, 1877.

11. William F. Cody, *An Autobiography of Buffalo Bill* (New York: Farrar & Rinehart, 1920), pp. 171–74.

12A. *San Francisco Chronicle,* May 13, 1880, p. 3.

12B. Frank Norris, *The Octopus* (Garden City NY: Doubleday, Duran, 1901), pp. 248–50.

CHAPTER 6. THE PEOPLE AND THE RESPONSE

1. Quoted in Samuel Carter, *Cherokee Sunset: A Nation Betrayed* (New York: Doubleday, 1976), pp. 247–49. The original document is housed with the John Ross Papers at the Gilcrease Institute of American History and Art, Tulsa OK.

2. Chief Seattle quoted in Charles Bagley, *History of Seattle* (Chicago: S. J. Clarke, 1916), p. 78.

3. Meninock's statement was introduced into evidence in a Washington court case called *State of Washington v. Towessnute,* 89 Wash 478 (1916). The statement was reproduced with additional historical analysis and comments in: (a) *Proceedings of the New Jersey Historical Society,* n.s. 13 (1928): pp. 477–79; and (b) *Washington Historical Quarterly* (July 1928): pp. 170–74.

4. Okute, 1911, quoted in Frances Densmore, *Teton Sioux Music,* Bulletin 61 (Washington DC: Bureau of American Ethnology, 1918), pp. 172–73.

5. Joseph, 1871, quoted in Helen Addison Howard, *War Chief Joseph* (Caldwell ID: Caxton, 1941), p. 84; and Chief Joseph, "An Indian's View of Indian Affairs," *North American Review* 128 (1879).

6. Luther Standing Bear, *Land of the Spotted Eagle* (Boston: Houghton Mifflin, 1933), pp. xix, 189–91. Reprinted by permission of Geoffrey M. Standing Bear, great-grandson of Luther Standing Bear.

7. *Black Elk Speaks,* ed. John G. Neihardt (Lincoln: University of Nebraska Press, 1932), pp. 8, 9, 62, 217. Reprinted by permission of the University of Nebraska Press. Copyright 1932, 1959, 1972, by John Neihardt. Copyright © 1961 by the John Neihardt Trust.

8. Quoted in W. F. Johnson, *Life of Sitting Bull and History of the Indian War 1890–1891* (N.p.: Edgewood, 1891), pp. 201–2.

9. *Geronimo: His Own Story,* ed. S. M. Barrett (New York: Dutton, 1970), pp. 170, 173.

10. Ten Bears, speech to the Congressional Peace Commission, October 10, 1867, quoted in R. N. Richardson, *The Comanche Barrier to South Plains Settlement* (Glendale CA: Clark, 1933), p. 303; and Quanah Parker, interviewed by Harry Stroud, *Indian Pioneer History* 87 (1875): 397 (a publication of the Oklahoma Historical Museum in Oklahoma City). Reprinted by permission of the Oklahoma Historical Society.

11. Wovoka quoted in Dee Brown, *Bury My Heart at Wounded Knee* (New York: Holt, Rinehart & Winston, 1970), p. 416. Originally published in *14th Annual Report of the Bureau of American Ethnology, 1892–1893* (Washington DC: Government Printing Office, 1896), pt. 2, p. 772. Wovoka did not speak English; his words were roughly translated by James Mooney, an employee of the Bureau of Ethnology of the Smithsonian Institution.

12. *Black Elk Speaks,* ed. John G. Neihardt (Lincoln: University of Nebraska Press, 1932), pp. 255–62. Reprinted by permission of the University of Nebraska Press. Copyright 1932, 1959, 1972, by John Neihardt. Copyright © 1961 by the John Neihardt Trust.

13. Choctaw and Chickasaw Nations of Indians, *Answer to Report of the Honorable Dawes Commission.* Pamphlet no. 7, 1895, National Archives.

14. George Catlin, *Letters and Notes on the Manners, Customs, and Condition of the North American Indians* (London, 1841), letter 10.

15. Charles Eaton Haynes, speech to the U.S. House of Representatives, 24th Cong., 1st sess., *Congressional Globe,* June 29, 1836.

16. Andrew Jackson, President's Annual Message of 1835, in *Compilation of Messages and Papers of the Presidents* (Washington DC, 1908), 3:171–73.

17. "The Folly of Making Indian Treaties," *Harper's Weekly* 20 (August 5, 1876): 630–31.

18. Thomas J. Morgan, *The Present Phase of the Indian Question* (Washington DC: Bureau of Indian Affairs, 1891), pp. 18–21.

19. Theodore Roosevelt, *Hunting Trips of a Ranchman* (New York: Putnam, 1885), pp. 17–19.

20. *The Dawes Act of February 8, 1887, U.S. Statutes at Large* 24 (1888): 388.

CHAPTER 7. ON BOTH SIDES OF THE TIN BADGE

1. Documents of 1851, quoted in Mary Floyd Williams, *History of the San Francisco Committee of Vigilance* (Berkeley: University of California Press, 1921), pp. 456–58, 460, 464–65.

2. Thomas J. Dimsdale, *The Vigilantes of Montana, or Popular Justice in the Rocky Mountains* (Denver CO, 1866), pp. 147–50.

3. Eugene Cunningham, *Triggernometry* (Caldwell ID: Caxton, 1971), pp. 421–24.

4. Wyatt Earp, as recorded in *Tombstone Epitaph,* October 27, 1881. Reproduced in Douglas D. Martin, *Tombstone's Epitaph* (Albuquerque: University of New Mexico Press, 1951), pp. 189–96.

5. Documents are quoted and reproduced in such biographies as Frazier Hunt, *The Tragic Days of Billy the Kid* (New York: Hastings House, 1956); J. W. Hendron, *The Story of Billy the Kid* (Santa Fe NM: Rydal Press, 1948); and the colorful but hopelessly biased work by Billy's killer, Pat Garrett, *The Authentic Life of Billy the Kid* (New York: Indian Head Books, 1994). On events of the time and place, a particularly good source is Robert N. Mullin, *A Chronology of the Lincoln County War* (Santa Fe NM: Press of the Territorian, 1966).

6. Jules Verne Allen, *Cowboy Lore* (San Antonio: Naylor, 1935), pp. 42–43.

7. George Armstrong Custer, *My Life on the Plains* (New York: Heldon, 1874), pp. 67–71.

8. John Wesley Hardin, *The Life of John Wesley Hardin, from the Original Manuscript, as Written by Himself* (Seguin TX: Smith & Moore, 1896), n.p.

9. Frank Canton, *Frontier Trails: The Autobiography of Frank Canton* (Boston: Houghton Mifflin, 1930; rpt. Norman: University of Oklahoma Press, 1966), pp. 36–42. New edition copyright 1966 by the University of Oklahoma Press, publishing division of the University.

CHAPTER 8. WOMEN OF THE AMERICAN WEST

1. Anthony Trollope, *North America* (Philadelphia: Lippincott, 1862), chap. 25.

2. Susan Shelby Magoffin, *Down the Santa Fe Trail and into Mexico: The Diary of Susan Shelby Magoffin, 1846–1847,* ed. Stella Drumm (New Haven: Yale University Press, 1926), pp. 1–107. Copyright © 1926, 1962 by Yale University Press.

3. Elizabeth Dixon Smith Geer, "Diary of a Woman on the Oregon Trail," *Transactions of the Oregon Pioneer Association of 1908* (Salem: Oregon Historical Society, 1908), n.p.

4. Catherine Haun, "A Woman's Trip across the Plains, 1849," manuscript diary, Huntington Library, San Marino CA.

5. Sarah Winnemucca, *Life among the Piutes: Their Wrongs and Claims* (Boston: Cupples, Upham; New York: Putnam, 1883), pp. 5–51.

6. *The Journals of Lewis and Clark* (New York: Bradford & Inskeep, 1814), August 19, 1805.

7. Pauline Lyons Williamson, 1885, Harry A. Williamson Collection, Manuscripts, Archives and Rare Books Division Schomburg Center for Research in Black Culture, New York Public Library, Astor, Lenox and Tilden Foundations; quoted in Cathy Luchetti, *Women of the West* (St. George UT: Antelope Island Press, 1982), pp. 115–18.

8. Elinore Pruitt Stewart, *Letters of a Woman Homesteader* (Lincoln: University of Nebraska Press, 1961), pp. 7–10.

9A. Helen Hunt Jackson, *A Century of Dishonor* (1881; rpt. New York: Indian Head Books, 1994), pp. 336–42.

9B. Bettie Gay, "The Influence of Women in the Alliance," in *The Farmers' Alliance History and Agricultural Digest,* ed. N. A. Dunning (Washington DC: Alliance, 1891), pp. 308, 311–12.

9C. Resolutions of the National American Woman Suffrage Association, Washington, DC, January 16–19, 1893. The most complete compilation of the documents of this and similar organizations, as well as writings by Elizabeth Cady Stanton, Susan B. Anthony, and other suffrage leaders, is *History of Woman Suffrage,* 6 vols. (New York: J. J. Little and Ives, 1922; rpt. New York: Source Book Press, 1970).

9D. Lilla Day Monroe Collection of Pioneer Stories, in the possession of Joanna L. Stratton, quoted in Stratton, *Pioneer Women: Voices from the Kansas Frontier* (New York: Simon & Schuster, 1981), pp. 253–67, reprinted with the permission of Simon & Schuster and International Creative Management, Inc. Copyright © 1981 by Joanna L. Stratton; and Carry A. Nation, *The Use and Need of the Life of Carry A. Nation* (Topeka KS: F. M. Steves, 1908).

9E. Martha White, "Work of the Women's Clubs," *Atlantic Monthly* 93 (May 1904), p. 614.

9F. Rheta Childe Dorr, *A Woman of Fifty* (New York: Funk & Wagnalls, 1924), pp. 118–20.

9G. *Muller v. Oregon,* 208 U.S. 412 (1908).

9H. The Consumers' League and the *Muller* Case, Rheta Childe Dorr, *What Eight Million Women Want* (Boston: Small, Maynard, 1910), pp. 2–6.

CHAPTER 9. WESTERNERS OF COLOR

1. Bret Harte, "The Heathen Chinee," in *Plain Language from Truthful James* (Chicago: Western News, 1870), pp. 33–35.

2. "John Chinaman," in *The California Songster* (San Francisco: Appelton, 1855), p. 44.

3. Oscar Lewis, *The Big Four* (New York: Knopf, 1938), pp. 71, 72–73, 74–75; and O. G. Villard, "Justice for the Chinese," *Christian Century* 60 (May 26, 1943): 633–34. Copyright 1943 Christian Century Foundation. Reprinted by permission from the May 26, 1943, issue of the *Christian Century.*

4. "A Chinese Massacre," *Los Angeles Daily News,* October 25, 1871.

5. *The Chinese Exclusion Act of May 6, 1882, U.S. Statutes at Large* 22 (1883): 58.

6. Hanayo Inouye, from the Issei Oral History Project, Inc., quoted in Eileen Sunada Sarasohn, *The Issei* (Palo Alto CA: Pacific Books, 1983), pp. 116–21.

7. Thomas Higginson, *Army Life in a Black Regiment* (Boston: Fields, Osgood, 1869), 131–32, 242–51.

8. Testimony of Henry Adams, 1877, 46th Cong., 2d sess., S. Rept. 693, pt. 2.

9. Letter to the editor, *Evening Day Book,* quoted in John Townsend, *The Doom of Slavery in the Union; Its Safety out of It* (Dallas TX, 1860).

10. Blanche Bruce, speech to the U.S. Senate, April 7, 1880, *Congressional Record,* 46th Cong., 2d sess., 1880, pt. 3: 2195–96.

11. Oral history of Laura Black Bear Miles, quoted in Cathy Luchetti, *I Do! Courtship, Love, and Marriage on the American Frontier* (New York: Crown, 1996), pp. 264–65. Reprinted by permission of Victor Orange, grandson of Laura Black Bear Miles.

12. James Henry Gleason, *Beloved Sister: The Letters of James Henry Gleason, 1841–1859* (Glendale CA: Arthur H. Clark, 1978), reprinted by permission of the Publishers; quoted in Cathy Luchetti, *I Do! Courtship, Love, and Marriage on the American Frontier* (New York: Crown, 1996), pp. 283–85.

13A. William F. Weeks, *Debates of the Texas Convention* (Houston: J. W. Croger, 1846), p. 157.

13B. J. Ross Browne, *Report on the Debates in the Convention of California on the Formation of the State Constitution in September and October, 1849* (Washington DC: John T. Tower, 1850), p. 63.

13C. "Behold the Friendship Existing for the Mexican Voters," the Brownsville (TX) *American Flag,* August 20, 1856.

13D. Antonio Maria Pico, February 21, 1859, document quoted in Robert Glass Cleland, *Cattle on a Thousand Hills: Southern California, 1850–1880* (San Marino CA: Huntington Library, 1951), pp. 238–43. Reprinted with the permission of the Henry E. Huntington Library. Copyright, 1941 by the Henry E. Huntington Library and Art Gallery; second edition, 1951.

13E. "Nuestra Platforma," *Las Vegas (NM) Daily Optic,* March 12, 1890.

14. Letter to the editor, trans. (French to Spanish) in *El Clamor Publico,* March 21, 1857; English trans. David Weber.

15. Juan Seguin, *Personal Memoirs of John N. Seguin, From the Year 1834 to the Retreat of General Woll from the City of San Antonio, 1842* (San Antonio: Ledger Book and Job Office, 1858), pp. iii–iv, 18–32.

CHAPTER 10. THE FAR-FLUNG BATTLE LINE

1. "Winning the West: The Setting and the Challenge," in *American Military History,* ed. Maurice Matloff (Washington DC: Center of Military History, U.S. Army, 1969), pp. 300–305.

2. William Barret Travis, response to demand for surrender of the Alamo, February 24, 1836, quoted in Henderson Yoakum, *History of Texas,* 2 vols. (New York: Redfield, 1856), pp. 76–77.

3A. James K. Polk, message to Congress, May 11, 1846, in *A Compilation of the Messages and Papers of the Presidents,* ed. James D. Richardson (Washington DC: Government Printing Office, 1896–99), 5:2287–93.

3B. Ulysses S. Grant, *Personal Memoirs of U.S. Grant* (New York: Charles L. Webster, 1885), 1:119–34.

3C. José Fernando Ramirez, *Mexico during the War with the United States,* ed. Walter Scholes, trans. Elliott Scheer (Columbia: University of Missouri Press, 1950), pp. 118–21.

3D. The Treaty of Guadalupe Hidalgo, February 2, 1848, in *Treaties and Other International Acts of the United States of America,* ed. Hunter Miller (Washington DC: Department of State, 1937), 5:207–36. See also *The Treaty of Guadalupe Hidalgo, February Second 1848,* ed. George P. Hammond (Berkeley CA: Friends of the Bancroft Library, 1949), p. 23.

4A. *Chicago Tribune,* April 29, 1861. See also *The Rebellion Record,* ed. Frank Moore (New York: Van Nostrand, 1861), 1:147–48.

4B. "Journal and Letters of Corporal William O. Gulick," ed. Max H. Guyer, *Iowa Journal of History and Politics* 28 (April 1930): 425. Reprinted by permission of the publisher.

4C. Gurdon Grovenor, 1863, quoted in William E. Connelley, *Quantrill and the Border Wars* (Cedar Rapids IA: Torch Press, 1910), pp. 362–65.

4D. W. R. Scurry, "Report of the Battle of Glorietta," in *Official Reports of Battles, as published by the order of the Confederate Congress at Richmond* (New York: Charles B. Richardson, 1863), pp. 186–89.

4E. Matthew Leeper Papers, July 11 and 21, 1862, quoted in Annie Heloise Abel, *The American Indian as Slaveholder and Secessionist* (Cleveland: Arthur H. Clark, 1919), pp. 354–55. Many of the Leeper Papers are reproduced in full in the appendix to Abel's book.

5. Patrick Edward Connor, c. 1868, "Statement in Medical History of Camp Douglas," manuscript quoted in Fred Roger, *Soldiers of the Overland* (San Francisco: Grabhorn, 1938), pp. 118–21.

6. Sarah Elizabeth Canfield, 1867–68, typescript, State Historical Society of North Dakota, Bismarck; quoted in Cathy Luchetti, *I Do! Courtship, Love, and Marriage on the American Frontier* (New York: Crown, 1996), pp. 82–85. Originally published as "An Army Wife on the Upper Missouri: The Diary of Sarah E. Canfield, 1866–1868," edited by Ray H. Mattison, *North Dakota History* 20, 4. Copyright 1953, State Historical Society of North Dakota. Used by permission.

7. Special Investigating Joint Committee, "The Sand Creek Massacre," 1864, from Reports of Committees, 39th Cong., 2d sess., 1866, Doc. 156, pp. 53, 73–74.

8. George Armstrong Custer, *Wild Life on the Plains and Horrors of Indian Warfare* (St. Louis MO: Continental, 1891), an expanded version of Custer's *My Life on the Plains* (1874).

9. *Helena Daily Herald,* July 2, 1876; *St. Paul and Minneapolis Pioneer-Press and Tribune,* July 6, 1876; and official report of General Philip Sheridan, in United States Secretary of War, *Annual Reports* (Washington DC: Government Printing Office, 1876), pp. 444–45. The Sheridan report was reproduced in John F. Finerty, *War Path and Bivouac, or Conquest of the Sioux* (Chicago, 1890), pp. 331–37.

10. Hamlin Garland, "General Custer's Last Fight as Seen by Two Moons," *McClure's Magazine* 11 (1898), p. 443.

11. Charles Cooper, "Buffalo Soldiers in the Desert," *New York Daily Tribune,* September 8, 1877. For additional information, see Captain Nicholas Nolan to Assistant Adjutant General, U.S. Army, Department of Texas, August 8, 1877. Both are in War Research Office, National Archives, Washington DC.

1. Theodore Roosevelt, "Ranch Life in the Far West: In the Cattle Country," *Century Magazine* 14 (February 1888): 200.

2. Emerson Hough, *The Story of the Cowboy* (New York: D. Appleton, 1898), pp. 1–20.

3. "Bunny," *Two Years a Cow-Boy & Life on the Prairie among the Indians & Back Woods of America* (London: London Literary Society, 1887), n.p.

4. John Baumann, "On a Western Ranche," *Fortnightly Review,* n.s. 41 (March 1887): 523–25.

5. Clarence Gordon, "Report on Cattle, Sheep, and Swine, Supplementary to Enumeration of Live Stock on Farms in 1880," in *Report on the Productions of Agriculture, Tenth Census* (Washington DC: Department of the Interior, 1883), 3:1071; and Andy Adams, *The Log of a Cowboy* (Boston: Houghton Mifflin, 1903), pp. 57–64.

6. Quoted in Clarence Gordon, "Report on Cattle, Sheep, and Swine, Supplementary to Enumeration of Live Stock on Farms in 1880," in *Report on the Productions of Agriculture, Tenth Census* (Washington DC: Department of the Interior, 1883), 3:1071; Charles J. Steedman, *Bucking the Sagebrush; or, The Oregon Trail in the Seventies* (New York: Putnam, 1904), pp. 255–59.

7. Solon Robinson in *New York Daily Tribune,* July 4, 1854.

8. *Prose and Poetry of the Live Stock Industry of the United States,* ed. James W. Freeman (Denver CO: Franklin Hudson, 1905), pp. 1–10.

9. Nat Love, *The Life and Adventures of Nat Love, by Himself* (Los Angeles, 1907), pp. 73, 93, 98–99.

10. Mary J. Jaques, *Texan Ranch Life: With Three Months through Mexico in a "Prairie Schooner"* (London: Horace Cox, 1894), n.p.

11. *Wichita Eagle,* May 28, 1874; Daniel Wilder, *The Annals of Kansas* (Topeka: Kansas Publishing, 1886), p. 94; and *Wichita Tribune,* August 24, 1871.

12A. James S. Brisbin, *The Beef Bonanza; or, How to Get Rich on the Plains* (Philadelphia: Lippincott, 1881), p. 43; and Joseph G. McCoy, *Historic Sketches of the Cattle Trade of the West and Southwest* (Kansas City MO: Ramsey, Millett, & Hudson, 1874), pp. 7–9, 383–85.

12B. *Galveston News,* January 10, 1886, quoted in J. Evetts Haley, *Charles Goodnight, Cowman and Plainsman* (Boston: Houghton Mifflin, 1936), pp. 327–28.

12C. David Dary, *Cowboy Culture: A Saga of Five Centuries* (Lawrence: University Press of Kansas, 1989), p. 278 (reprinted by permission of David Dary); and Ramon Adams, *The Cowman & His Code of Ethics* (Austin: Encino Press, 1969), pp. 11–12.

12D. "General Rules of the XIT Ranch," 1888, quoted in David Dary, *Cowboy Culture: A Saga of Five Centuries* (Lawrence: University Press of Kansas, 1989), pp. 303–7, from a printed copy at the Panhandle-Plains Historical Museum Research Center, Canyon TX. Reprinted by permission of David Dary.

INDEX

dominant culture (*continued*)
337, 339, 350–54, 355–57; and Native Americans, 201, 206, 224, 337, 347; shifting definitions of, 347

Dominguez, Manuel, 350

Dorr, Rheta Childe, 311–12, 314, 315

Douglas, Stephen, 69

Doza, Alexis, 43

Durant, T. C., 179, 180

Dust Bowl, 111

Dwamish Indians, 203

Earp, Wyatt, 250–53

Earp brothers, 249, 251, 252, 253

Eddy, Mary Baker, 296

Edmunds-Tucker Act, 59

education, 297; and homesteaders, 98–99; of Native Americans, 210, 235

Empire Mine, 144, 145

English people: and the American West, 414; as cowboys, 425, 426; on the cowboy, 414–15

ethnicity: and cowboys, 425–26; and mining, 157

Etulain, Richard, 145

Exodusters, 112, 333–36

expansionism, 6, 12, 25

Farmers' Alliance, 122, 126, 301

farming, 88; challenges of, 101–3; Chinese contributions to, 322; and cowboys, 433; as an honorable occupation, 103–5; and irrigation, 105–7; nostalgia for, 113–16; and political reform, 300–302; and women, 99–100, 104–5, 301

Farming for Profit (Read), 103

Fetterman, Captain William J., 212

Fetterman Massacre, 212–13

Ford, Robert, 259, 260

Fort Laramie Treaty, 216

forts, 386, 389–92

France, 2, 3, 366

Fremont, John C., 54

fur trade: contract for, 43–44; kinds of trappers in, 49–50; and the Missouri River, 41–42; and mountain men, 41, 48; and Native Americans, 51, 53; and profit, 45

Gall, Chief, 404

Garland, Hamlin, 98, 99, 402

Garrett, Pat, 253

Garrison, William Lloyd, 331

Gay, Bettie, 300–302

Geer, Elizabeth Dixon Smith, 279–80

General Federation of Women's Clubs, 310–11

Geronimo, 214

Ghost Dance, 213, 219–20, 233, 234, 236

Gibbon, John, 398, 399

Gleason, James Henry, 343

gold, 1, 15, 124; placer, 145; recovery of, 154–56; refining of, 156–57

Golden Spike Celebration, 179–80

goldfields: life in, 135–36

Goldmark, Josephine, 315

gold rush of 1848, 129–35, 139, 143, 157–61, 350, 352; and the Chinese, 316; and the Mexican-American War, 372; vigilantes in, 240

Goodnight, Charles, 423, 437–39

Goodnight-Loving trail, 423

Good Templars' Societies, 306

Gordon, Clarence, 417, 418, 423

Las Gorras Blancas, 353–54

Gould, Jay, 190

Granger Movement, 122

Grant, Ulysses, 232, 335, 364, 368–70

Great Railroad Strike of 1877, 190

Great Salt Lake basin, 59, 63, 66

Greeley, Horace, 63

Gros Ventre Indians, 236

Grovenor, Gurdon, 379

Guggenheim, Meyer, 146

Gulick, William, 378

Wister, Owen, 26

Wobblies. *See* Industrial Workers of the World

Woll, General Adrian, 357

women: African American, 290; diaries of, 271–80, 389–92; and farming, 99–100, 104–5, 301; in frontier forts, 389–92; and homesteading, 294–97; influence of, 141; among Japanese immigrants, 328–29; in mining camps, 140–42; Native American, 77, 285–89; as reformers, 297–315; reminiscences of journey west by, 280–85; roles played by, 270; Victorian views of, 297; and western exploration, 36, 77

Women's Christian Temperance Union (WCTU), 306, 307–8

Women's Trade Union League, 312

Woodruff v. North Bloomfield Gravel Mining Co., 147–51

Woods, Daniel B., 135

Worcester v. Georgia, 201–2, 229

Wounded Knee Massacre, 219, 220–22, 233, 235

Wovoka, 219–20

Wyoming Stockgrowers' Association, 267, 269

Wyoming Territory, 127

XIT Ranch, 440–44

Yakima Indians, 204–6

Yates, Richard, 376–77

Young, Brigham, 59, 63–66, 141, 376

Younger, Cole, 379

Younger, Jim, 379